THE
MAKING OF

Middle-earth

THE
MAKING OF

Middle-earth

A NEW LOOK INSIDE THE WORLD
OF J.R.R. TOLKIEN

CHRISTOPHER SNYDER

STERLING
New York

STERLING
New York

An Imprint of Sterling Publishing
387 Park Avenue South
New York, NY 10016

STERLING and the distinctive Sterling logo are registered trademarks of Sterling Publishing Co., Inc.

© 2013 by Christopher Snyder
For photographic copyright information, please see picture credits on page 338.

Produced by Laurie Dolphin for Authorscape, Inc.
Interior design by Amy Wahlfield

ISBN 978-1-4027-8476-7

Distributed in Canada by Sterling Publishing
c/o Canadian Manda Group, 165 Dufferin Street
Toronto, Ontario, Canada M6K 3H6
Distributed in the United Kingdom by GMC Distribution Services
Castle Place, 166 High Street, Lewes, East Sussex, England BN7 1XU
Distributed in Australia by Capricorn Link (Australia) Pty. Ltd.
P.O. Box 704, Windsor, NSW 2756, Australia

For information about custom editions, special sales, and premium and corporate purchases, please contact
Sterling Special Sales at 800-805-5489 or specialsales@sterlingpublishing.com.

Manufactured in China

2 4 6 8 10 9 7 5 3 1

www.sterlingpublishing.com

Frontispiece: *A ca. 1890 photochrom of Magdalen College, Oxford, where J. R. R. Tolkien and his fellow Inklings would meet on Thursday evenings.*

"*The making of things is in my heart from my own making by Thee.*"[1]

—J. R. R. TOLKIEN, *THE SILMARILLION*,
"OF AULË AND YAVANNA," 1977

CONTENTS

1 Learning his Craft

2 Tolkien's Middle Ages

3 "There and Back Again"

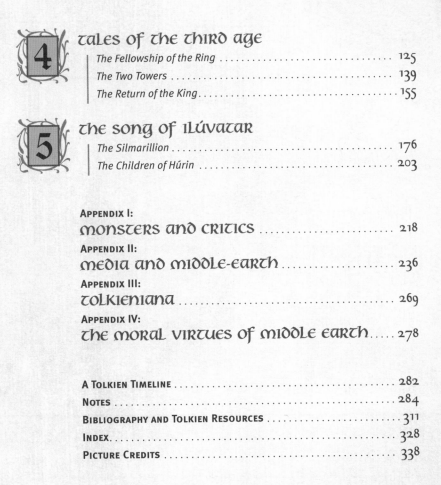

acknowledgments

Unlike most medievalists I have met, I did not have an appreciation for Tolkien as a young reader. I fell in love with the Arthurian legends as a teenager, became a professional historian, and only discovered the genius of Tolkien later in life. I owe a debt to all the Tolkien enthusiasts I have met during these years; to Peter Jackson, for kindling the flames; and to my Oxford Honors students for helping me focus my thoughts for this book. Special thanks are due to the staff of the Bodleian Library, the University of Oxford; the Emerson G. Reinsch Library, Marymount University; the Mitchell Memorial Library, Mississippi State University; and to Tom Shippey and Walter Hooper, for their help and encouragement.

This book in its final form would not have been a reality without the efforts of Joelle Delbourgo, my agent; Barbara Berger, my diligent and enthusiastic editor at Sterling Publishing; and the Tolkien Estate and publishers, with special thanks to Cathleen Blackburn and Stuart Patterson. Illustrated books like this one are a team effort, and the bulk of the work in this area was done by Sterling's Michael Fragnito, Editorial Director; Elizabeth Mihaltse, Art Director, Trade Covers; Chris Thompson, Art Director; Rodman Neumann, Managing Editor; and Elana Mitchel, Manager, Digital Asset Services; with assistance from packager Laurie Dolphin at Authorscape, interior designer Amy Wahlfield, and cover designer theBookDesigners.

Lastly, I thank my daughter Carys for reading Tolkien (and watching the films) with me, and give my love to my wife Renée for never complaining about this newest obsession. And Professor Tolkien, *in caelum observans*, I beg your forgiveness for all errors herein.

preface

" The world has changed. I feel it in the water. I feel it in the earth. I smell it in the air. Much that once was is lost, for none now live who remember it. "[2]

—GALADRIEL [CATE BLANCHETT] IN
THE FELLOWSHIP OF THE RING, THE MOVIE, 2001

MANY WHO HAVE READ the fictional works of J. R. R. Tolkien, or who have seen the trilogy of films made by Peter Jackson, would agree with the above sentiment of Galadriel. After our first encounter with Middle-earth, our world does not quite feel the same. We cannot look at gently rolling hills without thinking of the Shire, cannot watch autumn leaves turning gold without recalling Lothlorien, while the call of seagulls over the waves carries our spirits "into the West." Indeed, how many of us have looked hard into a mighty tree hoping to find the eyes of Treebeard peering out at us.

Tolkien's Middle-earth seems at first to be an utterly new and exciting creation. But on closer inspection, it is a very old world and dimly recognizable. Professor Tolkien—like his friend and colleague C. S. Lewis—was one living among us who *did* remember it. To be more accurate, he *recognized* this world in the languages, myths, and history of ancient and medieval Europe. Captivated as a child by what he later called "fairy stories," he became a professional medievalist and devoted his career to the study of early medieval language and literature, especially that of the Anglo-Saxons. The holder of no less than three

Water, earth, and sky: a bucolic scene photographed ca. 1890, in Devon, England, where Tolkien visited as a boy.

(!) professorships—two at Oxford University, Tolkien turned increasingly away from academic pursuits and instead channeled his immense learning into his fiction. Tolkien's fiction "lives" in such a vivid way to its readers because his books are grounded in a reality, albeit one that has become alienated from modernity. "We were born in a dark age out of due time," he wrote to his son Christopher, referring to the modern world, not the medieval period that many have dismissed as dark.[3] And for those of us who have been drawn into the adventures of Middle-earth and Narnia it is the medieval that feels like "home," as Tolkien once wrote, and "in unexplored desire we would still go home."[4]

There seems to be at least three *worlds* of J. R. R. Tolkien. There is the physical world in which he was born and educated, and in which he taught, wrote, made friendships, worshipped, and raised a family. These experiences—and places like Birmingham and Oxford—had an enormous impact on Tolkien the person as well as Tolkien the writer. The second world is the intellectual realm where Tolkien spent much of his time, beginning with his first fascination with fairy tales through his

adult obsessions with Northern languages and legends. This is the world of Beowulf and Brunhild, of Gawain and Fafnir, and the power and beauty of this world emanates from the very names of its places: Avalon, Heorot, Valhalla. Lastly, there is the world most familiar to Tolkien fans: Middle-earth, a land of elves and dark powers and Tom Bombadil. All three worlds will be discussed in this book, along with a fourth of which Tolkien had only a glimpse before he died: that of Tolkieniana, of fandom and franchise, culminating (as of this writing) in three of the most successful movies ever made.

FOR A LONG TIME THERE WAS ONLY ONE significant biography of J. R. R. Tolkien. It was written by Humphrey Carpenter in 1977 and based, in part, on interviews he conducted with Tolkien and his family and friends.[5] This biography is a companion and very similar in approach to Carpenter's *The Inklings* (1978), which deals with Tolkien alongside other members of his Oxfordian circle, especially the writers C. S. Lewis and Charles Williams. Carpenter felt that Tolkien deserved separate treatment, but wisely sought to publish the biography only after Tolkien's death, for Tolkien was not at all fond of the genre. Carpenter's biography has never been surpassed, though now it should be supplemented by the published letters of Tolkien, the recently discovered war record given full treatment by John Garth, and the invaluable two-volume reference work by Christina Scull and Wayne Hammond. Tom Shippey succeeds admirably in peering into the "inner life" of Tolkien the Philologist—philology, now called historical linguistics—being both Tolkien's passion and his profession, as it is for Shippey as well).[6] But the handful of competing biographies, many of which appeared around the time of Jackson's *Lord of the Rings* films, reveal little more than what Carpenter, Shippey, Garth, and Tolkien himself have provided us.[7]

Conversely, literary criticism of at least Tolkien's major works has never been lacking. As the modern literary genre of fantasy—virtually invented by Tolkien—has matured in the second half of the twentieth century, many academics have turned to serious and scholarly discussion of its major works. Those who have specialized in Tolkien studies (see Appendix I) have been aided in recent years by the publication of

annotated scholarly editions of both *The Hobbit* (1937) and *The Lord of the Rings* (1954–55) as well as the History of Middle-earth series (1983–96), edited by Christopher Tolkien, which traces the permutations of *The Lord of the Rings* and the "legendarium" (i.e., *The Silmarillion* and related stories of Middle-earth legends). The release of new Tolkien material, such as *The Children of Húrin* (2007) and *The Legend of Sigurd and Gudrún* (2009), provides yet more discussion for fans and critics alike.[8]

A few recent books have attempted to look at the whole Tolkien phenomenon, or at least at the varying reception of Tolkien's fictional works over the last few decades and of Jackson's films.[9] With the release of the three *Hobbit* films in 2012, 2013, and 2014, the name J. R. R. Tolkien may then be associated with one of the most successful film franchises in the history of cinema (alongside Harry Potter, James Bond, and Star Wars). Since Tolkien was overwhelmingly critical of an attempted animated version of the *Lord of the Rings* (he read the script in 1957–58) and thought that a live-action version could *never* be accomplished, one can only imagine his astonishment at the fact that his invented world is now equally as well known from cinematic images as it is from books.

Still, despite the continuing popularity of Tolkien's books and the flurry of attention surrounding the Jackson films, no one book has attempted to connect these modern literary and cinematic threads with the Middle-earth that Tolkien knew first, the one he found in the ancient languages and poetry of northwestern Europe. Long have we known the influence of works like *Beowulf* and *Sir Gawain and the Green Knight* upon Tolkien's fiction, but what of the historical cultures from whence these came? Historians and archeologists have, since the publication of *The Lord of the Rings*, revealed much about the cultures of the Celts, the Anglo-Saxons, and the Norse in the late Iron Age and the early Middle Ages. Tolkien himself embarked on such pursuits through his academic publications, seldom read by the fans of his fiction. *The Making of Middle Earth* will attempt to place Tolkien's scholarship *and* his fiction within the context of his wider pursuit of knowledge about the early inhabitants of the British Isles and of the remote Germanic-speaking realms on the Continent. Both the material and the literary cultures of these ancient peoples can help us to have a deeper appreciation of Tolkien's books and even their recent film and gaming adaptations.

In a famous 1936 essay, Professor Tolkien once excoriated historians for dismantling the masterful poem *Beowulf* in search of mundane clues about Anglo-Saxon society.[10] Let this book serve as an apology—not an *apologia*—from one historian who tries not to knock over towers in order to understand how they are built. In recent years archaeologists and historians have uncovered a few monuments that might even have prompted the professor to remove his ever-present pipe—if just for a moment—and take notice of the boldness and beauty, of the craft and ingenuity of his beloved Northern peoples.

1

Learning
his craft

from africa to birmingham

John Ronald Reuel Tolkien was born on January 3, 1892, in Bloemfontein, the capital of the Orange Free State, which was later incorporated into South Africa. His parents were Arthur Reuel Tolkien and Mabel Suffield, who had come to southern Africa a year earlier and were married in Cape Town. Mabel gave birth to two sons there, John Ronald (later known to his friends as Ronald) and Hilary. Arthur Tolkien, a bank manager, was the descendant of German immigrants who had come to England in the eighteenth century. His eldest son later took a linguistic interest in the family name, *Tolkiehn*, with its origins in Old Saxony, birthplace of "that noble northern spirit, a supreme contribution to Europe."[1] But two wars against Germany—and the virulent anti-Semitism of the Nazi period—somewhat tempered Ronald's pride in his German roots.[2]

Ronald Tolkien had a far greater interest in his mother's family, the Suffields, whose origins he believed lay in the Anglo-Saxon West Midlands county. "Though a Tolkien by name, I am a Suffield by tastes, talents, and upbringing, and any corner of that country [Worcestershire] (however fair or squalid) is in an indefinable way 'home' to me, as no other part of the world is."[3] It became literally home to him when, suffering from the torrid South African climate, Mabel moved back to the West Midlands, bringing Ronald and Hilary with her to live in Birmingham in 1895. Though meant to be a temporary move, it became permanent when the tragic news of Arthur Tolkien's death from rheumatic fever reached his family in February 1896.

Africa did not have a great influence on Tolkien the writer, given that he left the land of his birth at age three (and before the outbreak of the Boer war in 1899). He

Mabel Tolkien sent this hand-colored Christmas card from South Africa to her family, the Suffields, in Birmingham, in 1892. A nurse holds baby Ronald, then ten months old. Their cook and a servant pose with the Tolkiens.

King Edward's School, Birmingham, 1894; Tolkien was a student there from 1900–1902, and after a brief enrollment at a different school, he returned in 1903, graduating in 1911.

later recorded a few African memories, such as being bitten by a spider that gave him slight arachnophobia—a fear embodied by his menacing Middle-earth spiders. As a white, middle-class child surrounded by black servants, as well as an *Uitlander* (foreigner) in the eyes of the Dutch Boers, he offers an unusual colonial perspective. However, unlike near-contemporary writers such as Kipling and T. H. White, Tolkien showed little interest in the exotic lands where many British military and civil servants found themselves in the *fin de siècle*. Instead, he clung fiercely to his English roots and remained loyal to monarchy and empire.

Mabel Tolkien raised her boys—with little help from her family—in the tiny village of Sarehole, a few miles southeast of Birmingham. Mabel never cut the fair hair of Ronald and Hilary when they were toddlers, leading the local children to call them "wenches," an archaic term that greatly interested Tolkien in later years, during his work for the *Oxford English Dictionary*.[4] To him, turn-of-the-century Worcestershire (which at that time contained Sarehole) was a land of "good water, stones and elm trees and small, quiet rivers and . . . rustic people."[5] Both Ronald and Hilary would later recall their misadventures at Sarehole Mill, where the miller ("the Black Ogre") would steal their shoes when they dipped into the millpond and his son ("the White Ogre"—white from the milled flour) would chase them back home.[6]

In 1900, Tolkien obtained a place at King Edward's School in Birmingham, which had been his father's school. Because the school was

Previous pages: John Ronald Reuel Tolkien, ca. 1955.

*Ronald and Hilary
Tolkien, 1905.*

four miles from Sarehole and Mabel could not afford the train fare, she and the boys moved into the city, which Tolkien remembered as "dreadful."[7] That same year, Mabel Tolkien became a Roman Catholic, leading to a near complete separation from her family (her father was a Unitarian) as well as from the Tolkiens (many of whom were Baptists). She turned for support to Fr. Francis Xavier Morgan, a priest at the nearby Birmingham Oratory. When Mabel was hospitalized for diabetes in early 1904, Ronald went to stay with his Aunt Jane Neave near Brighton. Fr. Francis arranged for Mabel to convalesce in a cottage on the Oratory grounds, and her boys rejoined her there for a few months of idyllic living. But in November, she slipped into a diabetic coma and died at the cottage, with Fr. Francis at her side.

The premature death of his mother would have an enormous and lasting impact on Tolkien. One immediate result was that it drew him even more closely to the Church. In her will, Mabel had appointed Fr. Francis as her sons' guardian, but since they could not live with the priest in the Oratory, he arranged for the boys to stay with various relatives and allowed Ronald to continue his studies at King Edward's School. Every morning the two boys would go to the Oratory and have breakfast with Fr. Francis, after which they would help him serve mass before departing for school. Tolkien started to excel at King Edward's, winning a prize—a book on Roman history—on Speech Day in Autumn 1905, and becoming close to a group of like-minded schoolmates, including Christopher Wiseman, Rob Gilson, G. B. Smith, Vincent Trought, the brothers Wilfrid Hugh and Ralph Payton, Sidney Barrowclough, and T. K. "Tea-cake" Barnsley. At first it was rugby that brought these young men together, but soon they found that they shared a common interest in the history, literature, and art of the ancient and medieval worlds. In addition to the Greek and Latin of their studies, Tolkien became attracted to Old English and Gothic, Wiseman to Egyptian hieroglyphics, Smith to the Welsh language, and Gilson to early Renaissance art. During Tolkien's last term at King Edward's, he and his friends formed the Tea Club and Barrovian Society, or T.C.B.S.

> *"The fire's very cosy here, and the food's very good, and there are Elves when you want them. What more could one want?"*[8]

—BILBO DESCRIBING RIVENDELL IN *THE RETURN OF THE KING*

These "clandestine teas [and] secretive feasts,"[9] which began in the school library before moving to the tearoom at the local Barrow's Stores shop, was where he sharpened his wit and ad hoc critical abilities. It is also where he found his first intellectual community, a band of brothers who conspired against the modernist tendencies of the day. Tolkien's deep affection for these gifted young men made all the more tragic the premature death of Trought in 1912 and the loss of Barnsley, Ralph Payton, Smith, and Gilson in the Great War less than five years later.

It was also during these years that Tolkien met Edith Bratt. She was a fellow orphan and lodger at Mrs. Faulkner's house in Edgbaston, an area in Birmingham where Ronald and Hilary took up residence in 1908. Edith smuggled extra food to the boys and the three became close friends, and after many long walks and bicycle rides together the young couple declared that they were in love. Fr. Francis stepped in at this point, demanding an end to the relationship so that Tolkien could focus on his study for the Oxford entrance exams. He failed in his first attempt at an Oxford scholarship, but by the end of 1910 he had passed the Oxford and Cambridge examination and won a scholarship to study classics at Exeter College, Oxford. He wrote with the good news to Edith, now living in Cheltenham, but believed that he would have won a more prestigious scholarship had he not been distracted from Greek and Latin study by his obsession with Gothic.[10]

The young Edith Bratt, 1906.

OXFORD

GRADUATION FROM KING EDWARD'S SCHOOL included another prize-winning speech for Tolkien, as well as his playing the role of Hermes in Aristophanes' play *Peace* (in

Greek, of course). Following a walking tour of the Swiss Alps, Tolkien took up residence at Oxford's Exeter College in October 1911, his room overlooking Turl Street. He began his studies in Literae Humaniores— the honors course in classics, philosophy, and ancient history at Oxford—which then included classical history and philosophy in the original Greek and Latin. Tolkien chose comparative philology as his "Special Subject" (i.e., discipline specialization). In addition to attending lectures on Gothic by Joseph Wright, he was spending much time on both Welsh and Finnish, having recently read the Finnish epic *The Kalevala*. These languages and poems increasingly lured his attention away from his classical studies.

There were other distractions as well. Tolkien was active in Oxford's undergraduate extracurricular activities, including joining Exeter College's Rugby XV team and Boat Club, a debating society (the Stapledon), the Dialectical Society, and the Essay Club, of which he became president in 1914.[11] He also founded his own dining club, the Apolausticks, in 1912. This list does not even include the numerous teas, dinners, and concerts sponsored by his college and others in Oxford. Indeed, all of the fun and frivolity threatened to plunge Ronald Tolkien and other members of the T.C.B.S. into the world of the Oxford Aesthetes, the decadent and frivolous young men who Evelyn Waugh would later memorably describe in *Brideshead Revisited* and who both Tolkien and C. S. Lewis came to despise. Perhaps to counter this impression, Tolkien also joined King Edward's Horse, a territorial cavalry army regiment (of students drawn mostly from the colonies), which served for Tolkien as a continuity of the Officer Training Corps he had participated in with his friends at King Edward's School.

A recent photograph of Exeter College at Oxford, where Tolkien studied the Literae Humaniores.

At midnight on his twenty-first birthday, Tolkien wrote to Edith in Cheltenham to explain that his feelings for her had not changed and that they could now be married. Edith informed him that she had become engaged to another man, George Field, but agreed to meet with him in Cheltenham. At the end of this visit in January of 1913, Edith broke off her engagement to be with Tolkien, even agreeing to instruction in Catholicism. That February he took the Honour Moderations (examination in classics) and received discouraging Second-Class Honours (the second honors tier of British degree ranks), though his philology essay was praised. He was then advised to start attending lectures in English language and literature, and gravitated toward Old and Middle English, receiving instruction from (among others) eminent scholars A. S. Napier and Kenneth Sisam. He also continued in philology, the study of the structural and historical development of language, a field esteemed in the nineteenth century (especially among German scholars) and now all but extinct (historical comparative linguistics is its successor). Happier with his new field of study, Tolkien continued to see Edith whenever he could, and the two became formally betrothed (though without Fr. Francis's knowledge). They were not married, however, until March 22, 1916, for Tolkien had more than just his Oxford studies weighing on his mind. By August of 1914, Germany had invaded Belgium, and the War to End All Wars had begun.

the gReat waR

IN THE MICHAELMAS (i.e., autumn) term of 1914, there was much enthusiasm among Oxford students to join the British war effort. Almost all of Tolkien's T.C.B.S. friends volunteered. Back home, Hilary Tolkien signed up and would become a bugler in one of the Birmingham volunteer battalions in the Royal Warwickshire Regiment. For Ronald Tolkien, however, the decision to fight against Germany was neither quick nor easy. Despite his cadet training at King Edward's and Exeter—and mock battles on the rugby pitch—the elder Tolkien brother took great pride in his Germanic ancestry and was passionate in his study of the Germanic languages. He also wanted to complete his degree at Oxford and to begin his academic career so that he could support both Edith and himself. A temporary solution presented itself: he could receive army officer training while continuing his studies at Oxford until called up on active duty, hopefully after he had received his degree. Over the course of the academic year, Tolkien would settle into a daily routine of military drills in the mornings, lectures and tutorials in the afternoon, and a still-active social life in the evenings. Still, there were moments of despair and depression as he watched the majority of

In 1914, when this World War I recruitment poster was printed, Tolkien received army officer training while continuing his studies at Oxford.

his fellow Oxford students, and many of the young professors, leave the dreaming spires for the battlefields of France.

It was during this time, separated from Edith and his closest friends, that Tolkien began composing poetry in earnest. There was "Goblin Feet" (published in the volume *Oxford Poetry 1915*), "The Tides," the Lewis Carroll-esque "The Man in the Moon Came Down Too Soon," and "The Voyage of Éarendel the Evening Star." This last was inspired by his reading the following lines from *Crist II*, an Old English poem composed by the Anglo-Saxon poet Cynewulf in the eighth or ninth century (translation follows):

> *Eala Earendel! engla beorhtast*
> *ofer middangeard monnum sended*

> Hail Earendel, brightest of angels,
> Over Middle-earth sent to men.

These lines, as Tom Shippey has shown,[12] were the catalyst for Tolkien's "subcreation" of Middle-earth. ("Subcreation" is Tolkien's term—according to the OED—for inventing an imaginary secondary world.) From here on, he would focus his vague ideas about fairies and goblins into a cohesive universe of related tales, imbued with that same Northern spirit captured by Cynewulf, who had given Tolkien a name begging for explanation. Éarendel the Mariner would become the first hero of Middle-earth, and around his story would grow the great legendarium of which *The Lord of the Rings* and *The Silmarilion* are only a part. But in September 1914, the seed of these great works was a poem—a brief forty-eight lines of verse penned at Phoenix Farm in Gedling (Aunt Jane's new home), to which he gave the Old English title "Sciþfæreld Earendeles Æfensteorran" ("The Voyage of Éarendel the Evening Star").

Following a December meeting with T.C.B.S. members Wiseman, Smith, and Gilson—the inspirational Council of London—Tolkien also began his first systematic attempts at constructing a Gnomish language ("Gnome" becoming his preferred term for "Fairy") that he called "Quenya," based on the Finnish that he was now studying.

In June 1915, Tolkien sat for examinations in the School of English Language and Literature. No doubt the small number of students

A contemporary map of the Norse mythical realm of Midgard, which inspired the name "Middle-earth." Unlike Tolkien's Middle-earth, Vikings believed Midgard to be surrounded by a sea that was encircled by a great serpent, Jörgmungandr, with a land of ice to the north and one of fire to the south.

MIDDLE-EARTH

Tolkien wrote that "Middle-earth" was not a term of his own invention, but rather a modernization of a very old word for the inhabited world of men.[13] The location, nature, and even spelling of Middle-earth have confused many people. But Tolkien clearly had in mind the Norse Midgard, the mythic inhabitable land between the ice-covered land of the north and the region of fire to the south. It appears in Old English as *middan-geard*, in Middle English as *midden-erd* or *middle-erd*. In Tolkien's fiction Middle-earth is set in the midst of encircling seas. It is perhaps more than coincidental that Tolkien's own roots were in the Midlands of England.

remaining, and recent British setbacks in the war, dampened the usually boisterous celebrations that follow third-year exams at Oxford. After the examinations, he applied for a temporary commission in the regular army for the remaining period of the war, requesting to be posted to the 19th Battalion of the Lancashire Fusiliers, in which G. B. Smith and other Oxonians had been serving and training in North Wales. By July, Tolkien learned that he had received First-Class Honours in English, and that he had been appointed second lieutenant in the 13th Battalion of the Lancashire Fusiliers, much to the chagrin of Smith. Lt. Tolkien reported to Bedford later that summer for officer training.

Tolkien had begun his military training by breaking in horses for the King Edward's Horse regiment in Oxford. But in the Lancashire Fusiliers he was to break in men, and these not of the Oxbridge variety. As a junior officer, his duty was to drill the troops and prepare them for battle, treading "the dull backwaters of the art of killing."[14] But he chose infantry signaling as his specialty, with cryptography in particular making good use of his philological training. It was also a choice that might keep him from harm's way. By the end of January 1916, his closest T.C.B.S. friends—Wiseman, Smith, and Gilson—had all departed England for combat duty. It was not until June 6 that Tolkien left to join the British Expeditionary Force in France, arriving first at Étaples before joining his battalion at the front.[15] When the Battle of the Somme began on July 1, the 11th Battalion (to which he was now assigned) was held in reserve, but nevertheless fell under fire from a German field gun at Bouzincourt. Gilson and Payton were among the 400,000 British casualties of the Somme Offensive. On July 15, Tolkien's company finally went "over the top" into No Man's Land for an attack on Ovillers, which was captured the next day. In September, he was involved in the capture of a Saxon regiment at the Schwaben Redoubt during the Battle of Thiepval Ridge, and

Second Lieutenant Tolkien in uniform, 1916.

in October he also helped capture Regina Trench. Toward the end of the month, Lt. Tolkien was diagnosed with "trench fever" and transported to the British Red Cross Hospital at Le Touquet. Trench fever was caused by a bacterium transferred by the lice that were so common and numerous in the filthy trenches. On November 8, he was placed on the hospital ship HMHS *Asturias* and returned to England, to the Southern General Hospital set up at the University of Birmingham. Although eager to rejoin his company, Tolkien would experience lingering and often severe effects from the fever that would keep him in and out of army hospitals for months. Though he did not know it then, the Great War was over for J. R. R. Tolkien.

Page 573   *The War Illustrated, 29th July, 1916.*

Before and After Going Over the Top

British wiring party going up to the trenches. Circle inset: Some of the Lancashire Fusiliers fix bayonets prior to the assault on the enemy's positions, July 1st.

A tense moment in the trenches is when the roll-call is made after a charge, and the number of missing men is revealed by the absence of their voices. This photograph shows such a roll-call on the memorable First of July.

Troops of the Lancashire Fusiliers during the opening day of the Battle of the Somme, July 1, 1916. Tolkien's battalion would "go over the top" into No Man's Land two weeks later.

It was also to be over soon for G. B. Smith, due to deadly gas gangrene, which developed from shrapnel wounds he received on November 29 while on routine patrol not far from Bouzincourt. Not long before this, Smith had written an impassioned letter to his friend and fellow poet from King Edward's School, with a rather poignant sign-off: "May God bless you, my dear John Ronald, and may you say the things I have tried to say long after I am not there to say them, if such be my lot."[16] The belief of his closest T.C.B.S. friends in his own writing abilities, and the untimely deaths especially of Gilson and Smith, laid a heavy burden on Ronald Tolkien. All their boasts of greatness and promises of cultural reform would be mere youthful illusions if he survived yet did not publish his tales of ancient and enchanted lands. "You ought to start the epic," urged the other survivor, Christopher Wiseman. Back in the English countryside, with his wife by his side once more, J. R. R. Tolkien began systematically constructing the history of Middle-earth.

The title page from the 1913 edition of The Roots of the Mountains, *a novel by William Morris that influenced Tolkien. One of the earliest works of fantasy, it was originally published in 1889.*

THE ROOTS OF THE MOUNTAINS WHEREIN IS TOLD SOMEWHAT OF THE LIVES OF THE MEN OF BURG/ DALE THEIR FRIENDS THEIR NEIGHBOURS THEIR FOEMEN AND THEIR FELLOWS IN ARMS BY WILLIAM MORRIS

WHILES CARRIED O'ER THE IRON ROAD,
WE HURRY BY SOME FAIR ABODE;
THE GARDEN BRIGHT AMIDST THE HAY,
THE YELLOW WAIN UPON THE WAY,
THE DINING MEN, THE WIND THAT SWEEPS
LIGHT LOCKS FROM OFF THE SUN-SWEET HEAPS—
THE GABLE GREY, THE HOARY ROOF,
HERE NOW—AND NOW SO FAR ALOOF.
HOW SORELY THEN WE LONG TO STAY
AND MIDST ITS SWEETNESS WEAR THE DAY,
AND 'NEATH ITS CHANGING SHADOWS SIT,
AND FEEL OURSELVES A PART OF IT.
SUCH REST, SUCH STAY, I STROVE TO WIN
WITH THESE SAME LEAVES THAT LIE HEREIN.

LONGMANS, GREEN, AND CO.
LONDON, NEW YORK, AND BOMBAY
MDCCCCXIII

While Tolkien would later reject outright equation of battles and characters in *The Lord of the Rings* with figures and events in the World Wars, he did recognize some influence from his own wartime experiences. "The Dead Marshes and the approaches to the Morannon owe something to Northern France after the Battle of the Somme," he would confess many years later. "They owe more to William Morris and his Huns and Romans, as in *The House of the Wolfings* or *The Roots of the Mountains*."[17]

The last sentence is characteristic of Tolkien, who, like C. S. Lewis, rejected the notion from modern criticism that contemporary concerns outweigh those of the past. Yet Tolkien also admitted that writing was therapeutic for him during the dark and terrible days in the trenches. Writing in May 1944 to his son Christopher (in training with the Royal Air Force in South Africa), who was like his father in temperament and feeling depressed by military camp conditions, the elder Tolkien suggests:

> I think if you could begin to *write*, . . . you would find it a great relief. I sense amongst all your pains (some merely physical) the desire to express your *feeling* about good, evil, fair, foul in some way: to rationalize it, and prevent it just festering. In my case it generated Morgoth and the History of the Gnomes. Lots of the early parts of which . . . were done in grimy canteens, at lectures in cold fogs, in huts full of blasphemy and smut, or by candle light in bell-tents, even some down in dugouts under shell fire.[18]

What served as a positive distraction from the terrors at the front continued during Ronald Tolkien's almost two years of convalescence back in England. Sketches, notes, and poems from this period bring together the personal—new wife and home, loss of boyhood friends, horrific images from the Western Front—with the realm of Faërie, now taking shape through the language, cosmology, and history of the "subcreator" Tolkien. Many years later, he would create a hobbit named Frodo who was healed by Elves in a remarkable place named Rivendell, "the Last Homely House east of the Sea. . . . Merely to be there was a cure for weariness, fear, and sadness."[19]

Despite Tolkien's aversion to biographical criticism, there are many traces of the Great War that can be found throughout his Middle-earth works. There is, for example, the crucial relationship between Sam and Frodo. Many modern readers find it uncomfortable when they read the dialogue between Frodo and Sam that makes it clear there is a master-servant relationship between the two. Indeed, the Peter Jackson films play down this aspect of the story. Tolkien, however, supplies an explanation and context for Sam's role in *The Lord of the Rings*. "My 'Sam Gamgee' is indeed a reflexion of the English soldier," he told Humphrey Carpenter, "of the privates and batmen I knew in the 1914 war, and recognized as far superior to myself."[20] The batman was the personal servant of the officer in the English army. Originally the man who took care of the luggage and the packhorse, the batman had become more of a valet by the late Victorian period.[21] Tolkien found the company of

THE LOST GENERATION

While many scholars and critics have looked to Tolkien's wartime experiences to explain his fiction, it was not until the recent release of restricted records of British Army officers that one could speak with any specificity about the impact of the Great War on Tolkien. British author John Garth was the first to take full advantage of these records, along with private letters from both the Tolkien estate and several members of the T.C.B.S.; his book entitled *Tolkien and the Great War: The Threshold of Middle-earth* (2003) is a fascinating study of these members of the "lost generation."[22]

these working-class men, mostly miners and weavers from Lancashire, much preferable to that of the senior officers in his battalion.

"The Fall of Gondolin," later incorporated into *The Book of Lost Tales* (1984), was written as Tolkien was emerging from the grips of trench fever in early 1917. Garth describes the prose tale as a "dark and complex story of an ancient civilization under siege by nightmare attackers, half-machine and half-monster . . . [with] corpse-choked waters and smoke-filled claustrophobia."[23] In this struggle between good (gnomes) and evil (goblins) in the Faërie realm, we glimpse orcs and balrogs, medieval heraldry and William Morris, not to mention the iron dragons whose hollow bellies carry the enemy—a clear reference to the tanks newly employed on the Western Front. But it was the British who introduced tanks in the war, and so, as Garth points out, the goblins represent for Tolkien the evil in both camps.[24]

A British tank—an iron dragon—at the Battle of Thiepval Ridge, 1916, where Tolkien assisted in the capture of Regina Trench.

Tolkien perhaps avoided the post-traumatic symptoms faced by many returning veterans because, for him, there was a very gradual transition from army to civilian life. In December 1916, he was allowed to come home to Edith in Great Haywood, in the West Midlands,

where Edith had set up home shortly after their wedding. While con-valescing in late 1917, Tolkien was promoted to full lieutenant, and he expected to rejoin his company in France once he was cleared by the medical staff. On November 16, however, Edith gave birth to their first child—John Francis Reuel Tolkien—in Cheltenham (to which she had returned with her cousin Jenny), while Ronald was stationed with the 3rd Lancashire Fusiliers at Thirtle Bridge, in Yorkshire. Edith and the baby joined Ronald in Yorkshire later that month, but Ronald was transferred back to Staffordshire, to Penkridge Camp, in the spring of 1918. His family took up new residence at a cottage called Gipsy Green (in Teddesley Hay), sketched by Tolkien and memorialized as "Nomad's Green" in *The Book of Lost Tales*.[25] Further relapses of trench fever and other physical ailments kept Tolkien from returning to France, and instead he was posted at Brocton Camp, where he contracted gastritis. While Tolkien returned to the hospital, the remaining members of his original battalion were all killed or taken prisoner at the Third Battle of the Aisne (May 27–June 6, 1918) along the Chemin des Dames ridge north of Paris.[26] In October 1918, the army medical board finally gave Tolkien permission to seek civilian employment. Too late in the year for obtaining an academic appointment, he accepted an offer from his former tutor William Craigie to join the staff of the *Oxford English Dictionary*. The Tolkien family returned to Oxford shortly after the Armistice was signed on November 11, ending the Great War.

Tolkien the Scholar

"I HAVE SPENT MOST OF MY LIFE . . . studying Germanic matters (in the general sense that includes England and Scandinavia)," wrote Tolkien to his son Michael in 1941, "which I have ever loved, and tried to present in its true light."[27] Part of presenting these matters in their true light was, for the Oxford philologist, to devote his scholarly attention to detailed study of Germanic words and texts. Tolkien was taught foreign languages from a very early age by his mother, and so it is natural that his love of language would be associated with a beloved mother who was taken from him when he—and she—were young. But he was also an inventor of languages from an early age, and this gave him a particular affinity for philology. He was ideally suited, in other words, for work as a lexicographer working on the most important dictionary of the English language.

In 1919, Tolkien began work at the Oxford English Dictionary *in the Old Ashmolean building, shown here in a present-day photograph—it is now occupied by the Museum of the History of Science.*

In January of 1919, Tolkien joined the staff of the *Oxford English Dictionary* in the Old Ashmolean building on Broad Street. He was assigned entries beginning with the letter *W*, so one consulting the *OED* today might find his work under *walrus*, for example.[28] The modest salary paid by Oxford University Press led Tolkien to take on additional work as a tutor at the university, and in particular at the women's colleges Lady Margaret Hall and St. Hugh's. Flexible hours also allowed him to work on his first scholarly publication, the glossary for *Fourteenth-Century Verse and Prose* (1921), edited by his former tutor Kenneth Sisam.

According to American Tolkien bibliographer Wayne G. Hammond, over the course of his life Tolkien published one book of scholarship (plus two of collected essays), five critical editions and/or translations of Old and Middle English works, and about a dozen journal articles and other scholarly essays.[29] While respectable, this output is hardly that expected of a scholar who held three professorships (two at Oxford) and an academic career spanning some forty years. Much more scholarship could have been published (judging by his research notes) had he not, of course, devoted so much of his time to his family, his friends, his students, and his fiction. But then, he would not be J. R. R. Tolkien if he had only thought about his academic career. Still, Michael D. C. Drout, professor and chair of English at Wheaton, argues that while his scholarly output may not have been prolific, Tolkien's textual criticism—especially of *Beowulf* and *The Battle of Maldon*—were quite influential among generations of Anglo-Saxon scholars.[30]

"BEOWULF: THE MONSTERS AND THE CRITICS"

Tolkien read *Beowulf* for the first time (or at least the first time in Old English) at King Edward's School, and attended lectures on *Beowulf* by both Kenneth Sisam and A. S. Napier as an undergraduate at Oxford. As a professor at both Leeds and Oxford, he regularly lectured on the epic poem, and he wrote both an alliterative verse and a Modern English prose translation, the former left incomplete and the latter never published. On November 26, 1936, he delivered the Sir Israel Gollancz

Memorial Lecture at the British Academy in London, and it was titled "*Beowulf*: The Monsters and the Critics." Published the following year, this was to become one of the most important works of criticism ever written on the Anglo-Saxon epic.[31]

Tolkien begins his essay by taking a shot at those literary critics—even more numerous now than in his day—who seem to find the criticism to be more important than the literature itself. Admitting that he has not read everything ever written on *Beowulf*, he has nevertheless read enough to know that few scholars have been interested in the poem as a literary work, as opposed to a historical artifact from which they can mine bits of information about Anglo-Saxon culture. He illustrates this point with an allegory.[32] A man builds a great tower from stones that had once been part of an ancient building. His friends recognize the antiquity of the stones and knock the tower over in order to find hidden inscriptions, the date of the stones, or even a deposit of coal beneath them. "This tower is most interesting," they say, as they knock it over, but also, "What a muddle it is in!"[33]

The second attack launched by Tolkien in the essay is against those critics who complain that *Beowulf* is simplistic, centered on a one-dimensional hero fighting one-dimensional monsters. (By comparison, John Gardner's novel *Grendel* (1971) portrays a one-dimensional Beowulf while delving into the complex psyche of the monster Grendel.) Too many monsters, say these critics—"a wilderness of dragons"—and too little human affairs for a person of "correct and sober taste."[34] "A dragon is no idle fancy," retorts Tolkien, but rather in legend "a potent creation of men's imagination," and both ancient and modern poets took great interest in these "unfashionable creatures."[35] There are many heroes in literature, he points out, but very few good dragons, and the *Beowulf* poet gives us one that is both *draco* [Latin for dragon]—a bestial and terrifying worm—and *draconitas* ["dragon-ness"]—"a personification of malice, greed, destruction (the evil side of heroic life), and of the undiscriminating cruelty of fortune that discriminates not good or bad (the evil side of all life)." For Tolkien, Beowulf is not a common hero; he faces "a foe more evil than any human enemy," yet he is "incarnate in time, walking in heroic history, and treading the named lands of the North." While they may be unfashionable (at least among critics), neither hero nor dragon is silly, flat, or frivolous; indeed, it is their serious and realistic combat that will inspire the creation of Smaug, Túrin,

The hero Beowulf with the head of the monster Grendel; this illustration appeared in a 1908 book titled Stories of Beowulf, *by British children's author Henrietta Elizabeth Marshall.*

and Glaurung. Part of Tolkien's genius is that he makes his readers feel that they, too, are walking in heroic history.

If there is a central theme to the poem, it is for Tolkien "man at war with the hostile world, and his inevitable overthrow in Time."[36] Grendel, Grendel's mother, and the dragon are thus symbols of the hostile—be it in wild places or at court—and Beowulf is an Everyman who, though heroic, must ultimately lose the battle against Time. But for all its pessimism, the Anglo-Saxon poem is a fusion of Northern (pagan) courage—"perfect because without hope"—with a cosmology based on Scripture.[37] "A Christian was (and is) still like his [pagan] forefathers," writes Tolkien, "a mortal hemmed in a hostile world."[38] The *Beowulf* poet, a Christian, looks back into the heroic pagan past but recognizes there a tragedy that both traditions held to be true: that all earthly glory—no matter how grand—will end in night. The dawn offered through Salvation is assumed, but not treated, in the poem. Thus, Tolkien not only supplies a fresh critique of the first great work of English literature, he also attempts to reconstruct the worldview of Anglo-Saxon culture with one foot in the pagan past and the other in the Christian future, a worldview in which remarkable bravery and courage were displayed without hope of final victory, until the victory won on the Cross brought a ray of hope to the cold, dark Northern world. This *zeitgeist* of the barbarian heroic age would in turn provide a guiding spirit for both *The Lord of the Rings* and *The Silmarillion*.

"on fairy-stories"

In his *Beowulf* essay, Tolkien writes: "I will not here . . . attempt at length a defense of the mythical mode of imagination."[39] However, that is exactly what he *does* attempt in his essay "On Fairy-stories." This essay too began life as a lecture, and was written shortly after his *Beowulf* piece. On Wednesday evening March 8, 1939, Tolkien delivered the eleventh Andrew Lang Lecture in the United College Hall at the University of St. Andrews. Titled simply "Fairy Stories," it was first published (in 1947) as part of a collection of essays in honor of Charles Williams and still later (1964) as part of a short book called *Tree and Leaf* (with the short story "Leaf by Niggle").[40] From Tolkien's notes and newspaper accounts of the lecture, it is clear that his talk was significantly altered and expanded for publication.[41]

In the published essay, Tolkien begins with definitions. What are fairy stories? Are they different than fairy tales and nursery tales? What are fairies? In the OED, he tells us, the term *fairy tale* first appears in 1750, with three definitions listed: a tale or legend about fairies; an unreal or fantastic story; or a falsehood. Fairies, meanwhile, are defined as "supernatural beings of diminutive size" who work magic on men.[42] Tolkien rejects all of these meanings for his purposes. The diminutive fairy is a literary invention, he says, utilized by both William Shakespeare in *Midsummer Night's Dream* (ca. 1595) and Michael Drayton in his fairy poem *Nymphidia* (1627), and reaching the height of popularity—and frivolity—in

A beautiful fairy is depicted on the title page of The Red Fairy Book *(1890) by Andrew Lang, one of Tolkien's favorite authors of fairy stories.*

the flower fairies of the Victorian Age.[43] And while *fairy* is a relatively modern word, *Faërie* is an ancient concept preserved in many medieval stories. Faërie is Elfland, "the Perilous Realm itself," elusive, indescribable, unable to be "caught in a net of words."[44] While stories about Faërie may contain Fairies, Elves, or Dwarves, they do not have to. Tolkien excludes traveler's tales, dream fiction, and beast fables from his definition. Above all, fairy stories are not falsehoods or lies, and do not contain artificial plot devices. They are not primarily for children—and thus not the same as nursery tales—but are expressions of an adult longing or desire to create a world that is recognizable and yet immensely richer than our own. This is not just an act of subcreation for Tolkien, but a power that enables us to see lost beauties.

Tolkien argues that fairy stories, if well written, should share many qualities with other forms of literature. In addition to these, however, they also offer "Fantasy, Recovery, Escape, Consolation."[45] Fantasy here is defined as both the imagining of things strange and wonderful not actually present in what he calls the "Primary World" and the art of subcreating a "Secondary World" filled with such things, yet imbued with an "inner consistency of reality." It is, for Tolkien, "not a lower but a higher form of Art, [but] indeed the most nearly pure form, and so (when achieved) the most potent."[46] As potent as this human art is, the elves have a better one—Enchantment—that "can produce Fantasy with a realism and immediacy beyond the compass of any human mechanism."[47] Tolkien distinguishes this natural craft of the elves from Magic, the artifice of the Magician, who uses it to alter the Primary World for the purpose of power and domination. Faerian Drama is produced by elves (not men) within a fairy story (produced by men). Human Fantasy aspires to elvish Enchantment, even *if*—and Tolkien is always careful to add if—the elves are themselves a product of Fantasy. The dramas in the Perilous Realm have an even greater power and immediacy to the mortals within the story than the story has upon the reader. To those who say that Fantasy is childish folly, Tolkien answers that it is a "natural human activity," not in contradiction to reason but dependent upon it; it is "a human right" exercised because we ourselves were made, and "made in the image and likeness of a Maker."[48]

Tolkien next explores the Recovery, Escape, and Consolation aspects of fairy stories. Fantasy cleans our windows, he writes, so that we can see more clearly—Recover—those things that have been covered by "the drab blur of triteness or familiarity."[49] It also offers an Escape from the artificial to the natural. Utilizing the metaphor of the prisoner, Tolkien asks critics of fantasy if it is not natural for a prisoner to try to escape from a prison, to dream of escape, and talk to other prisoners about returning home?[50] As for the "Real Life"—the mass-produced existence from which fantasists are denounced for escaping—are cars more "real" than horses, or more "alive" than dragons and centaurs? Is a preference for describing trees and lightening rather than electric street lamps childish? Modernist realism may demand factories and machine-guns of its celebrated authors, but surely it is neither irrational nor irresponsible to prefer trees and castles and clouds.

Myth and Fantasy

any categorize—and sometimes dismiss—J. R. R. Tolkien as a fantasy writer. While this might be a convenient organizing principle for a modern bookstore, the genre of fantasy literature as we now recognize it did not exist when Tolkien first began composing his tales of Middle-earth. Indeed, an argument can be made that Tolkien himself *invented* modern fantasy writing. He was both a scholar of as well as a producer of myth. The English word *myth* is a Victorian creation, from the Latin *mythus* (Greek *muthos*), and the *Oxford English Dictionary* offers two very different definitions:

1. a traditional story, especially one concerning the early history of a people or explaining a natural or social phenomenon, and typically involving supernatural beings or events.

2. a widely held but false belief or idea.

While the second definition is more widely embraced in our day, Tolkien was interested in the first. By studying ancient myths, he sought understanding about the people who produced them; by writing his own, he acted as a subcreator, carrying on the tradition for modern audiences. Like ancient myths but unlike most modern fantasy, Tolkien's subcreation aimed for higher things than artistic novelty and creative ingenuity. "It was the only way that certain transcendent truths could be expressed in intelligible form," writes English-born writer and professor of humanities Joseph Pearce.[51] As Tolkien famously explained to C. S. Lewis in 1931 during an after-dinner walk they had with Hugo Dyson, a Lecturer in English at Reading University, Christianity was "the truest myth," the one played out in recorded history. Or, to put it another way, it was God's myth told directly to man as opposed to men's myths in which God used the mind of the individual poet to express Himself, "using such images as He found there."[52]

The Great Escape—from death—is the Consolation offered by many fairy stories, but not unique to them. The Happy Ending is, however, an essential part of all fairy stories for Tolkien. He invents a word to describe it: *eucatastrophe*, the "sudden joyous turn" in a story, the "good catastrophe."[53] Like theological grace, eucatastrophe is mysterious, not controlled by humans, and cannot be counted on to recur. The fairy story must allow for the possibility of tragedy—of grief and sorrow—for its Happy Ending to be believable and effective. But it also denies "universal final defeat," and gives its characters a "fleeting glimpse of Joy, Joy beyond the walls of the world, poignant as grief."[54]

This theological interpretation of the joy given by fairy stories is further explored in an epilogue attached to the essay. Here, Tolkien argues that the *evangelium*—the Gospel (OE *gōdspel*, "good tale"), the story of the Crucifixion and Resurrection of Jesus—is the greatest *eucatastrophe* of all. All fairy stories conceived before the Nativity were looking forward to it, all those written after the Resurrection are sanctified by it.[55]

As opposed to his *Beowulf* essay, "On Fairy-Stories" at first had little impact on academia. It is hardly mentioned by reviewers and critics until 1964, when it was published as part of *Leaf and Tree*. Tolkien's dismissal of the folklorists, who, in their categorization of motifs in fairy stories, "miss the soup for the bones," naturally evokes disagreement from academics of that ilk. Many academics also appear to be uncomfortable with Tolkien's overtly religious exegesis of fairy stories, and thus pass over the essay or this part of it in silence. Tolkien biographer Humphrey Carpenter criticized "On Fairy-Stories" for making too many points to be entirely cogent.[56] More recently, scholars have responded that Tolkien was not trying to prove a single thesis in the essay, but rather was surveying broadly critical thought on the subject of fairy stories and ultimately arguing that they constitute a legitimate literary genre.[57] Most important, however, is the fact that Tolkien himself felt that the ideas he developed in the essay contributed to his writing of *The Lord of the Rings*.[58] He described the book in his letters as a fairy story, and the novel's vivid depiction of the Perilous Realm and its compelling eucatastrophe almost seem to follow the blueprint laid out in "On Fairy-stories."

Tolkien the teacher

FEW SCHOLARS IN TOLKIEN'S DAY—and perhaps even fewer in our own—operated outside of academia. The academic career that Tolkien was so eager to begin meant ultimately landing a permanent teaching position. During the summer of 1920, he applied for the full-time position of Reader in English Language at the University of Leeds. With the department's Oxford connections and a good interview, Tolkien was offered the job. Edith gave birth to their second son, Michael, in October, and so Tolkien's family did not join him in the northern industrial town until early 1921. George Gordon, Professor of English at Leeds, took Tolkien under his wing and gave him the freedom to design the philological side of the English curriculum.

Tolkien also befriended a new lecturer named E. V. Gordon, who was to become his most significant collaborator. They worked together on a new edition of the Middle English poem *Sir Gawain and the Green Knight*, with Tolkien responsible for the text and Gordon for the notes, published by Clarendon Press in 1925. Tolkien's first significant scholarly contribution, this would serve as the definitive edition for two generations.

Tolkien and Gordon also collaborated on a very different kind of project: the Viking Club. This was a social gathering where undergraduate students met to drink beer, read Norse sagas, and sing comedic songs. Most of the songs were co-written by Tolkien and Gordon: funny stories about their students, nursery rhymes in Anglo-Saxon, and Norse drinking songs, they were published later as *Songs for the Philologists* (1936).[59] This, according to Carpenter, only increased their popularity as teachers and led to an unusually large number of undergraduates at Leeds specializing in philology.[60] Tolkien was also popular with the university administration and in 1924 a new chair was created just for him: the Professorship of the English Language. He was only thirty-two at the time of his appointment.

That same year Ronald and Edith welcomed a third child—Christopher Reuel Tolkien, named after Christopher Wiseman—and settled into a comfortable new house in Leeds. However, early in 1925, the position of Rawlinson and Bosworth Professor of Anglo-Saxon at Oxford opened up, and Ronald applied. Going up against much more

The Tolkien family moved to North Oxford in 1926, where they took up residence in this house on Northmoor Road.

senior candidates—including his former tutor Kenneth Sisam—Tolkien was appointed to the professorship. Assuming his new duties at Oxford that fall, including a professorial fellowship at the university's Pembroke College, Tolkien would continue teaching at Leeds as well for several months. In January 1926, the family moved to Oxford and took up residence on Northmoor Road in North Oxford, where they would live for the next twenty-one years. A baby girl—Priscilla Mary Reuel—was born to them there in 1929, and in his study the Rawlinson and Bosworth Professor would work on his lectures, revise his mythological cycle, and meet students for tutorials.

Due to his tendency to mumble and go off on tangents, Tolkien was by most accounts not a brilliant lecturer. However, when he recited poetry—especially *Beowulf*—he could move his audience with great passion, and C. S. Lewis recommended Tolkien's lectures to undergraduates for the insights contained in his many asides ("an inspired speaker of footnotes," he called Tolkien).[61] Although Tolkien enjoyed lecturing, his strengths as a teacher were most evident in tutorials (the opposite could probably be said of Lewis). When discussing texts one-on-one with students, he was affable, patient, and excited about both his own and his students' discoveries. He became a mentor to many Oxford students who studied English with him, including two generations of Anglo-Saxonists, such as Bruce Mitchell and Alan Bliss, and the poet W. H. Auden.

The notoriously low salary of an Oxford don, however, led Tolkien to seek other sources of income to support his large family. A common way for British academics to supplement their income was to serve as an external examiner, marking student papers from other schools and universities. He referred to this tedious job as "the examina-

A photochrom of Merton College, Oxford, ca. 1900. Where Tolkien held the post of Merton Professor of English Language and Literature from 1945–59.

tion treadmill." In the autumn of 1945, Tolkien was appointed to his third academic chair, as Merton Professor of English Language and Literature. Not only was this a prestigious appointment, it also meant a move to Merton College, and he found this fellowship more agreeable than that of Pembroke. Merton would be very good to Tolkien to his last days, spent in retirement looking out upon the beautiful Fellow's Garden and Christ Church Meadow. But on most Thursday evenings, he could be found across High Street, in the so-called New Building at Magdalene College, part of a new fellowship that would become Oxford's most famous.

the Inklings

In the below lines for an unfinished, untitled, undated poem that J. R. R. Tolkien wrote in Old English (translation follows), he parodies both his favorite poem, *Beowulf* (whose opening line is *Hwæt! we gardena in gear-dagum*), and his beloved group of Oxford friends—the Inklings—who gathered about the broad "Hlothwig," an Anglo-Saxon version of the name Lewis.

> *Hwæt! we Inclinga on ærdagum*
> *searoþancolra snyttru gehierdon. . . .*
> *Þara wæs Hloðuig sum, hæleða dyrost,*
> *brad ond beorhtword, cuþe he . . .*[62]

> Lo! We in olden days heard
> Of the wisdom of the cunning Inklings.
> How those wise ones sat together in their deliberations,
> Skillfully reciting learning and song-craft,
> Earnestly meditating. That was true joy!
> There was one Hlothwig, of men dearest,
> Broad and word-bright; he knew . . .

Tolkien, C. S. Lewis, and Charles Williams are the most famous of the Inklings, and for many, their writings have come to define the Christian, fantasist, and conservative/reactionary literary movement that took place at Oxford in the 1930s and '40s—which was contra- or anti-modernism and the Oxford Aesthetes—whose influence has only grown over the decades since Lewis's and Tolkien's deaths.

Tolkien first met C. S. Lewis at a gathering of the Oxford English faculty at Merton College on May 11, 1926. After tea, Tolkien approached Lewis, who had just recently been elected Fellow and Tutor at Magdalene College, to solicit his support for keeping language study in the English curriculum at Oxford.

> *"He is a smooth, pale, fluent little chap—can't read Spenser because of the forms—thinks language is the real thing in the school—thinks all literature is written for the amusement of men between thirty and forty. . . . Technical hobbies are more in his line."*[63]

—C. S. LEWIS, DIARY ENTRY ABOUT MEETING TOLKIEN, MAY 11, 1926

Despite Tolkien's lack of interest in Spenser and literary criticism, Lewis joined his side in the fight over the English curriculum and they were to prevail, keeping Old and Middle English works at the center of the Oxford English syllabus. Tolkien invited Lewis to attend meetings of the Kolbítar ("Coal-biters"), the informal faculty reading club Tolkien founded earlier that year for the purpose of reading and translating Icelandic sagas and other Old Norse works. Somewhat resembling the Viking Club he had cofounded with E. V. Gordon at Leeds, it was named for the Norse youths who lounged so close to the hearth fire in winter that they appeared to be biting the coal. Tolkien also became a member of the Oxford Arthurian society, founded by French scholar Eugène Vinaver in 1927, and the exclusive Oxford Dante Society (of which Lewis and Charles Williams were also members).[64]

Of all the societies and clubs that existed during the interwar years at Oxford (and Tolkien was a member of many of them), it was the group known as the Inklings that would have the widest and most lasting impact. Begun around 1931 by an Oxford undergraduate, Edward Tangye Lean, when he graduated in 1933 the club's only remaining members—Lewis and Tolkien—took it over as a sort of transformed Kolbítar, albeit wider in scope, to resemble the interests of Lewis, the Inklings' unofficial but undisputed center and master of ceremonies. Tolkien described the Inklings to his publisher Stanley Unwin in 1938 as "our literary club of *practising poets*—before whom the *Hobbit*, and other works (such as *the Silent Planet*) have been read."[65] John Wain, one of Lewis' former students, called it "a circle of investigators . . . meeting to urge one another on in the task of redirecting the whole current of contemporary art and life."[66]

Throughout the 1930s, Lewis and Tolkien would meet Monday mornings for a drink and a talk, "one of the pleasantest spots in the week," Lewis would recall.[67] This turned into a wider and bawdier gathering of Lewis's friends on Tuesdays, after morning classes and usually in the backroom of the Eagle and Child pub (aka the "Bird and Baby"). On Thursday evenings the group would meet in Lewis's rooms at Magdalene College (and occasionally in Tolkien's Merton rooms) for tea, a formal reading of (usually) an original work by one of its members, followed by beer and animated criticism. While the Tuesday morning sessions tended to be mostly drinking and banter in which outsiders sometime joined, the Thursday evening gatherings were more formal and could accurately be described as a writers group.[68] The "undetermined and unelected circle of friends who gathered about C. S. L.," as Tolkien put it,[69] included himself; Lewis's brother Warnie (Major Warren Lewis); Owen Barfield (a lawyer and writer); classicist Colin Hardie; Hugo Dyson and Nevill Coghill, both of whom were introduced to Tolkien while undergraduates at Exeter College; Rev. Adam Fox (a poetry professor and Dean of Divinity at Magdalene); Tolkien's youngest son and aspiring philologist Christopher Tolkien; C. E. Stevens (ancient history Tutor at Magdalene); Lord David Cecil

The Eagle and Child pub (aka the "Bird and Baby") today; during the 1930s, members of the Inklings would meet there often for literary discussions—and drinks.

C. S. Lewis

live Staples Lewis, known to his friends as "Jack," was born in Belfast in 1898. Close to his mother who died when he was only nine, Jack was sent by an emotionally distant father to a series of boarding schools in England and finally to a private tutor who prepared him for the Oxford exams. His undergraduate years at University College, Oxford, where he took First Class honors in "Greats" (ancient history and philosophy) and later English language and literature, was interrupted by a year in the trenches at the Western Front (he was wounded in April 1918 at the Battle of Arras). In 1925, Lewis was awarded an English fellowship at Magdalene College, where he stayed until Cambridge offered him a professorship in 1954. He married the American writer Joy Gresham Davidman in 1956 (he was devastated when she died of cancer in 1960), and lived for more than thirty years at a modest home outside Oxford known as the Kilns, often in the company of his brother Warnie. C. S. Lewis died on November 22, 1963, the same day both John F. Kennedy and Aldous Huxley died.

C. S. Lewis was by profession a medievalist, writing noteworthy literary criticism of, among other things, courtly romance and Milton's *Paradise Lost*. He became famous, however, as a radio lecturer and writer of Christian apologetics, making very public his adult conversion from atheism to Christianity. In the 1950s, his fame would extend beyond Britain with the publication of his beloved children's fantasy series, *The Chronicles of Narnia*. Lewis's friendship with fellow Oxford medievalist J. R. R. Tolkien led directly to his own conversion and to Tolkien's publication of *The Lord of the Rings*. While Lewis and the other Inklings affectionately called Tolkien "Tollers," in his writing Tolkien calls his friend and colleague "C. S. L." or simply "Lewis." Together (though not always in agreement), the writings of C. S. Lewis and J. R. R. Tolkien have come to define one of the great counter-movements in twentieth-century English literature and thought.

C. S. Lewis at Oxford, 1946.

(a biographer and sometime Oxford don); Cdr. James Dundas-Grant; R. E. Havard (Lewis's and the Tolkien family's physician); Fr. Gervase Mathew (a Dominican priest and lecturer at Blackfriars Hall College); the historian R. B. McCallum; John Wain (a novelist and later Professor of Poetry at Oxford); the Anglo-Saxonist C. L. Wrenn; and, from 1940 to his death in 1945, the enigmatic writer and editor Charles Williams.[70]

Much has been written about the Inklings, most—though not all—by later admirers. Many of its members were Oxford academics, most were Christian, and several were Roman Catholic; all were male. Most of the Inklings shared an interest in history and older literature, and a dislike of modern literary tastes. They "were academic in the best sense of the word" and "read imaginatively," recalled David Cecil in 1979. "The great books of the past were to them living in the same way as the work of a contemporary."[71] They were by no means all of one mind, however, and one of their hallmarks was unrestrained criticism of each other's ideas and writings. The truest common denominator was friendship with C. S. Lewis, and thus Lewis's move to Cambridge in 1954, his subsequent marriage to Joy Davidman, and his death in 1963, all contributed to the Inklings' demise.

If the T.C.B.S. was Tolkien's youth, the Inklings were his middle age. Clearly Lewis, in part, filled the role of intimate and critic that Wiseman, Smith, and Gilson had served for Tolkien. C. S. Lewis was also a medievalist and an Oxford don, and thus had more in common with Tolkien than did Wiseman in the postwar years, and Lewis's criticisms and suggestions were taken seriously by Tolkien. For Lewis, however, the intimacy had a different effect. "All of Lewis's fiction, after the two met at Oxford University in 1926," writes Colin Duriez in *J. R. R. Tolkien and C. S. Lewis: The Story of Their Friendship* (2003), "bears the mark of Tolkien's influence, whether in names he used or in the creation of convincing fantasy worlds."[72] While this may be a slight exaggeration, it is not far from the mark. Tolkien was aware that his (then-unpublished) writings were influencing Lewis's Space Trilogy.[73] He was also aware that the trilogy's central character, the philologist Dr. Elwin Ransom, bore a remarkable resemblance to himself.[74] He saw his ideas being "Lewisified," as he told his son Christopher in 1944, but appears not to have objected. Most important of all his influences on Lewis was Tolkien's explanation of Christianity as "the truest myth," made during a memorable late night walk with Lewis and Dyson on Addison's Walk in Magdalene Deer

Addison's Walk in Magdalen Deer Park at Oxford, where Tolkien and Hugo Dyson had a momentous walk with C. S. Lewis in 1931.

Park in 1931 (see page 21). Lewis recalled in his spiritual autobiography, *Surprised by Joy* (1955), that this conversation led directly to his own conversion to Christianity. Lewis attempted to repay this debt by constant encouragement of Tolkien in his Middle-earth writing, resulting in the publication of both *The Hobbit* and *The Lord of the Rings*.

In 1954, it was announced that a new chair had opened at Cambridge, Professor of Medieval and Renaissance Literature. Tolkien, who sat on the nominating committee for the chair, recommended Lewis and encouraged him to apply for it.[75] Lewis had been passed over three times for similar professorships at Oxford. While his new job and his growing relationship with Joy Davidman may have contributed to Lewis's drift away from Tolkien, "the similarities that united them," remarks Duriez, "were always stronger than the differences that separate them."[76] Tolkien wrote the poem "Mythopoeia" (1931) in part to explain subcreation to Lewis. In this poem, we see Tolkien as culture critic—a favorite role of Lewis's—praising ancient myth while blasting modernity for its lies and materialism.

Lewis, Tolkien, and Williams shared, as writers, what Anglican priest and Charles William Society secretary Richard Sturch has called Moralism, or a passionate interest in the goodness of humans and creation.[77] Unlike their modernist contemporaries, Tolkien and Lewis did not reject the bourgeois values held by the majority of their readers. Political conservatism and Christian ethics, patriotism, love of family and the countryside—these are hardly the defining characteristics of the works of modernists like Oscar Wilde, James Joyce, and Virginia Woolf. The Inklings were not disillusioned and tormented artists, nor were they bohemian rebels railing against the conventional morals of society. This does not mean, however, that they were incapable of creating characters in their works who *could* be described as such: Williams's novels are filled with them, and certainly Gollum could be said to be disillusioned and tormented. But it is the power of myth and poetry to bridge the gap between mortals and the divine that links and perhaps most defines the writings of Lewis, Williams, and Tolkien, as well as Barfield.[78]

fame and Retirement

ANOTHER THING THAT C. S. LEWIS AND J. R. R. TOLKIEN shared in common was unexpected and extraordinary fame. The fan letters that followed the publication of *The Hobbit* in 1937 grew exponentially with the release of *The Lord of the Rings* (1954–55). While first attempting to answer his fans with personal letters, eventually Tolkien had to employ a secretary and finally had to let his publisher send form letters.[79] Phone calls from American fans—often in the middle of the night—and uninvited visitors to his Oxford home led Tolkien to remove his number and address from publication. He was not well suited for celebrity—"my deplorable cultus" as he called it.[80] "Fame puzzled him," observed Carpenter, who was granted a lengthy interview in 1967. "Certainly let his readers be enthusiastic about the stories, but why should they make a fuss of him?"[81]

Financial success, however, allowed Tolkien to contemplate retirement from his teaching duties at Oxford. Retirement came at the age of sixty-seven, and on June 5, 1959, the retiring Merton Professor of English delivered a valedictory address at Merton College Hall.[82] In the address, Tolkien reflected upon the educational practices of the university during his career (decrying, for example, the increased emphasis on post-graduate research at Oxford) and on the battles fought between the "Lit and Lang" factions of the English faculty, battles that first brought him and C. S. Lewis together as allies. Most importantly, he defended his academic field, philology ("love of words"), against the misologists ("haters of words") who dominated modern literary criticism, dragging their students and readers down into a pit of dullness and linguistic ignorance. Despite the often-bitter tone of the address, Tolkien used his farewell to explain that because misology had become the norm, he *had* to go outside academe to show people the beauty and wonder of language and how words preserve "fragments of a noble past." As philologist Tom Shippey puts it, Tolkien's "utility for the lover of literature lies in the way he showed creativity arising from the ramifications of words . . . carrying within themselves very strong suggestions of 'the reality of history' and 'the reality of human nature.'"[83] If academic

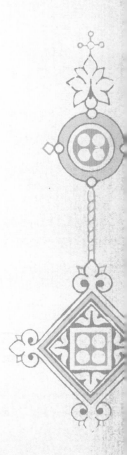

isolation was one of the themes of the valedictory address, the isolation continued for both Ronald and Edith Tolkien living in their Sandfield Road home in Headington, some two miles from the center of Oxford. Inklings gatherings had dwindled in number in the mid-1950s, and C. S. Lewis and Ronald Tolkien saw little of each other after Lewis's marriage to Joy Davidman, though Edith and Joy did become friends for a short while before the latter's death in 1960. The passing of C. S. Lewis in 1963 was very hard on Ronald—"an axe-blow near the roots," he called it.[84] Edith's health continued to deteriorate, and Ronald did not like to leave her alone for long. Never truly happy in Oxford, Edith convinced her husband to leave the city in 1968 for the Dorset coast, an area they had visited many times on holiday. Edith made many friends among the affluent elderly who vacationed at the Hotel Miramar in Bournemouth. The Tolkiens decided to purchase a house in Poole, near Bournemouth, where the author's whereabouts could be kept secret from over-adoring fans. They lived in the bungalow in relative luxury—for the first time in their lives—until Edith's death in November 1971.

The shock and grief Ronald experienced following Edith's passing might have been unbearable had it not been for two things: family and Oxford. He spent a lot of time visiting his brother Hilary and his children after Edith's death, and especially enjoyed playing with his grandchildren. But it was his return to Oxford that really lifted his spirits. Merton College offered him an extraordinary honor: a set of college rooms on Merton Street (with nearly free board) and the position of resident honorary Fellow. Other honors came to him at this time, including a trip to Buckingham Palace to receive the C.B.E. (Commander of the Most Excellent Order of the British Empire) from the Queen and honorary doctorates from Oxford and the University of Edinburgh.[85] Digestive troubles occasionally plagued him, but he felt well enough to travel back to Bournemouth to visit

The Merton Street college rooms where Tolkien lived after Edith's passing in 1971.

friends in August of 1973. During the visit he suffered from a bleeding ulcer, and in the hospital developed a chest infection. With his son John and daughter Priscilla at his side, J. R. R. Tolkien died on September 2, 1973. He was eighty-one years old.

Writing Tolkien

A BIOGRAPHICAL APPROACH TO J. R. R. TOLKIEN is necessarily fraught with difficulty. To begin with, one must deal with a scarcity of personal records, especially for the years between King Edward's and his first Oxford professorship. What survives is, for the most part, restricted by the Tolkien Estate, though both Carpenter and Garth were granted access to important early material. Then there is the attitude of the professor himself: "An author cannot of course remain wholly unaffected by his experience, but the ways in which a story-germ uses the soil of experience are extremely complex."[86]

Tolkien specialist Dimitra Fimi has defended the biographical approach to understanding his writings, partly on the grounds that Tolkien himself claimed to "hold the key" to the understanding of Middle-earth.[87] But she also cautions against accepting in its entirety the "biographical legend" that Tolkien created though his letters and various interviews. Tolkien did not do this because of egoism; rather, he apparently liked being mischievous and contrarian. He enjoyed challenging his readers and his critics just as he enjoyed challenging his students: ultimately challenge would lead to stronger argument and better understanding. Such is the pedagogical style of the typical Oxford tutorial, and such was the method of the *magister* in the medieval university, advocating a contrary position in order to draw a better thesis from his *discipulus*.

As his *Beowulf* essay teaches us, Professor Tolkien would ask us not what do his writings tell us about the author, but rather what can we learn from the context of the author's life that will help us to better understand his writings? One of the first biographical themes that become evident is nostalgia. Nostalgia certainly plays a prominent role in *The Lord of the Rings*: the elves have a longing for the Eldar Days, the Gondorians for Númenor, the hobbits for the Shire. In medieval Welsh poetry the word for this is *hiraeth*, which is hard to translate in English but means a sad longing for home or for a lost time and/or place. Critics have seen in this Middle-earth nostalgia Tolkien's own longing for a return to the golden years of his childhood and young adulthood, particularly when he lived with his mother and brother in Sarehole and visited his Aunt Jane Neave at Phoenix Farm.

There is also a sense of rootlessness in Tolkien's early biography, which had the effect of fostering a desire to establish deep roots for himself and his family. Leaving Africa and his father, leaving Sarehole, and his mother's death perhaps led him to cling to Edith, to the Church, and eventually to Oxford. Tolkien seems to have had little Tookish blood in him. Despite his having been born in Africa and receiving many invitations to lecture abroad, he traveled very little after returning from military service in France. He never visited the United States, though perhaps would have late in life had he been in better health.

The rolling, wooded Lickey Hills in Birmingham where Tolkien and his brother played as children inspired his creation of the Shire.

Other biographical issues are less clear. Was Tolkien a nationalist, a conservative, or a monarchist? It is difficult to find an appropriate label for the politics of Tolkien. As a schoolboy he declared himself a traditionalist, and argued that democracy ("hooliganism and uproar") has no place in international affairs.[88] He defended nationalism at Oxford during the outbreak of World War I and supported Irish Home Rule, but deplored the notion of superior races. "I am *not* a 'democrat,'" wrote Tolkien to a fan in 1956, "only because 'humility' and equality are spiritual principles corrupted by the attempt to mechanize and formalize them, with the result that we get not universal smallness and humility, but universal greatness and pride, till some Orc gets hold of a ring of power—and then we get and are getting slavery."[89] Cultural conservative and almost apolitical would perhaps best describe Ronald Tolkien, with a great sense of duty to King and Country, but also a skepticism and pessimism regarding formal politics which came from both theological principles and personal experiences with war and industrialization.[90]

Neither Tolkien nor Lewis lived to see a cultural reversal, a return to traditional values—a reversal that has yet to take place. Did Tolkien, therefore, see himself, as Galadriel did, fighting "the long defeat"?[91] In a sense his experience in the Great War could have felt this way, with so many of his friends and other young comrades having lost their lives before the German surrender. Tolkien, the T.C.B.S., and the Inklings were all fighting a long defeat against modernism, or so it may have seemed to Lewis and Tolkien despite the enormous success of the tales of Narnia and Middle-earth. And, as Tom Shippey has shown, Tolkien's profession—philology—has all but disappeared under the pressure from literary theory and postmodernist linguistics. Gandalf tells Frodo that among his peers he is the sole scholar of hobbit-lore, "an obscure branch of knowledge, but full of surprises."[92]

Of all these biographical details, it is the broad and prosaic category of "family and friends" (an alliteration Professor Tolkien would have liked) that emerges as the most incontrovertibly significant. From his mother came the love of language and myth, passions he shared with his closest friends at King Edward's and at Oxford. Later, the telling of his own tales to his children would lead directly to the publication of *The Hobbit*, and these readings as well as those to the Inklings gave him the confidence to share his invented world with a larger audience. The antithesis of the modernist bohemian, Ronald Tolkien seldom traveled abroad, avoided the big city, and was most creative while in conversation with his children, his close friends, and his students. Uncomfortable with fame, he found the greatest happiness in reading poetry and inventing languages. He neither embraced nor rejected his own century, but rather hoped to transform the modern with a great injection of the medieval. As Gandalf would say, "a fool's hope,"[93] perhaps, but nonetheless a noble one.

HIC ODO EPS

2

Tolkien's
middle ages

Back to the Sources

In modern literary theory so-called "source criticism"—the search for an author's source material—is not considered the highest or most original of academic pursuits.[1] Yet both C. S. Lewis and J. R. R. Tolkien rejected the more modern preoccupations of their English colleagues and contemporary critics, having little interest in Marxist, Freudian, and feminist interpretations of texts. We can only imagine Lewis's and Tolkien's bemused reaction to the Deconstructivism, Postcolonialism, and queer theory that now dominate literature departments. While all of these approaches can legitimately be applied to assessing Tolkien's fiction, the tremendous impact of ancient and medieval cultures upon Tolkien's "subcreation" cannot be dismissed. "I remain convinced," writes Tom Shippey, "that Tolkien cannot be properly discussed without some considerable awareness of the ancient works and the ancient world which he tried to revive."[2]

Tolkien fans and Tolkien scholars know this to be true, and since at least the 1970s have exerted much effort in piecing together the scraps of medieval myths and ancient languages from which Tolkien wove the tapestry of Middle-earth.[3] Today, we know even more about the cultures of the Anglo-Saxons, the Norse, and other Northern peoples in the nearly four decades since the professor's death, due to the important work done by historians and archaeologists. This includes their literature, of course, and Tolkien would be the first to point out that the duties of the medieval bard included communicating the truth through both myth *and* history.[4] *The Lord of the Rings* and *The Silmarillion* owe much to the high medieval phenomenon of chivalric romance, and, as critic Jane Chance has pointed out, even Tolkien's non–Middle-earth fiction is often a parody of such medieval genres as romance, lays, lyric, and fabliau (short, typically raunchy narratives).[5]

What follows is a survey of the ancient and medieval cultures that held the most appeal for Tolkien and that had the greatest impact on both his academic and popular writing. By no means is it a complete history of these periods. Furthermore, Tolkien's "Middle Ages" is idiosyncratic: it runs from the barbarian Iron Age to about the fifteenth century, but it also includes the great Gothic revival of the nine-teenth century. There is, however, a strand of continuity that runs, for example, from Sir Walter Scott's medieval-themed novels through Pre-Raphaelite paintings, Tennyson's Arthurian poetry, William Morris's novels and George MacDonald's fairy tales, to Tolkien's own fiction. It is what scholars now call "medievalism," a reimagining of the Middle Ages that blends contemporary preoccupations with the historical realities of medieval Europe. Both the medieval *and* medievalism had an enormous impact on Tolkien in his creation of the secondary world he called Middle-earth, which itself has now become one of the most famous examples of medievalism. In other words, Tolkien the academic was a *medievalist* who expanded our knowledge of the Middle Ages, while Tolkien the writer of fiction extended and expanded the scope of *medievalism* at a time when few people thought the medieval world had anything to teach the modern one.

> "*I am historically minded.*
> *Middle-earth is not an imaginary world.*"[6]

—J. R. R. TOLKIEN, "NOTE ON AUDEN'S REVIEW OF
THE LORD OF THE RINGS," 1956

ANCIENT GREECE AND ROME

THE GREAT ANTIQUITY OF MIDDLE-EARTH is glimpsed in its fallen stone monuments and in the primitive Púkel-men of *The Return of the King*, who appear to be Tolkien's version of Paleolithic hunter-gatherers. For historians, however, the ancient world begins with the advent of writing, which occurred before 3000 BC in Mesopotamia and shortly thereafter in Elam (modern-day Iran), Canaan, and Egypt. Progressing from the mundane business accounts kept on the first cuneiform tablets, ancient scribes would go on to record such mythic and religious texts as *The Epic of Gilgamesh*, the Egyptian *Book of the Dead*, and the Old Testament. Since the eighteenth century archaeologists have added much to our understanding of the Sumerians, Babylonians, Assyrians, Israelites, and other peoples of the ancient Near East. With a few exceptions, however, the philologist J. R. R. Tolkien showed little interest in these peoples

Previous pages:
A detail from the Bayeux Tapestry, showing Odo, Bishop of Bayeux, leading his troops. The ca. 1070s embroidered cloth depicts the Battle of Hastings (1066) and the events surrounding the Norman conquest of England.

A bas-relief of Ptolemy IV Philopator (reigned ca. 221–205 BC), at the Temple of Deir-el-Medina in Luxor, Egypt. The pharaoh wears an Atef crown, symbolic of Osiris, which inspired the tall winged helmets of the Númenóreans and Gondorians.

and their languages. Following the Second Vatican Council (1962–65), he was asked to contribute English translations to the Jerusalem Bible, the Roman Catholic translation of the Bible published in 1966. However, only the brief Book of Jonah can be said with certainty to be Tolkien's work.[7] He also claimed to have modeled the Númenóreans (and thus the Gondorians as well) on the historical Egyptians, from their tall winged helmets (see left) to their obsession with royal ancestry, lavish tombs, embalming, and massive sculpture and architecture.[8]

Tolkien often professed an admiration for aspects of Mediterranean cultures. In a 1968 letter to the *Daily Telegraph*, he admitted to a love of Romance languages, particularly Latin and Spanish.[9] Mabel Tolkien was the first to give Latin lessons to her son Ronald, before he even started school. He learned both Greek and Latin while at King Edward's School in Birmingham, as Classical texts were at the center of the school's curriculum. English poetry was given to the students primarily so that they could practice translating it into Latin. To amuse himself, Ronald would make up Greek-style words, and his closest friends at King Edward's were boys who shared his interest in Greek and Latin.[10] Tolkien began his studies at Exeter College, Oxford, in Classics. In 1913, he took Classical Moderations, specializing in Greek philology, but was encouraged by his tutors to switch to English after receiving only second class honours on his examinations.

Although Tolkien's love for "Northerness" (he disliked the term "Nordic") was evident, in *J. R. R. Tolkien: Myth, Morality, and Religion* (1984), author and philosophy professor Richard Purtill reminds us that Tolkien's first literary adventures were in Classical literature. Purtill argues that Tolkien's Valar are closer to the Olympian gods than they are to the Norse.[11] There is a Roman god of the Underworld named Orcus, but it is not clear if this influenced Tolkien's conception of the subterranean orcs.[12] "[I] first discovered the sensation of literary pleasure in Homer," Tolkien wrote in 1953.[13] Certainly the myth of Atlantis influenced Tolkien in his story of the destruction of Númenór, a great human civilization swallowed up by the sea. Tolkien described Quenya, his invented High Elvish language, as "Elven-latin," and said

that its two main ingredients—Finnish and Greek—were languages that gave him "'phonaesthetic' pleasure."[14]

Whereas Classical languages and mythology had a significant early impact on Tolkien, he never expressed much interest in the history or politics of Greece and Rome. He appears to have agreed with Plato's criticism of ancient Greek democracy, reminding us that the term *democratia* was the near equivalent of "mob rule" for the philosophers.[15] Roman politics did not grab Tolkien either, and his sympathies may have lain rather with the barbarians in the conquered provinces. "I should have hated the Roman Empire in its day (as I do)," he wrote in 1944, "and remained a patriotic Roman citizen, preferring a free Gaul and seeing good in Carthaginians."[16] While the western half of the Roman Empire fell in the fifth century AD, the eastern half survived as the Byzantine Empire, and remained until the Turks took Constantinople in 1453. Similarly, in *The Lord of the Rings*, the northern Númenórean kingdom of Arnor vanished while the southern kingdom of Gondor grew in power until it was eventually diminished, as Tolkien explained, "to decayed Middle Age, a kind of proud, venerable, but increasingly impotent Byzantium."[17]

The Germanic-speaking barbarians[18] who conquered the Western Roman Empire particularly fascinated Tolkien. Though for years barbarians from Germany and the eastern steppes were recruited for the Roman army, the Gothic defeat of the Romans at Adrianople (Edirne, Turkey) in AD 378 necessitated a new strategy: treaties with entire tribes to fight for Rome instead of against it.[19] Thus did the Visigoths first enter Italy and southern France as allies or "federates" (*foederati*) of Rome. In 406, however, the Rhine River froze and allowed several groups of hostile barbarians—in particular the Alans, the Vandals, and the Suevi—to invade Gaul (modern France) and pillage their way to the Pyrenees. Tolkien may be referring to this event when, in *The Fellowship of the Ring*, he describes the Brandywine River as freezing over during the Fell Winter, which allowed the white wolves to cross into Buckland.[20] The western emperor Honorius refused

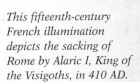

This fifteenth-century French illumination depicts the sacking of Rome by Alaric I, King of the Visigoths, in 410 AD.

GOTHIC INFLUENCES

Of all the groups of barbarians in Western Europe, the Goths and the Anglo-Saxons interested Tolkien most. He taught himself the Gothic language and their runic alphabet, known as futhark, describing Gothic as "the first [language] to take me by storm." Shippey suggests that the language haunted him his entire life.[21] Gothic names appear in the northeastern Middle-earth kingdom of Rhovanion and among the early leaders of the Rohirrim,[22] and Gothic cavalry may have inspired Tolkien's depiction of the Riders of Rohan. While he was supposed to be studying the Classical languages in his first years at Oxford, Tolkien was falling in love with the languages of the barbarians.

the increasing demands of the Visigothic federates; after a long siege, they sacked Rome in 410; Attila brought the Huns into Italy in 452; the Vandals, after crossing to North Africa, launched a naval invasion and sacked Rome in 455; and the Ostrogoths under Theodoric seized all of Italy in 493. Barbarian kingdoms eventually would replace all of the provinces of the Western Roman Empire.[23]

CELTIC BRITAIN AND IRELAND

ROME'S FIRST ENCOUNTER WITH northern barbarians dates back to ca. 390 BC, when Gauls sacked the young city well before it was the heart of a great empire. When Rome finally conquered its greatest rival, Carthage, at the end of the Second Punic War (218–201 BC), it began constructing an empire by linking Mediterranean civilizations, including eventually Greece and Egypt. Julius Caesar (100–44 BC), however, made his military reputation with victories against the Celtic-speaking kingdoms of Gaul and Britain and some of the German tribes living along the Rhine. Unlike the Greeks and Egyptians, the Celts and Germans did not leave great written records of their achievements in the Iron Age. We must settle for what archaeology can tell us about their cultures, as well as Classical observers like Caesar and Tacitus, until the Christian church spread Latin among these barbarians in the early Middle Ages. By the eleventh century, great written epics were being produced in the Celtic and German lands, and it is on these medieval works that Tolkien focused his academic expertise.

In the Iron Age, Celtic-speaking people inhabited Britain, Ireland, and Gaul. It is not technically correct to call all of them "Celts," for no ancient author ever used that term for inhabitants of the British Isles (Caesar uses "Celtae" to describe one group of tribes in Gaul).[24] Contemporary archaeologists avoid the term entirely, but clearly there are linguistic and cultural similarities between these neighboring peoples.[25] During the late Iron Age, rich and powerful kingdoms began to develop in Central Gaul and southeastern Britain, spurring conquests by Julius Caesar (Gaul, 58–50 BC) and Claudius (Britain, AD 43). Scotland and Ireland remained, for the most part, outside of Roman control, but even here there is much evidence of trade with Rome (and of raids of Roman provinces). Rome founded cities, paved roads, and built stone fortifications in the western provinces, but much of the native cultures also survived more than four hundred years of imperial rule.

The Brittonic Age (AD 400–600)

Roman control of Britain officially came to an end around the time of the Visigothic sack of Rome in AD 410, when the Western Roman emperor Honorius wrote to the British towns telling them to see to their own defenses. This they did, for both Britain and Gaul had been suffering from decades of raids by barbarians beyond the frontier, including the Irish, the Picts (from Scotland), and the Saxons.[26] The Brittonic (or Brythonic) Age is an appropriate label for this period because the now-independent Britons controlled most of Britain and because nearly all of our historical sources for the fifth and sixth centuries come from Romano-British or "Brittonic" (to use the linguistic term) writers.[27]

Around the year 429, the Britons, under the influence of a British tyrant named (in later sources) Vortigern, turned for military aid

Europam, Sive Celticam Veterem . . . is a map showing the ancient Celtic regions of Europe according to sixteenth-century scholars; it was created in 1595 by Abraham Ortelius, the noted cartographer, cosmographer, and publisher from Antwerp.

to groups of Germanic mercenaries (probably from the Rhineland). Vortigen, along with a council of Britons, invited the newly arrived Saxons to settle in the eastern parts of Britain to protect British towns and villas from Picts and other raiders. Before long, however, these "Saxons" turned against their British employers. The original Germanic mercenaries were joined by other warriors from the continent, now probably accompanied by civilians, sparking a war—the Battle of Mons Badonicus (Badon Hill), ca. 500—that ultimately lead to the creation of England. The sixth-century British historian Gildas described the Saxon's revolt in apocalyptic terms, in his *De Excidio et Conquestu Britanniae* ("On the Ruin and Conquest of Britain"):

> The barbarians push us back to the sea, the sea pushes us back to the barbarians: between these two kinds of death, we are either drowned or slaughtered. . . .

> All the major towns were laid low by the repeated battering of enemy rams . . . as the swords glinted all around and the flames crackled. It was a sad sight. In the middle of the squares the foundation-stones of high walls and towers that had been torn from their lofty base, holy altars, fragments of corpses, covered (as it were) with a purple crust of congealed blood, looked as though they had been mixed up in some dreadful wine-press. There was no burial to be had except in the ruins of houses or the bellies of beasts and birds.[28]

Compare this with Tolkien's description of the siege of Gondor in *The Return of the King*, led by orcs who had crossed the river at Osgiliath, burning houses and barns and battering the Gate of Gondor with "the great ram" Grond. Gildas writes that, in the wake of the Saxon revolt, many Britons left for lands "over the seas" (Brittany and Galicia), "singing psalms instead of sea-shanties." This sad departure recalls that of the elves in *The Lord of the Rings* (like the Britons, the "first born"), leaving in the White Ships from the shores of a besieged Middle-earth.

Most Britons stayed, however, seeking refuge in ancient hill forts. The great craggy citadels that dot the coasts of Cornwall (e.g., Tintagel) and western Scotland (e.g., Dumbarton and Dunadd) compare to such Middle-earth strongholds as Minas Tirith and Helm's Deep, while Glastonbury Tor in Somerset recalls Amon Sûl (Weathertop) (see pages 46–47).

British resistance was led by the warlord Ambrosius Aurelianus, and Gildas records a great victory over the invaders at the Battle of Badon Hill, which was attributed in later sources to King Arthur. But the Britons had to settle for a truce with the barbarians, and by the end of the sixth century we can discern tribal or ethnic groupings of Saxons and other Germanic peoples—the Angles and possibly the Jutes—emerging in much of lowland Britain. These small groups were led by charismatic warlords who expanded their landholdings by moving both west and north from Kent, Essex, and Northumbria. A series of battles and expansions in the late sixth and early seventh centuries effectively cut off from one another the British kingdoms of Dumnonia (encompassing Devon and Cornwall), Wales, and northern Britain, just as the northern Dúnedain people, for example, were cut off from their southern kin in Gondor. Some have suggested that Lindon, a "land of music" in the far west of Middle-earth, is the equivalent of the areas settled by the remnant of the surviving British population, with Forlindon being Wales and Harlindon as Cornwall, both separated from the Shire (Oxfordshire) by mountain ranges.

MEDIEVAL CELTIC LITERATURE

While study of the Anglo-Saxons tended to dominate historiography during the late 1700s and early-to-mid 1800s, a Romantic fascination with the Celts began to grow slowly in the mid-nineteenth century. New editions of medieval Irish and Welsh literature appeared during this time in Britain and Ireland and at Oxford, the Jesus Professorship of Celtic was created in 1877. It is hard to describe Tolkien's relationship with things "Celtic." In his 1955 essay "English and Welsh," he begins by ridiculing modern fascination with the Celts (an attitude shared by many of his Oxbridge contemporaries) and ends by expressing his lifelong devotion to the Welsh language, which formed the basis of his second invented Elvish language, first called Gnomish and later Sindarin.[29] In a 1937 letter to publisher Stanley Unwin he confessed that he felt "a certain distaste" for Celtic things, "largely for their fundamental unreason. They have bright colour, but are like a broken stained

Carrocks and Crannogs

ondly remembering several holidays spent on the rocky coast of Cornwall, Tolkien may have borrowed the Cornish word for rock, *carrek*, for the shape-shifter Beorn's great rock, "the Carrock," in *The Hobbit*.[30] The Old Welsh form *carrecc* influenced the Old English (Northumbrian dialect) *carr* and the Middle English form *carrock*, "a heap of stones," which can mean either a burial marker (or cairn, found most often in Celtic-speaking regions) or an isolated rocky hill.[31]

There was great variety in medieval Celtic settlements and abodes. Unlike the masonry of the great Roman towns and fortresses, native houses and small settlements were nearly always built of timber or wickerwork, as were the buildings in Rohan. In Ireland, Wales, and northern Britain, people often lived in dwellings on artificial sites called *crannogs*, which were constructed on islets or piles in lakes beginning in the Bronze Age. Many crannogs were stockaded, and had footbridges to the mainland that could be retracted for defensive purposes. Most crannogs in this region contained just one or a small number of dwellings, while some Iron Age examples from the Continent may have been considerably larger. The community of Esgaroth, or Lake-town, in *The Hobbit*, is a much larger settlement of this type.

A historic reconstruction of the 2,500-year-old Oakbank crannog on Loch Tay, Perthshire, Scotland.

The settlement of Dumbarton, in Scotland, was built on a volcanic rock overlooking the River Clyde. Dating back to the Iron Age, it was the center of the ancient kingdom of Strathclyde from the fifth century until 1018.

Glastonbury Tor, the site of an Iron Age settlement that dates back to ca. 300–200 BC, is a hill in Glastonbury, England surmounted by the medieval St. Michael's Tower. The hill was often surrounded by floodlands and mist, even appearing as an island at times, and thus is heavily steeped in myth.

glass window reassembled without design. They are in fact 'mad.'"[32] Yet, in a later letter to Milton Waldman of the London publisher Collins, Tolkien said that he wanted the *Silmarillion* to have "the fair elusive quality that some call Celtic (though it is rarely found in genuine, ancient Celtic things)."[33] On more than one occasion Tolkien used the medieval Welsh idiom for fairies, "fair folk" (*Y tylwth teg*), to describe the Elves of Middle-earth.[34]

In addition to his expressed love of the Welsh language, Tolkien drew direct inspiration from such medieval Welsh literature as the *Mabinogi*, as well as Breton lays.[35] In 1930 he composed an original poem called "The Lay of Aotrou and Itroun" (Breton for "Lord and Lady"), in which the hero makes a deadly deal with a Breton enchantress or *corrigan*. This rhyming and alliterative poem was later published by Tolkien's friend, Gwyn Jones, a Celticist acclaimed for his English translation of the *Mabinogi*.[36] The "Four Branches" of the *Mabinogi*, ancient Welsh mythological tales dealing with the theme of youth, were collected and published by the English translator Lady Charlotte Guest along with related Arthurian tales in her *Mabinogion* (1838–49).

Tolkien owned no less than four scholarly editions of the *Mabinogi*, in addition to Lady Guest's translation.[37] In a draft of his essay "On Fairy-stories" (see pages 18–22) Tolkien refers to the hero from one of the Welsh Arthurian romances in the *Mabinogi*: "I had [as a child] a deep longing to see and speak to a Knight of Arthur's Court whom I should have regarded much as Peredur did."[38] Peredur is the title character in the Welsh Grail romance *Peredur son of Efrawg*, a naïf (and the Welsh equivalent of the French Perceval) who has never before seen a knight.

Also associated with the *Mabinogi* is the earliest Arthurian prose tale in Welsh, *Culhwch and Olwen*. In the tale, Culhwch, the hero, is given a series of seemingly impossible tasks by Olwen's father, Ysbaddaden Chief Giant, before he will consider allowing Culhwch to marry her. Tolkien follows this folklore motif in the *Silmarillion* tale of Beren and Lúthien, where the Elvish king

The beginning page of Culhwch and Olwen, *from an 1894 edition of* The Mabinogion, *Welsh mythological tales and Arthurian tales published by Lady Charlotte Guest in 1838–49.*

YSTORI KULHWCH AC OLWEN,

NEU

HANES Y TWRCH TRWYTH.

KILYD mab kelydon wledic auynnei wreic kyn-mwyt ac ef Sef gwreic avynnawd goleudyd merch anlawd wledic. Gwedy ywest genthi. mynet ywlat yggwedi malkawn a geffyt ettiued. Achaffel mab ohonunt trwy wedi y wlat. Ac ar awr y dellis beichogi. ydeuth hitheu yggwylltawc heb dy anhed. Pan dyuu y thymp idi. ef a dyuu

Sindarin and Welsh

n the first O'Donnell Lecture in Celtic Studies, delivered in Oxford on October 21, 1955, J. R. R. Tolkien announced that Welsh held a special place for him, and indeed for many English-speaking people. "It is the native language to which in unexplored desire we would still go home."[39] The second of his invented Elvish tongues—Sindarin or "Grey-Elven"—was deliberately modeled on British-Welsh "because," as he wrote in 1954, "it seems to fit the rather 'Celtic' type of legends and stories told of its speakers."[40] Here are some examples of possible Welsh influence on Sindarin:

BORROWED WORDS

W *daeron*, "birds" > S *Daeron*, a minstrel of King Thingol

W *hen*, "old" > S *hen*, "eye"

W *arth*, "bear" (e.g. *Arthur*, "bear-man") > S *arth*, "royal"

HOMONYMS (SIMILAR SPELLING, DIFFERENT MEANING)

W *Lleu* (**Ir** *Lug*), Celtic god ("Long-Arm") > S *lhúg*, "snake"

W *Aeron*, a god of battle > S *aearon*, "great ocean"

W *caer*, "fortress" > S *cair*, "ship"

W *glen, glyn* "fair" > S *glîn*, "gleam"

W *tor(r)*, "peak" > S *tûr*, "mound"

MUTATIONS OF INITIAL CONSONANTS (LENITION*)

W *dyn*, "man" > *hen ddyn*, "old man"

W *ci*, "dog" > *corgi*, "dwarf dog"

S *parf*, "book" > *i-barf*, "the book"

SOFT CONSONANTS PAIRED WITH NASAL CONSONANTS

W *llawenydd, afon*

S *lhaw, cirith*

*Lenition is the mutation of initial consonants; thus the hard "d" in the first example is softened to a "th" sound (dd) when an adjective is added.

Thingol tells Beren that he must retrieve one of the Silmarils from Morgoth himself in order to win Lúthien's hand in marriage.

Tolkien was not proficient in the Gaelic tongues, and considered Old Irish to be "wholly unattractive."[41] Nevertheless, he owned a great many books on Irish language and literature. His poem "Imram" (1946) is a verse reworking of the Latin prose *Navigatio sancti Brendani* (*The Voyage of St. Brendan the Navigator*) (ca. early tenth century), itself a famous example of the medieval Irish adventurous voyage genre called *imram*.

A figurative map of St. Brendan's voyage from 1621; Tolkien's poem "Imram" (1946) is a verse reworking of the ca. early tenth century Latin prose work The Voyage of St. Brendan the Navigator.

The greatest literary epic of medieval Ireland is the *Táin Bó Cúailnge* (*The Cattle Raid of Cooley*), the central story of the Ulster cycle of myths. The *Táin* focuses on the conflict between King Ailill and Queen Medb of Connaught and the Ulster hero Cú Chulainn; neither Medb nor Cú Chulainn have clear parallels in Middle-earth. However, the thrones of turf on which Aragorn, Éomer, and Imrahil sit before Aragorn's coronation recall the traditional seat of Conchobar, legendary king of the Ulstermen.[42] The Púkel-men or Wild Men (also called Woses, from the Middle English word *wodwos*) who aid the Riders of Rohan before the Battle of the Pelennor Fields may owe something, linguistically at least, to the Old Irish *púca*, or "spirit," which may be the ultimate origin

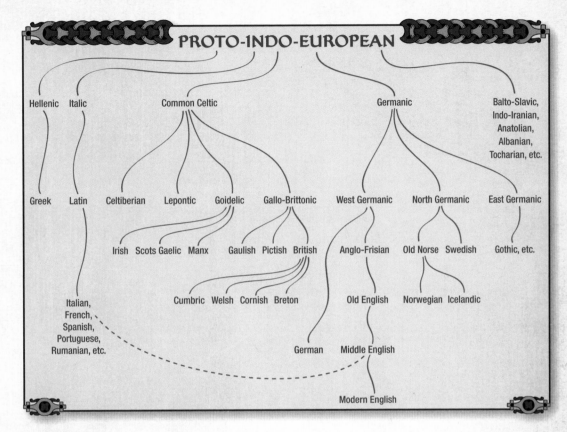

PROTO-INDO-EUROPEAN

Hellenic · Italic · Common Celtic · Germanic · Balto-Slavic, Indo-Iranian, Anatolian, Albanian, Tocharian, etc.

Greek · Latin · Celtiberian · Lepontic · Goidelic · Gallo-Brittonic · West Germanic · North Germanic · East Germanic

Irish · Scots Gaelic · Manx · Gaulish · Pictish · British · Anglo-Frisian · Old Norse · Swedish · Gothic, etc.

Italian, French, Spanish, Portuguese, Rumanian, etc. · Cumbric · Welsh · Cornish · Breton · Old English · Norwegian · Icelandic

German · Middle English

Modern English

A "language tree" showing the relationship of some of the Indo-European languages. While Tolkien had a reading knowledge of many of these languages, he specialized in the Anglo-Saxon (Old English) and Middle English languages and literature.

of the English sprite Puck (Old English *pucca*).[43] For Druadan Forest, the home of the Púkel-men, Tolkien could have had in mind the Greek root *drú* ("oak") or Old Irish *druí* (usually translated "druids," Celtic priests often associated with sacred oak trees). The Elves apparently called the Púkel-men *Drúedain*, which would have meant something like "the untamed allies." Many scholars, following Celticist Kenneth Jackson, now believe that *druid* derives ultimately from a Common Celtic word for "wisdom." Is there a hidden wisdom in Tolkien's Wild Men of the Woods?

The Anglo-Saxons and Old English

Anglo-Saxon England

"The *Engle* [English] have the true tradition of the fairies," wrote J. R. R. Tolkien in *The Book of Lost Tales*, "of whom the *Íras* [Irish] and the *Wéalas* [Welsh] tell garbled things."[44] Himself an Englishman of German descent, Tolkien responded from an early age more to the myths and languages of the Germanic peoples than to either the Celtic or the Mediterranean. He found in them a "noble northern spirit," and nowhere "was it nobler than in England, nor more early sanctified and Christianized."[45] But Tolkien found the mythology of the Anglo-Saxons—whom he loved most—to be frustratingly impoverished. Around 1951, in an attempt to get both *The Lord of the Rings* and *The Silmarillion* published, Tolkien wrote a lengthy letter to Milton Waldman at Collins illuminating the impetus for his Middle-earth projects, explaining that he was "grieved by the poverty of my own beloved country; it had no stories of its own (bound up with its tongue and soil), not of the quality that I sought."[46]

Why was it that Tolkien and other scholars had such difficulty finding early or uncorrupted Anglo-Saxon myths? Christian Latin and Norman French had replaced or altered much of early pagan English culture. When the Anglo-Saxons first came to Britain very few could read or write. They brought with them from the Continent names of Northern deities, stories about elves and dwarves and giants, and even long epic tales like *Beowulf*. But very little of this oral material survived or was chosen to appear in written form after the Anglo-Saxons adopted the Latin alphabet and the new monotheistic faith beginning around AD 600. Yet through his scholarship, Professor Tolkien discovered peculiar Old English words that he believed, according to his own philological theory, could be "opened up" to reveal ancient tales of dragons and goblins and heroes.

In a January 1945 letter to his son Christopher, Tolkien confessed to being enthralled by Frank M. Stenton's classic history *Anglo-Saxon England* (1943), which he describes as "an intriguing story of the origins of our peculiar people."[47] "I'd give a bit for a time machine," he writes, a sentiment shared by most historians of early Britain. Nearly seventy years after Stenton wrote his book, early Anglo-Saxon Britain remains "a period filled with most intriguing Question Marks," to use Tolkien's phrase. For example, we do not know much other than the names of the earliest Anglo-Saxon kings in Britain. Hengist (or Hengest) and Horsa are said to have been two brothers, descended from the deity Woden, who brought three keels of warriors to the island at the invitation of the British king Vortigern.[48] Since *hengest* and *horsa* are simply the Old English words for "stallion" and "horse," historians have tended to dismiss this as an unhistorical echo of some lost myth. Tolkien may be playing with this notion in naming the two Fallohide brothers who founded the Shire Marcho and Blanco, also derived from Old English words for "horse" (Old English *mearh*, "horse," *blanca*, "white horse").[49]

Of the other early Anglo-Saxon kings, some of them—like Cerdic, king of Wessex—strangely bear Celtic names. All of this points to our failure to understand the nature and details of the *adventus Saxonum*, the coming of the Saxons to Britain. Historians and archaeologists continue to debate when the first Saxons arrived on the island (was it as early as the fourth century?), in what numbers did they come (was it a few ships or in the tens of thousands?), and how they were able to overcome large numbers of Britons and seize towns and some of the best farmable land on the island. Did many Britons cooperate with the newcomers, as some scholars are now suggesting, giving up their own language and culture for the higher status of being "English"?

Unfortunately, the smoke does not clear for English historians until after 597, when the Roman priest Augustine began his missionary work in the kingdom of Kent. We know the story of St. Augustine of Canterbury, and of his disciples who went into Northumbria, because these details are preserved by the "Father of English History," the Northumbrian monk *Bæda*, better known as the Venerable Bede (ca. 673–735). In Bede's time, England was divided into seven petty kingdoms known as the Heptarchy: Kent, Sussex, Wessex, East Anglia, Mercia, Northumbria, and Essex. At first, Anglo-Saxon kings were chiefly warlords with some sacral duties. By the late sixth century a *bretwalda* (or "Britain-ruler") sometimes ruled as an "overking," as the King of Gondor once did with the kingdoms of the West. The title, or at least a similarly wide authority, seems to have passed in succession from Æthelberht of Kent to Rædwald of East Anglia, then to a series of rulers of Northumbria, of Mercia, and finally of Wessex. Archaeologists believe that it is Rædwald (d. 625) who is buried in the largest of the mounds at Sutton Hoo, in which excavators found remnants of a ship with arms and armor and luxury items that have come to virtually define the Anglo-Saxon style of ornamental dress.[50]

A page from Historia ecclesiastica gentis Anglorum (Ecclesiastical History of the English People), *a history of the Anglo-Saxons by the Northumbrian monk Bede finished in 731 AD.*

> " . . . Offa was famous
>
> Far and widely, by gifts and by battles,
>
> Spear-valiant hero; the home of his fathers
>
> He governed with wisdom, whence Eomær did issue
>
> For help unto heroes, Heming's kinsman,
>
> Grandson of Garmund, great in encounters. " [51]
>
> —BEOWULF, LINES 1957–62

The Anglo-Saxon kings continued their expansionist wars against the Britons during the sixth and seventh centuries. During this time, the Anglo-Saxons' adoption of Christianity, codification of laws, and diplomatic and trade relations with the continental Franks turned these

This ceremonial helmet was part of the Sutton Hoo treasure excavated from an Anglo-Saxon cemetery, in Suffolk, England, in 1939.

The helmet worn by Karl Urban, who portrayed the character Éomer in Peter Jackson's The Lord of the Rings *films, bears a striking similarity to the helmets discovered at Sutton Hoo.*

warlords into dynasts of more or less stable states. This does not mean, however, that they did not fight one another, nor that they were safe from intra-dynastic strife.

A collection of objects from the Staffordshire Hoard, discovered in 2009 in what was the heart of the Midlands Anglo-Saxon kingdom of Mercia. Nearly a hundred swords or seaxes (battle knives) are included. The only nonmilitary items are four or five gold crosses, the largest likely an altar or processional cross.

Northumbrian monarchs like Edwin (ruled 616–33) and Oswald (ruled 634–42) sparked a great flowering of monastic art and scholarship in their vast kingdom, continuing into the eighth century, of which Bede and the illuminated Lindisfarne Gospels (ca. 700) are just two examples. Offa of Mercia (ruled 757–96), who styled himself "King of the English," minted millions of English pennies, corresponded with Charlemagne, received legates from Pope Adrian I, and constructed the massive Offa's Dyke—stretching nearly 150 miles roughly along the current border of England and Wales—as a defense against Welsh raids. But it was the rulers of Wessex who would ultimately unify the Anglo-Saxon kingdoms due to the necessity of joint resistance against the Viking onslaught. Alfred the Great (ruled 871–99) defeated the Vikings at the Battle of Edington (878), began the creation of the English navy, established thirty garrisoned fortified towns called *burhs* linked by *hereweges* (army roads) across his kingdom, and sponsored an educational revival through the proliferation of both Latin *and* Old English texts (Alfred himself did an English translation of the sixth-century Roman philosopher Boethius).[52] Alfred spent months undercover in the Somerset fens, assembling troops, before defeating the fearsome Viking host. An unexpected monarch (he had four elder brothers) and inspirational leader who united disparate peoples, Alfred is perhaps one of the inspirations for Tolkien's Strider/Aragorn.

It is however in Rohan, not Gondor, that we find the truest incarnation of the Anglo-Saxons in Middle-earth. Although both Rohan ("Horse Country") and Rohirrim ("Horse Masters") are Sindarin words, the language of the Rohirrim is Old English or archaized

Names of the Rohirrim

NAMES*	ENGLISH TRANSLATION
Dernhelm**	helmet of secrecy
Dwimorberg	ghost mountain
Edoras	dwellings
Éomer	excellent [with?] horse
Éomund	horse-guardian
éored	cavalry
Eorl	earl, nobleman
Éothain	horse-soldier
Éowyn	one who delights in horses
Grayhame (OE græghama)	gray covered
Gríma	mask
Guthwine	battle-friend (Éomer's sword)
Háma (OE hām)	home, house
Isengard	iron yard
Láthspell (OE laðspell)***	ill news
Mearas, "lords of horses"	horses (from OE mearh); famous, excellent (from OE mǣre)
Riddermark (OE ridda-mearc)	boundary of the horsemen
Thengel (OE þengel)	prince
Théoden	lord of the people
Théodred (OE þeod-ræd)	counsel of the people
Wormtongue (OE wyrm-tunge)	serpent's tongue, sarcastic person

* The names not followed by Old English words in parentheses are themselves Old English
** Éowyn took this name as her disguise
*** Grima insulted Gandalf by calling him this name

modern English. Many of their names (see table on opposite page) contain a form of an Old English word for "horse" (*eoh*), and the Rohirrim refer to themselves as Éothéod ("Horsefolk") or Eorlingas ("Eorl's people"), after their first leader.[54] Just as the Anglo-Saxons originally came from the North and were granted lands by the Britons, so too did the Rohirrim come from the North and were granted land—Calenardhon, by Cirion of Gondor. Whatever their Germanic origins, however, the Anglo-Saxons did not make much use of cavalry in Britain.

> *" The Rohirrim are more akin to the ideas the Angles had of themselves in their legends, and the virtues of the Riders are the same virtues which the Angles admired and respected: courage, loyalty, generosity, self-reliance. "*[55]

—EDMUND WAINWRIGHT, *TOLKIEN'S MYTHOLOGY FOR ENGLAND: A MIDDLE-EARTH COMPANION* (2004)

OLD ENGLISH LITERATURE

No Anglo-Saxon writings survive from the period before the Anglo-Saxons' conversion to Christianity, and most of the prose we possess comes from the Wessex of King Alfred.[56] The earliest-recorded Old English poem is "Cædmon's Hymn" (ca. 658–80; recorded in the eighth century) to God the Creator, by the Anglo-Saxon monk Cædmon; his story is preserved in Bede's *Ecclesiastical History*. The majority of Old English poetry survives in four manuscripts dating from around AD 1000, the most important of which are *Beowulf* and the *Exeter Book*. These formulaic-style poems were originally oral compositions put down on paper by poets (*scops*) who had learned to write; the poems' structured half-lines employ alliteration and synonyms, revealing that they were meant to be performed. Kennings, contrast, and ironic understatement also characterize Anglo-Saxon poetry, but rhyme is rare.

One quality of much Old English poetry is melancholy—a cold and often grim view of life. We see this in two of the most widely read Old English poems, included in the *Exeter Book*: "The Ruin" (ca. eighth century) and "The Wanderer" (date unknown). Like the Hobbits gazing at the fallen ancient Númenórean monuments, the poet of "The Ruin" wonders at the ruins of a Roman town:

> *Wrætlic is þes wealstan, wyrde gebræcon;*
> *burgstede burston, brosnað enta geweorc.*
> *. . . Eorðgrap hafað*
> *waldend wyrhtan forweorone, geleorene,*
> *heardgripe hrusan, oþ hund cnea*
> *werþeoda gewitan.*

> Wondrous is this wall of stone, by Fate broken;
> The fortifications have fallen, crumbled this work of giants.
> . . . Earth's embrace holds
> The mighty workers of the walls, decaying, gathered in
> The hard grip of the ground, while a hundred generations
> Of man have passed away.[57]

The ruins of the Roman Baths and Abbey in Bath, England, thought by many to have inspired the ca. eighth century Old English poem "The Ruin."

In *The Fellowship of the Ring*, Tolkien reworks these lines from "The Ruin"; Legolas hears the stones of Hollin lamenting the departed Elves who once erected fair buildings in what was Eregion: "fair they wrought us, high they builded us; but they are gone."[58] Existential questions and life/death contrasts abound in another Old English elegy, *The Wanderer*:

> Hwær cwom mearg? Hwær cwom mago?   Hwær cwom maþþumgyfa?
> Hwær cwom symbla gesetu?   Hwær sindon seledreamas?
> Eala beorht bune!   Eala byrnwiga!
> Eala þeodnes þrym!   Hu seo þrag gewat,
> genap under nihthelm,   swa heo no wære.

> Where is the horse? Where is the rider? Where has the gift-giver gone?
> Where are all the guest-seats? What happened to all the joys of the hall?
> Alas the bright beaker! Alas the mailed warrior!
> Alas the mighty prince! How the time has fled,
> Vanished under the night-helm, as if it never were.[59]

Compare this excerpt with this line from the poem of Rohan recited by Aragorn as he passes the burial mounds at Edoras: "Where now the horse and the rider? Where is the horn that was blowing?"[60] Both the Old English original and Tolkien's adaptation are examples of *ubi sunt . . . ?* poems, in which the poet observes sadly the passing of time. (The entire phrase in Latin, *Ubi sunt qui ante nos fuerunt*, translates as "Where are those who were before us?") Tolkien utilizes both alliteration and rhyme in his poem.

Not surprisingly, much of what survives of Anglo-Saxon poetry is Christian verse. Tolkien claims that the beginning of his *Silmarillion* tales came when he first read the ca. ninth century poem *Crist* (also known as *Christ I* or *The Advent Lyrics*), preserved in the *Exeter Book*. Here he found the lines *Eala Earendel engla beorhtast | ofer middengeard monnum sended*, "Hail Earendel, brightest of angels, | Over Middle-earth sent to men." As mentioned in the previous chapter, in 1914, Tolkien wrote the poem "The Voyage of Earendel" in response to the *Crist* poem, so as to give a "respectable" origin-story for Earendel (see further discussion in Chapter Five).

The Poets of Middle-earth

olkien spent much of his life reading, editing, and translating Anglo-Saxon poetry. He also composed original poetry in both Old English and modern English using Anglo-Saxon verse forms and techniques such as the ones below:

HALF-LINES

"*Oft Scyld Scēfing   sceaþena þrēatum*" (*Beowulf*, line 4)
"Ents the earthborn, old as mountains" (*LOTR*, p. 586)

ALLITERATION

"he would pierce and parry before his prince" (*The Battle of Maldon*, line 16)
"spear shall be shaken, shield be splintered" (*LOTR*, p. 838)

KENNINGS (COMBINATION OF TWO NOUNS TO FORM A POWERFUL METAPHOR)

Ring-giver, whale-road, word-horde (from *Beowulf*)
Wide-walkers, sword-day, league-fellows (*LOTR*, pp. 586, 838, 849)

LITOTES (INTENTIONAL, IRONIC UNDERSTATEMENT)

"Small pleasure they had in such a sword-feast" (*Beowulf*, line 562)
"nothing was further from our thoughts than inconveniencing goblins" (*The Hobbit*, p. 60)

Another important Old English work, *The Dream of the Rood* (ca. eighth century), is a different kind of religious poem, a dream-vision. Here the wooden cross (Old English *rood*) from Calvary addresses his audience:

> *Rod wæs ic aræred.   Ahof ic ricne cyning,*
> *heofona hlaford,   hyldan me ne dorste.*
> *þurhdrifan hi me mid deorcan næglum.   On me syndon þa dolg gesiene,*
> *opene inwidhlemmas.*

> A cross was I erected. I raised up the mighty king,
> Heaven's lord, to stoop I did not dare.
> They pierced me with wicked nails. On me were visible wounds,
> Gaping gashes of hate.[61]

Treebeard speaks similarly of "wanton hewing" when he curses Saruman and the orcs for chopping down the trees of Fangorn Forest.[62]

In *The Hobbit*, Tolkien pays tribute to yet another form of Old English poetry: the riddle. Ninety-six riddles have been preserved in the *Exeter Book*, metaphorical riddles dealing with war, religion, and the everyday life of the laborer. In the chapter "Riddles in the Dark," Bilbo and Gollum engage in a battle of wits rather than swords (see pages 107–9 for a full discussion of this episode). Tolkien's riddles, it should be noted, are much shorter than those in the *Exeter Book*, and many of them rhyme. He reworked one of these *Hobbit* riddles in Old English and, together with a similar invented riddle, mischievously published it in 1923 in a Leeds University publication under the title "Two Saxon Riddles Recently Discovered."[63]

Beowulf

From the entire corpus of Old English literature, one work alone is widely known. It is still taught in most universities and continues to generate new editions and translations (and even commercial films). This work is also responsible for eliciting a response from J. R. R. Tolkien that would establish his academic reputation, a critical essay as influential today as it was when it first appeared in 1937. The work, of course, is *Beowulf*, and the essay is "*Beowulf*: The Monsters and the Critics" (see pages 16–18).

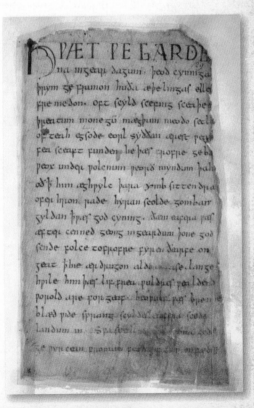

The date of composition for *Beowulf* is unknown, for though the poem itself contains much early material we can only date the sole manuscript in which it survives—Cotton MS Vitellius A.15—to around AD 1000.[64] With 3,182 unrhymed, alliterative half-lines, *Beowulf* is the longest extent Old English poem. It is the story of a band of Geatish warriors who arrive in Denmark to aid the Danish king Hrothgar and his people, who have been terrorized by a monster named Grendel. The leader of the Geats, Beowulf, tears Grendel's arm off in a struggle inside the great hall of Heorot, mortally

The beginning page of Beowulf, *Cotton MS Vitellius A.15, ca. 1000 AD.*

wounding the beast, and the Geats are rewarded with great riches by Hrothgar (described by the poet with the kenning "ring-giver"). What then follows is an even more amazing adventure as Beowulf plunges into a deep lake lair to defeat and kill Grendel's furious mother. The final episode of the poem takes place many years later, when Beowulf is an aged king back in his homeland in Geatland (modern-day southern Sweden). A dragon that has been hoarding treasure emerges from his lair to terrorize the countryside, and with the help of only one loyal companion the king is able to slay the dragon. Beowulf, however, dies in the struggle and is honored by his people with a lavish funeral.

Although there are some Christian elements in the story (it was almost certainly written by a Christian scribe), *Beowulf* is essentially an ancient pagan tale that was brought to England from Scandinavia by Anglo-Saxon immigrants. Before Tolkien, few literary critics considered *Beowulf* to be a great literary epic, and so the poem fell into the hands of historians and archaeologists in the twentieth century who mined it for clues about the culture of the early Anglo-Saxons. In "*Beowulf*: The Monsters and the Critics," Tolkien criticized scholars for excavating a poem which he considered to be a cohesive and artistic masterpiece. Critics who tend to dismiss *Beowulf*'s monsters, Tolkien argued, are missing the serious intentions of a learned Christian poet: namely, as noted in chapter one, to examine "man at war with the hostile world and his inevitable overthrow in Time."[65] While not everyone agreed with Tolkien, he managed to persuade many English departments to require *Beowulf* as part of their curricula, and this in turn has kept the poem in print and even generated several new translations, most notably the recent one by Nobel laureate Seamus Heaney (1999).

Old English scholars, to be fair, have long recognized the beauty and complexity of *Beowulf*. The poem begins memorably with a description of the funeral of the legendary Danish king Scyld Scefing:

> *hi hyne þa æthæron   to brimes faroðe,*
> *swæse gesiþas,   swa he selfa bæd,*
> *þenden wordum weold   wine Scyldinga*

> They carried him to the seashore,
> His beloved companions, just as he bade them,
> While the lord of the Scyldings still wielded words[66]

Was Tolkien thinking of this episode, and the Sutton Hoo ship burial, when he described how Aragorn, Legolas, and Gimli laid out the body of the fallen Boromir in a boat and sent him on his own death voyage?

Tolkien found his orcs lurking in line 112 of *Beowulf*: "there sprang ogres and elves and demons (*eotenas ond ylfe ond orcneas*)." The Anglo-Saxon *orcneas* (literally "demon-corpses") are more like zombies than goblins. The word itself may derive from the Latin *orcus* (Orcus was the Roman god of the underworld), but of that Tolkien was not convinced.[67] They also appear in Old Norse as þyrsa (ogres). Note that in the *Beowulf* line, the orcs are in the company of elves and *eotenas*—usually translated as ogres or giants; in Middle-earth the eotenas become "ents," the race of giant tree shepherds. The latter also appear in the phrase *orþanc enta geweorc*, "the skillful work of ents," in the Old English poem *Maxims II*. Théoden's hall, Meduseld, also appears in *Beowulf* as a generic description, "mead-house," while Gríma Wormtongue owes something to the

The scene in The Hobbit *where Bilbo creeps into the dragon Smaug's lair to steal a cup mirrors the end of* Beowulf, *where a servant sneaks into a dragon's cave to steal a precious vessel (shown here). This illustration appeared in* Stories of Beowulf, *by British author Henrietta Elizabeth Marshall, 1908.*

character Unferð, the warrior who challenges Beowulf's reputation in Heorot. Éomer says "*Westu Théoden hál!*" ("May you be healthy, Théoden!"), just as Beowulf declared *"Wæs þu, Hrōðgār, hāl!"*

At the end of *Beowulf*, a servant of one of the Geatish lords sneaks into a dragon's cave to steal a precious vessel. Tolkien certainly had this in mind when he wrote the chapter "Inside Information" for *The Hobbit*, when Bilbo's theft similarly provokes a dragon attack. But the episode was also the inspiration for an earlier Tolkien poem, "The Hoard," written in 1922 and then titled "Iumonna Gold Galdre Bewunden," from line 3052 of *Beowulf*. Tolkien also drew and painted episodes from *Beowulf*, some of which can be found in his sketchbook, *The Book of Ishness* (see Appendix II).

In the 1930s, Tolkien would attempt to write a poem in modern English but utilizing the *Beowulf* meter—unrhymed but alliterative. This was his "The Fall of Arthur," (see page 81). Years before this, at Leeds, Tolkien also attempted both an alliterative verse translation of *Beowulf* in modern English and a modern English prose translation, but he was dissatisfied with both and both remain unpublished. He did, however, write a long preface to the 1914 modern English translation of *Beowulf* by scholar John R. Clark Hall when it was revised by Tolkien's friend and colleague C. L. Wrenn and published in 1940. Tolkien's fascination with Anglo-Saxon alliteration would also lead to his composing *The Homecoming of Beorhtnoth Beorhthelm's Son* (1953), an alliterative verse-drama continuation of *The Battle of Maldon*, a fragmentary eleventh-century poem that narrates the heroic defeat in 991 of the Earl of Essex by a Viking host.[68] Tolkien's accompanying criticism of the Old English poem focuses on such themes as pride, heroism, and chivalry, themes he would later explore in his Middle-earth fiction.

anglo-saxons and normans

At the time that *Beowulf* was being inscribed in the Cotton manuscript, England was more or less a unified Christian state. This was the work of Alfred the Great and his Wessex successors, but the descendants of Alfred's Viking enemies would play their part as well. The Danish king Cnut (or Canute) the Great ruled England from 1016–35, and Edward the Confessor (ruled 1042–66), the son of a Norman queen, spent much of his early life in Normandy and named as his successor his cousin, William II, the duke of Normandy (who would become known as William the Conqueror). The dukes of Normandy were descendants of Rollo, a Norse adventurer who forced the king of France to grant him land and title in 911. By the eleventh century, the Normans had adopted Christianity, the French language, and feudal politics. Still, Edward's Norman advisors were unpopular with the English nobility, especially with Earl Godwin of Wessex and his sons. When Edward died childless in January of 1066, Godwin's son, Harold, was crowned king by the English nobles and William invaded in September to fight for the throne. The issue was settled when Harold was defeated and killed at the Battle of Hastings on October 14, 1066[69]—one of the great "turning points" in English history, and Tolkien certainly saw it as such for English language and culture.

Two scenes from the Bayeux Tapestry (ca. 1070s): the image at right depicts William II, the duke of Normandy, seated in the center between his half-brothers Odo, the Bishop of Bayeux, left; and Robert, Count of Mortain, right. All three are clad in mail armor. Top; William's invasion fleet at the Battle of Hastings.

The VIKINGS AND OLD NORSE

SOME HISTORIANS VIEW THE VIKINGS as the last wave of barbarian invaders to hit Western Europe, a ninth-century version of the pagan terror that threatened the Roman Empire back in the fourth and fifth centuries. Like the Goths, the Franks, and the Anglo-Saxons, the Vikings eventually adopted Christianity and other cultural attributes of the more "civilized" lands that they conquered. Again, with Christianity came an alphabet with which the Norse scribes could record a wealth of Scandinavian myths and heroic sagas. The resultant body of literature, most of it in Old Norse, was a favorite of Tolkien's and provided him with numerous names and stories that would make their way into Middle-earth.

"Viking" (Old Norse *vikingr*) is the popular name given to Scandinavian warriors who were active throughout the North Atlantic in the ninth to twelfth centuries.[70] Whether due to a warming climate change that began ca. AD 950, which melted previously icy seas and inspired wanderlust, or a desire for adventure and plunder, thousands

BATTLE OF HASTINGS

A unique source of information about the dramatic events surrounding the Battle of Hastings is the Bayeux Tapestry (ca. 1070s), which narrates military and political events and shows us arms, armor, and clothing from the period. Tolkien admitted that he did not focus on the details of the clothing worn by characters in Middle-earth, but commented of the Rohirrim that "the styles of the Bayeux Tapestry (made in England) fit them well enough."[71] While the tapestry may or may not have been made in England (it was certainly commissioned by William's half-brother Odo, the Norman Earl of Kent and Bishop of Bayeux), the mail armor depicted on the tapestry was likely worn by both Harold's and William's men at Hastings. Whether Professor Tolkien liked it or not, the Anglo-Saxon and Norman/French aristocracies had grown culturally very similar in the eleventh century, and both were far removed from their respective barbarian pasts.

of farmers from Denmark, Norway, and Sweden went on seasonal campaigns or raids on neighboring territories. The success of these raids was due to the Viking ship, which employed an innovative clinker construction (overlapping planks) allowing for more flexibility in rough seas and narrow rivers. The dragon prow of the Viking ship (other animals were also used) added to the "terror of the Northmen"—a reputation for animal-like ferocity—which these pagan warriors perhaps exploited with acts of brutality on soldier and civilian alike. Isolated monasteries like Iona, in the Scottish Hebrides, and Lindisfarne, in northern England, were particularly vulnerable to Viking attacks, and hence the monastic chroniclers made much of Viking violence in their accounts.

But there is another side to the Viking Age, one that revisionist historians have grasped. Viking camps often turned into fortified trading posts, and these in turn provided rural Ireland and Russia, for example, with their first real cities (Dublin, Waterford, Wexford, Limerick, Cork, Novgorod, Kiev, Smolensk). In an age of isolated economies, the Vikings were truly international, founding kingdoms in the British Isles, France, and Sicily and trading outposts in Greenland and Iceland; they even maintained partnerships with the Byzantines and Arabs. We now possess archaeo-

Drawings of a ca. early-ninth-century Viking sword from Norway.

logical proof that Norse explorers did reach North America, their Vinland settlement attributed to Leif Eriksson. Viking swords were yet another advance for the early Middle Ages, and Scandinavian art employed animal and plant motifs to great effect in jewelry and wood and stone carving.

The vibrant pagan artistic tradition can perhaps be seen best in Old Norse literature.[72] Whereas very little is known about the gods and myths of the Anglo-Saxons and the Goths, many facets of Viking religion were recorded via runic inscriptions on runestones, amulets and jewelry, weapons, and other items; and preserved in poetry. The Viking pantheon includes Allfather, wise Oðin, who ruled Asgard from his palace of Valhalla; the simple-minded thunder god Thor; the fertility deities Frey and Freya; the beautiful and nearly invulnerable god Balder; and the trickster Loki. We also glimpse the dangerous Frost Giants, the vicious wolf Fenrir, and the enormous serpent of Midgard.

The intertwined threads of religion, heroic epic, and historical fiction in Norse sagas are often hard to disentangle. Court poets called skalds preserved ancient materials and delivered them to audiences eager for thrilling stories of violence and sea adventure. Most of the surviving Norse myths come from Iceland and are in Old Icelandic, which is identical to Old Norse. There are sagas about Scandinavia, France, and the British Isles, but the majority concern Iceland. Tolkien first read Old Norse at King Edward's School, and chose Scandinavian Philology as his Special Subject in the Oxford English School. At Leeds he taught Old Icelandic and cofounded (with E. V. Gordon) the Viking Club, where professors would gather with undergraduates to drink beer, recite sagas, and sing comic songs (see page 23). A more serious endeavor was his Kolbítar ("Coal-biters") group at Oxford, where he led faculty colleagues in careful translation of the major works of Old Norse (see page 26). In 1933, Tolkien was made an honorary member of the Icelandic Literary Society.

The most venerable body of this Icelandic material is the twelfth-century collection of verse known as the *Elder Edda* or *Poetic Edda*. Tolkien made great use of this material in his fiction, including lifting the names of eleven of the dwarves—and Gandalf—from a poem in the *Elder Edda* called the "Völuspá" ("Prophecy of the Völva, or Sibyl," see page 99). Tolkien admitted to basing Gandalf's character in part on the wise and crafty Oðin as he appears in the *Edda*.[73] In addition to looking to Anglo-Saxon riddles for inspiration in his creation of the famous riddle contest between Bilbo and Gollum in *The Hobbit* (see pages 61 and 107–9), Tolkien may also have been inspired by Norse verse. Riddle contests appear in at least two Old Norse works—the "Vfthrúdismal" ("Lay of Vafthrúdnir") in the *Elder Edda*, and *Hervarar saga ok Heiðreks*

The figure shown on this gold bracteate, or medallion, from the Germanic Iron Age, is believed to depict Oðin.

(*The Saga of King Heidrek the Wise*)—both involving a disguised Oðin, and there was also a thriving riddle tradition in medieval Iceland.

In *The Return of the King*, Tolkien mimics the verse style of the *Poetic Edda* in Théoden's rallying cry before the Battle of the Pelennor Fields: "Spear shall be shaken, shield be splintered, / A sword-day, a red day, ere the sun rises!"[74] Compare this to the below verse from the "Völuspá":

> Hard is it in the world,
> great whoredom,
> an axe age, a sword age,
> shields will be cloven,
> a wind age, a wolf age,
> ere the world sinks.[75]

Another collection of Icelandic material was produced ca. 1225–40 by the scholar Snorri Sturluson. This work is known as the *Prose Edda*, but much material overlaps with the *Elder Edda*. In both works there is a distinction between *ljósálfar* ("light elves") and *dökkálfar* ("dark elves"), with the latter—who dwell beneath the earth—usually interpreted as dwarves. Tolkien borrows the distinction but reworks it for *The Silmarillion*.[76] Also found in the *Prose Edda* is the gold ring Draupnir, made by the dwarves for Oðin, which magically produces eight copies of itself every ninth night.

Though he had first discovered the *Silmarillion*'s Eärendil in the Old English poem *Crist* (see page 59), Tolkien later found an explanation of the name in Old Norse literature and equivalents in other Germanic myths. In the *Prose Edda*, the hero appears as Aurvandil, a companion of the god Thor. When the god offers to carry the hero across a frozen river in a basket, Aurvandil's toe, sticking out of the basket, freezes. Thor then snaps it off and tosses it into the sky, where it becomes a star named *Aurvandils tá*, "Aurvandil's toe." This same figure, as Orendel, appears in a German poem ca. 1200 as a prince, who is shipwrecked on the way to the Holy Land, is rescued by a fisherman, and eventually marries a woman named Breide ("Bright").[77] Morning star, mariner-prince, messenger: Tolkien simply combines them all to come up with a more appealing explanation for Earendel than a frozen toe, and builds upon his early poem to give us perhaps the central figure of the entire *Silmarillion*: Eärendil.

> *"I adopted him [Eärendil] into my mythology—in which he became a prime figure as a mariner, and eventually as a herald star, and a sign of hope to men."* [78]

— J. R. R. TOLKIEN, FROM AN UNSENT LETTER ADDRESSED
TO A "MR. RANG," AUGUST 1967

The most influential of all the Icelandic heroic sagas is the *Völsungasaga* (late thirteenth century), the story of the Völsungs, which first appears in partial form in the *Elder Edda*. Tolkien recalls that as a child he had greatly enjoyed reading "The Story of Sigurd" from the *Völsungasaga* as it was retold by Andrew Lang in his *Red Fairy Book* (1890).[79] In the *Völsungasaga*, Sigurd, like Bard in *The Hobbit*, is a hero who slays a dragon, has the ability to understand birds, and begins his career in relative obscurity.[80] The *Völsungasaga* also features the reforging of a sword—Gram—given to Sigurd for the killing of the dwarf-turned-dragon Fáfnir, and the cursed ring Andvarinaut, possessed by Loki and later by Fáfnir. Sigurd ultimately slays Fáfnir by piercing his soft belly from below, as does Túrin Turambar when he slays the dragon Glaurung in *The Silmarillion*.

In the 1920s and '30s, Tolkien worked on two poems, "The New Lay of the Völsungs" and "The New Lay of Gudrún," in an attempt to unify the stories in the *Völsungasaga*. These original poems were edited by Christopher Tolkien and published in 2009 as *The Legend of Sigurd and Gudrún*.

Tolkien was not the only Oxonian drawn to these tales. C. S. Lewis describes in *Surprised by Joy* his first childhood encounter with "Northernness," after reading, in Henry Wadsworth Longfellow's *Tegner's Drapa* (1847), the lines "I heard a voice that cried / Balder the beautiful / Is dead, is dead—."[81] Tolkien's former pupil, the poet W. H. Auden, shared his own translations of Old Icelandic with his professor and coauthored (with Paul B. Taylor) a collection of these titled *The Elder Edda: A Selection* (1969), dedicating it to Tolkien. In his review of *Lord of the Rings*, Lewis recognizes "that hard, yet not quite desperate,

An illustration by English illustrator Arthur Rackham of Sigurd slaying Fáfnir, from The Land of Enchantment, *1907.*

insight into Man's unchanging predicament by which heroic ages have lived. It is here that the Norse affinity is strongest: hammer-strokes, but with compassion."[82]

MIDDLE ENGLISH LITERATURE

IN 1929, TOLKIEN PUBLISHED a philological article on two Middle English religious tracts, titled "*Ancrene Wisse* and *Hali Meiðhad*." In this scholarly piece, as Tom Shippey has shown, Tolkien argued that *Ancrene Wisse* was a product of Herefordshire, a shire (county) in the far west of England whose linguistic traditions were not much disturbed by foreign invasion and innovation.[83] While in the twelfth and thirteenth centuries much of the rest of England—and the English language— were succumbing to the influence of the Normans and the French language, there were still parts of medieval England like the West Midlands that retained much of their Anglo-Saxon heritage, perhaps with a bit of Welsh tradition mixed in. Through scholarly study of the Middle English literature from this region, Tolkien was able to both make important contributions to his academic field and find several figures and themes for his created "secondary world."

Middle English is a label used to describe various forms of the English language spoken in Britain between roughly 1066 and 1470. The literature from this period varies greatly, from archaic Anglo-Saxon epic to French-influenced courtly romance. Tolkien taught most of the major works of this period, and much of his scholarly publication concerned Middle English literature. In fact, his first book and first published academic piece was *A Middle English Vocabulary*, for Oxford's Clarendon Press in 1922. The book, which he wrote while working for the *Oxford English Dictionary*, was a companion volume to Kenneth Sisam's *Fourteenth Century Verse and Prose* (1921). Tolkien's glossary has remained to this day a standard reference tool for students of Middle English.

Perhaps the first major work of Middle English is one that could also be described as the last Anglo-Saxon epic: *Brut*, written ca. 1200 by the English priest Laȝamon (Lawman or Layoman). This poem, which utilizes both alliteration and rhyme, continues a tradition begun in the *Historia Brittonum* (*History of the Britons*, possibly complied or revised by ninth-century Welsh monk, Nennius) of narrating the adventures of Brittonic kings—from their legendary founder, Brutus of Troy (hence the title *Brut*), to the successors of King Arthur. In Laȝamon's *Brut*, Arthur after his last battle tells his successor Constantine that he is being carried off

> . . . *to Aualun; to uairest alre maidene.*
> *to Argante þere quene; aluen swiðe sceone.*
> *and heo scal mine wunden; makien alle isunde.*

> . . . to Avalon, to the fairest of all maidens,
> to Argante, their queen, an elf exceedingly radiant.
> And she shall my wounds make all sound.[84]

Both Galadriel and Arwen are radiantly beautiful healers of fairy realms, and Tolkien borrowed from the *Brut* the name for Éowyn's sword, *dwimmerlaik*.[85] This was a poem that Tolkien and C. S. Lewis both taught and likely discussed at some length.[86]

pearl and sir orfeo

One of the most subtle and moving works of Middle English is the alliterative poem *Pearl*, written anonymously in the late fourteenth century. It contains the story of a father who, grieving over the death of his young daughter, has a sudden vision of Paradise in which he is greeted by a maid arrayed in pearls. The maid, it turns out, is his daughter grown to maturity, who assures him that she is now blissful as the bride of Christ. Tolkien first encountered the poem at King Edward's School, and later studied it at Oxford. One of the attractions for him is that it was written in the West Midland's dialect of Middle English, and thus from the land of his mother's people. While teaching the poem at Leeds, Tolkien wrote *The Nameless Land* (first published in 1927 and later retitled *The Song of Ælfwine*), which he claimed was directly inspired by *Pearl*.[87] Tolkien's modern English translation of *Pearl* did not appear until after his death, in 1975, and was broadcast in Britain on Radio 3 in May of 1978.[88]

As with with *Pearl*, Tolkien also worked for many years on both a Middle English edition and English translation of the poem *Sir Orfeo*. Written ca. 1330, *Sir Orfeo* is a Middle English version (perhaps via a French adaptation) of the classical Greek myth of Orpheus in the Underworld. Here Orfeo is a king and harper whose wife Heurodis is magically abducted by the king of Faërie to his realm; Orfeo, in disguise, sings for the Faërie king to win a favor and get her back. Unlike the Greek tale, *Sir Orfeo* has a happy ending. In 1954, Oxford University Press published an edition of the poem written by Tolkien's student, A. J. Bliss, part of a monograph series of which Tolkien was an editor.

sir gawain and the green knight

Tolkien's modern English translations of *Sir Orfeo* and *Pearl* were published in 1978 together with his translation of *Sir Gawain and the Green Knight*. But long before this, Tolkien had made a great contribution to his field by producing, together with his Leeds colleague E. V. Gordon, the definitive Middle English edition of the poem, which was published by Oxford University Press in 1925.[89] Written by the same poet who composed *Pearl*, *Sir Gawain* is a long and complex poem comprised of both alliteration and rhyme. It narrates the story of the strange Green Knight who barges into Arthur's court challenging the king and his knights to the "beheading game"—a theme in early literature thought to represent renewal. Young Gawain is the only knight who will take up the challenge, but though successful in removing the head of the intruder, the Green Knight, unfazed, picks up his head and demands that Gawain appear at the Green Chapel on New Year's Day to receive his blow in turn as part of the game.

As with the *Pearl*, Tolkien had discovered this Middle English classic while at King Edward's School, and recited it at T.C.B.S. meetings. He often taught the poem and lectured on it at Oxford, and it was the subject of his 1953 W. P. Ker Lecture at the University of Glasgow.[90] Tolkien loved the language of the poem, and his fondness for *Sir Gawain*'s alliteration can be seen in his own Arthurian poem, "The Fall of Arthur" (see page 81). When Aragorn brings his forces to the Black Gate in *The Return of the King*, the Mouth of Sauron greets

One of twelve miniatures added in ca.1410 to the late-fourteenth-century manuscript Sir Gawain and the Green Knight *(Cotton Nero A X, art.3), shows Gawain and the beheaded Green Knight (holding his own severed head) at King Arthur's court.*

him with scorn, saying, "Is there anyone in this rout with authority to treat with me?"[91] Compare this with the first words of the Green Knight when he appears before Arthur: "Where is the governor of this gang?" The hobbits' journey through dangerous and enchanted forests is perhaps an echo of Gawain's journey to the Green Chapel, where:

> Sumwhyle wyth wormez he werrez, and with wolues als,
> Sumwhyle wyth wodwos, þat woned in þe knarrez,
> Boþe wyth bullez and berez, and borez operquyle,
> And etaynez, þat hym anelede of þe heʒe felle;[92]

> At whiles with worms he wars, and with wolves also,
> at whiles with wood-trolls that wandered in the crags,
> and with bulls and with bears and boars, too, at times;
> and with ogres that hounded him from the heights of the fells.[93]

While words from *Sir Gawain* such as *etaynez* (Ents) and *wodwos* (woses) were obvious inspirations for Tolkien, scholars have also noted parallels between *Sir Gawain* and *Lord of the Rings* in their utilization of absentee villains (Morgan le Fay and Sauron) and the ultimate failures of the two heroes—Gawain and Frodo—to live up to their promises.[94] The qualities of loyalty and gallantry demonstrated by Gawain are also, perhaps, evident in Aragorn.

Of course, the most famous of all the works in Middle English is Geoffrey Chaucer's *The Canterbury Tales* (ca. 1387–1400). Though many consider Chaucer England's first great poet, Professor Tolkien did not share this opinion. In 1938, British poet laureate John Masefield invited Tolkien to perform, as Chaucer, some lines from "The Nun's Priest's Tale" at Oxford's *Summer Diversions* arts festival. Tolkien wrote to Masefield, complaining that focusing on Chaucer would give the erroneous impression that he was the "first English poet," and before him all English poetry "was dumb and barbaric."[95]

And yet, it was Chaucer who had served as a sort of "gateway" to other Old and Middle English texts for Tolkien, via his King Edward's School tutor, George Brewerton.[96] Tolkien later published a paper on the dialects in Chaucer's "Reeve's Tale," and could recite from memory that poem as well as "The Nun's Priest's Tale."[97] Dimitra Fimi has pointed out that Tolkien may also have shared one very important sentiment with Chaucer: a sadness over the departure of the elves/ fairies from this world.[98] As the Wife of Bath memorably tells us,

> In th'olde dayes of the Kyng Arthour,
> Of which that Britons speken greet honour,
> Al was this land fulfild of fayerye.
> The elf-queene, with hir joly compaignye,
> Daunced ful ofte in many a grene mede.
> This was the olde opinion, as I rede—
> I speke of many hundred yeres ago.
> But now kan no man se none elves mo.[99]

KING ARTHUR AND THE MATTER OF BRITAIN

TOLKIEN SEEMS TO HAVE had mixed feelings about the Arthurian legends. Though fond of them since childhood, and receiving great acclaim for his edition of *Sir Gawain*, Tolkien steered clear of direct borrowing from Arthuriana in his Middle-earth writings. They were not, from the beginning, English, but rather native Brittonic stories that fell under Christian, French, and chivalric influences from the twelfth and thirteenth centuries, "associated with the soil of Britain but not with English." Tolkien felt that the Faërie elements of Arthurian romances were "too lavish, and fantastical, incoherent and repetitive," and too "involved in . . . the Christian religion." The story of Arthur was also too often presented as historical fact, which he felt was inaccurate and unfair.[100]

These are very interesting comments coming from a devout Catholic, a lifelong reader of Arthurian legends, and a medievalist who gave us the standard critical edition of a key Arthurian text. But let us take Tolkien's points one at a time. First, he states correctly that the Arthurian legends are first associated with Britain but not with the English language. They are, in fact, called "The Matter of Britain" (*la matière de Bretagne*) by medieval poets who drew on both historical and Celtic mythological material to construct the Arthurian romances that were so popular from the twelfth to fifteenth centuries. Though we have no proof that Arthur was ever a historical figure, he is almost always depicted as a British warrior or king fighting *against* the Anglo-Saxons. Arthur's first literary appearance is in the ninth-century *Historia*

Brittonum, where he is credited with twelve great victories over the Saxons, culminating in the Battle of Badon Hill. Another Latin work, the tenth-century *Annales Cambriae*, from Wales, dates Badon Hill to 518 and states that "Arthur and Medraut (Mordred)" fell at the Battle of Camlann in 539.[101] Though Arthur appears in Welsh poems around this time, it was not until 1136 that a full account of his activities is given, in a historically questionable but highly popular work titled *Historia Regum Britanniae* (*History of the Kings of Britain*) written by the Oxford clerk Geoffrey of Monmouth. Geoffrey's *History* inspired many Old French versions of Arthuriana: from *Roman de Brut* (ca. 1155), by the Norman poet Wace; to the romances by twelfth-century poet Chrétien de Troyes; to the thirteenth-century Vulgate Cycle (also known as the Prose Lancelot), the five-part prose work that makes the Holy Grail an essential element of the Arthurian saga. The French romances in turn inspired the great Arthurian epics in English, including Sir Thomas Malory's *Le Morte D'Arthur* (1485), Edmund Spenser's *The Fairy Queene* (1590–96), Lord Alfred Tennyson's *Idylls of the King* (1856–85), and T. H. White's *The Once and Future King* (1958).

An 1868 illustration of Arthur and Merlin by French engraver Gustave Doré, from Lord Alfred Tennyson's Idylls of the King, *an epic Arthurian cycle of twelve narrative poems published between 1842 and 1888.*

"Why," asks Tom Shippey, "should Englishmen take interest in a Welsh hero committed to their destruction, and known anyway via a French rehash?"[102] This brings us to Tolkien's second point, that the legend is too lavish, fantastical, and incoherent. Geoffrey of Monmouth, for example, has Arthur conquering not only the Saxons, but also the Scots, the Irish, the Danes, the Norwegians, the Gauls, and the Romans! In Geoffrey's *History*, as well as in vernacular poems and tales like *Culhwch and Olwen*, Arthur also slays giants, hunts dragons, giant boars, and monstrous cats, and does not die but is carried off to the Faërie realm of Avalon. It is true that the Welsh and Breton Arthurian material contains much that is magical and monstrous, remnants of a paganism long since gone. But surely Tolkien would not have objected to this? On the contrary, his third point is that the Arthurian legends are too *Christian*. Indeed, Arthur was considered by medieval artists and writers to be the greatest of the Three Christian Worthies—that is, the three greatest Christian kings—Arthur, Charlemagne, and the crusader Godfrey of Bouillon. And the legend of the Holy Grail, although containing elements of pagan magic, gained popularity because of its association with the Last Supper, the Crucifixion, and the explicitly Christian quests of Arthurian knights like Perceval and Galahad.[103]

Tolkien cannot have meant that the Arthurian legends were too Christian for his enjoyment, only that they were too directly related to Christian history for him to have included them explicitly in his subcreation. For him, good art and fairy-stories should convey the moral truths of history and Christianity without simply borrowing events from the "primary world." Still, many readers and scholars have identified Arthurian elements in Tolkien's fiction. Tolkien himself described Frodo's departure with the elves to the Undying Lands in the West as "an Arthurian ending," i.e., similar to the departure of Arthur to Avalon, where he is joined on a ship by Elves or queens.[104] Both Frodo and Arthur leave to be healed of their "grievous wounds," and both voyages may be symbolic of death. The shards of the great sword Narsil— which was reforged for Aragorn as Andúril—recall the broken swords of the Grail romances, such as the Sword of Solomon made whole by Sir Galahad in the thirteenth-century Vulgate *Quest of the Holy Grail*.

Edmund Wainwright points to the many similarities that Aragorn shares with both Arthur and the historical king Alfred the Great.[105] Many of the Arthur/Aragorn similarities—royal mother and father, raised in obscurity or exile, fights to gain his rightful throne—simply match the list of hero attributes famously compiled by FitzRoy Somerset, 4th Baron Raglan, known as Lord Raglan, in his book *The Hero: A Study in Tradition, Myth and Drama* (1936). But there is another similarity—one of character—that is not found in every mythic hero. Arthur and Aragorn are both fierce and mighty warriors, yet there is also a gentleness and humility about them. For Arthur, this trait is not in the original Welsh material, but is rather a chivalric trait highlighted by Thomas Malory (where it is also apparent in Lancelot) and made central in the Arthurian novels of Tolkien's contemporary, T. H. White.

Scholars are divided on the influence that the literary Merlin had on Tolkien's creation of Gandalf. Like the Merlin of the romances, Gandalf is fond of disappearing (*The Hobbit*) and appearing in disguise (*The Lord of*

the Rings). "May you ever appear where you are most needed and least expected!" said the Elvenking of Mirkwood to Gandalf,[106] though this could easily be said of Merlin in *Le Morte D'Arthur*. Like Merlin, Gandalf is mentor to heroes and to kings: Bilbo, Frodo, Pippin, Aragorn, and Faramir all receive tutelage and advice from him. In origin, Gandalf is an Istari Maia (helper spirit) and thus immortal; Merlin was said to have been sired by a demon and to be entombed by the Lady of the Lake— not dead but sleeping—in an enchanted tree or cave. And, of course, both Merlin and Gandalf are accomplished wizards, using magic to aid heroes and kingdoms. When Tolkien's editor Rayner Unwin announced the birth of his son, whom he named Merlin, and told Tolkien that the name was more appropriate for a child than was Gandalf, Tolkien replied, "I am sure you are right: Gandalf was always old . . . Not a name for a child of Men!"[107]

Tolkien was not, however, above outright borrowing of Arthurian names, though he sometimes altered them slightly to avoid direct associations. The "Broseliand" in an early version of Tolkien's unfinished poem *The Lay of Leithian*, for example, is the enchanted Forest of Brocéliande in Breton Arthurian stories, though later Tolkien changed it to Beleriand, where it described a region in Middle-earth; similarly he uses "Avallon" in the story *The Fall of Númenor* to refer to the island of Tol Eressëa, but later changes it to "Avallónë," where it becomes the name of a city on the island.[108] In *The Return of the King*, the cavalry of Prince Imrahil are called "the swan-knights of Dol Amroth," echoing the epithet borne by Lohengrin, son of Parzifal, in an early thirteenth-century Grail romance of that name by German knight and poet Wolfram von Eschenbach.[109] Other influences are less obvious. Tolkien's "Westernesse" is, he tells us, inspired by the Arthurian kingdoms of Logres (modern England) and Lyonesse (a mythical land said to once be part of Cornwall that supposedly sank under the sea).[110] The Vulgate Cycle of Arthurian romances uses a narrative technique

German manuscript illustrator Diebold Lauber created this drawing for a ca. 1443–46 edition of Parzifal, *the early thirteenth-century Grail romance by German knight and poet Wolfram von Eschenbach.*

Magic and Machines

hen Galadriel shows her mirror to Frodo and Sam in *The Fellowship of the Ring*, she explains, "For this is what your folk would call magic, I believe; though I do not understand clearly what they mean; and they seem to use the same words of the deceits of the Enemy."[111] Tolkien did not invent wizards, but he certainly explored magic in a more nuanced way than, say, the *Harry Potter* series does. He also linked magic and machines in a unique way, with a distrust of the latter that may seem downright medieval to some.

When Tolkien was presented with the present of a new home tape recorder in the 1950s, the first thing he did was to recite into it the Lord's Prayer (in Gothic, of course) in order to exorcise the demons he said must be living in it!

John Garth has suggested that Tolkien's distrust of machines can be traced, in part, to his and other British soldiers' reactions to the new machines of war introduced at the Western Front during the Great War, particularly flame-throwers and tanks. In his prose tale *The Fall of Gondolin* (1917), for example, Tolkien describes the goblins employing brass dragon battering rams, flame-throwing fire dragons, and iron dragons carrying Orcs in their hollow bellies moving "on iron so cunningly linked that they might flow . . . around and above all obstacles before them."[112] The internal combustion engine "seen through enchanted eyes," writes Garth, "could appear as nothing other than a metal heart filled with flame."[113]

Tolkien wrote to his son Christopher during the Second World War with evident disgust for "the abominable chemists and engineers" who were putting even more powerful weapons in the hands of modern tyrants.[114] Both the orcs and the Uruk-hai were bred of sorcery and science. The former, created in "the subterranean heats and slime" by Melkor, had hearts of granite and deformed bodies, their foul faces unable to smile but they laughed like "the clash of metal."[115] The latter were creations of Saruman, a genetic experiment (possibly breeding orcs with men) to yield more powerful demons who could travel in daylight. Treebeard memorably describes Saruman as having "a mind of metal and wheels; and he does not care for growing things, except as far as they serve him for the moment."[116]

The flame thrower utilized by an Italian soldier in this photograph in the August 24, 1918, edition of Leslie's Weekly *newspaper was a likely inspiration for Tolkien's flame-throwing fire dragons.*

called *entrelacement*, an "interlacing" of story threads in a complex and intricate pattern within one overarching narrative. Tolkien, who had read much French medieval romance while working on his edition of *Sir Gawain*, employs this device throughout *The Lord of the Rings*.[119] Although some have criticized Tolkien for using this decidedly old-fashioned style of narrative, others have argued that the technique supplies a subtle cohesion to the complex plot of the epic.[120]

MALORY'S *LE MORTE D'ARTHUR*

"Whoso pulleth out this sword of this stone and anvil, is rightwise king born of all England." This famous line first appears in *Le Morte D'Arthur*, written by Sir Thomas Malory while in prison during the closing years of the War of the Roses and published by England's first printer, William Caxton, in 1485. Malory traces the story of Arthur from his conception at Tintagel Castle to his departure for Avalon and the subsequent deaths of Guinevere and Lancelot. For Malory, Arthur was an *English* king, at the center of the greatest collection of knights the world has ever known: the Fellowship of the Round Table. The magnum opus of Arthurian romances, *Le Morte D'Arthur* was a text much discussed and admired by J. R. R. Tolkien and C. S. Lewis.[121]

Tolkien's "high style"—the chivalric speech of characters like Aragorn and Faramir—is quite similar to Malory's prose style. The name of Malory's Sir Balan appears twice in Tolkien's writings. *Balan* is the Sindarin word for "One with Power," equivalent to *Vala* in Quenya (High Elvish); Balan is also said to have been the original name of Bëor, founder of the eldest House of Men. Both the glowing sword Sting and Andúril, "The Flame of the West," resemble Arthur's sword Excalibur, which, according to Malory, shone like thirty torches, and both Andúril and Excalibur have magical scabbards.[122]

Though mostly a creation of French poets, Lancelot—or at least Malory's Lancelot—may have contributed to Tolkien's creation of Aragorn. Both Lancelot and Aragorn are royal exiles, uncrowned princes who wander the forests in rough guise. Whereas Aragorn as the ranger Strider cannot be united with his immortal love Arwen, Lancelot as *le Chevalier Mal Fait* ("The knight that hath trespassed") is driven away from Camelot by a madness brought on by his love for Guinevere, the queen who cannot be fully his. Lancelot alone can heal the Hungarian knight Sir Urre, who had been cursed by a sorceress with wounds that would not heal; he does so by "searching his wounds" with his hands. Similarly, the healing hands of the king allow only Aragorn to heal Éowyn.

"The Fall of Arthur"

Though he may have wanted to keep Camelot and Middle-earth distinctly separate entities, Tolkien was inspired to try his hand at an original Arthurian poem in the early 1930s.[123] Titled "The Fall of Arthur" (*fall*, perhaps, to distance himself from Malory's *morte*), it survives in what was thought to be an unfinished handwritten manuscript containing 954 lines.[124] A few lines were quoted in Humphrey Carpenter's *Biography*, and the author of the present book was given access to a page of the manuscript. In October 2012, it was announced by the publisher HarperCollins that a complete work, edited by Christopher Tolkien, would be published the following year. Though writing in modern English, Tolkien clearly mimics the verse style of the *Beowulf* poet, with alliterative half-lines and kennings. Surely the professor would have noticed the irony of writing poetry about Arthur in the language and style of his enemies!

The poem begins with Arthur and Gawain returning to Britain from the Continent—where they have been fighting a war against the Saxons—in order to face the usurpation of Mordred. The two ponder the wisdom in asking for Lancelot's help against Mordred. While Arthur considers rapprochement with Lancelot, Mordred lusts after Guinever [*sic*]:

> His bed was barren; there black phantoms
> of desire unsated and savage fury
> in his brain had brooded till bleak morning.

And the Queen herself is described unflatteringly as a vixen, a

> lady ruthless,
> fair as fay-woman and fell-minded,
> in the world walking for the woe of men.[125]

This may be the only one of Tolkien's works that deals significantly with sexual lust and adultery, two themes that are prominent in the French Arthurian romances of the twelfth century and in Malory.

¶Here foloweth the syxth boke of the noble and worthy prynce kyng Arthur.

¶How syr Launcelot and syr Lyonell departed fro the courte for to seke auentures/ ⁊ how syr Lyonell lefte syr Launcelot slepynge ⁊ was taken. Capm.j.

None after that the noble ⁊ worthy kyng Arthur was comen fro Rome into Englande/ all the knyghtes of the roūde table resorted vnto ꝑ kyng and made many iustes and turneymentes/ ⁊ some there were that were good knyghtes/ whiche encreased so in armes and worshyp that they passed all theyr felowes in prowesse ⁊ noble dedes ⁊ that was well proued on many. But in especyall it was proued on syr Launcelot du lake. For in all turneymentes and iustes and dedes of armes/ bothe for lyfe and deth he passed all knyghtes ⁊ at no tyme he was neuer ouercomen but yf it were by treason or enchauntement. Syr Launcelot encreased so meruaylously in worshyp ⁊ honour/ wherfore he is the first knyght ꝑ the frensshe booke maketh mencyon of/ after that kynge Arthur came from Rome/ wherfore quene Gueneuer had hym in grete fauour aboue all other knyghtes/ and certaynly he loued the quene agayne aboue all other ladyes and damoyselles all the dayes of his lyfe/ and for her he

A page from a 1529 edition of Sir Thomas Malory's Le Morte D'Arthur, *published by London printer Wynkyn de Worde.*

Tolkien does not speak much about modern Arthurian literature. He read T. H. White's *Sword in the Stone* shortly after it was published in 1938, and also, as might be expected, the Arthurian cycle of poems by fellow Inkling Charles Williams. "I actively disliked his Arthurian-Byzantine mythology," said Tolkien of Williams's *Taliessin through Logres* (1938) and *Region of the Summer Stars* (1944), for which C. S. Lewis wrote an accompanying essay.[126] "I seldom find any modern books that hold my attention," he once told the *Daily Telegraph*, excepting Isaac Asimov and Mary Renault.[127] It is doubtful that the most recent trend among Arthurian writers—realistic historical fiction—would have held any more appeal for him.

VICTORIAN FAIRY TALES AND THE GOTHIC REVIVAL

WHAT TOLKIEN CALLS "FAIRY-STORIES" (see pages 18–19) continued to hold an attraction for him throughout his life. Though many derive from the Middle Ages, most fairy tales, as they are usually termed, come to us from collections published in the nineteenth century.

"The essence of fairy-stories is that they satisfy our heart's deepest desire: to know a world other than our own, a world that has not been flattened and shrunk and emptied of mystery."[128]

—THEOLOGY PROFESSOR AND AUTHOR RALPH WOOD,
THE GOSPEL ACCORDING TO TOLKIEN, 2003

Furthermore, since the 1980s, social and cultural historians have redefined fairy tales as complex creations by adults that blend sometimes ancient oral traditions with contemporary socioeconomic concerns. Thus, they should not be simply dismissed as "tales for children." Some fairy tales come directly from the great nationalist folklore collections—the Brothers Grimm (Germany), Sir Walter Scott (Scotland), Hans Christian Andersen (Denmark)—others are Romantic or Victorian retellings of medieval tales. Fairy tales, Arthurian poetry and

The cover of Kinder-und Hausmärchen (Children's and Household Tales) *by Jacob and Wilhelm Grimm, illustrated by Paul Meyerheim in 1886*

paintings, and new translations of medieval epics all form part of the great Gothic Revival that swept Europe and America in the mid to late nineteenth century. J. R. R. Tolkien and C. S. Lewis formed much of their literary and aesthetic tastes on these works, which they first encountered as boys in the *fin de siècle*.

Tolkien cites Andrew Lang and George MacDonald as particular favorite authors of the genre, but we know that he also read the Brothers Grimm, George Dasent, Edith Nesbit, John Francis Campbell, Charles Perrault, Lewis Carroll, Beatrix Potter, and Kenneth Grahame.[129] However, Tolkien harbored an intense dislike for the Victorians' tendency to view fairies as twee, diminutive creatures, an unfortunate trend he believed could be traced back to the writings of William Shakespeare and Michael Drayton in the Elizabethan era (see page 19). Perhaps this is why, of all the fantastic nineteenth-century literature, he preferred the more adult tales of Finnish philologist Elias Lönnrot and English designer and writer William Morris, grounded as they were in authentic mythological material of the Northern peoples.

finnish and the kalevala

The political liberalism of the late eighteenth century—which witnessed revolutions throughout the Western hemisphere from America to France—gave speed to a cultural nationalism that swept through Europe in the first half of the nineteenth century. The music, dress, and stories of the *Volk* ("the people") were an important part of nationalist expression, especially in countries or regions that were under political rule of other regimes. Finland, long controlled by Sweden and then Russia, was one such land, and its young nationalist movement had a member named Dr. Elias Lönnrot. In 1835, Lönnrot was to provide his country with its first significant work of literature—*The Kalevala*—and a century later this work would have an enormous influence on the Oxford philologist who created Middle-earth with a heavy dose of Finnish names and myths.[130]

Lönnrot wrote his master's thesis on Finnish mythology in 1827, at the age of 25. It was titled "On Väinämöinen, a Divinity of the Ancient Finns." In 1835, he released his first collection of Finnish folk songs, arranged in thirty-two cantos, called the *Old Kalevala*. He would later expand this to fifty cantos and include traditional wedding songs and rural spells, and this version, published in 1849, is known simply as *The Kalevala*. Less unified than other national epics, and more a product of peasant culture than aristocratic, *The Kalevala* tells many stories in many voices, but contains a wildness and magic that have made it appealing to many. Tolkien discovered an English translation while at King Edward's School, and at Oxford in 1914 he began writing *The Story of Kullervo*, a retelling in both prose and verse of a story in *The Kalevala* that would haunt him for many years. This is the story of Kullervo the hapless, son of Kalervo, who spends his entire life seeking revenge on his murderous uncle Untamo. Kullervo's every act is disastrous, none worse than seducing his own sister (though he does not know her) and leading to her suicide. After his entire family is destroyed, Kullervo himself resorts to suicide, asking his sword to slay him.

Tolkien attempted his retelling of the Kullervo story in the style of William Morris's romances, but left it unfinished. Later he would

An illustration from the saga of Kullervo from an 1875 Finnish edition of The Kalevala.

change the characters' names and give the tale a Middle-earth setting, the result being "Turambar and the Foalóke" (originally called "Of Túrin Turambar") one of the earliest written parts of *The Book of Lost Tales*, published separately in 2007 as *The Children of Húrin* (see Chapter Five). Túrin becomes a more appealing character than Kullervo, but Tolkien preserves the sense of doom and tragedy. *The Silmarillion* also contains many episodes and characters directly inspired by material from *The Kalevala*. There is, for example, the story of the magician Väinämöinen, who fills the northern region of Finland with such sweet music that the moon and the sun come down from the sky to hear it, settling in two trees where they are then captured by the evil witch Louhi. This is echoed in the *Silmarillion* story of the Two Trees of Valinor, which are destroyed by Morgoth and Ungoliant, and the subsequent creation of the sun and moon to replace the light of the dead trees. A mysterious object in *The Kalevala* called the Sampo has a story similar to that of the Simarils. Väinämöinen's ability to control nature with his songs may be the inspiration of the similarly powerful songs of Tom Bombadil in *The Lord of the Rings*.

Ultimately, however, it was the Finnish language itself that would have the greatest impact on Tolkien's writing. Soon after arriving in Oxford in 1911, Tolkien found *A Finnish Grammar* (1870), by diplomat and linguist Sir Charles Eliot, in the Exeter College Library. The language "intoxicated" him and distracted him from his study of the Classics at Oxford.[131] Though he never mastered Finnish, he continued to resort to the original language of *The Kalevala* as he worked on his Kullervo story. More importantly, Finnish became the basis for his invented Quenya, the language of the High Elves.

WILLIAM MORRIS AND THE PRE-RAPHAELITES

IN MANY PARTS OF EUROPE, nationalism went hand in hand with Romanticism. The Romantic Age began in the last quarter of the eighteenth century, dominated the first half of the nineteenth century, and in some areas—particularly music—lasted until the end of that century. Reacting against Enlightenment values and industrialization, Romantic artists embraced folktales and folk music, mythology, and medieval or "Gothic" themes. Arthurian legends became very popular again, with illustrated editions of Malory published alongside new and very popular Arthurian poetry by Alfred Lord Tennyson, William Morris, and others.

In 1848—a year of nationalist revolutions across Europe—a group of seven young men from the Royal Academy of Art in London rejected the strict Neoclassicism of their older peers and formed the Pre-Raphaelite Brotherhood. For subject matter they found inspiration in Classical mythology and medieval romance, believing that medieval and early Renaissance art was far superior to later styles. They tried to follow the dictate of English art critic (and later Pre-Raphaelite admirer) John Ruskin:

> Go to nature in all singleness of heart, and walk with her laboriously and trustingly, having no other thought but how best to penetrate her meaning, and remember her instruction, rejecting nothing, selecting nothing and scorning nothing; believing all things to be right and good, and rejoicing always in the truth.[132]

Original members of this group included the painters Dante Gabriel Rossetti, William Holman Hunt, and John Everett Millais. Later they were joined by painter Arthur Hughes and William Morris and his partner, fellow designer Edward Burne-Jones. Other painters who associated with or were influenced by the Pre-Raphaelites include Ford Madox Brown, Elizabeth Siddal (Rossetti's model and eventual wife), and John William Waterhouse.

"The Pre-Raphaelites have enormous powers of imagination, as well as of realization." [133]

—JOHN RUSKIN, *LECTURES ON ARCHITECTURE AND PAINTING* (1854).

We do not know how much Tolkien approved of the Pre-Raphaelite movement, but there are clues that he had some sympathies.[134] He compared his Tea Club and Barrovian Society (T.C.B.S.) to the Pre-Raphaelite Brotherhood, to which members Michael and Christina Rossetti usually referred as the P.R.B.[135] T.C.B.S. member Rob Gilson spoke with great enthusiasm about John Ruskin at gatherings of the

MORRIS AS
HEROIC BARD

In appearance, Morris rather looked like a hobbit but saw himself more as a chivalric hero. While painting the Oxford murals, he even commissioned a suit of armor from a local blacksmith and wore it to dinner to amuse his artist friends. In 1871, Morris took a trip that Tolkien would have envied—to Iceland, where he was welcomed as a great bard—though he took the trip partly to escape Rossetti's open affair with his wife Jane. Morris's daughter May recalled of that summer: "my Father was away North, and while he was riding among the black wastes and crossing the great rivers of that land of wonder we were basking by our gentle uneventful Thames."[136] English professor Marjorie Burns argues that Morris's descriptions of his travels in the *Icelandic Journals* (1911) parallel in several instances the adventures of Bilbo in *The Hobbit*, and many scholars have commented on the resemblance of the Shire to the utopian Nowhere in Morris's *News from Nowhere* (1891).[137]

King Edward's School Literary Society. Tolkien attended a meeting of the Exeter College Essay Club in 1913 at which a paper was read on Dante Gabriel Rossetti as artist and poet, and in February 1952, he attended a dinner of the Society of Medieval Languages and Literature at Balliol College to hear author John Bryson present a paper on the P.R.B. as Oxford undergraduates.[138] Tolkien wrote to Rayner Unwin in 1972 that he found comfort in the Fellow's Garden at Merton College, which reminded him of a Pre-Raphaelite painting.[139]

We do know that Tolkien had great admiration for one Pre-Raphaelite: William Morris. Morris had, like Tolkien, been an undergraduate at Exeter College, and it was there that Morris met Edward Burne-Jones (who was from Birmingham *and* went to King Edward's School) and discovered Ruskin and the Pre-Raphaelites. Burne-Jones introduced Morris to Dante Gabriel Rossetti in 1856, and the next year Rossetti invited Ned and Topsy (as the two great friends came to be known) to help him paint ten murals from the *Morte D'Arthur* (their favorite book) at the Oxford Union Society. There they met and befriended the student and aspiring poet Algernon Swinburne and a local Oxford beauty named Jane Burden, who would become Morris's model for the Arthurian wall paintings and, in 1859, his wife. The three artists also founded a design firm together, which later became the famous Morris & Co and produced medieval-themed wallpaper, tiles, tapestries, furniture, and stained-glass windows (including a Tristram and Iseult series inspired by Malory). A leader in the Arts and Crafts Movement, in the 1880s Morris also became a leader of the Socialist movement in England, and was founder of the Society for the Protection of Ancient Buildings.

Birmingham Museum and Art Gallery has one of the finest collections of Pre-Raphaelite paintings, drawings, and stained glass in the world, which it began collecting soon after it opened in 1885.[140] Native son Edward Burne-Jones is well represented in the museum, and in the year of its opening, Burne-Jones was also commissioned to design the stained glass window in St. Philip's Cathedral in Birmingham. As a student at Exeter College, it is likely that Tolkien would have seen a tapestry designed by Burne-Jones and Morris titled *The Adoration of the Magi* that hangs in the College Chapel.

It was William Morris's writings, however, that would be of most interest to Tolkien. When he won the Skeat Prize for English in 1914,

Tolkien used the prize money to purchase a book of Welsh grammar and three books by Morris: *The Life and Death of Jason* (1867), *The House of the Wolfings* (1889), and *The Story of the Volsungs and Niblungs* (1870).[141] For the latter, and for *The Story of Grettir the Strong* (1869), Morris had collaborated with native Icelander Eiríkr Magnússon, then living in London. Magnússon would ultimately publish six volumes of their saga translations, while Morris would also retell the Icelandic *Laxdaela Saga* in verse in his epic poem *The Earthly Paradise* (1868–70). Evidence suggests that Tolkien would have read these and many of Morris's romances, including *The Roots of the Mountains* (1889) and *The Sundering Flood* (1897), as well as Morris's translation of *Beowulf* (1895), *The Defence of Guenevere and Other Poems* (first published 1858), and at least two biographies of Morris. In 1941, Tolkien delivered a lecture at Oxford titled "William Morris:

The Adoration of the Magi, *a tapestry by Edward Burne-Jones and William Morris that hangs in the chapel at Exeter College, Oxford (1890), was likely seen often by Tolkien as a young student.*

The Story of Sigurd and the Fall of the Nibelungs."[142] He was particularly fascinated by Morris's technique of adapting older legendary material and bringing it to modern audiences in a mixture of archaic prose and verse. As a poet Morris explored many different meters and, like Tolkien, composed songs. Both men favored octosyllabic rhyming couplets.

William Morris wrote of the Dale and of Mirkwood, of trolls and of "Gunnlaug the Worm-tongue." In *The Well at the World's End* (1896) he gives us a "Gandolf" and a "Silverfax" (which likely inspired the name of Gandalf's great white horse, Shadowfax).

andrew Lang

THE FIRST TIME TOLKIEN encountered William Morris's name may have been in Andrew Lang's *Red Fairy Book*, where Lang states in his preface that his story of Sigurd was "condensed by the Editor from Mr. William Morris's prose version of the 'Volsunga Saga.'"[143] Tolkien read the *Red Fairy Book* as a child, and perhaps because it was given to him by his mother it held a special place for him throughout his life. It was here that he discovered Norse myth and, more specifically, dragons.[144] There was an Oxford connection here as well. The Scottish-born Andrew Lang came to Oxford in the late 1860s, where he received a First Class in Honour Moderations (preliminary examinations) and also in Greats (Classics). In 1870, he became a full Fellow of Merton College and taught at Oxford for another five years before marrying and moving to London to pursue a career in journalism.

But it was as a writer of fiction and scholar of mythology that Lang would make his name. Best known for his twelve books of fairy-stories and other tales for children, Lang also wrote poetry, novels, and serious studies of myth and folklore. In several articles and books, Lang refuted the mythological theories of nineteenth-century German phi-lologists Jacob Grimm and Max Müller, namely that folklore was not "the debased residue of a higher mythology, but that higher or literary mythology rests on the foundation of folklore."[145] Lang was a founder and president of both the Folk-lore Society and the Society for Psychical Research, but he was also a harsh critique of such late Victorian fads as faith healing and mind reading.

Tolkien revised and expanded his 1939 Andrew Lang Lecture "On Fairy-stories" for *Essays Presented to Charles Williams* (1947) and again for *Tree and Leaf* (1964). In the lecture/essay, Tolkien agrees with Lang that the diminutive fairies so popular with Victorians are tiresome and artificial, symbolic of their creators' patronization of their young readers.[146] As discussed in Chapter One (see page 19), however, he attacks Lang's notion that fairy stories are specifically for children—who, according to Lang, have tastes most like our "naked ancestors." More important, "On Fairy-stories" is the earliest and most complete version of Tolkien's unique theory of "subcreation." Tolkien rejects Lang's belief that fairy stories try to convince children that such marvelous things can happen in the real, or "primary," world. On the contrary, writes Tolkien, the creator of the fairy story is a sub-creator, creating a "secondary world" (God being the Creator of the primary world) in which children *and* adults can enter and, under its spell, find that world to be true. The spell—the "glamour of Elfland," as he calls it—awakens a powerful desire, only partially filling it. Children like fairy stories not because they are children, writes Tolkien, but because they are human.[147]

An example of "the diminutive fairies so popular with Victorians"—this illustration by English American artist Reginald Bathurst Birch is entitled "The fairy king and queen drawn by ten beetles." It was included in "A Fairy-ring Inhabited," a story by Henry Hawthorne that appeared in an 1897 edition of the American children's magazine St. Nicholas.

George MacDonald

GEORGE MACDONALD (1824–1905) was a Scottish writer and poet who wrote several contemporary novels set in Scotland; two fantasy novels for adults, *Phantastes* (1858) and *Lilith* (1895); and both books and shorter tales for children, including *At the Back of the North Wind* (1871), *The Princess and the Goblin* (1872), *The Princess and Curdie* (1883), and "The Golden Key," a story published in *Dealings with the Fairies* (1867). *The Princess and the Goblin* and "The Golden Key" were particular favorites of Tolkien's. Like both Tolkien and C. S. Lewis, MacDonald lost his mother early in life.[148] MacDonald's literary reputation and his circle of literary and artist friends, however, was wider than Tolkien's, and included Lewis Carroll, John Ruskin, and Edward Burne-Jones as well as Alfred Tennyson, Charles Dickens, Henry Wadsworth Longfellow, and Walt Whitman. MacDonald has been called both "the grandfather of the Inklings" and the true founder of modern fantasy.[149]

Goblins, illustrated by English pre-Raphaelite artist Arthur Hughes for an 1888 edition of George Macdonald's The Princess and the Goblin, *one of Tolkien's favorite fairy stories.*

George MacDonald was a deeply religious man and a devotee of German Romanticism. Like Tolkien, MacDonald believed that spiritual yearning—*sehnsucht*—could be evoked by myth and fairy stories. MacDonald became a famous preacher and lecturer, and the strong narrative voice that he uses in his children's fiction can be seen at certain places in *The Hobbit*.[150] Tolkien acknowledged on several occasions that the goblins in MacDonald's fantasy novels influenced his own depiction of goblins and orcs, and that his own ents (probably also Old Man Willow) owe something to the anthropomorphic Ash, Beech, and Alder in MacDonald's *Phantastes*.[151] MacDonald and Tolkien both rewrote the Man in the Moon nursery rhyme, and Tolkien's *Smith of Wooton Major* (1967) owes its origin to his abandoned effort to write a new edition of MacDonald's "The Golden Key." MacDonald's fiction and his essay "The Fantastic Imagination" (1893) provided Tolkien with important material for reflection in his lecture/essay "On Fairy-stories."

"[The fairy-story] may be used as a Mirour de l'Omme ['Mirror towards Man']; and it may (but not so easily) be made a vehicle of Mystery. This at least is what George MacDonald attempted, achieving stories of power and beauty when he succeeded . . . and even when he partly failed."[152]

—J. R. R. TOLKIEN, ON WHAT BOTH HE AND MACDONALD ATTEMPTED TO DO IN THEIR RESPECTIVE SUBCREATIONS, FROM "ON FAIRY-STORIES," 1939.

Re-reading late in life the stories that had so moved him as a child, Tolkien became more critical of MacDonald, especially of his tendency toward didacticism. Still, both Tolkien and C. S. Lewis revered George MacDonald for his storytelling abilities. Like Virgil in Dante's *Purgatorio*, MacDonald serves as Lewis's heaven-sent (and Scottish-accented) guide in his fantasy *The Great Divorce* (1945). In *Surprised by Joy*, Lewis wrote that his own imagination was "baptized" by reading MacDonald as a boy.

The Northern Land

BOTH TOLKIEN AND C. S. LEWIS were first inspired by Victorian retellings of Northern myth; both men went on to study the languages and literature of Northern cultures; and both were directly inspired by these myths to write new works of fiction that reached great levels of popularity and commercial—if not always critical—success. "Like Walter Scott or William Morris before him," writes Shippey, "[Tolkien] felt the perilous charm of the archaic world of the North."[153] Priscilla Tolkien perceived that her father was responding to what he believed was an overwhelming presence of the land and climate of northwestern Europe in northern myth:

> The ideas aroused by the sufferings of long, hard cruel winters, the dazzling beauty of the short flowering of Spring and Summer, and the sadness of seeing this once more pass back into the darkness. . . . Such a climate also nourished the virtues which he held in such high regard: heroism and endurance, loyalty, and fidelity, both in love and war.[154]

The Northern land, be it England or Scandinavia or Iceland, held the language and the history which called out incessantly to J. R. R. Tolkien. From schoolboy to soldier to aging Oxford professor, Tolkien sought to understand the land and its myths and struggled to bring them forth again for the modern reader.

3

"There and back again"

J. R. R. TOLKIEN was a natural and gifted storyteller. He made up stories with his brother when they were children, he wrote narrative poetry as an Oxford student and as a soldier at the Western Front, he recited and explicated myth to his students at Leeds and Oxford, and he told stories to his four children in the 1920s and '30s. The Tolkien children were regaled with tales about the rogue Bill Stickers, the toy dog Rover, and the hale and hearty Tom Bombadil, and Father Christmas himself wrote them letters about his adventures with the North Polar Bear (the letters to his children, "sent from the North Pole" at Christmas time, were written by Tolkien between 1920 and 1942 and published in 1976 in *The Father Christmas Letters*).[1] The elder boys, John and Michael, recalled their father reading to them in his study each Christmas a long tale about a small creature with furry feet.[2] This was in 1928 or thereabouts, and by 1933 his younger children, Christopher and Priscilla, were drawn into the circle as the tale reached completion. In 1932, Tolkien shared a manuscript of this tale with his friend C. S. Lewis, who wrote to another friend that he "had a delightful time" reading it. Four years later, Tolkien lent the manuscript to an Oxford grad working for the London publisher Allen & Unwin, and eventually the script made its way to chairman Sir Stanley Unwin. For a reviewer Unwin turned to his own son, ten-year-old Rayner, who wrote a formal report to his father recommending publication. Rayner earned a shilling for his review, and Tolkien was given a contract. On September 21, 1937, the children's tale was published by Allen & Unwin under the title *The Hobbit, or There and Back Again*.

HOBBITS AND DWARVES

"IN A HOLE IN THE GROUND there lived a hobbit." This sentence was scribbled on a blank page in a School Certificate examination book by a bored and tired professor who was laboriously grading a stack of papers on a hot summer day. After writing that famous first sentence, he commented years later, "I thought I better find out what hobbits were like."[3] Well, they are a bit like the Snergs in E. A. Wyke-Smith's *The Marvellous Land of Snergs* (1927), a dwarf-like, good-natured race who love to eat. Tolkien admitted that the Snerg character Gorbo, "the gem

looked at him for quite half a minute. His eyes did not twinkle any more. They were very kind, and there was the beginning of a good smile on his lips.

Una put out her hand. "Don't go," she said ; "we like you."

"Have a Bath Oliver," said Dan, and he passed over the squashy envelope with the eggs.

"By Oak, Ash, and Thorn," said Puck, taking off his blue cap, "I like you too. Sprinkle a little salt on the biscuit, Dan, and I'll eat it with you. That'll show you the sort of person *I* am. Some of us"—he went on, with his mouth full—"couldn't abide salt, or horse-shoes over a door, or mountain-ash berries, or running water, or cold iron, or the sound of church bells. But I'm Puck!"

He brushed the crumbs carefully off his doublet and shook hands.

"We always said, Dan and I," Una stammered, "that if it ever happened we'd know

"AT LAST HE BEGAN TO LAUGH."

An illustration of the sprite Puck by British artist Claude Shepperson, from Rudyard Kipling's book of short fantasy stories Puck of Pook's Hill. *The stories were published in the* Strand *magazine with Shepperson's illustrations from January to October 1906; Puck may be one of the inspirations for certain hobbit attributes.*

of dunderheads," may have been an unconscious influence for Bilbo Baggins, the protagonist of his tale.[4] A similar acknowledgment was made regarding the bland, bourgeois protagonist in Sinclair Lewis's 1922 novel *Babbit*. The name Bilbo is both an invented first name as well as a type of nickname—like Gorbo—once common in England. Bilbo is also a real surname that survives mostly in the American South, as well as the name of a type of sword blade made in Bilbao, Spain.[5] Still, it is most likely to have been chosen by Tolkien because of its alliteration—Bilbo Baggins—and as appropriate to the protagonist of his children's story. "Baggins" is English dialectical slang for something substantial eaten between meals, for example afternoon tea, of which Bilbo is very fond.[6] As for the hobbit's appearance, this may owe something to Puck in Rudyard Kipling's *Puck of Pook's Hill* (1906): "a small, brown, broad-shouldered, pointy-eared person with a snub nose, slanting blue eyes, and a grin that ran right across his freckled face."[7]

Previous pages:
A family trip to Switzerland in 1911, where Tolkien passed through the Lauterbrunnen Valley, influenced the geography of The Hobbit's *Rivendell and the Misty Mountains. This photochrom of the Lauterbrunnen was taken ca. 1890.*

The origin of hobbits

Tolkien believed that he was inventing hobbits when he wrote that first sentence in the Oxford examination book. However, he likely first encountered the word *hobbit* in *A New Glossary of the Dialect of the Huddersfield District* (1928), by Walter E. Haigh, for which Tolkien himself wrote the preface. He may have also seen the word in a list in *The Denham Tracts*, a collection of folklore writings by Michael Aislabie Denham (and edited by Dr. James Hardy) published in two volumes (1892 and 1895) by the Folklore Society in London.[8] *Hobbit* appears with *bogies* and *hobgoblins* in *The Denham Tracts* list, and is defined in the index as "a class of spirits." While the name is certainly similar to those of many country spirits in British folklore—such as hobs, hobthrusts, and hobyahs—Tolkien writes in Appendix F of *The Lord of the Rings* that the name derives from Old English *holbytla*, or "hole-builder." There is another small hole-dweller with a similar-sounding name—the rabbit—and indeed Bilbo is called (derisively) a rabbit by several characters in *The Hobbit*. Tolkien himself was firm on the point—"Certainly not rabbit"—and acknowledges that Sinclair Lewis's *Babbit* (1922) may have been an influence. But as Tom Shippey and Michael Drout have pointed out, rabbits do not appear in the English language until the fourteenth century because they were imported around that time from the Continent.[9] They would thus have been alien or unknown creatures to the Anglo-Saxons, just as the hobbits are to most of the inhabitants of Middle-earth.

Tolkien's hobbits live in quite comfortable holes, and Bilbo Baggins's—called Bag End—was more comfortable than most. Bilbo might be described as a country squire, a well-to-do bachelor of the English gentry (the non-noble landowners). He owns a very nice piece of property in Hobbiton which, in hobbit terms, is an impressive "country house" (we find out later in *The Lord of the Rings* that his Sackville-Baggins relations greatly desire it). Bag End is replete with several pantries and even entire rooms that serve as closets for his clothing. Bilbo is a collector of fine things, keeps a tidy home, and enjoys sitting outside and smoking his pipe. He does not, however, seem to work or have a specific job. He has his meat delivered by a butcher. He is polite, well dressed, and strictly maintains his privacy.

But there is another side of Bilbo lurking behind his conventional Baggins exterior: he is half Took, a hobbit family known for their unexpected adventures and rumored fairy blood. Bilbo had a mother named Belladonna (Italian for "beautiful lady") Took, an example of the exotic element in Tookish naming practices.[10] Still, it took an unexpected wizard and an "unexpected party" to awaken the Tookish blood in Bilbo. The wizard Gandalf—an old man with a blue pointed hat, a gray cloak, and a walking staff—appears before Bilbo like an eccentric Oxford tutor, lecturing the hobbit on semantics and word connotation and offering to send him on an adventure, "Very amusing for me, very good for you—and profitable too, very likely, if you ever get over it." He is followed by thirteen dwarves, all with colorful hoods, eager to sing and eat Bilbo's food. Thus does the unexpected party begin.

> *"I don't much approve of The Hobbit myself . . . newfangled hobbits and gollums (invented in an idle hour)."*[11]
>
> — J. R. R. Tolkien, letter to G. E. Selby, December 14, 1937

concerning dwarves

Tolkien's source for Gandalf and the dwarves is the Old Norse work the *Elder Edda* (see Chapter Two, pages 67–68). Specifically, it is the "Dvergatal" ("Catalogue of Dwarves") from the first poem in the *Edda*, called the "Völuspá" ("The Prophecy of the Sibyl"):

> . . . the race of dwarfs
> Out of Brimir's blood / and the legs of Blain.
> There was Motsognir / the mightiest made
> Of all the dwarfs, / and **Durin** next;
> Many a likeness / of men they made,
> The dwarfs in the earth, / as Durin said.
> Nýi and Niði, / Norðri and Suðri,
> Austri and Vestri, / Alþjófr, **Dvalinn**,
> Nar and **Nain**, / Niping, **Dain**,
> **Bífur**, Báfur, / **Bömbur**, **Nóri**,
> Órinn, Ónarr / **Óinn**, Miöðvitnir.

The Races of Middle-earth

or the most part, Tolkien preferred to capitalize when referring to the races of Middle-earth in general terms—Elves, Men, Dwarves, and Hobbits. (For the purposes of this book, to avoid confusion between going back and forth between capitalized and lowercase words, these terms will be lowercased.) Elves are "a race similar in appearance (and more so the further back) to Men, and in former days of the same stature."[12] In the appendices to *The Lord of the Rings*, Tolkien writes that the elves were "high and beautiful, . . . tall, fair of skin and grey-eyed, though their locks were dark, save in the golden house of Finarfin."[13] In a letter from 1956, he further explains that "Elves and Men are just different aspects of the Humane. . . . The Elves represent, as it were, the artistic, aesthetic, and purely scientific aspects of the Humane nature raised to a higher level than is actually seen in Men."[14] Men in Middle-earth can be dark-haired (the Númenóreans) and swarthy (the Southrons) or fair-haired and fair-skinned (the Rohirrim). Hobbits are called Halflings by the Númenóreans because they were, in the early days, about half their height—three and a half feet; Númenórean men often reached seven feet. Dwarves are not much taller—usually four feet—but are much stockier

> *"In spite of later estrangement Hobbits are relatives of ours: far nearer to us than Elves, or even than Dwarves. And the world being after all full of strange creatures beyond count, these little people seemed of very little importance."*[15]

—PROLOGUE, "CONCERNING HOBBITS,"
THE FELLOWSHIP OF THE RING

than hobbits and are bearded. In *The Silmarillion* we find out that the dwarves were created by Aulë and made hardy, stubborn, and long-lived in order to withstand the assaults of Morgoth. Orcs were "squat, broad, flat-nosed, sallow-skinned."[16] At first, Tolkien felt that orcs were mutated from elves who were captured and tortured by Morgoth. After *The Lord of the Rings* was published, however, he admitted that the orcs were problematic and "require more thought." "Orcs were beasts of humanized shape (to mock Men and Elves) deliberately perverted/converted into a more close resemblance to Men."[17] Though Tolkien makes much of the differences between the races of Middle-earth, he is not happy that there is discord among men and among all the free peoples. "Indeed," states Haldir in *The Fellowship*, "in nothing is the power of the Dark Lord more clearly shown than in the estrangement that divides all those who still oppose him." Thus racial discord can be traced back to Morgoth and Sauron. Despite what many critics have written, Tolkien preferred a multicultural Middle-earth where even miscegenation is seen as a positive (e.g., Beren and Lúthien, Valacar and Vidumavi, Aragorn and Arwen, and Faramir and Éowyn).[18]

Some of the races of Middle-earth: two dwarves (Richard Armitage as Thorin Oakenshield, far left, and Ken Stott as Balin, far right), a high elf (Hugo Weaving as Elrond), a wizard (Ian McKellan as Gandalf), and a hobbit (Martin Freeman as Bilbo Baggins)—in a scene from the Peter Jackson film The Hobbit: An Unexpected Journey *(2012).*

Vigg and **Gandálfr**, / Vindálfr, **Þrain**,
Þekk and **Þorin**, / **Þror**, Vit and Lit,
Nyr and Nyrath,— / now have I told—
Regin and Rathsvith— / the list aright.
Fíli, **Kíli**, / **Fundin**, Váli,
Heptifili, / Hannar, Sviur,
Frar, Hornbori, / Fræg and Loni,
Aurvang, Jari, / **Eikinskjaldi**.
The race of the dwarfs / in Dvalinn's throng
Down to Lofar / the list must I tell;
The rocks they left, / and through wet lands
They sought a home / in the fields of sand.
There were Draupnir / and Dolgthrasir,
Hár, Hugstari, / Hléþjolfr, **Glóinn**,
Dóri, **Óri**, / Dufur, Andvari,
Skirfir, Virfir, / Skafith, Ai.[19]

The names bolded here in the "Dvergatal" are the ones that Tolkien borrowed wholesale for *The Hobbit*, along with one he turns into an epithet: Eikinskjaldi, "Oakenshield." Durin, though not one of Thorin's company, is described later in *The Hobbit* as "the father of the fathers of the eldest race of dwarves, the Longbeards," a reference perhaps to the Lombards (Longobardi or Langobardi in Italian), a Germanic tribe who migrated to Italy, and who were contemporaries of the Goths and Saxons.[20] But notice too that Gandalf is here in the list of dwarves. The earliest surviving manuscript (ca. 1928–30) of *The Hobbit*, six handwritten pages from Chapter One, shows that Tolkien originally had Gandalf as the head dwarf, while the wizard was then named Bladorthin.[21] But the name Gandalf, which translates as "wand-elf," suggested a different role. While the dwarves' appearance and actions owe much to nineteenth-century fairy-tales (especially *Snow White*), Gandalf bears some similarities to an old bearded man on a German postcard owned by Tolkien.[22]

The sudden appearance of a cranky wizard and questing dwarves in a quiet and cozy hobbit neighborhood is, for the reader, a shock, registered by Bilbo's reaction to his uninvited guests. Michael Drout has argued that Bilbo is a mediator for us, the readers.[23] Culturally Bilbo is familiar enough to us—he speaks more or less the way we do (Tolkien

When it was dark, the masters of the house came home. These were seven dwarfs, who dug in the mountains all day for treasure. They lit their seven candles when they came in, and then they saw that some one had been in the house. The first dwarf said, "Who has been sitting in my chair?" The second of them said, "Who has been eating from my plate?" The third dwarf said, "Who has taken some of

my bread?" The fourth said, "Who has been drinking out of my little cup?" The fifth said, "Who has used my little fork?" The sixth said, "Who has been cutting with my little knife?" The seventh said, "Who is this lying upon my bed?" Then the others all came crowding up to him, bringing their candles with them. They held their candles up so that the light fell upon Snow-White, and when they saw her, the whole seven cried out with one voice, "What

In The Hobbit, *the dwarves' appearance and actions owe much to nineteenth-century fairy-tales such as* Snow White; *here, in an 1885 version of the story from* Three Fairy Princesses, *British artist Caroline Paterson depicts the dwarves—with their long beards and caps—gathering around the sleeping form of* Snow White.

calls the hobbits "relatives of ours"), he likes the comforts of home, he responds to monetary inducements—and so becomes our interpreter of the heroic world of Gandalf and Thorin and Smaug. As Bilbo begins the journey he is not at all comfortable in the unfamiliar surroundings and with the unfamiliar company, and thus at first resists the attempts of Gandalf and the dwarves to get him to join their adventure. But his character develops along the way to the Lonely Mountain, experiencing what modern critics might call "psychological growth" (Tolkien would *never* have used that phrase). Bilbo leaves behind his provincialism, eventually embracing his Tookish desire for adventure and displaying heroism in combat with the spiders of Mirkwood and in crawling through the tunnel toward the dragon. Conversely, the heroic but stubborn Thorin, thoroughly aristocratic, learns in the end to appreciate some of the middle-class values of hobbits, as he admits on his deathbed to Bilbo.

Trolls and Goblins, Gnomes and Elves

If Bilbo and his fellow hobbits are merry and middle class, the trolls and the orcs that Bilbo encounters are crude, working-class bullies. Tolkien emphasizes this with the common names and vulgar dialect of the trolls (uniquely in *The Hobbit*):

> "Blimey, Bert, look what I've copped!" said William. . . .
> "Lumme, if I knows! What are yer?"[24]

While the goblins in *The Hobbit* are less uncouth in their speech, Tolkien does use this technique again with the orcs in *The Lord of the Rings*. Some have suggested that the crude language of these creatures is a reflection of what Tolkien heard from soldiers in the trenches during the Great War. In any event, the three trolls of *The Hobbit* are fairy-tale trolls: they are large and ugly, violent and stupid, but they do talk and have personalities. The trolls of medieval literature and Scandinavian folklore can be monsters who dwell in mountains and forests (e.g., in *Beowulf* and *Sir Gawain and the Green Knight*) or even enchanted fiends (the Old Norse verb *trylla* means to bewitch or enchant), but the comic man-eaters of *The Hobbit* owe more to Jacob Grimm and Andrew Lang.

Equally comic are the first elves who appear in *The Hobbit*, invisible singers of frivolous songs who mock Bilbo and the dwarves as they approach Rivendell. Gandalf calls them "Good People" with "over merry tongues," recalling the euphemisms for fairy in Irish and Welsh folk tradition (as in Irish *daoine maithe*, "the good people," and Welsh *tylwyth teg*, "the fair folk"). Similarly, the disappearing Elves of Mirkwood are very like the "trooping fairies" one encounters in Irish folklore, whose processions and revelry are medieval, aristocratic, and rarely glimpsed by humans.[25] Elrond of Rivendell, however, bears little resemblance to his elven subjects. He is described as a descendent of elves and of the men of the North; noble and fair in face, as strong as a warrior and as wise as a wizard.[26] Tolkien called this passage "a fortunate accident," because it sets up the

Swedish artist John Bauer was well known for his illustrations of trolls, which appeared in numerous early editions of the fairy-tale annual Bland tomtar och troll (Among Gnomes and Trolls), *and with which Tolkien may have been familiar. This illustration accompanied* The Boy and the Trolls, *by Walter Stenström, in a 1915 edition of the annual.*

Elrond Half-elven of *The Lord of the Rings* and *The Silmarillion*; for though he took the name Elrond from his early legendarium material (1926's "Sketch of the Mythology"), he had not as yet connected Bilbo's world fully to Middle-earth.[27]

In *The Hobbit*, Elrond's wisdom is illustrated when he explains the names and origins of the swords taken from the trolls' lair. Named swords are of course commonplace in medieval legend; thus Thorin's Orcrist (Sindarin "Goblin-cleaver") and Gandalf's Glamdring ("Foe-hammer") join such hero-weapons as Arthur's Excalibur ("From Steel," from the Latin *caliburnus*), Beowulf's Hrunting (Old English "Thrusting"), and Sigurd's Gram (Old Norse "Wrath"). Elrond also explains to the dwarves the meaning of the runes on Thror's map, including the "moon-letters" that can only be seen when the light of the moon shines behind them. Like Bilbo, Tolkien "loved maps . . . [and] runes and letters and cunning hand-writing."[28] The runes Tolkien employs in *The Hobbit* are, by his own admission, an alphabet similar to the runes of Anglo-Saxon inscriptions, such as those found on the so-called Franks Casket—a small Anglo-Saxon whalebone box discovered in France in the nineteenth century and now in the British Museum (see right).[29]

The purpose of the Franks Casket—which was constructed in the first half of the eighth century AD in Northumbria—is unknown, though reliquary and jewelry box have both been suggested. Its panels contain scenes of Roman, biblical, and Germanic pagan inspiration, including Titus's capture of Jerusalem, the Adoration of the Magi, and Weland the Smith at his forge (this hero appears in both Anglo-Saxon and Eddic literature). The panels also contain the same Anglo-Saxon runes that Tolkien employed on the cover of The Hobbit *and on Thror's map.*

MOUNTAINS, RINGS, AND RIDDLES IN THE DARK

AFTER BILBO'S PARTY LEAVES Rivendell, they head northeast to the Misty Mountains. Tolkien admits that his description of the mountain pass, with its tumbling stones and "thunder-battles," is based on a hiking trip he took with his aunt and brother in the Swiss Alps in 1911.[30] The name "Misty Mountains," Shippey notes, comes from a line in the Eddic poem "Skirnismál," where they are associated with trolls.[31]

From Goblin to Elf

ver the course of his career—from the time he began writing his earliest poetry and sketches to his great works *The Lord of the Rings* and *The Silmarillion*—Tolkien changed both his nomenclature and his description of the beings of Middle-earth. His childhood poetry dealt often with fairies; in this he was no doubt influenced by Andrew Lang and other Victorian writers. By the time Tolkien went off to war, however, he had shifted his usage to *gnomes*. Though possibly related to the Greek *gnōmē*, "thought, intelligence," it is more likely that the sixteenth-century German-Swiss physician and alchemist Paracelsus invented the word *gnomus* to describe a mythologicial species of pygmies who dwelled within the earth.[32] These creatures are closer to Germanic dwarves than to Tolkien's tall and noble elves. In the 1915 poem "Goblin Feet," Tolkien used the terms *goblin*, *fairy*, and *gnome* interchangeably. He would, in later poems, settle on *elves*, using *gnome* then as a term for one specific group of elves, the Noldor, itself a Quenya word meaning "the Knowledgeable." And the word *goblin*, which Tolkien employs in *The Hobbit* and in his early poetry, is replaced by *orc* in *The Lord of the Rings*. (Orcs are mentioned only once in the original edition of *The Hobbit*, while goblins appear only ten times in *LOTR*). The reason for his change in terminology is not entirely clear. The use of the term *fairy* to describe a homosexual man dates back to the mid-1890s, but Tolkien never says that this influenced him. More likely it is his preference for Germanic words (Old English *ælf, dweorg, orc*) over French (*faerie, gobelin*). In a letter published in the *Observer* on February 20, 1938, in reply to a reader who had inquired about the etymology of the names and terms in *The Hobbit*, Tolkien stated—with a wink—that "*elf, gnome, goblin, dwarf* are only approximate translations of the Old Elvish names for beings of not the same kinds and functions."[33] C. S. Lewis discusses the confusion over the names, sizes, temperaments,

The stone-giants Bilbo sees across the ravine, who toss boulders at each other in sport, may have been the inspiration for a similar episode in C. S. Lewis's Narnia book *The Silver Chair* (1953). Both Tolkien's and Lewis's giants ultimately derive from the English *eten* (Old English *eoten*, Middle English *eten* and *etayn*), a large monster (often translated as "ogre" or "giant") who appears in both *Beowulf* and *Sir Gawain and the Green Knight*.[34] In *The Hobbit*, goblins first make their appearance in the Misty Mountains, grabbing Bilbo and the dwarves and singing (or croaking) rhythmically as they carry their prisoners underground. *The Hobbit*'s goblins, who also appear in the Tolkien's Father Christmas letters at about this time (the early 1930s), owe more to the writings of George MacDonald and

and origins of these mythical beings in the chapter titled "The *Longaevi*" ("longlivers") in his posthumously published lecture-collection, *The Discarded Image* (1964). He first describes the three most common historical perceptions of the "long-living" elves/fairies as evidenced in old literature and myths:

1. Evil, terrifying creatures of night.
2. Tiny wild beings who revel and dance.
3. Beautiful, vital female beings of human size; High Fairies.

He then elaborates on "four rival theories of their nature; attempts, which never reached finality, to fit even these lawless vagrants into the Model [of Medieval cosmology]."

1. They are a distinct "species" of sentient beings between angels and humans.
2. They are "demoted" angels, lesser spirits assigned to "the airy region" or various places on the earth.
3. They are ghosts.
4. They are fallen angels (i.e., demons or devils).

The second category in the rival theories, demoted angels, is explored by Lewis in his *Space Trilogy* and also by Tolkien in *The Silmarillion*, though in the latter they are called Valar and Maiar rather than elves. The elves, dwarves, and hobbits of *The Lord of the Rings* and the fauns, dwarves, and giants of *The Chronicles of Narnia* seem closest to the species of sentient beings between angels and humans.

Algernon Blackwood, an early twentieth-century English writer known for his ghost stories, than to medieval sources.[35]

Bilbo is separated from the dwarves after Gandalf's slaying of the Great Goblin and the company's flight into the dark tunnels beneath the mountains. He eventually makes his way to an underground pool where he finds a ring (not knowing, of course, that it was *the* ring) and its most recent master, "old Gollum, a small slimy creature."[36] Bilbo's encounter with Gollum and their "riddle game"—Chapter Five, "Riddles in the Dark"—comprise a sort of narrative core for *The Hobbit*. Bilbo, separated from Gandalf and the dwarves, is left to his own devices in a contest with his antithesis. Gollum is like Bilbo in that he

GOLLUM

Tolkien's initial description of Gollum in *The Hobbit*—small and dark—does not correspond to all of the illustrations of the creature that appeared in editions of the book, and of course in *The Lord of the Rings* Gandalf does tell us who Gollum is and from whence he came. Tolkien described a small slimy creature called Glip in his 1928 poem collection *Tales and Songs of Bimble Bay*, and may in part have been influenced by the golem, an artificial creature, often monstrous, of Jewish religious texts and folklore. Tolkien scholar Douglas Anderson has suggested that Old Norse *gull* (or *goll*), which could mean both "gold" and "finger-ring," is a more likely source.[37] In his entirety, however, Gollum remains one of Tolkien's most original creations.

A sculpture of the slimy bug-eyed creature Gollum, holding his favorite food, raw fish. It was created by the New Zealand prop company Weta Workshop, which worked on The Lord of the Rings *and* The Hobbit *film franchises.*

is small and clever and always hungry. But even in his original guise, Tolkien depicts Gollum as a kind of anti-hobbit: he is slimy rather than furry; treacherous in his "home," not courteous; and Bilbo's polite bourgeois language contrasts with the hissing, suspicious speech of Gollum. Two things bring these two very different creatures together: riddles and a ring.

Shortly after the publication of *The Hobbit*, Tolkien wrote a letter to the London newspaper the *Observer* concerning his riddles: "There is much work to be done here on the sources and analogues."[38] With tongue firmly in cheek, Tolkien notes that it was unlikely that Bilbo or Gollum had made up any of the riddles, and prompts us to seek the true "sources and analogues." We find them to be the fascinating Anglo-Saxon riddles found in manuscripts like the *Exeter Book*. Other sources include Old Norse riddles, nursery rhymes, and Tolkien's own writings.[39]

"I don't know where he came from, nor who or what he was. He was Gollum— as dark as darkness, except for two big round pale eyes in his face."[40]

—NARRATOR FROM *THE HOBBIT*, ON GOLLUM

Tolkien revised the chapter "Riddles in the Dark" significantly in 1951 to bring Gollum and the ring in line with their depictions in

The Lord of the Rings. He changes the terms of the contest, for example, from Gollum giving Bilbo a present if the hobbit wins, to Gollum showing Bilbo the way out of the cave. These changes and others were required because Tolkien had developed the ring itself—it went from being a magical but almost unnecessary plot device to becoming the One Ring that drives the entire plot of *The Lord of the Rings.* In a conversation between Gandalf and Frodo in *The Lord of the Rings*, Gandalf explains that both Gollum and Bilbo lied about how they obtained the ring because they were under its power.[41]

Magical rings abound in ancient and medieval literature. The Ring of Gyges, which Glaucon describes to Socrates in Book II of Plato's *Republic*, turns its wearer invisible when worn with its decorative face turned to the inside, as does the ring given to the Arthurian knight Yvain in Chrétien de Troyes' *Yvain: The Knight of the Lion.* Many Arthurian romances feature magic rings that make the wearer invincible in battle or invulnerable to wounds. Rings or other objects that confer invisibility are found in many fairy tales, including "The Story of Sigurd" in Andrew Lang's *The Red Fairy Book*—the tale of Sigurd/Siegfried from *The Völsungasaga* (see page 69) and *The Nibelungenlied* (a related Middle High German epic poem circa 1200). Andvaranaut, the Ring of the Nibelungs, is a cursed ring that Sigurd/Siegfried removes from the dragon Fáfnir's hoard. In *The Hobbit*, Tolkien clearly had the invisible type of ring in mind, though in *The Lord of the Rings* he may have combined the invisible and cursed rings in a similar way to the talisman in the Ring of Gyges myth, which had the power to corrupt and enslave its wearer, no matter how noble.[42]

The "Riddles in the Dark" episode concludes with Bilbo displaying an act of both courage and pity. Refusing to kill Gollum while invisible—"not a fair fight"—Bilbo instead leaps over the wretched creature to make

Fáfnir guards his hoard, which includes the cursed ring, in an illustration from "The Story of Sigurd" in Andrew Lang's The Red Fairy Book *(1890).*

THE STORY OF SIGURD   359

and flayed off the skin, and took it to the house of Otter's father. Then he knew his son was dead, and to punish the person who had killed him he said he must have the Otter's skin filled with gold, and covered all over with red gold, or it should go worse with him. Then the person who had killed Otter went down and caught the Dwarf who owned all the treasure and took it from him.

Only one ring was left, which the Dwarf wore, and even that was taken from him.

Then the poor Dwarf was very angry, and he prayed that the gold might never bring any but bad luck to all the men who might own it, for ever.

Then the otter skin was filled with gold and covered with gold, all but one hair, and that was covered with the poor Dwarf's last ring.

But it brought good luck to nobody. First Fafnir, the Dragon, his exit, "Not a great leap for a man, but a leap in the dark."[43] Though his courage is more that of the common soldier than the mythic hero, Bilbo's sense of fairness in a fight and compassion for the enemy resembles the chivalric code of the Arthurian world. Few in reality ever lived up to the knightly ideals, as C. S. Lewis once pointed out in an essay on chivalry, but that does not invalidate them.[44]

BEORN

AFTER GETTING PAST GOLLUM and the goblin guards, and escaping the tunnels into the light, Bilbo is reunited with Gandalf and the dwarves. But their happy reunion is soon interrupted by the howling of wolves, evil packs that lived in the shadow of the mountains. Tolkien calls them "wild Wargs," reaching into his philological bag to find an old Germanic word that meant both "outlaw" and "wolf" (Old English *wearg*, Old High German *warg*).[45] The Wargs are contrasted by the eagles who appear to rescue Bilbo's party, an ancient and noble race of birds.[46] A symbol of imperial Rome, the eagle was considered in the Middle Ages the greatest of the raptors; only an emperor was permitted to carry and hunt with an eagle according to the *Book of Saint Albans* (1486), which contained essays on hunting, hawking, and heraldry. The eagle episode in *The Hobbit* may have been inspired by Chaucer's unfinished poem, "The House of Fame" (ca. 1379),[47] with its eagle dream-guide. The role of the eagles as rescuers was so appealing to Tolkien that he would return to it again in *The Lord of the Rings*.

The eagles deposit Gandalf, Bilbo, and the dwarves near the Carrock. Tolkien's choice of name for the hill near Beorn's home, and the philological comments made by Gandalf, are a bit confusing. As mentioned in the previous chapter (see page 46), Tolkien may have borrowed directly the Cornish word *carrek* (rock) for the Carrock, or else he may have inherited the Celtic word through Middle English versions[48] *carrock*, *currick*, *corrock*, *currok*, *curragh*, and *cirock*, for "a heap of stones," meaning either a cairn or a rocky hill. It is not certain whether Tolkien had only one or several of these meanings in mind.

The encounter with Beorn begins with the comic tone used in the trolls scene, but turns dark as Bilbo discovers what happens to Beorn at night. For Beorn is a shape changer, a werebear. In the earliest versions of *The Hobbit* manuscripts he is called "Medwed . . . a skin-changer," and has similarities to the North Polar Bear in Tolkien's

Father Christmas Letters.[49] The name Beorn is an Old English word for "man" or "warrior," but its similarity to the Old Norse *björn*, "bear," suggests that it too originally referred to the animal.[50] Tom Shippey reminds us that the name Beowulf is often explained as "Bee's-wolf," that is, one who devours honey—a bear.[51] In the Old Norse *Saga of King Hrolf Kraki* there is a man-bear named Bjorn whose curse is to live as a bear during the day and a man at night. Tolkien's description and drawings of Beorn's hall, not surprisingly, closely resemble Anglo-Saxon and Norse mead halls, the most famous of which is Hrothgar's hall in *Beowulf*, Heorot.

An artist's rendering of an Anglo-Saxon or Norse mead hall, a great feasting hall such as the one featured in Beowulf, *which is similar in description to Beorn's hall in* The Hobbit.

Next, Bilbo, Gandalf, and the dwarves take their places at a long table in Beorn's hall. As they prepare to sup, Bilbo witnesses a strange procession of animals—white ponies, gray dogs, white sheep, black rams—standing on their hind-legs and carrying torches in their mouths.[52] At first this appears to be a gathering of the kind of anthropomorphized animals one finds in early fantasy and children's writers like Lewis Carroll and Beatrix Potter. But the ritualistic solemnity of the scene, and the fact that the animals do not talk or interact with Bilbo's party, suggests another source. Both Celtic and Norse deities are often accompanied by animal servants and messengers. The Celtic horned god Cernunnos is depicted on the Gundestrup Cauldron—a silver vessel from circa 200 BC–AD 300 discovered in Denmark—holding a snake and being served by deer and other beasts. Odin has his ravens,

Detail from the silver vessel known as the Gundestrup Cauldron, ca. 200 BC–AD 300, depicting the Celtic horned god Cernunnos holding a snake and being served by deer and other beasts—perhaps a model for the animal procession scene at Beorn's hall. The cauldron was discovered in a peat bog in Denmark in 1891.

Hugin and Munin, who bring him news of the world (as the old raven Roäc does for Thorin). The embroidered cloth borne by the rams suggests a medieval tapestry or manuscript page with animal ornament, such as the highly stylized decorative work in the Book of Kells (ca. 800) and the Lindisfarne Gospels (early eighth century), illuminated manuscripts from the British Isles.

MIRKWOOD and Lake-cown

"REMEMBER YOU ARE OVER the Edge of the Wild now,"[53] warns Gandalf as they leave Beorn's hall for the journey through Mirkwood forest. Mirkwood is derived from an ancient word—the Old English *mirce*, "dark" and "gloomy;" it is also, likely, at least a subconscious borrowing from William Morris (who featured a Mirkwood in his *A Tale of the House of the Wolfings*, 1889).[54] In *The Hobbit*, Mirkwood turns out to be the home of goblins, hobgoblins, orcs, spiders, and, worst of all, the Necromancer. Tolkien tells us no more here about hobgoblins, orcs, and the Necromancer, except—as Gandalf mentions before he leaves Bilbo and the dwarves—that the latter is a "black sorcerer" living in a "dark tower."[55] We only find out later, in *The Lord of the Rings*, that Sauron is the Necromancer and that Gandalf's mission is to drive Sauron from Mirkwood. Abandoned by their wizard guide, the company must cross an enchanted stream where they encounter startled deer fleeing from a huntsman's horn. In the Arthurian legends, the sudden appearance of a beautiful hart or stag marks the beginning of a great adventure. Such awaits Bilbo and company, who are soon led off the path by the momentary and mysterious appearances of a band of wood-elves. Tolkien's narrator in his early poem "Goblin Feet" (1915) had similarly and frustratingly pursued a band of trooping fairies (to use Yeats's phrase), while the beautiful fairy women of Arthurian romance can often be found alongside forest streams and lakes. Anderson suggests that the Middle English poem "Sir Orfeo" (see page 72), which Tolkien himself translated, was the most likely source for the fairy hunt.[56]

The dwarf Bombur, who had fallen into the enchanted stream and become a victim of its spell, awakens to describe a beautiful dream he has had of a great, endless feast in the land of Faërie. "A woodland king was there with a crown of leaves, and there was a merry singing, and I could not count or describe the things there were to eat and drink."[57] Celtic myth is full of such dream visions and journeys, and they made their way into medieval French and English poetry. Bilbo, meanwhile, experiences a breathtaking vision of thousands of "black emperor" butterflies, followed by a heroic encounter with giant spiders. Using his ring, his elvish dagger, Sting, and taunts of "Attercop!" and "Old Tomnoddy!" Bilbo manages to fight off several of the spiders and free the dwarves who had been caught. The word *attercoppe*, "poisonheads," is found in the twelfth- or thirteenth-century Middle English poem "The Owl and the Nightingale," which also features a taunting.[58]

No sooner is the battle of the spiders over than the dwarves are caught again, this time by wood-elves. Tolkien goes to great length to explain them:

> These are not wicked folk. If they have a fault it is a distrust of strangers. Their magic was strong. . . . They differed from the High Elves of the West, and were more dangerous and less wise. For most of them . . . were descended from the ancient tribes that never went to Faerie in the West. . . . and after the coming of Men they took ever more and more to the gloaming and the dusk. Still elves they were and remain, and that is Good People.[59]

While Tolkien would later revise this passage slightly, in the original edition published in 1937 he includes the terms *Faerie*, *Elves*, and *Gnomes* in his description of the wood-elves, and refers to them using the Irish euphemism Good People. The Elvenking who imprisons the dwarves is not named in *The Hobbit*; we find out in *The Lord of the Rings* that he is Thranduil, father of Legolas. His vegetal crown—woodland flowers in spring, red leaves and berries in autumn—and his oaken staff suggest the Green Men carved in medieval churches or, even older figures, the Druids of the Iron Age, who performed rituals involving sacred oaks.

Bilbo is literally "over a barrel" in his escape from the wood-elves, and he and his dwarf companions float down river to the country of Dale and a settlement of men called Lake-town or Esgaroth. Tolkien describes it as a "busy wooden town" constructed on huge piles of forest trees in the lake.[60] As mentioned on page 46, lake-dwellings such as that described by Tolkien are an ancient phenomenon in Celtic-speaking lands. Excavated examples in Switzerland, Ireland, Scotland, and Wales may have influenced Tolkien's depiction of Lake-town.

Green Men

S o-called "Green Men" (also foliate heads, foliate masks) were employed as decorative ornamentation in medieval manuscripts and as carvings on churches and other buildings. Early Roman examples suggest the origin to be Bacchus, but the motif was popular in Britain and Ireland from the early Middle Ages. Traditionally, Gothic and later examples of Green Men have been interpreted as evidence of lingering paganism in Christian Europe, referencing elves or nature spirits. Architectural historian Richard Hayman has recently suggested, however, that they depict demons, and like the Sheela na gig carvings in Ireland and Britain of crouching women with exposed vulvas (*síle ina giob*, Irish for "old lady on her haunches"), were grotesque figures meant to frighten churchgoers with images of sin and death.[61]

Above and below: two of the green men gargoyles of Oxford.

A Sheela na gig carving at the twelfth-century Romanesque Church of St. Mary and St. David, in Kilpeck, Herefordshire, England.

Esgaroth is ruled by the Master, a thoroughly modern man who did not "think much of old songs, giving his mind to trade and tolls, to cargoes and gold, to which habit he owed his position."[62] He is comparable to the governor Gumpas in C. S. Lewis's *Voyage of the Dawn Treader*, who had "statistics" and "graphs" and argued that slavery was "an essential part of the economic development of the islands." "I think we have had enough of governors," said King Caspian as he replaces Gumpas with the loyal Lord Bern, "kneeling with his hands between the King's hands and taking the oath to govern the Lone Islands in accordance with the old customs, rights, and usages of governors."[63] Here Lewis has combined a physical element of feudal ceremony (the homage) with language about rights and customs akin to that in the Magna Carta (1215) and the Scottish declaration of independence, the Declaration of Arbroath (1320).

In *The Hobbit*, it is the people of Esgaroth who cry for the captain Bard ("grim-voiced and grim-faced") to be their king. The scheming Master declares that the citizens of Lake-town "have always elected masters from among the old and wise, and have not endured the rule of mere fighting men." "We will have King Bard!" replied the citizens. "We have had enough of the old men and the money-counters!"[64] Tolkien scholar John Rateliff suggests that Lake-town is Tolkien's only oligarchy, a republic ruled by merchant guilds with an elected "Master" (similar to Florence and Venice in late medieval Italy), also the title held by the chief administrator in many Oxford colleges.[65]

smaug

THE MASTER OF LAKE-TOWN is paralleled by the dragon living under the mountain. Both are cunning, suspicious creatures and both are greedy for gold. But the awesome power of Smaug[66] the Magnificent places him in the company of the mighty dragons of Germanic myth. "I desired dragons with a profound desire," said Tolkien of his first encounter with them, as a child reading Andrew Lang's *Red Fairy Book*. "Of course, I in my timid body did not wish to have them in the neighborhood. But the world that contained even the imagination of Fáfnir was richer and more beautiful, at whatever cost of peril."[67]

Neither do Thorin and the rest of the dwarves wish to face a dragon, and so turn to their burglar once more for assistance. One of the great moments in *The Hobbit* is Tolkien's description of Bilbo crawling in the dark toward the dragon:

> He was trembling with fear, but his face was set and grim. . . .
> Soon he thought it was beginning to feel warm. "Is that a
> kind of glow I seem to see coming right ahead down there?"
> he thought. . . . It was at this point that Bilbo stopped.
> Going on from there was the bravest thing he ever did. . . .
> He fought the real battle in the tunnel alone, before he ever
> saw the vast danger that lay in wait.[68]

One can feel the excitement building in Tolkien's prose, even hear a father's voice rising dramatically as he exclaims to his children that the red-golden light at the end of the tunnel is "The glow of Smaug!"

The enormous winged serpent sleeping on a great pile of treasure has a surprising effect on the hobbit. "His heart was filled and pierced with enchantment and with the desire of dwarves; and he gazed motionless, almost forgetting the frightful guardian, at the gold beyond price and count."[69] Bilbo seizes "a great, two-handled cup, as heavy as he could carry," and fled from the cave. Many alert readers have spotted the source of this episode in *The Hobbit*: the theft that awakens the dragon-terror at the end of the poem *Beowulf* (see Chapter Two, page 63). Though Tolkien did not deny this, his reply to a 1938 letter in the *Observer* shows how he saw himself simply continuing in the tradition of subcreators. "It is difficult to think of any other way of conducting the story at that point," he wrote. "I fancy the author of *Beowulf* would say much the same."[70]

Bilbo's return visit to the dragon hoard includes a lengthy conversation with Smaug, who uses the interview to discover the invisible hobbit's true identity. A likely source for this episode, as Shippey has pointed out, is the conversation between the hero Sigurd and the dragon Fáfnir in the poem "Fáfnismál" in the *Elder Edda*.[71] The riddling self-descriptions offered by the hobbit (clue-finder, web-cutter, barrel-rider, etc.) are another nod to the Anglo-Saxon and Norse riddle tradition. But Bilbo's cockiness and wordplay with Smaug is also reminiscent of that of Homer's Odysseus as the burglar Nobody in the cave of the Cyclops Polyphemus. Here Odysseus taunts Polyphemus after blinding the giant and escaping the cave, leading to the curse of Poseidon that provides the tragic pathos of *The Odyssey*. Bilbo also escapes the cave but *his* hubris leads to the destruction of Lake-town and, indirectly, to the tragic deaths of the Battle of Five Armies.

Dragons

ragons are a commonplace creature in both Western and Eastern mythology. In the West, they almost uniformly appear as great winged serpents capable of vast destruction (fire-breathing only one of their terrible weapons) but also possessing intelligence and sometimes magic. Dragons appear in Greco-Roman myths, and of course feature prominently in medieval art and literature. Medieval Christians associated them with the serpent in the Garden, depicted St. Michael battling a seven-headed version at the Apocalypse, and feared that their souls might be devoured by dragons in Hell. Both Tolkien and Lewis were drawn particularly to the dragons of Germanic myth, of which Fáfnir and the dragon of *Beowulf* are the most notable. In a 1965 BBC interview, Tolkien said that dragons "comprise human malice and bestiality together so extraordinarily well, and also a sort of malicious wisdom and shrewdness—terrifying creatures!"[72]

Lewis focused on greed as the defining characteristic of dragons in *Voyage of the Dawn Treader*, where thinking "dragonish thoughts" can transform one into a dragon. Tolkien was already developing the story of the wingless dragon Glaurung when he was writing *The Hobbit*, while the dragon Chrysophylax Dives is featured in his *Father Giles of Ham* (1949).

A carving of the scene from the Sigurd legend from the The Völsungasaga, where the hero kills the dragon Fáfnir; on the wooden doorway from the ca. late twelfth-century Hylestad church, which was located in Setesdal, Norway.

A print from the Apocalypsis Sancti Johannis, a book of woodcuts and religious text printed in Germany, ca. 1467. The page depicts two scenes from the Book of Revelation: on the top (12:3–12:7), Michael and his angels fight the seven-headed dragon; on the bottom (13:1–13:2), Saint John sees a similar seven-headed beast rising out of the sea.

Smaug's dragon hoard contained many and diverse treasures: gold and silver, great jewels, golden harps, mighty weapons and spectacular armor, and the prized white gemstone of the Dwarves, the Arkenstone (from Old English *eorclan-stān*, "precious stone"). The assemblage recalls that from the royal ship burial at Sutton Hoo (see Chapter Two, pages 53–54). However, the mound containing the ship burial at Sutton Hoo was not excavated until 1939, two years after *The Hobbit* was published.

endings

THE SLAYING OF SMAUG by Bard, the gold lust and greed exhibited by the dwarves once they are exposed to the treasure, Thorin's violent treatment of Bilbo, and the outbreak of war: all of these moments at the end of *The Hobbit* can be described by one of Tolkien's favorite Germanic words—grim. This Middle English word, from Old English *grimm*, "fierce," appears frequently in *Beowulf* (more than thirty times) and in the Eddas and sagas (where it is a personal name). It is the most oft-used descriptor of Bard, and Thorin looks and talks that way under the spell of the treasure. The Old Norse version of the word, *grimr/grimmr*, "hooded one," which appears as a descriptor or even epithet of Odin, is the likely origin of the many Grim names—e.g., Grimsbury, Grim's Hill, Grimsditch—in the English countryside.

There is even a change in Bilbo at the end of the book. Though he does not fall completely under the spell of the treasure, he does pocket the Arkenstone and then uses it in political negotiations. At Thorin's deathbed, he is even able to shed his bourgeois colloquialisms for the high, epic language appropriate for addressing a dying king:

> "Farewell, good thief," [Thorin] said. "I go now to the halls of waiting to sit beside my fathers, until the world is renewed. Since I leave now all gold and silver, and go where it is of little worth, I wish to part in friendship from you. . . .

> Bilbo knelt on one knee filled with sorrow. "Farewell, King under the Mountain!" he said. "This is a bitter adventure, if it must end so; and not a mountain of gold can amend it. Yet I am glad that I have shared your perils—that has been more than any Baggins deserves."

"No!" said Thorin. "There is more in you of good than you know, child of the kindly West. . . . Some courage and some wisdom, blended in measure. If more of us valued food and cheer and song above hoarded gold, it would be a merrier world. But sad or merry, I must leave it now. Farewell!"[73]

There is much here in this moving passage, one of the finest written in *The Hobbit*. It begins with Thorin addressing Bilbo with a paradoxical title—good thief—but one that elevates him from the status of "burglar" which he is usually called by the dwarves.[74] Thorin's description of the afterlife is similar to that promised to elves and men in *The Silmarillion*, and echoes the idea of Valhalla as home for fallen Norse heroes. On one very important point does it differ, however: Thorin believes that gold and silver will have no worth in the afterlife, which is closer to a Christian than a pagan Germanic

A detail from an eighteenth-century Icelandic manuscript shows Valhöll (Valhalla), the hall of the gods and home of fallen heroes in Norse mythology.

belief. On the other hand, Tolkien's assertion here of the worth of hobbit values—good food, cheer, and song—recalls the more earthly side of medieval culture, one often overlooked by modern observers but celebrated in both the high culture (chivalric romances) and low (carnival) of the Middle Ages.

The clarity and wisdom that Thorin has gained on his deathbed are expressed in words that recall, of all things, Aristotle's "virtue ethics." In the *Nicomachean Ethics*, Aristotle prescribes the pursuit of virtue (*areté*, "excellence") through habituating the "golden mean"—the middle between two extremes. The virtue of courage (*tharsos*), for example, lies between the extremes of cowardice and rashness. Similarly, the intellectual virtue of prudence or practical wisdom (*phronesis*) is acquired through practicing moderation and observing those who live well.[75] Thus Thorin is, at the climax of the novel, telling the reader that Bilbo has the habits that make one "merry" or happy in the Aristotelian sense, that he has demonstrated his excellence (in cleverness and courage), and that he is about to be rewarded with a return to the Shire where he can enjoy the fellowship of others in good food and good cheer.

The Hobbit ends with many partings and a return journey to the Shire (though we do not learn the name of Bilbo's country until *The Lord of the Rings*). This cyclical plot structure—reflected in the words to Bilbo's song, "The Road Goes Ever On"—becomes an important one for Tolkien, who adopts it again for *The Lord of the Rings*. One could say that it is almost Tolkienian, though the professor was probably aware that he was following a pattern often seen in fairy-stories and children's literature. It is a most satisfying ending to a long journey, akin to sitting in a comfy chair next to the fire and smoking a pipe. And that is exactly where the story ends, with Bilbo and Gandalf in good cheer sharing some tobacco and telling stories of far distant lands.

TOLKIEN EXPRESSED SOME REGRET for the "talking down to children" tone at the beginning of *The Hobbit*. "I had not [at that time] freed myself from the contemporary delusions about fairy-stories and children," he wrote in 1961 to his Aunt Jane."[76] In 1967, he admitted to an interviewer that "*The Hobbit* was written in what I should now regard as bad style, as if one were talking to children. There's nothing my children loathed more."[77] (See Appendix II for further discussion of *The Hobbit* as a work of juvenile fiction, and the reaction of critics to it as such.)

Many critics noticed the change of tone as *The Hobbit* progresses toward the themes of politics and war, some seeing this narrative inconsistency as a flaw. But the change in tone also reflects the character development of the protagonist, for Bilbo is in a sense spiritually immature, choosing the comforts of his cozy little hole over adventure in the world of the tall people. That is, until Gandalf shows up to give him a little nudge out the door and helps him see his hidden talents. The changing narrative tone of *The Hobbit* "keeps pace with the hero's journey," wrote C. S. Lewis in 1937, in his anonymous *Times Literary Supplement* review of the book.[78]

Tolkien scholar Jane Chance has compared the intrusive narrator in *The Hobbit* to a know-it-all critic, and suggests that Tolkien used this device the way Chaucer inserted himself as one of the tale-telling pilgrims in *Canterbury Tales*.[79] Lewis uses the same device throughout *The*

Chronicles of Narnia. Yet Tolkien ultimately rejected the notion that *The Hobbit* was a children's book. "Anything that was in any way marked out in *The Hobbit* as for children, instead of just for people, [my children] disliked—instinctively," he later reflected. "I did too, now that I think about it."[80] The wide appeal and lasting impact of *The Hobbit* show that the work was able to overcome this shortcoming, if one could call it that. The public demand for "more hobbits!" would also lead Tolkien to embark on a more ambitious project, one that would take him from fairy-story to fantasy epic. Nearly twenty years later Tolkien would finish *The Lord of the Rings*, bringing together Gandalf and the hobbits with the quite serious and ultimately tragic story of the elves that he had been working on since his undergraduate years in Oxford.

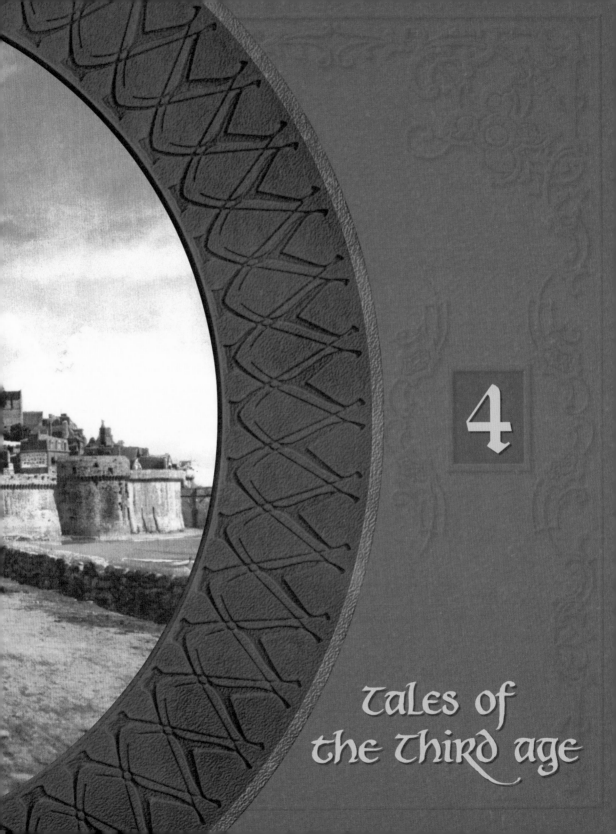

4

Tales of
the Third age

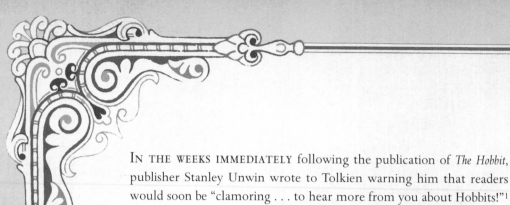

IN THE WEEKS IMMEDIATELY following the publication of *The Hobbit*, publisher Stanley Unwin wrote to Tolkien warning him that readers would soon be "clamoring . . . to hear more from you about Hobbits!"[1] "I cannot think of anything more to say about *hobbits*," replied Tolkien, but he *was* interested in sharing stories about the world "into which the hobbit intruded."[2] When Tolkien turned over to Allen & Unwin parts of what would later become *The Silmarillion* and *Farmer Giles of Ham* in November 1937, the publisher respectfully declined pursuing it as a single book but suggested that sections of it could be useful in producing more hobbit adventures. As Tolkien turned his mind from the grand epic narrative of his legendarium in order to satisfy this demand for "more hobbits," he found on this new adventure that a terrifying wraith had materialized on the path. The sudden appearance of Black Riders in these early drafts of *The Lord of the Rings* marked this as a very different kind of book. "Thus, the new story," writes Bradley Birzer, "was rapidly transformed from a delightful and whimsical children's sequel to *The Hobbit* into an adult story that wrestled with questions of enormous theological and philosophical import and subtlety."[3]

The new story would also have to wait seventeen years before it appeared in print. There were several reasons for this. Tolkien's scholarship and college obligations took up most of his time during term, while summer was busy with grading examinations and giving extra lectures in order to supplement his modest professorial salary. Medical bills and university tuition for his children necessitated this extra work. As Britain drifted closer to another war with Germany, Tolkien's new hobbit adventure also grew darker, and he struggled with direction. He shared drafts privately with his son Christopher and with C. S. Lewis, and read bits at Thursday-night gatherings of the Inklings, who proved to be harsh critics. The result was several false starts, stops, and significant rewrites. The aged Bilbo perhaps expressed Tolkien's frustration at the end of *The Lord of the Rings* when he says: "And when I have time to write, I only really like writing poetry."[4] The war and health problems (including, possibly, depression[5]) delayed things even more, but by October 1949, he had essentially completed the Rings saga. Still, it was not the type of book that Allen & Unwin had requested, and Tolkien began negotiating with Milton Waldman from the London publisher Collins. The book languished at Collins and Tolkien returned (with tail somewhat tucked) to Allen & Unwin in 1952. Rayner Unwin's enthusiasm for the book led to a contract, but because of rising costs and a postwar paper shortage, *The Lord of the Rings* would have to be published in three volumes, a division not of Tolkien's design; he never saw the epic as a trilogy. When the first volume, eventually named *The Fellowship of the Ring*, at last appeared in print in July 1954, its first chapter bore the title "A Long-Expected Party." Tolkien fans, friends, and editors would have found that an entirely appropriate description of *The Lord of the Rings* itself.

The Fellowship of the Ring

CONCERNING HOBBITS

Volume I of *The Lord of the Rings* bore several titles early on, including *The Shadow Grows* and *The Return of the Shadow*.[6] When Tolkien at last settled on *The Fellowship of the Ring*, he liked that it fit well with the title of the last chapter: "The Breaking of the Fellowship." The prologue satisfies the demand for "more hobbits" as well as serving as a summary of Bilbo's finding of the Ring and encounter with the dragon. The section "Concerning Hobbits" expands upon the hobbit-lore given at the beginning of *The Hobbit*. Tolkien here uses a literary conceit from the Middle Ages, saying that the lore is a selection from the *Red Book of Westmarch*—a book of hobbit history started by Bilbo to recount his adventures and later expanded by Frodo, Sam, and Sam's heirs and collected into a library of lore. The name of the book recalls such medieval Welsh manuscripts as the *Black Book of Carmarthen* and the *Red Book of Hergest*, which are collections (dating to the thirteenth and fourteenth centuries, respectively) of Arthurian and very early folk material.

Tolkien wrote that hobbits avoided machinery except for forge-bellows, handlooms, and water mills, such as this old one in Derbyshire, photographed ca. 1890.

In this material from Bilbo's library we first learn the name of his country, the Shire, so-named by the hobbits living under the authority of the Thain. This Shire (Old English *scīr*, "district"), though a colloquial name for an English county, may be an homage to the idealized Sarehole of Tolkien's youth. He loved the West Midlands, both the land and its dialect, and thus the Shire is in the west of Middle-earth. In Sarehole, he and his brother explored the unspoiled woods and played in the millpond. Hobbits, he writes in the prologue, avoid the use of machines other than the forge-bellows, the water mill, and the handloom.[7] The Thain (Old English *ðegn*, "vassal or retainer"—one who "retained" or held the lands of the king) of the Shire resembles the late Anglo-Saxon thanes, gentry who served as administrators and tax collectors for the king, with occasional military obligations as well.[8] This usage is similar to the Shirriff (i.e., sheriff, from Middle English *shire-reeve*), who appears a bit later in the prologue. Many of the other place names mentioned in the early part of *The Fellowship*—such as Mirkwood, Bree, and Westernesse—have medieval origins, as of course does the setting Middle-earth (see page 9).[9]

Shown here in a ca. 1912 photograph, the Honorable Victoria Mary Sackville-West, Lady Nicolson—Vita Sackville-West—may have been Tolkien's inspiration for the Sackville-Bagginses, especially Lobelia.

Tolkien is clearly having fun with the naming of the Shire-folk in the prologue and first chapters of *The Fellowship*. There are the Three Tribes—Harfoots ("hairy feet"), Stoors ("large/strong ones"), and Fallohides ("paleskins")—all Old English names and perhaps a reference to the Angles, Saxons, and Jutes who are, in Bede's *Historia*, called the original three tribes of English settlers in Britain. Marcho and Blanco Harfoot are the Hengist and Horsa of the Shire[10] (see page 52). Isumbras Took is an homage to the hero of the Middle English romance *Sir Isumbras*. Old Master Gorbadoc takes his name from a legendary king of the Britons (Gorboduc) who appears in Geoffrey of Monmouth's *Historia Regum Britanniae*. The "Sackville" in Sackville-Baggins—the snobby cousins of Bilbo and Frodo—is French via Norman; Tolkien rarely used French or Romance names, so "Sackville" can be considered a pretentious hobbit surname and, perhaps, an unflattering reference to Virginia Woolf's aristocratic lover Vita Sackville-West. Sancho Proudfoot's first name is a nod to Miguel de Cervantes's character from *Don*

Quixote. Tobold Hornblower is a combination of Shakespeare's Tybalt from *Romeo and Juliet* and C. S. Forester's protagonist Horatio Hornblower. Isengrim is the Norse name of the wolf in the twelfth-century *Le Roman de Renart* (compare Maugrim, the wolf-captain in C. S. Lewis's *The Lion, the Witch, and the Wardrobe*). Fredegar "Fatty" Bolger was inspired by *The Chronicle of Fredegar*, an account of events in Frankish Gaul ca. AD 564–641; in early drafts Fatty's first name was Hamilcar, after Hamilcar Barca, father of the Carthaginian general Hannibal. The name Sam Gamgee is thought to derive from *gamgee*, the old Birmingham colloquial word for cotton wool, which in turn came from Gamgee tissue, a cotton-wool surgical gauze invented by Birmingham physician Dr. Sampson Gamgee in 1880.[11] With great surprise and delight did Tolkien receive, in 1956, a letter from a Mr. Sam Gamgee of Brixton Road, London, inquiring about the history of the character with his same name.[12]

Both C. S. Lewis and Rayner Unwin (thirteen years old at the time), reading an early draft of *The Fellowship* in 1938, advised Tolkien that there was too much hobbit and too little adventure in the early chapters. "I must plainly bow to my two chief (and well-disposed) critics," he wrote to Stanley Unwin. "The trouble is that 'hobbit talk' amuses me privately . . . more than adventure."[13] Some of this hobbit talk, however, sets up the adventures that are to come. When we first meet Sam, for instance, he is at the Green Dragon Inn in the Shire, trying to explain to his neighbors—who think he is being ridiculous—about dragons, ents, and the fair folk.

Sam's attitude toward the elves is likely representative of the attitude of some medieval Englishmen toward them, and perhaps that of Tolkien himself: "'They are sailing, sailing, sailing over the Sea, they are going into the West and leaving us,' said Sam, half-chanting the words. . . . He believed he had once seen an elf in the woods, and still hoped to see more one day."[14] Not everyone in the Middle Ages, however, felt so drawn to them: others believed that elves caused madness and disease, or—like Gimli did before he met Legolas and Galadriel—that they worked mischievous enchantments and were not to be trusted.

We also learn more about Gollum early on in the *The Fellowship* when Gandalf explains to Frodo the history of the Ring. Gollum's original name was Sméagol (Old English *smēagan*, "penetrate, scrutinize," and *smygel*, "retreat, burrow"), and he came from a respectable family, from a hobbit-like race of river folk:

SOCIAL CLASS

The class difference between the friends Frodo, Merry, and Pippin on the one hand, and the gardener Sam on the other, is evident in the names themselves, although Sam will eventually rise above his nickname and, later in life, become mayor of the Shire. Thus the reality of social hierarchies, and the common sense of the common Englishman, are themes established at the very outset of the novel.

The most inquisitive and curious-minded of that family was called Sméagol. He was interested in roots and beginnings; he dived into deep pools; he burrowed under trees and growing plants; he tunneled into green mounds; and he ceased to look up at the hill-tops, or the leaves on trees, or the flowers opening in the air: his head and his eyes were downward.[15]

In other words, Sméagol was the opposite of Sam, the simple gardener who appreciates growing things and elves and songs without the obsessive need to know the "roots and beginnings." Is this Tolkien's warning to his fellow academics? Like Saruman with the *palantír* (a crystal-ball-like seeing stone), "His knowledge is deep, but his pride has grown with it",[16] Sméagol "put his knowledge to crooked and malicious uses"[17] once he began wearing the Ring.

A statue of Pepin (Pippin) the Great in Würzburg, Germany; the first Carolingian king of the Franks was likely the namesake of Peregrin "Pippin" Took.

> *" One Ring to rule them all,*
> *One Ring to find them,*
> *One Ring to bring them all*
> *and in the darkness bind them."*[18]

—TRANSLATION OF PART OF THE INSCRIPTION
ON THE ONE RING, DISPLAYED ONLY
WHEN PLACED IN FIRE

In the early chapters of *The Fellowship* Tolkien introduces a new Ring-bearer: Frodo Baggins. Like Tolkien, Frodo was an orphan who was adopted by a kindly bachelor, his cousin Bilbo. Originally Tolkien had thought this new adventure would be given to a son of Bilbo's named Bingo, whose friends were named Odo, Frodo, and Vigo.[19] However, this rhyming cast of hobbits was replaced by Frodo, Sam, Merry (Meriadoc Brandybuck), and Pippin (Peregrin Took). While Samwise is an English nickname (Old English *sāmwīs*, "half-wise, simple"), Frodo (Old English *frōd*, "old, wise") is from the Germanic heroic tradition (a King Frōda appears in *Beowulf*). Meriadoc is an aristocratic name from early medieval Brittany, and Pippin was the name of the first Carolingian king of the Franks.

The Power of the One Ring

hen Bilbo found the ring in *The Hobbit* it gave him invisibility, like Plato's Ring of Gyges and that in Chrétien de Troyes' *Yvain* (see page 109). In *The Fellowship*, however, we also learn that this ring is a Great Ring, a Ring of Power that gives its wearer unnatural long life, though a mortal who possesses the ring suffers tormenting attenuation, and, as Gandalf explains to Frodo "does not die, but . . . he *fades*." Moreover, this is the Ruling Ring, which gave Sauron the ability to control the wearers of the other rings. For Gollum and the Ringwraiths—also called the Nazgûl, the black riders who serve as Sauron's terrible servants—this means ultimate servitude and loss of self. Is Tolkien using the One Ring to comment on the effects of power itself? Tom Shippey brings to our attention one very interesting Anglo-Saxon proverb: *Man deþ swá hé byþ þonne hé mót swá hé wile,* "Man does as he is when he may do as he wishes."[20] The power of invisibility allows the wearer of the One Ring to do as he or she wishes; but, as Gandalf, Galadriel, and Elrond suggest, this is not a good thing. Still, there is something about hobbits that makes them resistant to the evil of the Ring. Because Bilbo began his ownership with pity for Gollum, rather than with violence, he took little hurt from carrying the Ring for so long. A natural aversion to power over other people, perhaps, gives hobbits some protection against the Ruling Ring. But most immune to its powers is Tom Bombadil. Already very old, Bombadil neither desires the Ring, nor does it make him invisible when he places it on his finger. He is "Master of wood, water, and hill," but master of no man but himself.

TOM BOMBADIL

Sam is set apart from the provincial, unimaginative hobbits in the Green Dragon Inn because he received "a proper education"—listening, as a lad, to Bilbo tell stories about elves and dragons. "Me, sir!" he exclaims when Gandalf orders him to go on the journey with Frodo. "Me go and see Elves and all! Hooray!"[21] Then he burst into tears. Such is the proper response to an invitation to Faerie.[22] Sam gets his wish before leaving the Shire when he, Frodo, and Pippin encounter the elven-host of Gildor of Rivendell passing through the wood under the light of the moon and the stars. Not only does Gildor supply Frodo with news and advice, but he fortifies the company with good cheer by filling their bottles with a golden honey-wine that resembles mead.

The master of good cheer, however, is Tom Bombadil. After rescuing the hobbits from the evil tree Old Man Willow, he takes them

Old Man Willow: Willows dangle over the River Cherwell, which flows from North Oxford past Magdalen and Merton Colleges into the Isis (the name for the Thames in this area). The river is a popular destination for "punting"; here punts are tied up along the Magdalen Bridge.

back to his house in the Old Forest near the Withywindle River, where they are greeted by his lady, Goldberry, "daughter of the River." Tom, larger than a hobbit but smaller than a man, is described as having "a blue coat and a long brown beard; his eyes were blue and bright, and his face red as a ripe apple, but creased into a hundred wrinkles of laughter."[23] Goldberry had "long yellow hair rippled down her shoulders; her gown was green, green as young reeds, shot with silver like beads of dew."[24] In a 1937 letter to Stanley Unwin, Tolkien described Bombadil as "the spirit of the (vanishing) Oxford and Berkshire countryside," while Shippey sees in him a bit of the Green Knight in *Sir Gawain*.[25] Later in *The Fellowship* Elrond tells us that Bombadil is very old and goes by other names: Iarwain Ben-adar ("oldest and fatherless" in Sindarin), Forn (Old Norse, "ancient"), and Orald (Old English, "very ancient").[26] Referring to the hobbits' visit to the House of Bombadil, Tolkien wrote in a 1958 letter to science fiction enthusiast Forrest J. Ackerman, "Goldberry represents the actual seasonal changes in [the river-] lands."[27] The muddy river, which Tolkien calls the Withywindle ("winding river bordered by willows"), is likely the Cherwell River in North Oxford.[28]

Bombadil rescues the hobbits a second time on the Downs, where Frodo and his companions wander in the fog and end up captives of the Barrow-wights, wraith-like creatures who haunt the barrows. The insular tradition of burials accompanied by prestige goods under mounds or "barrows" stretches from the Neolithic to the Viking Age. There are several possible candidates for sites near Oxford that might have influenced Tolkien in his depiction of the Barrow-downs. On the border of Oxfordshire near the village of Little Rollright are several ancient monuments, including a single and oddly shaped megalith (the King Stone), a small group of standing stones that once formed the entrance to a Neolithic chamber tomb (the Whispering Knights dolmen), and an impressive stone circle (the King's Men).[29] Oxfordshire also has Wayland's Smithy, identified as Welandes smiððe in an Anglo-Saxon charter of AD 855; the site is linked to the fairy blacksmith Wayland (Old English Wēland) of Germanic mythology. The bordering county of Wiltshire has perhaps the greatest concentration of Neolithic and Bronze Age monuments in all of Britain, including the stone circles of Avebury and Stonehenge and the communal chambered tomb of West Kennet, while south of Oxfordshire there is Nine Barrow Down, a linear barrow cemetery of round barrows on the Purbeck Ridgeway in Dorset.

Wayland's Smithy, a Neolithic long barrow on the Berkshire Downs, was a favorite holiday destination of the Tolkiens.

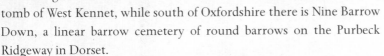

"Frodo [saw that] all those hills were crowned with green mounds, and on some were standing stones, pointing upwards like jagged teeth out of green gums."[30]

—From Book One, Chapter VIII, "Fog on the Barrow Downs," *The Fellowship of the Ring*

Inside the barrow Frodo sees his companions lying as if dead bedecked with gold crowns and chains, surrounded by weapons and other treasures. This could be the description of almost any ancient pagan royal burial, from the great mounds over the Hallstatt chieftains to that covering King Rædwald at Sutton Hoo (see page 53). But Merry, Pippin, and Sam also had one long naked sword lying across their throats. Here is a reflection perhaps of Thomas Malory's tale of Sir Pelleas, who leaves Camelot in amorous pursuit of a lady who wants nothing to do with him. Instead she sleeps with his friend Sir Gawain, and when the young Pelleas finds them lying in bed together asleep he contemplates killing them both, but instead places his naked blade across their throats as a symbol of their betrayal.

Der Erlkönig is portrayed here by the nineteenth-century German painter and physiologist Carl Gustav Carus, a friend of Goethe.

Tom Bombadil then arrives; after freeing the hobbits and chasing out the wight who was haunting the mound, Bombadil outfits the company with leaf-shaped daggers, ornamented with serpent forms, from the barrow treasure. Leaf-shaped swords and daggers are typical of the Bronze Age and early Iron Age rather than medieval. Bombadil and the hobbits ride across a deep dike and bank that Tom says was once the boundary of an ancient kingdom.

BREE

After bidding farewell to Tom Bombadil, the hobbits make their way to the town of Bree under Bree-hill and the Prancing Pony inn, where they are supposed to meet Gandalf. Instead, they encounter the tall, mysterious Strider, a Ranger from the North—one of the Dúnedain, a race of men descended from the Númenóreans who patrol the boundaries of Eriador in Middle-earth. He stands apart from the men of Bree (Welsh *bre*, "hill"), who are said to be "brown-haired, broad, and rather short, cheerful and independent,"[32] having lived in this part of the West long before hobbits and other men arrived. Here, again, is a probable reference to the ancient Britons or the Welsh. Strider, who Tolkien originally called "Trotter" (and who was originally a hobbit), is able to resist taking the Ring and instead offers his service to Frodo: "If by life or death I can save you, I will."[33] A letter that Gandalf leaves with the innkeeper Barliman Butterbur eventually reveals Strider's true identity—he is Aragorn, son of Arathorn, a friend of Gandalf's that the hobbits should trust. Aragorn shows the hobbits proof of his identity by showing them the "blade that was broken."[34] Tolkien here would undoubtedly have had in mind the tale of the sword Gram, the sword of Sigmund in the *Völsungsaga* that is broken by Odin but later reforged and given to Sigurd, slayer of the dragon Fáfnir (see page 69).[35]

The episode on Weathertop, where Frodo is stabbed by the Lord of the Nazgûl after putting on the Ring, and the subsequent flight to the ford, recalls the Goethe poem "Der Erlkönig" (1782), set to music by Schubert and others. In the poem, a frightened child is carried home on horseback by his father.

The Pubs of Middle-earth

lthough the Green Dragon closed its doors in 1926 and there is no record of a Prancing Pony, Oxford has more than its fair share of pubs today. The Inklings have made the "Bird and Baby" (the Eagle and Child) famous, but Tolkien and his friends also frequented the Lamb and Flag (across St. Giles Street), the King's Arms (on the corner of Holywell Street and Parks Road), and the White Horse (beside Blackwell Books on Broad Street). Gandalf "put a good word"[36] on Old Barliman's beer to make it good. In the Middle Ages, some thought elves or angels were responsible for fermentation; the small amount of wine or spirit that evaporates in the barrel is still called the "angel's share."

An early engraving of a medieval brewery; in the Middle Ages, some people believed that elves or angels were responsible for the process of fermentation.

"Mein Sohn, was birgst du so bang dein Gesicht?"
"Siehst, Vater, du den Erlkönig nicht?
Den Erlenkönig mit Kron und Schweif?"
"Mein Sohn, es ist ein Nebelstreif."

"My son, why do you hide your face so anxiously?"
"Father, do you not see the Elf-king?
The Elf-king with crown and train?"
"My son, it is a wisp of fog."[37]

Like Frodo on Weathertop, the boy can clearly see a malicious spirit who is trying to seize him, and like Frodo he receives a wound from the fiend. But while Frodo makes it to Rivendell safely and is healed, the son is dead in his father's arms by the time they reach their home. Based on a Danish folktale, "Der Erlkönig" features a malevolent elf who tries to seduce and abduct children, as in the popular medieval belief in fairy "changelings" who are exchanged for human children.

RIVENDELL

As in *The Hobbit*, Tolkien's description of Rivendell and the Misty Mountains was based on memories of his trip with his brother, Aunt Jane, and family friends to Switzerland in 1911. Rivendell, situated in a lush river valley, resembles the Lauterbrunnen Valley through which Tolkien passed on his way to the icy peaks and snowy crevasses of Silberhorn, which reappear as the mountain pass of Caradhras (Sindarin, "red horn") in *The Fellowship*.[38] In the feasting hall at Rivendell, seated at "high table" (as in Oxford college dining, where fellows and their guests sit at a raised table on a dais), we meet Elrond and his daughter Arwen. Elrond ("Star-dome") is a further development of the wise master we met in *The Hobbit*, and we are told for the first time that he is the son of Eärendil. Although Arwen is a Sindarin name ("noble maiden"), Tolkien admitted that it is also a Welsh word; *Arwyn* is actually, in Wales, a common male personal name, meaning "fair, beautiful." When Frodo and Sam fall asleep while the elves are "merrymaking" in the Hall of Fire, we are reminded of the enchanted sleep of Bombur in Mirkwood, both based on the common medieval trope of the fairy spell.

The Council of Elrond that follows the feast has the feel of a faculty meeting: lots of people talking, full of arcane and fascinating bits of information, and interminable! Here the hobbits meet the dwarf Gimli, son of Glóin; Legolas, son of King Thranduil of Mirkwood; and Boromir, son of the steward of Gondor, Denethor. They hear the names and deeds of ancient kings, and ancient weapons that also bear names, like Aiglos, the Spear of Gil-galad, and Narsil, the Sword of Elendil (see page 105 for more on named swords of medieval heroes). These compare to Rhongomyniad or Rhongomiant (Welsh, "Spear Slayer"), the name of Arthur's spear in medieval Welsh literature, and the magical spear Gáe Bolg (Old Irish, "Death Spear"), carried by Irish hero Cú Chulainn. The hobbits also learn that Isildur, Elendil's son, vowed to keep the One Ring "as weregild for my father, and my brother."[39] The Old English word *wergild* is literally translated as "man-price"—money paid to a victim's family after a homicide in order to curtail blood feuds in the early Middle Ages (and used by the Vikings in order to extract ransom money for prestige hostages). During the council, Gandalf tells the participants that he had been held captive by the wizard Saruman in Orthanc (Old English *orþanc*, "skillful work"), the black tower of Isengard, and was rescued by "Gwaihir the Windlord, swiftest of the Great Eagles."[40] Gwaihir is another Sindarin name (literally "wind-lord") that is homophonic with medieval Welsh names like Gwythyr, Gwrhyr, Gwawrddur, Gwyr, Gweir, Gwyar, and Garanhir, all of which are from *Culhwch and Olwen* (see page 48). *Culhwch* contains a scene in which one of Arthur's men, Gwrhyr, the Interpreter of Tongues, questions the Eagle of Gwernabwy, "the oldest animal in this world, and the one who has traveled the farthest."[41] Later, Gwrhyr himself takes the shape of a bird. The wizard Radagast the Brown is called by Gandalf in this chapter a "master of shapes and changes of hue,"[42] and is a special friend to birds.

Of all the speeches at the Council of Elrond, perhaps it is one given by a missing member that is most interesting. Gandalf sought the aid of Saruman the White against Mordor but found that his old friend had other designs:

"*A new Power is rising. Against it the old allies and policies will not avail us. . . . As the Power grows, its proved friends will also grow; and the Wise, such as you and I, may with patience come at last to direct its courses. . . . We can bide our time, we can keep our thoughts in our hearts, deploring maybe evils done by the way, but approving the high and ultimate purpose: Knowledge, Rule, Order. . . . There need not be . . . any real change in our designs, only in our means.*"[43]

—Saruman, Book Two, Chapter II, "The Council of Elrond,"
The Fellowship of the Ring

The name Saruman is from the Old English *searu-man*, "man of cunning." But it is modern, rather than medieval, ideas that he is expressing. When we read this speech it is hard not to think of the Nazis and the

War and Glory

he debate between isolationism and intervention appears several times in *The Lord of the Rings*. Early on in *The Fellowship*, Gaffer Gamgee gives a clear statement of the position taken by most in the Shire:

> *"Elves and dragons!* I says to him. *Cabbages and potatoes are better for me and you. Don't go getting mixed up in the business of your betters, or you'll land in trouble too big for you."*[44]

Isolationism also appears to be the default position of the ents. Treebeard tells Merry and Pippin that he has not troubled with the Great Wars of elves and men and wizards. "I am not altogether on anybody's *side*, because nobody is altogether on my *side*."[45]

Éomer takes a similarly isolationist stance when he encounters Aragorn, Legolas, and Gimli: "We desire only to be free . . . keeping our own, and serving no foreign lord, good or evil."[46] Aragorn, however, will allow for no fence-sitting, and tells Éomer to relay a message to Théoden: "Open war lies before him, with Sauron or against him. None may live now as they have lived, and few shall keep what they call their own."

Eventually, both the ents and the Rohirrim are moved to take action against Saruman. Not surprisingly, Gandalf and the elves are firmly on the side of Aragorn and intervention. After Gandalf has given Frodo a nudge out the door, the hobbit encounters an elf named Gildor on the edge of the Shire. "The wide world is all about you," he counsels Frodo. "You can fence yourselves in, but you cannot for ever fence it out."[47]

Most hobbits have never seen war, and Sam's first glimpse of it—in the Harad attack on Faramir's rangers—is neither heroic nor romantic:

> He was glad that he could not see the dead face [of the Harad soldier]. He wondered what the man's name was . . . and if he was really evil of heart, or what lies or threats had led him on the long march from his home; and if he would not really rather have stayed there in peace.[48]

Sam's reaction here is modern rather than medieval. It is the reaction of a civilian, or perhaps of a young soldier in the Great War seeing his first casualty in No Man's Land. Sam serves here, like Bilbo in *The Hobbit*, as an interpreter of the epic and heroic world of medieval romance for the modern reader.

appeasement of Hitler being promoted by many in Britain when Tolkien was beginning *The Lord of the Rings*. Gandalf, like Churchill, was buying none of this. While not political allegory, this is political commentary, and Saruman is recommending a Machiavellian strategy for addressing modern tyranny.[49] Elrond suggests another strategy—the Ring must be destroyed—and Frodo offers to take it into the fires of Mount Doom, where it was forged. "This is the hour of the Shire-folk," exclaims Master Elrond, "when they arise from their quiet fields to shake the towers and counsels of the Great."[50]

Appeasement: In September 1938, a year after Tolkien began his work on The Lord of the Rings, *English prime minister Neville Chamberlain flew to Munich to meet with Adolf Hitler in an unsuccessful effort to negotiate peace with the German Führer.*

MORIA

The Nine Walkers, the Fellowship of the Ring, set out from Rivendell on a path that takes them to the Misty Mountains and through the Mines of Moria. Deep in the mines they encounter orcs, black Uruks from Mordor (huge orcs with incredible strength), a cave-troll, and a balrog. In *The Silmarillion*, balrogs are fire demons who serve the evil Morgoth (see page 181). This one, "Durin's Bane" as Gimli calls him, is described as a dark form, of man-shape or greater, with a streaming mane of fire, in one hand a flaming blade and in the other "a whip of many thongs."[51] While there is no obvious source for this creature, Shippey suggests that Tolkien had in mind the mythic Norse fire giant Múspell.[52]

LOTHLÓRIEN

With Gandalf having fallen in battle with the balrog, the rest of the company flee Moria and into the Golden Wood of Lothlórien, "the heart of Elvendom on earth." There Celeborn and Galadriel rule over the Galadhrim, the "Tree-people." The Lord and Lady are very tall, "grave and beautiful," and "together through the ages of the world [they] have fought the long defeat."[53] Indeed, there is a sadness that clings to the great beauty of Lothlórien. Like spring flowers and autumn leaves, it cannot last. Galadriel refuses the Ring when Frodo offers it to her, only to announce that she "will diminish, and go into the West."[54] She bestows gifts on the members of the company, including a magical scabbard for Aragorn (as the Lady of the Lake does for King Arthur) and three golden hairs from her own tresses for the adoring Gimli (à la Lancelot and Guinevere).[55] While Galadriel plays the roles of gift-giving lord and courtly lady, she also bestows blessings and light, like the Virgin Mary.[56]

The last stage of the journey in *The Fellowship* takes the company down the great river Anduin, past the Gates of Argonath, toward Minas Tirith. The Argonath, "Pillars of Kings," were the ancient guardians of Númenor, colossal stone statues of warrior-kings, "silent wardens of a long-vanished kingdom."[57] Such monumental sculpture belongs to the ancient world rather than the medieval. Famed are the giant statues of the pharaohs in Egypt (many of which can still be seen) and the Colossus of Rhodes, one of the Seven Wonders of the Ancient World. This statue of the Greek god Helios, erected ca. 292 BC and destroyed in 226 BC in an earthquake, was so large that its legs allegedly straddled the island's main harbor.[58] The Romans also erected monumental sculpture, especially the late Roman and early Byzantine emperors. Near the Argonath is Amon Hen, the "Hill of the Eye." Fleeing from Boromir, who had tried to seize the Ring, Frodo found himself on the ancient Seat of Seeing on Amon Hen (*hen* means "old" in Welsh). Putting the Ring on he could now see across all of Middle-earth—Mirkwood, Moria, Lórien, Harad, Rohan, Gondor, and even Mordor—and everywhere he looked he glimpsed the signs of war.

This sixteenth-century German engraving depicts the Colossus of Rhodes, which supposedly stood over one hundred feet tall.

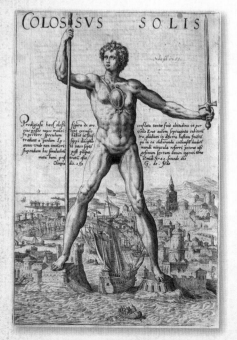

The first volume of *The Lord of the Rings* ends with Frodo determined to go alone to Mount Doom. Sam, however, is equally determined to accompany him, and nearly drowns in the river trying to reach Frodo's boat. It is a comic scene—"Of all the confounded nuisances you are the worst, Sam!" complains Frodo as he hauls

A giant hand that was once part of the Colossus of Constantine, a statue erected by the Roman emperor Constantine the Great in ca. 314 AD, and which is now in fragments. It is estimated that the seated figure would have been about 40 feet high.

his companion into the boat—but it is also poignant, as the two hobbits realize that they may never see Strider and the rest of their companions again. Still there is hope, and it resides in the humble gardener: "Yet we may, Mr. Frodo. We may," says Sam.[59]

The Two Towers

Volume Two of *The Lord of the Rings* was at first to be called *The Ring in the Shadow*, then *The Shadow Lengthens*; finally Tolkien settled on *The Two Towers*.[60] He liked the ambiguity of the title: "it might refer to Isengard and Barad-dûr, or to Minas Tirith and B[arad-dûr]; or to Isengard and Cirith Ungol."[61] There are many towers in the saga, but Volume Two references are mainly to Orthanc (Isengard) and Cirith Ungol. The artificial division of the three volumes leaves the middle novel with two books (three and four) and two entirely separate narratives, the first devoted to the conflict between Rohan and Isengard and the second the journey of Frodo and Sam to Mordor.

The Death of Boromir

Book Three begins where Book Two left off, with Aragorn looking for Frodo but finding instead that his camp has been attacked by orcs from both Isengard and Mordor. Hearing the Horn of Gondor blowing, he rushes back to camp and finds Boromir sitting against a tree and

> . . . pierced with many black-feathered arrows; his sword was still in his hand, but it was broken near the hilt; his horn cloven in two was at his side. Many Orcs lay slain, piled all about him and at his feet.
>
> Aragorn knelt beside him. Boromir opened his eyes and strove to speak. . . .
>
> "Farewell, Aragorn! Go to Minas Tirith and save my people! I have failed."
>
> "No!' said Aragorn, taking his hand and kissing his brow. "You have conquered. Few have gained such a victory. Be at peace! Minas Tirith shall not fall!"[62]

Tolkien's scene very closely parallels the death of Roland in the Old French eleventh-century heroic poem, *La Chanson de Roland* (*The Song of Roland*):

An illumination illustrating the Song of Roland, *from the* Grandes Chroniques de France, *manuscripts compiled between the thirteenth and fifteenth centuries that chronicle the royal history of France.*

But Roland felt that death had made a way
Down from his head till on his heart it lay;
Beneath a pine running in haste he came,
On the green grass he lay there on his face;
His olifant and sword beneath him placed,
Turning his head towards the pagan race,
Now this he did, in truth, that Charles might say
(As he desired) and all the Franks his race; —
"Ah, gentle count; conquering he was slain!" —
He owned his faults often and every way,
And for his sins his glove to God upraised.

But Roland feels he's no more time to seek;
Looking to Spain, he lies on a sharp peak,
And with one hand upon his breast he beats:
"Mea Culpa! God, by Thy Virtues clean
Me from my sins, the mortal and the mean,
Which from the hour that I was born have been
Until this day, when life is ended here!"
Holds out his glove towards God, as he speaks
Angels descend from heaven on that scene.

The count Roland, beneath a pine he sits;
Turning his eyes towards Spain . . .[63]

Like Roland, Boromir makes a full confession and ends his life in defense of his companions (Merry and Pippin, who are nevertheless taken by orcs). Aragorn, Gimli, and Legolas then give Boromir a hero's send-off by placing his body with his weapons—and those of his vanquished foes—in a boat and sending it over the Falls of Rauros, a ship-burial that recalls that of Scyld Scefing in *Beowulf*.

rohan

Aragorn, Legolas, and Gimli vow to hunt down the orcs who have taken Merry and Pippin captive, and set off in a pursuit that takes them to the grassy uplands of Rohan—the Riddermark, "Land of the Horsemen." Aragorn tells Gimli that the Rohirrim "are proud and willful" men, but also "true-hearted, generous in thought and deed; bold but not cruel;

wise but unlearned, writing no books but singing many songs."[64] Soon enough they encounter the Riders of Rohan and their captain, Éomer son of Éomund. These "mail-clad men, swift, shining, fell and fair to look upon," wore their flaxen hair long and braided, bore swords and spears and shields, and rode upon great warhorses.

As discussed in Chapter Two, Tolkien's depiction of Rohan and the Rohirrim owes much to Gothic and Anglo-Saxon culture (see pages 56–57). Rohan, however, is not a Germanic name, but rather an ancient aristocratic surname from Brittany. "I was aware of this, and liked its shape," wrote Tolkien in 1967. "But nothing in the history of Brittany will throw any light on the Eorlingas."[65] Yet the Bretons were renowned in the early Middle Ages for their light cavalry, equipped with throwing spears, and their chieftains for amassing a great deal of wealth in their rural strongholds.[66] The Carolingians had to construct the March of Brittany—a fortified border region— in order to keep the Bretons from raiding their territory. The most famous count of the Breton March was Roland, the eighth-century historical figure behind *La Chanson de Roland.* Eventually the Breton lords became vassals of the king of France, just as the chieftains of Rohan served as vassals to Gondor. And like the Rohirrim, the Bretons were fond of equine personal names, like Marrec (Breton, "Horseman") and Guivarc'h ("Worthy of a Stallion").

Edoras and Meduseld are indisputably Germanic words.[67] Old English *eodor* can mean "enclosure" or "house" but also "prince, lord." *Meduseld* means "mead-hall" and is found in *Beowulf.* For Théoden, king of Rohan, Tolkien went to one of the many Old English words for "king," or more literally "king of the people" (*þéo-den*). But there is a cognate or word of similar origin in *thiudans*; sixth-century Roman historian Jordanes notes in his work *Getica* (AD 551) that *thiudans* was the title of the sacral or priestly king of the Goths, as opposed to the *reiks,* or "warlord." Ironically, although Théoden's name is derived from "sacral king," he serves as the warlord of the Rohirrim, while it is ultimately Aragorn who is the sacral healer of the people (in the House of Healing) and the land.

Royal burial mounds line the road to Edoras, each covered with flowers called *simbelmynë* (Old English "always remembered"); these barrows are closer in description than the one at Weathertop to Anglo-Saxon and Viking pagan burials. Éowyn, the White Lady of Rohan, carries the wine-cup to Théoden and his guests in the hall (as does Wealhþeow with the mead-cup in *Beowulf*) and offers it with the Old English blessing, *Ferthu Théoden hál!* ("Health be with thee, Théoden!"). Yet Éowyn is also courageous and noble, she receives a sword and corselet from Théoden, and in *The Return of the King* she calls herself a "shield-maiden" (Old Norse, *skjaldmær*) and longs for battle. Éowyn, who is in love with Aragorn but eventually becomes angry with him for spurning her, resembles the Valkyrie Brynhildr whom Sigurd rescues (by cutting off her corselet) in the *Prose Edda*.

> "Éowyn came forward bearing wine. . . .
> As she stood before Aragorn she paused suddenly
> and looked upon him, and her eyes were shining.
> And he looked down upon her fair face and smiled;
> but as he took the cup, his hand met hers,
> and he knew that she trembled at the touch.
> 'Hail Aragorn son of Arathorn!' she said.
> 'Hail Lady of Rohan!' he answered, but his face
> now was troubled and he did not smile." [68]

—FROM BOOK THREE, CHAPTER VI, "THE KING OF THE GOLDEN HALL," *THE TWO TOWERS*

fangorn

After a long and important conversation with the Riders,[69] Aragorn follows the trail of the kidnapped Merry and Pippin into Fangorn Forest. The two hobbits though, had already escaped unseen after several Rohirrim slew their orc captors, and while wandering alone in Fangorn they encounter an ent named Treebeard. According to Tolkien, the ents owe their name to an Old English word for giants, as, for example, in the old English elegy *The Wanderer*, line 87: *ealda enta geweorc idlu stodon*, "the old creations of giants stood desolate."[70] Treebeard in particular was "a large Man-like, almost Troll-like, figure, at least fourteen foot high, very sturdy, with a tall head, and hardly any neck."[71] He is the spirit of the forest (Fangorn is Sindarin and translates as "Treebeard"), a parallel to Tom Bombadil in the Old Forest. He tells Merry and Pippin about the betrayal of Saruman and, at the entmoot—an ent council meeting—decides to abandon his isolationist position and march to war against Isengard. Ultimately, Merry and Pippin will help the ents attack Orthanc and destroy Saruman's power in Isengard.

Aragorn and his companions do not find the hobbits in Fangorn, but rather meet up with an unexpected figure clothed in white, whom they mistake for Saruman the White. It is none other than Gandalf, who—resurrected from his fall in Moria and combat with the balrog— is no longer Gandalf the Grey, but now Gandalf the White.[72]

AVENGING ANGEL

Tolkien was adamant in stating that Gandalf really "died" and was sent back, with greater wisdom and power, to exhort and aid the enemies of Sauron. Tolkien also says that Gandalf the White is comparable to an angel,[73] and indeed in his role in the War of the Ring he is like the avenging angels of medieval iconography: shining like the sun, swift in coming, often flying (though he needs the eagles for his wings), brandishing a mighty sword, slaying demons and terrible beasts.

Tolkien thought of Gandalf the White as an avenging angel or saint similar to those depicted in medieval iconography. Here, Saint Michael brandishes his sword over the defeated dragon in this painting by Netherlandish artist Josse Lieferinxe, created ca. 1500.

helm's deep and isengard

As the Rohirrim ride from Edoras to Helm's Deep, Tolkien gives us a lengthy description of the fortress, incorporating elements from many medieval defenses. Far up into the Deeping-coomb (valley) the riders come to Helm's Dike, "an ancient trench and rampart scored across the

God and the Cosmology of Middle-earth

here is no direct reference to heaven or hell in either *The Hobbit* or *The Lord of the Rings*. Many, however, have read symbolic references to heaven. There is, for example, the vision that Frodo has in the house of Tom Bombadil:

> Frodo heard a sweet singing running in his mind: a song that seemed to come like a pale light behind a grey rain-curtain, and growing stronger to turn the veil all to glass and silver, until at last it was rolled back, and a far green country opened before him under a swift sunrise.[74]

Frodo's vision in the house of Bombadil becomes reality at the very end of *The Return of the King*, when he is aboard the white ship sailing "into the West," a metaphor for death in medieval Irish literature.

In *The Two Towers*, Faramir describes to the hobbits a custom of Gondor that seems to be a religious ritual. Before they eat, Faramir and his men turn and face west in a moment of silence. "We look towards Númenor that was," says the young captain, "and beyond to Elvenhome that is, and to that which is beyond Elvenhome and will ever be."[75]

In light of the absence of any specific references to God and religion in *The Lord of the Rings*, it is remarkable to see Tolkien writing a year after its full publication, that his book "is about God, and His sole right to divine honour. The Eldar and the Númenóreans believed in The One, the true God, and held worship of any other person as an abomination. Sauron desired to be a God-King," and was thusly punished.[76]

Like the ancient Egyptian god-kings, the pharaohs, Sauron was eventually defeated by the Faithful—Eléndil and his son Isildur—with some divine assistance. This is just one of many exoduses in *The Silmarillion*.

coomb."[77] As with the dike the hobbits cross near Bree (see page 132), this reflects the early medieval defenses employed by the Britons and Anglo-Saxons. The rest of Helm's Deep resembles the Norman motte-and-bailey castle (built on a mound or motte, with a surrounding wall enclosing a courtyard or bailey) and its more elaborate medieval successors. A causeway and ramp lead through Helm's Gate and the thick two-story Deeping Wall, and finally to the Hornburg, the keep of this Middle-earth castle. The Uruk-hai use explosives to breech the wall,

This scene from the Bayeux Tapestry (ca. 1070s) [above] depicts troops trying to burn down the battlements on the motte or mound of the Château de Dinan in Brittany, during the Battle of Dinan in 1065; [right] the motte-and-bailey fortification of Château de Dinan as it looks today.

which mirrors the introduction of gunpowder during the Hundred Years' War (ca. 1337–1453), the war that effectively ended "cavalry and castle," which had dominated medieval warfare.

Even more modern is the conversation that Gandalf, Théoden, and others have with the defeated Saruman at Orthanc after the battle of Helm's Deep. Orthanc is also a fortress—but as it turns out, not a very medieval one. Here Saruman's wizardry takes the form of political rhetoric, similar to the enchantment of a twentieth-century politician. Saruman asks Théoden, whose lands and people he has just attacked, to be a friend and ally, and the very sound of his voice is enough to win over some of the Riders in attendance. Éomer and Gimli see through the deception, however. "The words of this wizard stand on their head," growls the dwarf, while Éomer calls him "an old liar with honey on his forked tongue." Saruman replies in a mellifluous voice:

> Come, Éomer, Éomund's son! . . . Slay whom your lord names as enemies, and be content. Meddle not in policies which you do not understand. . . . Yet with some [the House of Eorl] have after [war] made peace, none the worse for being politic.[78]

Good and Evil

verything is black and white in *The Lord of the Rings*, goes the complaint. Tolkien casts everything, including his characters, as good or evil. These characters lack the psychological complexity of characters in the best modern novels, or even the best fantasy. Moreover, as one anonymous reviewer wrote, though "all right-thinking hobbits, dwarves, elves, and men can combine against Sauron," Tolkien "never explains what it is they consider the Good."[79]

In actuality, Tolkien is, to the dismay of most of his critics, quite interested in the nature of good and evil.[80] Far from being a relativist, these concepts are *real* to him, not mere manifestations of class struggle, patriarchal religions, or unevolved psyches. Yet, unlike many of his fantasy imitators, he is not simplistic in his portrayal of good and evil. This is especially true of *The Lord of the Rings*, and in particular with characters like Frodo, Gollum, Boromir, and Saruman.

Does evil exist as an external power, competing with the good, or is it an internal manifestation of fallen man (or fallen elf), causing a struggle within every soul?[81] The One Ring is, on the surface, an external object of power; it has its own character, its own characteristics, and is feared in and of itself (even when Sauron is seemingly out of the picture). But its power works on those who wear it, possess it, or come physically near it. It magnifies, or distorts, powers within the Ring-bearers—Isildur, Sméagol, Bilbo, Frodo—and threatens to do so with those who are tempted to wear it—Gandalf, Boromir, Galadriel.

Both Tom Shippey and Peter Kreeft have identified the two competing views of evil, which Shippey labels the Boethian and the Manichean. The first denies the existence of evil as an external force, or explains it as merely temporal, a tool that God uses to instruct us. The second sees good and evil in cosmic conflict, with humans forced to choose sides in the battle. "Nothing is evil in the beginning, or by nature," writes Kreeft. "Morgoth was one of the Ainur, Sauron was a Maia, Saruman was the head of Gandalf's order of Wizards, the Orcs were

What Saruman means is *politique*, the political philosophy developed in sixteenth-century Europe that subordinates religion and other traditional values to bring internal stability to the state or to promote its interests internationally.[87] This early modern political philosophy runs counter to the heroic values of Éomer and the Rohirrim. Let the politicians decide policy, not the warriors, advises Saruman. Théoden is not fooled, and sees Saruman as a "corrupter of men's hearts" and a puppet of Mordor. "Dotard!" replies Saruman. "What is the House of Eorl but a elves, the Ringwraiths were great Men, and Gollum was a Hobbit."[82] God created all natural things and they are, therefore, good "by nature." Evil cannot create, it can only twist, pollute, or pervert. This is especially important to keep in mind when considering the orcs, for it is tempting to view them as a simplification of evil, mindless and soulless beings who form a violent and faceless mass akin to the all-too-common dehumanization of enemy soldiers during times of war. But early in *The Silmarillion*, Tolkien explains that they were originally elves with free will, who *chose* to hide from the Valar, and in their "turning away from the good" their souls became twisted by Morgoth into dark and perverted slaves. They become anti-elves, as ugly as the elves are beautiful. Even when the elves and men of Beleriand banded together to defeat Morgoth in the Eldar Days, "the Elves deemed that evil was ended forever," explains Elrond succinctly, "and it was not so."[83]

"In my story," wrote Tolkien in 1956, "I do not deal in Absolute Evil. I do not think there is such a thing, since that is Zero."[84] No "rational being" is wholly evil, explains Tolkien. Even Morgoth and Sauron, after all, were created good before their respective falls, and both even began with some good intentions. "Nothing is evil in the beginning," states Elrond. Pride and the lust for domination came to define Morgoth and Sauron, but they were exercising free will when they stepped onto the path of tyranny.

Denying absolute evil in Middle-earth is not to say that evil does not exist at all. "The Real Absence of goodness," is how Joseph Pearce describes the seeming paradox.[85] This is essentially the Augustinian position on Evil, for St. Augustine argued that a willful turning away from God is a disorder—in fallen man and fallen angel—that we call evil.[86] If evil is real in Middle-earth, what are its characteristics? Tolkien's list would probably include pride, despair, lust for power or domination, and destruction of the natural, of green and growing things.

thatched barn where brigands drink in the reek, and their brats roll on the floor among the dogs?"[88]

With Gandalf, Saruman takes a different tactic, appealing to his "noble mind" and their "high and ancient order." Together they can restore order without aid from commoners, who should be grateful for the wizards' lead and council. "For the common good I am willing to redress the past, and to receive you," he tells Gandalf. We the readers are, like the Riders, tempted to believe that Gandalf *will* climb the

ПРИВЕТ ГЕРОЙСКИМ ВОИНАМ СОВЕТСКОГО СОЮЗА ОТ БРИТАНСКИХ СОЮЗНИКОВ БОРЮЩИХСЯ С НИМИ

МЫ ВСЕГДА С ВАМИ В УДАЧАХ И НЕУДАЧАХ ВМЕСТЕ ДОБЬЕМ РАЗГРОМИМ УНИЧТОЖИМ НАШЕГО ВРАГА

Tolkien did not literally equate the British, the Soviets, and the Nazis with Rohan, Isengard, and Mordor, yet, during the writing of The Lord of the Rings, *he watched as Britain joined forces with Stalin's totalitarian state to defeat the German war machine. The British-Soviet alliance is idealized here in this Russian war propaganda poster from World War II.*

tower and that these two "reverend and wise" men will settle the dispute through some complex solution that we "ill-mannered children or stupid servants"[89] could not possibly understand. Does not even Plato suggest that only the philosopher-king will rule justly? Significantly, Saruman's spell is broken by laughter—Gandalf's laughter—and mirth is followed by mercy. Even now Gandalf offers freedom to Saruman, in hope that the wizard will turn from Mordor and save himself—dare we say, save his soul.

Tolkien spends a great deal of space on this scene. He found himself, at the time of writing, watching the rise of a dictator who used the power of his voice to move the masses (and convince not a few politicians from other countries including, at first, Tolkien's own), whose defeat was only possible through Britain's alliance with another totalitarian state that itself used political propaganda to gain support while covering up the many atrocities it had committed. Although Saruman is trying to convince Rohan to ally with Isengard to fight Mordor, Tolkien does not want us to literally *equate* the Nazis and the Soviets with Isengard and Mordor; he does, I believe, want to contrast these "progressive" modern ideologies with the retrograde values of Rohan and the Fellowship, derived, as the latter were, from medieval heroic and chivalric ideals.[90]

The reappearance of gollum

In Book Four, Tolkien leaves Rohan and Saruman behind and turns the narrative to the journey of Frodo and Sam toward Mount Doom. In the first chapter, Gollum accidently reveals himself to the hobbits, and Frodo shows pity toward him, making Gollum take an oath to serve as their guide through Mordor. Tolkien here presents a sort of reverse version of Rudyard Kipling's poem "Gunga Din" (1892): Frodo and Sam (equivalent to the British soldiers) are fair and gentle masters, while Gollum/Sméagol only gives the appearance of loyalty and servitude, and ultimately tries to take his master's life rather than save it.

At the beginning of *The Fellowship*, when describing Bilbo's encounter with Gollum, Gandalf gives Frodo a long discourse on mercy, or pity:

> "What a pity that Bilbo did not stab that vile creature. . . . "
>
> "Pity? It was pity that stayed his hand. Pity, and Mercy: not to strike without need. . . . He took so little hurt from the evil, and escaped in the end, because he began his ownership of the Ring so. With Pity."
>
> "I am sorry," said Frodo. "But I am frightened; and I do not feel any pity for Gollum."
>
> "You have not seen him," Gandalf broke in.
>
> "No, and I don't want to. . . . He deserves death."
>
> "Deserves it! I daresay he does. Many that live deserve death. And some that die deserve life. Can you give it to them? Then do not be too eager to deal out death in judgement. For even the very wise cannot see all ends. I have not much hope that Gollum can be cured before he dies, but there is a chance of it. And he is bound with the fate of the Ring. My heart tells me that he has some part to play yet, for good or ill, before the end; and when that comes, the pity of Bilbo may rule the fate of many—yours not least."[91]

Frodo acts at first as we might, out of instinct, and is quick to judgment. But Gandalf *has* seen Gollum, and heard his story, and has seen much more of the world than has Frodo. Interestingly, Gandalf defines pity here in almost chivalric terms: not to strike without need. Tolkien thought this lesson of Gandalf's so important that he returns to it again in *The Two Towers*. When Frodo first encounters Gollum at Emyn Muil, he recalls Gandalf's speech, which Tolkien reiterates word for word. "For now that I see him," Frodo tells Sam, "I do pity him."[92]

the dead marshes

In Chapter II, "The Passage of the Marshes," Gollum sings a song that includes the fish riddle he had used against Bilbo in *The Hobbit*. Hearing the song, Sam is reminded of their lack of food; worrying that Gollum might murder Frodo and him in their sleep and eat them, he vows to stay awake and keep watch while Frodo sleeps. When he falls asleep

MERCY AND REDEMPTION

Ultimately, pity, or mercy, is the device upon which *The Lord of the Ring*'s eucatastrophe—good catastrophe—depends. Because Frodo takes pity on Gollum and shows him mercy on several occasions, Gollum survives to the end of the journey and is there to wrest the Ring from Frodo when he declares, at the Crack of Doom, that he is unwilling to give it up (see page 168). Tolkien thus "interlaces" Gollum through the narrative (a medieval technique) and builds a complex plot-labyrinth (a postmodern technique) where Frodo's original choice leads ultimately to a happy conclusion, but not in an obvious and predictable way.

Dead Faces in the Water

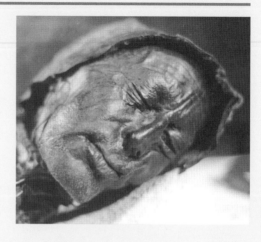

he Tollund Man is an incredibly well-preserved body from ca. 300 BC found in 1950 in a Danish peat bog. The chemical cocktail in the decaying bog preserved the man's sheepskin cap, along with a leather rope around his neck, suggesting that he was a human sacrifice. Some, though not all, of the many "bog bodies" found in Ireland, Britain, and northwestern Europe—mostly from the Iron Age—show signs of similarly gruesome deaths. Features discovered on some of the bodies—such as manicured fingernails or costly ornaments—indicate noble birth. Could they have inspired the specters in the Dead Marshes? Tolkien may or may not have read about bog bodies (which have turned up since the nineteenth century), but he certainly knew the cultures that produced them. Perhaps they informed this passage from the Dead Marshes chapter:

> Wrenching his hands out of the bog, [Sam] sprang back with a cry. "There are dead things, dead faces in the water," he said with horror. . . .
>
> Gollum laughed. "The Dead Marshes, yes, yes: that is their name," he cackled. "You should not look in when the candles are lit."
>
> "Who are they? What are they?" asked Sam shuddering, turning to Frodo. . . .
>
> "I don't know," said Frodo in a dreamlike voice. "But I have seen them too. In the pools when the candles were lit. They lie in all the pools, pale faces, deep deep under the dark water . . . grim faces and evil, and noble faces and sad."[93]

as well—for nine hours straight—Sam later reproaches himself with names "drawn from the Gaffer's large paternal word-hoard."[94] Tolkien uses here "word-hoard"—a kenning found in Anglo-Saxon poems like *Beowulf*—to describe the vocabulary of the would-be poet Sam and his oft-quoted father, Gaffer Gamgee.

Faramir, Captain of Gondor

After passing through the Dead Marshes, the three arrive at the forbidding Black Gate of Mordor. Heavily guarded and seemingly impassible, Frodo insists he must bring the ring to Mordor to complete his task and thus will go to the gate. Sam, of course, accepts his fate and says he will go with Frodo. However Gollum convinces the hobbits that there is another way into Mordor, and leads them to a secret passage at the high mountain pass and tower Cirith Ungol. Along the way, they encounter a company of soldiers from Gondor led by their captain, Faramir, son of Denethor. Tolkien paints the character of Faramir with colors from the chivalric palette used on his brother, Boromir. But the harsh lines of Boromir are softened in the depiction of the younger captain, a scholar-knight who has been tutored by none other than Gandalf, or Mithrandir, as he is known in Gondor. For example, when Frodo believes that Faramir is trying to trick him with lies, the latter makes his code of honor clear: "I would not snare even an orc with a falsehood."[95] And Faramir responds to Sam's brash defense of Frodo with a stern warning of patience: "Were I as hasty as you, I might have slain you long ago. . . . But I do not slay man or beast needlessly, and not gladly even when it is needed."[96]

Whereas Boromir was impatient to have his father recognized as king of Gondor, Faramir possesses the patience, wisdom, *and* martial abilities of a good king. When Faramir surmises that the cause of Boromir's rift with the fellowship was some sort of "mighty heirloom" belonging to Sauron, he tells Frodo that

> I would not take this thing, if it lay by the highway. Not were Minas Tirith falling in ruin and I alone could save her, so, using the weapon of the Dark Lord for her good and my glory. No, I do not wish for such triumphs.[97]

And yet, unlike his brother, Faramir is not at all tempted to grasp power when it lies before him. Later, when he learns that the "heirloom" is in fact the One Ring, he reassures Frodo:

> *Not if I found it on the highway would I take it* I said. . . . Even though I knew not clearly what this thing was when I spoke, still I should take those words as a vow, and be held by them.[98]

While Boromir is modeled on the eponymous hero of *La Chanson de Roland*—impetuous but courageous—Faramir is more like Oliver—Roland's wise and prudent fellow knight and confidant. Faramir is a medieval prince who fights only in defense and who seeks the restoration of the City for the aesthetic and academic gifts it has to offer:

> "War must be, while we defend our lives against a destroyer who would devour all; but I do not love the bright sword for its sharpness, nor the arrow for its swiftness, nor the warrior for his glory. I love only that which they defend: the city of the Men of Númenor; and I would have her loved for her memory, her ancientry, her beauty, and her present wisdom."[99]

The word *ancientry* used here is apropos to both Tolkien and Faramir: an English word with a medieval feel (the first known use is in 1580), it sums up all of the history and antiquity of a place. As Frodo, Sam, and Gollum approach the Cross-roads and the path leading to the Stair of Cirith Ungol, they come across a huge seated figure carved in stone,

> . . . still and solemn as the great stones of Argonath. The years had gnawed it, and violent hands had maimed it. Its head was gone. . . .
>
> The old king's head . . . was lying rolled away by the roadside. "Look, Sam!" [Frodo] cried, startled into speech. "Look! The king has got a crown again!"
>
> The eyes were hollow and the carven beard was broken, but about the high stern forehead there was a coronal of silver and gold. A trailing plant with flowers like small white stars had bound itself across the brows as if in reverence for the fallen king, and in the crevices of his stony hair yellow stonecrop gleamed.
>
> "They cannot conquer for ever!" said Frodo.[100]

Compare Tolkien's lines to these, from the poem "Ozymandias" (1817), by Percy Byshe Shelley:

> Half sunk, a shattered visage lies, whose frown
> And wrinkled lip and sneer of cold command

A colossal statue of Ramesses II lies in ruin at the Ramesseum necropolis on the site of the ancient city of Thebes, which inspired Shelley's "Ozymandius" (Greek for one of the names in Ramesses's title, see poem excerpt on pages 152 and 154)—and perhaps the giant headless statue of a king encountered by Frodo, Sam, and Gollum on the Cross-roads. The photograph was taken ca. 1910.

Tell that its sculptor well those passions read
Which yet survive, stamped on these lifeless things,
The hand that mocked them and the heart that fed.
And on the pedestal these words appear:
"My name is Ozymandias, King of Kings:
Look on my works, ye mighty, and despair!"[101]

shelob the great

Tolkien's childhood fear of spiders, which he visited in a lighthearted way in Mirkwood of *The Hobbit*, returns in the much darker form of Shelob, the terror that closes *The Two Towers*. His description of her is both gruesome and memorable:

> There agelong she had dwelt, an evil thing in spider-form. . . .
> How Shelob came there, flying from ruin, no tale tells, for
> out of the Dark Years few tales have come. But still she was
> there, who was there before Sauron, and before the first stone
> of Barad-dûr; and she served none but herself . . . bloated
> and grown fat with endless brooding on her feasts, weaving
> webs of shadow; for all things were her food, and her vomit
> darkness. Far and wide her lesser broods . . . spread from glen
> to glen. . . . But none could rival her, Shelob the Great, last
> child of Ungoliant to trouble an unhappy world.[102]

The only way to combat Shelob's darkness is light—the phial of Galadriel—and the near berserker (Old Norse *ber-serkr*, "bear-shirt") fighting of Master Samwise. The uncanny ability to become insanely violent in battle was, as did Beorn in *The Hobbit*, was a phenomenon of the Viking world. It can also be glimpsed in early medieval Irish literature, particularly with the battle frenzy (Irish *ríastrad*) of the hero Cú Chulainn.[103]

Returning to himself after the battle with Shelob, Sam sees the lifeless body of Frodo lying wrapped in webs and must make a tough decision: stay and attend to the burial of Frodo, or go on alone with the quest to destroy the ring. "Don't leave me here alone!" he cries over Frodo's body. "Don't go where I can't follow!" Then anger surged inside of Sam, writes Tolkien, "and he ran about his master's body in a rage, stabbing the air, and smiting the stones, and shouting challenges."[104]

Now more like Achilles mourning the death of Patroclus in Homer's *The Iliad*, Sam's displays of bravery and grief are a fitting end to *The Two Towers*. Like Tolkien and his school friends who went off to the Western Front with images of medieval warfare filling their minds, Sam the aspiring poet finds his courage in the darkest, most unromantic of places; and despite his prowess in battle, is still confronted with the loss of his dearest friends.

The Return of the King

FOR VOLUME THREE of *The Lord of the Rings*, Tolkien suggested two titles: *The War of the Ring* and *The Return of the King*. He preferred the former, for he felt that the latter told the readers up front how the whole story was going to end! Unwin prevailed and thus did Tolkien accept *The Return of the King* as the title for Books Five and Six.

Minas Tirith, Chivalry, and Feudalism

Book Five begins with the ride of Gandalf and Pippin to Minas Tirith. Unlike Edoras and Helm's Deep, the citadel of Minas Tirith bears no obvious resemblance to one single historical structure, but rather has elements of many. Its seven levels, with a winding road reaching the pinnacle, recall Mont Saint-Michel in Normandy, which was constructed first as a citadel of the Armorican Britons in the fifth/sixth centuries AD. Later, under the Franks, it became a Benedictine abbey.

Minas Tirith contains elements of the winding road and multilevel ramparts of Mont Saint-Michel in Normandy [far left] and the remnants of the zigzag ramparts of the Maiden Castle hill fort in Dorset [left].

However, the layout of the walls and gates at Minas Tirith, forcing riders to zigzag their way up the citadel, parallels a defensive technique used in the construction of Iron Age hill forts like Maiden Castle in Dorset.

In the great stone city of Minas Tirith we meet an ancient royal culture that expresses itself through chivalry as well as architecture. Tolkien describes in great detail the livery of the Guards of the Citadel, with its heraldic device of seabird (white wings on helmets), white tree blossoming, many-pointed stars, and a silver crown (on black surcoats). The knights of Prince Imrahil of Dol Amroth are no less finely arrayed, entering Minas Tirith "with gilded banners bearing his token of the Ship and the Silver Swan."[105] Gandalf and Pippin enter the Great Hall of Minas Tirith to find a grieving Steward Denethor. In a moving scene of redemption, a suddenly serious Pippin offers his service to Denethor "in payment of my debt," that is to repay Denethor for the loss of his son Boromir, who fell in battle protecting the hobbits. "Swear to me now!" replies Denethor as Pippin grasps the hilt of his sword lying on his lap, Tolkien shifting his prose to mimic that of feudal ceremony:

> "Here do I swear fealty and service to Gondor, and to the Lord and Steward of the realm . . . from this hour henceforth, until my lord release me, or death take me, or the world end. So say I, Peregrin son of Paladin of the Shire of the Halflings."
>
> "And this do I hear, Denethor son of Ecthelion, Lord of Gondor, Steward of the High King, and I will not forget it, nor fail to reward that which is given: fealty with love, valour with honour, oath-breaking with vengeance."[106]

Compare this formal language with that of Fulbert, bishop of Chartres, writing ca. 1020 to William V, Count of Poitou and Duke of Aquitaine:

> Whoever swears fidelity to his lord should always have six things in mind: safe, secure, honest, useful, easy, possible. Safe, namely, lest he injure his lord with his own body. Secure lest he not injure his secret interests or his defenses through which his lord can be secure. Honest lest he not injure his lord's justice or in other matters which seem

to pertain to his honesty. Useful lest he injure his lord's possessions. Easy or possible, lest that the good, which his lord could easily do, he would make difficult, and that what would be possible, he would make impossible for his lord. A faithful man should pay heed to these examples. It is not sufficient to abstain from evil, unless he may do what is good. It remains that he faithfully give his lord counsel and help in the aforementioned matters, if he wishes to be worthy of his benefice (fief) and safe in the fidelity that he has sworn. The lord also ought to render his duty to his faithful man in all things. If he does not, he may be thought of as faithless, just as he, who in consenting or telling lies will be perfidious and perjurious.[107]

There is a parallel episode to the one with Pippin and Denethor later in *The Return of the King*, with Merry and Théoden:

> "You shall be my esquire, if you will. Is there gear of war in this place, Éomer, that my sword-thain could use?" . . .
>
> "There are no great weapon-hoards here, lord," answered Éomer. . . .
>
> "I have a sword," said Merry. . . . Filled suddenly with love for this old man, he knelt on one knee, and took his hand and kissed it. "May I lay the sword of Meriadoc of the Shire on your lap, Théoden King?" he cried. "Receive my service, if you will!"
>
> "Gladly will I take it," said the king; and laying his long old hands upon the brown hair of the hobbit, he blessed him. "Rise now, Meriadoc, esquire of Rohan of the household of Meduseld!" he said. . . .
>
> "Like a father you shall be to me," said Merry.[108]

Here the language (sword-thain, weapon-hoard) is that of the Anglo-Saxon world, before the Normans brought feudalism to England, and Merry offers his service out of love while for Pippin it is to repay a debt and save his honor. Yet otherwise the ceremony is very similar, and both Merry and Pippin seem instinctively to know what to do and say on such an occasion.[109]

Aragorn and Éowyn

As the narrative turns from Minas Tirith to Rohan, much more is revealed of the characters of both Aragorn and Éowyn. Aragorn becomes more grim and lordly as war approaches, and yet he pauses to reveal a softer side as he watches Théoden, Éomer, and Merry depart for Dunharrow: "There go three that I love, and the smallest not the least."[110] When he rides ahead with the Dúnedain to Éowyn's camp, he meets her fierce love with courtesy. "Then it was kindly done, lord, to ride so many miles out of your way to bring tiding to Éowyn," she tells him. "Indeed," replies Aragorn, "no man would count such a journey wasted."

The mood changes when Aragorn tells Éowyn that he must depart from the Rohirrim and take the Paths of the Dead. When she protests and offers to ride with him, Aragorn engages a stereotypical double standard about women:

> "Lord," she said, "if you must go, then let me ride in your following. For I am weary of skulking in the hills, and wish to face peril and battle."
>
> "Your duty is with your people," he answered.
>
> "Too often have I heard of duty," she cried. "But am I not of the House of Earl, a shieldmaiden and not a dry-nurse? . . . All your words are but to say: you are a woman, and your part is in the house. But when the men have died in battle and honour, you have leave to be burned in the house, for the men will need it no more. But I am . . . not a serving-woman. I can ride and wield blade, and I do not fear either pain or death."[111]

In this lengthy dialogue—one of the longest in the entire novel—Tolkien gives Éowyn the last word. Many readers would say that she has the greater argument. Tolkien plucks a shieldmaiden from Norse myth and places her in a situation where she can speak the grievances of a modern woman without it seeming anachronistic or inappropriate. However just her case, still she loses the company of Aragorn and realizes that, despite his courtesies toward her, she never did hold his heart.

The one person who can relate to Éowyn is Merry. He has been parted from his dearest friend, and though accepted as Théoden's sword-thain, is forbidden by the king to ride to battle at Minas Tirith.

Éowyn, disguised as a male soldier named Dernhelm, takes the hobbit on her own horse. Merry's desire to perform valorous deeds in defense of his friends is an echo of her own feelings, and together they make an unorthodox—but soon to prove effective—team on the battlefield.

The Pelennor

Pippin is less eager for battle back at Minas Tirith, and scarcely able to look as the Nazgûl swoop screeching across the Pelennor Fields outside the city. His companion, Beregond, however, is encouraged by the sight of the approaching Faramir. "The Lord Faramir!" he cries. "Brave heart!"[112] Though Mel Gibson has made the description synonymous with William Wallace, it actually relates to his successor in the Wars of Scottish Independence, Robert the Bruce. After King Robert's death in 1329, Sir James Douglas and other companions of the Bruce carried his mummified heart on a Crusade to the Holy Land, but, cut off by Moors in Spain, threw the silver casket containing the heart at their attackers with the words, "Lead on brave heart, as ever thou was wont to do."[113]

The admiration for Faramir is not shared by his father. "Ever you desire to appear lordly and generous as a king of old," scolded Denethor.[114] The steward is interested in ends, not means, and is even willing to sacrifice another son in a desperate attempt to hold the garrison of Osgiliath. Yet he walks—and even sleeps—clad in a mail shirt and girt with a sword, capable of going into battle if he judged it to be the best strategy. With Gandalf, Denethor plays a competition of wills and wisdom, thinking that because he has a Seeing Stone he can outmatch the wizard. Gandalf does not take the bait, but calmly reminds the steward that the enemy is lacking in one area—cavalry—the measure of success for over five hundred years in medieval European warfare.

At Stirling Castle in Scotland, a statue of the fourteenth-century king of Scots Robert the Bruce, who was known as Braveheart, like the brave Gondor captain Faramir.

The theme of despair runs through this part of the narrative. During a sortie where the last mounted men in Gondor, with Gandalf at their helm, overtake the foe—for the moment—Faramir is critically wounded and brought back to Denethor unconscious and broken. Part of Denethor's despair is that he has lost one son and another lies dying, meaning that his line will come to an end; he cannot see the nobility of Faramir's character, only that of his blood. "Mean folk shall rule the last remnant of the Kings of Men," he laments.[117] The Lord of the Nazgûl, who has broken into the city using a wolf-head battering ram drawn by huge beasts, is called both "shadow of despair" and the "Captain of Despair" by Gandalf, whom Denethor calls "the Grey Fool, [whose] hope has failed."[118] Denethor refers literally to Frodo's quest—the fool's hope—which at this point in the narrative is in peril but has not in fact failed. Nevertheless Denethor releases Pippin from his service and prepares to immolate himself and his youngest son (who is ultimately saved by Gandalf), an act madder than that of Dido, queen of Carthage, who legendarily threw herself on a pyre to stay faithful to her first husband and avoid marriage to a Berber king.

"Denethor *was* tainted with mere politics," wrote Tolkien in 1955. "If he had survived as victor, even without use of the Ring, he would have taken a long stride towards becoming himself a tyrant."[119] Denethor was overly concerned with authority in Gondor, in contrast to Gandalf, who states "the rule of no realm is mine. . . . But all worthy things that are in peril as the world now stands, those are my care."[120]

The suicide of the mythological Greek hero Ajax, shown here on a reproduction from an ancient Greek vase. The tale of Ajax may be an inspiration for the story of Denethor and his sons.

Gandalf, meanwhile, has perhaps met his match in the Black Captain—the Nazgûl Lord, the Witch-king of Angmar—and his sword of flames. Then comes the cavalry. Significantly for Tolkien's geography, it is out of the North that a people—a horse people—comes to the aid of civilized Gondor. The ride of the Rohirrim first takes Théoden's cavalry through the lands of the Púkel-men, who offer to guide the Rohirrim along a secret road to Minas Tirith. Though the news about the siege of the city is dire, Théoden's response is the opposite of that of Denethor. Where the steward told Pippin to abandon his oath of service, the king tells his riders, "Oaths ye have taken: now fulfill them all, to lord and land and league of friendship"[121] (with alliteration apropos). The two leaders' respective ends are also a study in contrasts: Denethor's suicide and his attempt to burn Faramir, versus the heroic old king who rides to put out the fire engulfing Minas Tirith; Théoden falls in battle against the Black Captain's winged fell beast, but only after rousing his warriors to arms and himself defeating the chieftain of the Haradrim. "*Hope he rekindled*," went his funeral song, "*and in hope ended*."[122]

The only thing standing between the fallen king and the fell beast is the slender rider Dernhelm. The Witch-king says scornfully:

"Hinder me? Thou fool. No living man may hinder me!"

Dernhelm laughed. . . . "But no living man am I! You look upon a woman. Éowyn I am, Éomund's daughter. You stand between me and my lord and kin. . . . "

Suddenly the great beast . . . fell down upon Éowyn . . .

Still she did not blench: maiden of the Rohirrim, child of kings, slender but as a steel-blade, fair yet terrible. A swift stroke she dealt, skilled and deadly. The outstretched neck [of the beast] she clove asunder, and the hewn head fell like a stone.[123]

It is then Merry's turn to save his lord and his disguised patron. Stabbing the Witch-king in the knee, Merry distracts him just enough for Éowyn to collect herself and drive her own sword into the face of the Ringwraith lord, fulfilling the prophecy that he would be killed by no living *man*.

Théoden departs from this world with hope: "I go to my fathers. And even in their mighty company I shall not now be ashamed."[124] This farewell is an echo of the similarly pagan death-vision of Thorin in *The Hobbit*. For the elegy for the fallen soldiers at Pelennor, Tolkien employs alliteration, meter, and kennings inspired by Anglo-Saxon poetry:

> We heard of the horns in the hills ringing, the swords shining in the South-kingdom. Steeds went striding to the Stoningland as wind in the morning. War was kindled.[125]

When Éomer beholds his king dying and then his sister seemingly following suit, he cries, "Death take us all! . . . Ride, ride to ruin and the world's ending!"[126] Tolkien knew well the cold and bleak eschatology of the Anglo-Saxons and the Norse—their belief in the forthcoming end of the world, the Ragnarök—and this Northerness comes through clearly here with the Rohirrim. Yet even in such "fell mood" Éomer does not give in to despair, but rather waves his sword in defiance of the black ships approaching.[127]

The houses of healing

Aragorn is the embodiment of the ideal medieval monarch. He is first revealed as the true king of Gondor when he enters the Houses of Healing and displays "the healing hands of the king."[128] The herb-master of the city believes this to be an old wives' tale, harking back to "rhymes of old days which women such as our good Ioreth still repeat without understanding."[129] "[G]o and find some old man of less lore and more wisdom," replies Aragorn. In other words, myths and old wives' tales *do* hold truth, though the learned often dismiss their wisdom.

Faramir, "the wizard's pupil," wakes from his death-sleep and immediately recognizes the royalty that has saved him:

> "My lord. You called me. I come. What does the king command?"
>
> "Walk no more in the shadows, but awake!" said Aragorn. "You are weary. Rest a while, and take food, and be ready when I return."
>
> "I will, lord," said Faramir. "For who would lie idle when the king has returned?"[130]

Mûmakil, Variags, and the Black Ships

he last volley from the enemy at Pelennor is a host of strange men and weapons from the south and east of Gondor, many of which, as Hammond and Scull point out, were inspired by ancient and/or medieval origins.[131] From Harad came giant war elephants, which Tolkien calls *mûmakil*, capable of carrying many armed men on their artillery platforms. Alexander the Great encountered such war elephants in India, while Romans faced the invading pachyderms of the Greek general Pyrrhus and the Carthaginian Hannibal. The inspiration for Tolkien's Variags of Khand is perhaps the Varangians, a name for Scandinavians who invaded Eastern Europe in the ninth and tenth centuries. Lastly, Tolkien's black ships or *dromunds*, piloted by the Corsairs of Umbar, are likely modeled on the *dromons* or galleys of the Byzantine navy, also used by the Italians who transported knights to the Holy Land during the Crusades.[132] Aragorn's flying of the Gondorian standard from the black ships recalls the legend of the Greek king Theseus, who, after killing the Minotaur in Crete, forgot to exchange the black sail on his ship for the white—indicating his survival—upon returning to Athens, causing his father Aegeus to commit suicide. This story was inspiration for a similar episode in the medieval tragedy of Tristan and Isolde.

The war elephants of the Harad recall those of Hannibal; this ca. 1600 AD print shows the Roman troops of the general Scipio Africanus, on horseback, arrayed against the forces of Hannibal, astride elephants, during the battle of Zama, ca. 202 BC, near Carthage, Tunisia.

Faramir's response is nearly biblical in the language Tolkien employs to show the loyalty and humility of Denethor's younger son. Whereas Boromir at first doubted Aragorn's claim and questioned the need for a king of Gondor, Faramir acts as the true steward of the city, ready and willing to turn over authority to the rightful king (which he does prior to Aragorn's coronation in Book Six).

The healing of Éowyn is a more difficult task for Aragorn, for he knows that simply healing her body will not remove the darkness that lies deep within her. Her brother believes that this is a broken heart, caused by Aragorn's rejection at Dunharrow. Gandalf, however, offers another explanation for her malady:

> "My friend . . . you had horses, and deeds of arms, and the free fields; but she, born in the body of a maid, had a spirit and courage at least the match of yours. . . . But who knows what she spoke to the darkness, alone, in the bitter watches of the night . . . the walls of her bower closing in about her, a hutch to trammel some wild thing in?"[133]

Drawing on images of Joan of Arc, Tolkien makes a statement for women's rights, or at least offers to the men an illustration of the double standard that they have long enjoyed. Éowyn wants the same opportunities and experiences of any man from the Mark, and even yearns for a glorious death in battle like Théoden. Then she meets her fellow convalescent, Faramir, whose gentleness and wisdom bring about a slow change in Éowyn. As Faramir looks upon her with affection, "it seemed to him that something in her softened."[134]

While Éowyn still fears being trapped in a cage, and sees her convalescence in those terms, sharing it with Faramir lessens the pain and gradually she begins to trust this man, tall and courteous. The romance of Faramir and Éowyn is like a medieval version of the tale of Theseus and his abduction and subsequent marriage to the Amazonian warrior queen Hippolyta (or in some tellings, her sister Antiope). While Tolkien himself later wrote that Éowyn was brave but not Amazonian, and that her relationship with Faramir was valid even though it progressed quickly and did not go through the stages of courtly love,[135] he casts their roles too well. Faramir has Lancelot's courtesy and prowess if not his fanaticism, but also a philosopher's love of wisdom and beauty. He can talk of love and battle with the words of the troubadour: renown, puissant, valiant. Éowyn, from the uncivilized North, longs to be a warrior, whether Amazon or Valkyrie, but also wants the love of a great man. When the right man finally offers his heart to Éowyn, she relinquishes her role as shieldmaiden in exchange for that of healer. Each gives the other something that was missing, and they stand—and talk—together as equal partners.

Finally, for Merry, his heroic deeds at Pelennor are followed by a simple request for pipeweed. "But," he tells Aragorn in the Houses of Healing, "it is the way of my people to use light words at such times and say less than we mean. We fear to say too much."[136] Is this Tolkien's way of saying that the English are emotionally repressed?

ARAGORN

"We all know what a true king is," writes the philosopher Peter Kreeft. "Something in us longs to give him our loyalty and fealty and service and obedience. He is lost but longed for and some day will return, like Arthur. In the *Lord of the Rings*, Arthur's name is 'Aragorn.'"[137] Aragorn rides out of the Paths of the Dead under the White Mountains, mustering an army of ghosts to defeat the Corsairs of Umbar and ride on to glory at the Battle of the Pelennor Fields. This may have been based on the European myth of the Wild Hunt—a spectral horde that rampages across the land terrifying all in its path. In his encyclopedic work *Otia Imerialia* (*Recreation for an Emperor*, ca. 1212), English chronicler Gervase of Tilbury related the common belief in medieval Britain that the phantom riders of the Wild Hunt were the ghosts of Arthur's knights. Aragorn raises the banner of the kings of Gondor on his ship and wields Isildur's blade remade in battle, and yet Aragorn chooses to pitch his tent outside the city rather than enter as king. Even when his most powerful vassals—Éomer and Imrahil—urge him to declare himself, even when he displays the healing hands of the king, Aragorn returns to the guise of the Ranger. This pairing of prowess and humility is what makes all want to follow and serve him, and many want his love and companionship. Thus did Arthur build Camelot and draw to him the greatest knights and ladies of the realm.

Aragorn's greatest test, perhaps, comes before the Black Gate of Mordor. After being mocked by the Mouth of Sauron—who waves Frodo's mail and elven cloak, and Sam's sword, in Aragorn's face—

The Four Loves

n C. S. Lewis's book *The Four Loves* (1960), Lewis, acting as a Christian Platonist, constructs a paradigm using four Greco-Roman concepts of "love": Affection (*storge*), Friendship (*philia, amicitia*), Eros/Venus ("being in love"/sex), and Charity (*agapē, caritas*). Tolkien arguably explores all of these loves—and others—in his major works of fiction.

There are many examples of familial affection in *The Lord of the Rings*: Elrond and Arwen, Bilbo and Frodo, Denethor for Boromir, Boromir and Faramir, Éomer and Éowyn, Théoden and his niece and nephew. Brotherly bonds are particularly strong and present in *The Silmarillion*, (see Chapter Five) sometimes too strong, as in the case of the sons of Fëanor. Father-daughter bonds can also be destructive when possessiveness and jealousy enter in, as with Thingol and Lúthien. Tolkien would have had countless ancient and medieval examples of familial affection, both praiseworthy and destructive, to draw upon.

Tolkien's own strong bonds of male friendship—with members of the T.C.B.S. and later the Inklings—would naturally be expected to emerge in his fiction. Bilbo develops real friendships with Gandalf and some of the dwarves (especially Balin) in *The Hobbit*, but it is in *The Lord of the Rings* that we see the strongest bonds between males. Sam and Frodo is the most obvious bonding, but also Aragorn and Boromir, Aragorn and Legolas and Gimli, Legolas and Gimli, Aragorn and Éomer, Merry and Pippin, and of course the Fellowship of the Ring as a whole. While in depicting the Fellowship Tolkien likely drew inspiration from Greek myth (e.g., Jason and the Argonauts), the historical Germanic *comitatus* ("warband," as exemplified in *Beowulf*), and the Arthurian Knights of the Round Table, the pairing of male friends in long marches and combat situations was likely drawn from his own wartime experiences.

The bond between brothers in arms as depicted by Tolkien's Fellowship of the Ring is exemplified by King Arthur and the knights of the Round Table, shown here in an engraving after a ca. fourteenth-century manuscript illustration.

The Greek word *philos* can also be used for intense enjoyment of activities and created things. Tolkien is somewhat ambivalent on the love of created things. Take Bilbo's response as he listened to the dwarves sing: "[He] felt the love of beautiful things made by hands and by cunning and by magic moving through him, a fierce and jealous love, the desire of the hearts of dwarves."[138] Ultimately the dwarves' greed will lead to war and to the death of their leader; and yet, their song about the dragon's hoard is what awakens Bilbo's Tookish blood and leads him to an appreciation of travel and a desire to see natural wonders like mountains and forests. While elves and dwarves naturally take pride in their craftsmanship, *The Silmarillion* also shows the danger of becoming prideful and possessive of one's accomplishments (e.g., with Fëanor, who defies the will of the Valar because of his love for the silmarils he has created; and with the dwarves who murder for the Nauglamir, the necklace they craft to hold the silmarils).

Tolkien is frequently criticized for his lack of inclusion (and assumed lack of understanding) of romantic love, not to mention sex, in his novels. While this is a fair criticism of *The Hobbit* (then again, he would hardly have wanted to tell his young children erotic stories), *The Lord of the Rings* does have two strong romances set within the context of war: Aragorn and Arwen, making sacrifices for one another (though admittedly mostly in the appendices); and Faramir and Éowyn, a swift pairing but nonetheless a complex and interesting romance. *The Silmarillion* has several romantic couples, with Beren and Lúthien being central to the whole narrative. As for Venus, she makes only off-screen appearances in Middle-earth (though as a planet she likely inspired the Star of Eärendil). Tolkien left it to other modern writers to explore the mysteries of sexual love.

As Christians, both Lewis and Tolkien would have held *agape*, "selfless love," above all others. Gandalf and Boromir, and to an extent, Frodo, all sacrifice their lives for their companions. Sam is certainly willing to do this for Frodo, Faramir for his city, and Aragorn for all the free peoples of the West.[139] Here Tolkien can bring together the sacrificial and ascetic dimensions of early Christianity with the heroism of Anglo-Saxon warrior society. The opposite, self-love, though embraced in a modern secular age, is certainly not a medieval virtue. Tolkien explains the paradox within Gollum: "He hated [the Ring] and loved it, as he hated and loved himself."[140] Gollum and Sauron, who possessed the Ring longer than any other, are the most self-absorbed characters in *The Lord of the Rings*, but there are many others (Saruman, Wormtongue, Denethor) who are self-deluded because they trust too much in their own knowledge and powers.

Isildur's heir stands firm and fierce, drawing up his outnumbered host to challenge the Dark Lord. Yet at the end of Book Five it is not Aragorn whom we follow on the battlefield of Cormallen, for Tolkien shifts the narrative perspective to Pippin, just as he had done with Bilbo during the Battle of the Five Armies in *The Hobbit*. There, just before losing consciousness, Bilbo cries, "The Eagles are coming!"[141] In *The Return of the King*, Pippin hears the same hopeful cry just before he is crushed by a troll and all goes dark.

eucatastrophe

As Arthurian tales often depart from Arthur's doings in order to narrate the adventures of his knights, so does Book Six of *The Lord of the Rings* leave Aragorn's host and return us to the tower of Cirith Ungol, where the orcs had carried Frodo after finding him lying paralyzed from the sting of Shelob. Sam's rescue of his master is something of a parody of chivalric romance, with orcs killing each other and fleeing from Sam's shadow, mistaking him for a large elf-warrior.[142] When dealing in this episode with the Ring, however, Tolkien turns serious, describing its attempted seduction of Sam and Frodo's harsh reception of his devoted rescuer: "Give it to me!" cries Frodo, holding out a trembling hand to Sam, who has kept the Ring safe. "You can't have it . . . you thief!" Frodo is part addict, part Norse hero, telling Sam, "You cannot come between me and this doom."[143] For the reader it is simply heart wrenching to see Sam, who has struggled so valiantly to rescue Frodo, be hurt to tears by the one he loves most.

In the slow ascent of the two hobbits up Mount Doom, we leave behind the world of heroic myth and chivalric romance.[144] Tolkien's description of the seemingly endless march of the orcs, the weight of the hobbits' gear, their constant search for water, and the barren landscape all point to his own experiences at the Western Front. As they begin to ascend the desolate mountain, Frodo declares, "No taste of food, no feel of water, no sound of wind, no memory of trees or grass or flower . . . I am naked in the dark."[145] They are in purgatory, and the only way out for Frodo is to be carried by his faithful servant up to the Crack of Doom. Once there, however, Frodo makes a surprising declaration: "I have come. . . . But I do not choose now to do what I came to do. I will not do this thing. The Ring is mine!"[146] This catastrophe—Frodo *chooses* to put on the Ring and claim it for his own—coincides with the attack of the trolls at the Black Gate. At the same moment, both Sam and Pippin (our narrative perspective on the events) are knocked unconscious to the ground. It truly seems that all hope is lost.

But as Tolkien explains in his essay "On Fairy-Stories," readers of the fantastic expect to be drawn back from the brink of tragedy, to be consoled by a happy ending which offers them a glimpse of joy.[147] He calls this the *eucatastrophe*, an escape from death and final defeat through some unexpected outside force or turn of events. Gandalf had described to Frodo this possibility back in the Shire when Frodo was first given the Ring (see page 149). Bilbo spared Gollum and left the Ring to Frodo, which made possible the two coming together, and Frodo also showed pity on Gollum. This led ultimately to Gollum biting off Frodo's finger to get the Ring and Frodo to struggle with him, leading unintentionally to the Ring (and Gollum) falling into the flames of Mount Doom.

If this seems to be more than coincidence, consider that Frodo and Sam would still have died after the loss of the Ring in the flames had Gandalf not been sent to Middle-earth and to the Shire, and had he not done a service to the eagles (in *The Hobbit*, it is noted that he healed the Lord of the Eagles' arrow wound[148]), which led to their coming to his aid and to the rescue of Frodo and Sam. Whatever power sent Gandalf, it both respects the free will of Bilbo and Frodo *and* seems to have "meant" for things to happen a certain way. Tolkien here is trying to reconcile, on the one hand, the ancient pagan concepts of fate and doom that permeated the Northern myths he so loved, and on the other hand the medieval Catholic understanding of grace and free will, as articulated especially by Christian theologians Augustine of Hippo and Thomas Aquinas. Middle-earth is Tolkien's ideal medieval world where both pagan and Christian can coexist without contradiction.

many partings and the scouring of the shire

"Long live the Halflings! Praise them with great praise!" The rescue of the Ring-bearers, and their grand reception by the Captains of the West, are described in language full of chivalric and Christian elements. Knights in bright mail saluting, trumpets blaring, a minstrel singing . . . even the eagle-lords have vassals! Tolkien is at his most effusive here: "Their hearts, wounded with sweet words, overflowed, and their joy was like swords, and they passed in thought out to regions where pain and delight flow together and tears are the very wine of blessedness."[149]

The celebrations, the coronation of King Elessar (Aragorn), and his marriage to Arwen Undómiel are all staged by Tolkien according to the agricultural calendar. The end of Mordor coincides with the end of winter, the reviving of Frodo and Sam (on April 8) with the beginning of spring, the wedding with Midsummer's Day, and the parting from friends in Gondor with the beginning of autumn. Gandalf's conversation with Aragorn on the mountain above Minas Tirith is about the blooming of a new White Tree, an offshoot of the original, and is thus symbolic of the pending royal marriage and continuing the new dynasty. Both the fertility of the land and that of the king are quintessential medieval concerns; they are inextricably linked in the Arthurian tale of the Fisher King, whose wounds cause impotence that extends to his kingdom, which becomes a barren wasteland until he is healed.

Gandalf tells Aragorn that the Third Age is over, and the Fourth Age will be dominated by men. As the narrative bids a fond (if ponderous) farewell to Gondor, Rohan, Fangorn, and Rivendell, Tolkien also leaves the Middle Ages behind and returns us to the modern world of the Shire, now industrialized thanks to the schemes of Lotho Sackville-Baggins (the "Chief") and Saruman ("Sharkey"). In addition to ugly architecture, barricades, despotic rules, and prisons, part of Sharkey's plan is forced collectivization in the Shire: "It's all these 'gatherers' and 'sharers,'" explains a frightened hobbit to Frodo, Sam, Merry, and Pippin. "They do more gathering than sharing, and we never see most of the stuff again."[150] But what began as greed and gluttony turns to revenge and wanton destruction. In his final moments, Saruman, once the greatest wizard of his order, stands for nothing but nihilism; he is worse than a beggar, he is a knifeman.

In contrast to the miserable end of Sharkey at the hands of his maltreated servant Wormtongue, is the elevation of the four hobbits, especially Merry and Pippin. The Raising of the Shire is a bold and masterful act of politics and warfare. Before the hobbits part ways with Gandalf, he tells them that they are ready to put their own affairs in order, it "is what you have been trained for."[151] After proving themselves to be brave on the battlefields of men, these two hobbits show that they have grown up and are ready to command. They have become "lordly" to the inhabitants of the Shire, and this is reflected in the titles that they eventually assume (as noted in *The Lord of the Rings* appendix, Merry becomes Master of Buckland, and Pippin, the Thain).

Fate and Free Will

o encourage Frodo, Gandalf explains to him that there are powers at work other than those that serve the Dark Lord: "Bilbo was *meant* to find the Ring, and *not* by its maker. In which case you also were *meant* to have it. And that may be an encouraging thought."[152] When Frodo tells Gandalf that he does not understand, we can sympathize. Tolkien, in writing that "something else" was at work and italicizing *meant*, appears to be dipping his toe in the water but not plunging in. Is Gandalf talking about fate? About God? "Fate" (a classical concept) is occasionally mentioned in *The Lord of the Rings*, but more common is the word "doom" (a medieval term).

In a recently published philological note, Tolkien himself draws attention to the linguistically connected Sindarin words *amar*, "world," and *amarth*, "fate" (Quenya *umbar*), making the point that the Eldar saw fate as the fixed, unalterable (by its inhabitants) way of the physical world, or at least of Earth. This fate "affected an individual person," and was "not open to modification by his free will." What has been preordained from creation can be moved or destroyed, but cannot—even by the Valar—be *changed* into something else. Tolkien gives the example of Bilbo being *fated* to find the Ring, but retaining his will in deciding what to do with it, just as Frodo was *fated* to be the Ring-bearer, but not to necessarily destroy it. Tolkien saw *umbar* as a "net-work of 'chances,'" but the ultimate relationship of free will to the *foreknowledge* of the Creator, Ilúvatar, "was not resolved by the Eldar."[153]

As Tolkien artist David Cremona writes, "Ilúvatar, as ever, does not compel or predestine, but his plans are far-seeing and the roads to his ends, many."[154] We, as mortal readers, proceed along a linear path and expect the immortal to follow along. But while stories may be a way for elves and men to express truth, linear narrative cannot ultimately encompass and explain metaphysical realms. If the medieval Faërie world seems illogical and unexplainable, how much more confused would we be if we were confronted with the heavenly realm from which both the Faërie world and our physical world proceed.

"Political action cannot keep Middle-earth safe for elves" in the Fourth Age, writes Peter Kreeft, "but it can still keep it safe for Hobbits," that is, for us.[155] Is the Scouring of the Shire, then, Tolkien calling us to war? The hobbits are divided on the issue: Merry, Pippin, and Sam take up arms to defend the Shire, but Frodo declares his pacifism. "I do not wish for any sword," he declares on the field of Cormallen during the celebrations. In pain from wounds that will never heal, Frodo's response to war is not unlike that of many soldiers returning from combat, and

Themes and Concerns

ew York University medieval historian Norman Cantor, admittedly "not an enthusiast of *The Lord of the Rings*,"[156] identifies three ways that he sees how the novel has captured important (but often overlooked) aspects of medieval civilization:

1. It describes the condition of endemic warfare and the fear of armed bands attacking villagers;

2. It describes a long and arduous journey undertaken by a common soldier with one or two companions (Frodo and Sam) rather than that of a great nobleman with an armed retinue; and

3. It shows that the little peoples of the medieval world could be heroic, too.[157]

While Cantor's observations are not far from the mark, he ignores Tolkien's sympathetic portrayal of such nobles as Aragorn, Éowyn, and Faramir, and Frodo at least was more country squire than cleaver peasant. The culture of the medieval European aristocracy—feasting, love poetry, hunting, warfare—is what we find in Rivendell, in Rohan, and in Gondor. The return of the king—Aragorn—ensures the survival of chivalry as well as that of village culture, epitomized by the "comings and goings" of the Shire.

Summing up *The Lord of the Rings* is no easy task, and Tolkien does not simplify things in his commentary on the novel. Power is certainly an important theme, as is Hope (and its opposite, Despair). Addiction and mechanized warfare are modern concerns that Tolkien explores in the novel. Courage, the importance of keeping oaths, and martial valor are more medieval themes present throughout the work. Fellowship and Love are timeless ideals and important to Tolkien, and all Four Loves—affection, friendship, eros, agapé—can be seen in the relationships between the major characters.[158] But there is one more type of love, love for one's country, which is central to the hobbits' quest in particular. Like *The Hobbit*, *The Lord of the Rings* begins and ends in the Shire. The people, the homes, the pipeweed, and the beer of this green and pleasant land are ever present throughout the narrative, despite all the great battles and politics of the Big Folk. To quote Sam, or Peter Jackson's version of the hobbit, the Shire is simply what's "worth fighting for."[159]

Chivalrous love—one of the themes central to The Lord of the Rings—*personified in this illustration from the* Codex Manesse, *an early fourteenth-century Middle High German poetry anthology. The couple shown here could be Éowyn and Faramir.*

though it was not Tolkien's personal view he seems at least to have recognized it among his fellow combatants in the Great War and respected it. In *The Lord of the Rings*, Tolkien even viewed Tom Bombadil as a "natural pacifist."[160] But Frodo's pacifism is also tied to his great capacity for pity. Even after Saruman has attempted to stab him, Frodo will not let Sam strike at the fallen wizard: "I would still spare him, in the hope that he may find [his cure]."[161]

Like the Arthurian knight Gawain in *Sir Gawain and the Green Knight*, Frodo returns from his successful quest feeling a sense of personal failure and seeking redemption.[162] But redemption is not to be found at home, among his own people and friends. The healing of Frodo will require a special grace, one granted by the elves who, as a race, also share Frodo's sense of doom and need for redemption. The novel comes to a close at the Grey Havens, where Bilbo and Frodo, granted a place on the last ships sailing for the West, say goodbye to their Shire friends:

> "But," said Sam, and tears started in his eyes, "I thought you were going to enjoy the Shire, too, for years and years, after all you have done."
>
> "So I thought too, once. But I have been too deeply hurt, Sam. I tried to save the Shire, and it has been saved, but not for me."[163]

"Such epiphanies are quintessentially modernist, and never without sorrow" for wartime authors, writes author Patchen Mortimer.[164] Coming to terms with the changes modernity has brought to his own Shire, Tolkien turns to Gandalf to sum up all of the feelings that the author, the hobbits, and the readers are feeling: "'I will not say: do not weep; for not all tears are an evil.'"[165]

With these, his last words in *The Lord of the Rings*, Gandalf instructs us about the grieving process that comes with saying goodbye to friends, family, and beloved places. The intense poignancy produced from the intersection of emotion and intellect is, according to C. S. Lewis, a defining characteristic of humanity, and here, as often is the case with Tolkien, hobbits show us what it means to be human.[166]

5

The song
of Ilúvatar

THE TREMENDOUS COMMERCIAL SUCCESS of *The Lord of the Rings* led, as with *The Hobbit*, to a demand for more tales of Middle-earth. No sequel would ever appear, at least none written by J. R. R. Tolkien. Instead, Tolkien returned again and again to his early "gnomish" material, that which had inspired his poems and invented languages when he was a student at Oxford and a soldier in the war. These tales, which span from the creation of Middle-earth to the tales of the Third Age related in *The Hobbit* and *The Lord of the Rings*, are known collectively by Tolkien scholars as his legendarium, or "The Silmarillion." While no prose versions of this material appeared in print during J. R. R. Tolkien's lifetime, his son and literary executor Christopher has published four collections posthumously: *The Silmarillion* (1977), *Unfinished Tales* (1980), *The History of Middle Earth* (twelve volumes, 1983–96), and *The Children of Húrin*.

This chapter will examine the two most cohesive, *The Silmarillion* and *The Children of Húrin*. The first is a complex, controversial, and grand narrative. It has elicited a wide array of responses from readers, including disparaging remarks from many Tolkien enthusiasts, while a large number have never even read or at least finished the book. *The Children of Húrin*, though appearing in brief form in earlier published works, is a more confined and conventional narrative, but has appeared so recently that it has yet to generate much criticism. What follows is a discussion of the ancient and medieval source material that served in part as inspiration for the two novels. I would argue that an understanding of how this material relates to Tolkien's legendarium should play not a little role in determining the literary merit of these two posthumous works.

the silmarillion

IN 1913, WHILE AN UNDERGRADUATE at Oxford, Tolkien came across a series of Old English religious poems from the *Exeter Book* (see pages 8, 57–59, 61). He was struck by a passage in one of these poems, by Cynewulf, called *Crist: Eala Earendel engla beorhtast | ofer middengeard monnum sended*, "Hail Earendel, brightest of angels, | Over Middle-earth sent to men."

"I felt a curious thrill," he wrote long after reading the poem, "as if something had stirred within me, half waken from sleep. There was something very remote and strange and beautiful behind these words, if I could grasp it, far beyond ancient English."[1] A year after his discovery of *Crist*, while on holiday at his aunt's house in Nottinghamshire, he composed "The Voyage of Earendel the Evening Star." It begins:

> Earendel sprang up from Ocean's cup
> In the gloom of the mid-world's rim;
> From the door of Night as a ray of light
> Leapt over the twilight brim,
> And launching his bark like a silver spark
> From the golden-fading sand
> Down the sunlit breath of Day's fiery death
> He sped from Westerland.[2]

When soon after this his friend G. B. Smith asked him what the poem was about, Tolkien replied, "I don't know. I'll try to find out."[3] For the next sixty years he spent much time trying to find out, frustratingly trying to convince friends, publishers, and even himself that a great mythology for England could be constructed from these and other poems inspired by Old English, Norse, and Finnish texts. Both *The Hobbit* and *The Lord of the Rings* were tangents, even distractions from this greater quest. At the time of his death in 1973, no great mythology of Earendel and his ancient elvish kin had appeared. Four years later, in accord with Tolkien's will, his son Christopher (assisted by Canadian writer Guy Gavriel Kay) edited and published *The Silmarillion*, and at last Tolkien fans could see in a grand, nearly biblical narrative the cosmology and ancient tales of Middle-earth that had started it all.

Between "The Voyage of Earendel" and *The Silmarillion* there are a more than a dozen poems (most unpublished), several watercolors, and a handful of prose sketches (not published until 1983's *Book of Lost Tales*). Thanks to the release of *The History of Middle-earth*, Tolkien scholars can now reconstruct much of the process by which J. R. R. Tolkien tried to shape a continuous narrative and Christopher Tolkien ultimately succeeded in transforming this material into the published work known as *The Silmarillion*. Rather than detail this long and complex

Previous pages:
An illustration by Gustave Doré from the 1866 edition of John Milton's Paradise Lost. *Entitled "This greeting on thy impious Crest receive," it shows the seraph Abdiel attacking Satan for inciting revolt, similar to the rebellion and descent of Melkor/Morgoth in* The Silmarillion.

sequence of events, I want to focus on two key structural decisions: the framework and "transmission" of the tales, and the overall geography of *The Silmarillion*.

J. R. R. Tolkien had tinkered with the notion that the legendarium was a collection of elvish history and myth recorded by Bilbo during his eighteen years' residence in Rivendell.[4] Another conceit considered by Tolkien was that these tales were taught by the elves to an Anglo-Saxon mariner named Ælfwine, or that Ælfwine was the translator of tales written by elvish loremasters, first recorded by men of Númenor. Such complex transmission history is typical of medieval manuscripts, and as a conceit is used by modern writers like Umberto Eco (*The Name of the Rose*, 1980) and Michael Crichton (*Eaters of the Dead*, 1976).

If the entire subcreation of Middle-earth begins with the discovery of the Earendel verse, then it makes sense for Tolkien to envision a world where mariners sail to mysterious western islands. Such was the destiny of the Angles and Saxons who came to Britain, and later the Vikings who sailed to the British Isles, Iceland, and Greenland. English Tolkien scholar Rhona Beare notes that Beleriand, the part of Middle-earth in which most of the events of *The Silmarillion* take place, was given by Tolkien a maritime climate very similar to England's; and likewise, the Great Sea to the West bears a resemblance to the Atlantic (e.g., "grinding ice" fills its northern parts).[5] The centrality of trees in *The Silmarillion*—especially the Two Trees, which gave first light to the Earth—is also in accord with Norse creation myths, which feature the ash tree Yggdrasil, whose roots support the whole universe, and first man—Ask—himself made out of an ash tree. But Tolkien became troubled that his flat earth, only later "bent," contradicted scientific fact. This represents the greater struggle of an author who sought to bring the verisimilitude and narrative drive of the modern novel, done successfully in *The Lord of the Rings*, to the larger "parent" myth without sacrificing the antique language and romance structure of *The Silmarillion*. If father and son ultimately fell short of achieving this, they nevertheless

Tolkien envisioned a world where mariners sailed to mysterious western islands—such as the Vikings did. Here, a Viking ship is depicted on this carved stone from Gotland, Sweden.

have given the world rare beauties and unforgettable images of Middle-earth that resonate all the more—for careful readers—because these things ultimately derive from a rich historical sourcebook.

the creation of arda

Christopher Tolkien decided that *The Silmarillion* should consist of five distinct parts of his father's legendarium—Ainulindalë, Valaquenta, Quenta Silmarillion, Akallabêth, and "Of the Rings of Power and the Third Age"—as well as genealogies, notes, and maps. The first part, Ainulindalë, means "The Music of the Ainur." Here Eru ("the One") first makes the Ainur ("Holy Ones"), "the offspring of his thought."[6] Eru communicates to the Ainur through music, eventually sharing his vision of the creation of Eä, the material world or universe. Eru would send the Flame Imperishable into the heart of the Void and from it would come Arda ("the Realm," or Earth) as a globe within the Void.[7] The Creation comes about through song, begun by Eru or Ilúvatar, as he is known in Arda, and then it continued in both song and deed by the Ainur. For some of the Ainur go out into the Void to perform their part in the creation of Arda, and there they later became known as the Valar to the Children of Ilúvatar (elves and men). The greatest of the Ainur is Melkor, but his was from the beginning a strong note of discord in the choir of Ilúvatar. Pride, anger, and envy enter the mind of Melkor, and he tries to seize a portion of Arda to make a kingdom for himself: "But he desired rather to subdue to his will both Elves and Men, envying the gifts with which Ilúvatar promised to endow them; and he wished himself to have subjects and servants . . . and to be master over other wills."[8]

The second part of *The Silmarillion*, the Valaquenta, is an account of the names and attributes of the Valar and the Maiar (lesser spirits) that survives in elvish lore. The Valar number seven lords and seven queens, and they are listed by their original elvish names: Manwë, Ulmo, Aulë, Oromë, Mandos, Lórien, and Tulkas; Varda, Yavanna, Nienna, Estë,

In Norse creation myths, the roots of the great ash tree Yggdrasil support the whole universe. This illustration of Yggdrasil is from a seventeenth-century Icelandic manuscript.

Vairë, Vána, and Nessa. Though originally in their company, Melkor was no longer considered one of the Valar; the Noldor, or Deep Elves, refuse to utter his name and thus call him Morgoth, the "Dark Enemy of the World."

Manwë is given the lordship of Arda, and the winds and the clouds are his delight. His queen is Varda, Lady of the Stars, and light is her power and joy. Elves love Varda above all the Valar, and name her Elbereth. Manwë and Varda live together in Valinor, in the west above the tallest mountain on Earth. Next in might to Manwë is Ulmo, Lord of Waters, who dwells alone in the deep seas of Arda. Aulë, a great smith and craftsman, is lord of the substances of the earth and what lies beneath it. His spouse is Yavanna, the Giver of Fruits, tall and green-robed mistress of all things growing from the earth. Mandos and Lórien are brethren—the Fëanturi—masters of spirits whose true names were Námo and Irmo. Námo is keeper of the Houses of the Dead (also called Mandos), and his spouse is Vairë the Weaver. Irmo is the master of visions and dreams, and he lives in the gardens of Lórien with his spouse Estë, the gray lady and healer of hurts and weariness. Nienna is sister to the Fëanturi, and she mourns ever for the hurts of the world, but brings wisdom to all who sorrow. Greatest in strength is Tulkas the Valiant, the golden-haired, ruddy-faced champion of the Valar. His spouse is Nessa, sister of Oromë, swift of foot and delighting in dance. Oromë, Lord of the Forest, is the grim hunter of monsters and fell beasts, and is married to Vána, Ever-young, younger sister of Yavanna. "All flowers spring as she passes and open if she glances upon them," it is said of Vána.[9] This recalls the description of Olwen in *Culhwch and Olwen*: "Four white clovers would spring up in her track wherever she went. Because of that she was called Olwen (White-track)."[10]

According to the Valaquenta, with the Valar came other spirits, the Maiar, who are from the same order of beings but of lesser degree. The Maiar function as: "servants and helpers [to the Valar] . . . seldom [have they] appeared in form visible to Elves and Men."[11] While most of their names are not known by the Elves, a few are especially remembered and honored: Ilmarë, handmaid of Varda; Eönwë, banner-bearer and herald of Manwë; Ossë, vassal of Ulmo and master of the seas of Middle-earth; his wife Uinen, Lady of the Seas; and Melian and Olórin, who dwell in Lórien. There are other spirits who were drawn to Melkor before his fall, as well as Maiar who were corrupted by his lies and came into his service. He is served by fire-demons called Valaraukar or balrogs, by dragons and other monstrous beasts, and by a Maia named Gorthaur the Cruel. The latter was Melkor's greatest lieutenant and successor, known to elves and men as Sauron.

The eighteenth-century English astronomer Thomas Wright created this schema of the Pythagorean solar system as part of a portfolio published in 1742 entitled "A synopsis of the universe, or, the visible world epitomiz'd." Its elaborate swirling orbits populated by celestial beings evokes the "music of the spheres" theorized by Pythagoras (see next page) as well as the "music of the Ainur" that created the world of The Silmarillion.

In these tales of creation and cosmic order, *The Silmarillion* is comparable to the most ancient Near Eastern and Western myth traditions, such as those of Mesopotamia, Egypt, and Greece. Creation through music, in particular, can be traced back to Pythagorean philosophy and its medieval interpretation, the "music of the spheres."[12] The nature associations and rank-ordering of spiritual beings also reflects the Roman, Celtic, and Norse pantheons. But the rebellion and descent of Melkor/Morgoth is directly inspired by the Book of Genesis and its medieval commentaries. Of the latter, Tolkien would have been particularly drawn to two Anglo-Saxon poems in the Junius 11 MS (Bodleian Library, Oxford) known as *Genesis A* and *Genesis B*. These are verse elaborations of the story of Creation and the expulsion of Adam and Eve from Eden. While *Genesis A* (early eighth century) sticks close to the script, *Genesis B* (ninth century) is notable for its novel and expansive account of Lucifer's rebellion against God and his subsequent exile. Compare the following excerpts to each other and to the beginning of *The Silmarillion*:

GENESIS A

[These angelic hosts] had no knowledge of
working evil or wickedness, but dwelt in innocence   20
forever with their Lord: from the beginning they wrought
in heaven nothing but righteousness and truth, until
a Prince of angels through pride strayed into sin: then
they would consult their own advantage no longer, but
turned away from God's loving kindness. They had   25
vast arrogance, in that by the might of multitudes they
sought to wrest from the Lord the celestial mansions,
spacious and heaven-bright. Then there fell upon
them, grievously, the envy, presumption, and pride
of the Angel who first began to carry out the evil plot,   30
to weave it and promote it, when he boasted by word—
as he thirsted for conflict—that he wished to own the
home and high throne of the heavenly kingdom to the
north.[13]

The below excerpt from *Genesis B* brings to mind the vivid portrait of Satan in John Milton's *Paradise Lost* (1667). Indeed, Milton may have seen the Junius 11 manuscript before composing his epic. But in *The Silmarillion*, the First War is not in heaven but rather at—and fully intertwined with—the creation of earth.

Fallen angels being cast into the mouth of Hell; a detail from MS. Junius 11 (Oxford, Bodleian Library).

GENESIS B

One in particular had he created so shining
so mighty in his thinking;   he let him wield so much power,
highest next to Him in Heaven-Kingdom.   He had him so brightly created,
so winsome were his ways in heaven,   that came to him from the Lord's company   255
that he was like the light of the stars.   He should have loved the work of the Lord.
he should have held dear to himself his joys in heaven and should have thanked his Lord
for those delights that He shared with him in that light; then would He have permitted
him for a long time to wield power.
But he turned himself to a terrible thing;   he began to heave up trouble against Him,   260
against that highest Heaven's Ruler,   who sits on the saintly throne.
Dear was he to Our Lord;   yet God might not be deluded
that his angel began   to become over-spirited.
He raised himself up against his Superior,   sought hate-speech;
boast-words began.   He did not wish to serve God;   265
he said that his body was   light and shining,
bright-white and hue-luminous.[14]

The Elder Days

The Quenta Silmarillion, consisting of twenty-four chapters, is by far the largest part of the book. Though its subtitle is "The History of the Silmarils," it relates all of the major events and figures between the first war of the Valar against Morgoth in the Elder Days and the voyage of Eärendil into the heavens. It is dominated by the great elf-lords of the First Age; man enters but late into the picture. Nevertheless, the romance of the mortal Beren and the elf-maid Lúthien form the heart of this great saga, and their fate is intertwined with that of the enigmatic jewels knows as Simarils.

Before Arda was fully shaped, Melkor was at war against the Valar, who were ultimately able to defeat him at this primordial stage through the coming of Tulkas the Strong into the "Little Kingdom"[15] of Arda. Tulkas's wrath and laughter are his weapons, and they force Melkor to retreat for a while into the Void. After the Valar subdue the fires of the First War by burying them under the mountains of Arda, light is provided by two lamps crafted by Aulë and placed on top of lofty pillars erected amid the great seas to the north and the south of Middle-earth. In this constant light many things begin to grow, great and small, plant and beast—it is the Spring of Arda. But when the Valar rest from their labors on the Isle of Almaren, in the middle of the Earth where the lights meet and mingle, Melkor returns to the north with a host of fiends and constructs the fortress of Utumno deep under the earth. Melkor's presence begins to cause plants to rot, waters to turn foul, and violent beasts to roam the earth. Filled with pride and arrogance, Melkor once more attacks the Valar, this time by destroying the pillars and lamps and causing great destruction in the Spring of Arda.

With their abode in Middle-earth destroyed, the Valar depart west across the Great Sea and build a new home in the Land of Aman. On the shores of Aman they raise the Pelóri, the highest mountains on Earth, and on top of their highest peak Manwë sets his throne so that he and Varda can look out upon the whole Earth. Behind the mountain ramparts the Valar build their new home, Valinor, and it exceeds their original creation in Middle-earth because all living things and even stone and water are hallowed by the Valar, the Deathless. Upon a green mound in their new city, watered by the tears of Nienna and nourished by the song of Yavanna, two saplings arise and grow to become the Two Trees of Valinor: Telperion, whose dark green leaves gave off a silver light,

The Valar and Some Parallels in European Mythology

THE SILMARILLION	GRECO-ROMAN	CELTIC	GERMANIC
Manwë ("swift birds . . . come and go at his bidding")	Zeus/Jupiter		Oðin
Varda	Hera/Juno		Frigga
Melkor			Loki
Ulmo ("he made music on his horns of shell")	Poseidon/Neptune	Manannán mac Lir	Ægir
Aulë	Hephaestus/Vulcan		
Yavanna	Demeter/Ceres	Lug/Lleu	Freya
Námo/Mandos	Hades/Pluto	Donn/Arawn	Hel
Vairë	The Fates		The Norns
Irmo/Lórien	Morpheus		
Estë	Panacea		
Nienna	Athena/Niobe?		
Tulkas	Ares/Mars?		Thor, Tyr
Nessa	Artemis/Diana		Skaði
Oromë	Pan?		Freyr
Vána	Chloris/Flora	Cernunos	

and Laurelin, with young green leaves glittering gold. The waxing and waning of the Two Trees occur in a twelve-hour cycle, and thus begins the Count of Time on Earth during the days of the Bliss of Valinor.

It is at this time that Ilúvatar sees Arda and thinks it is beautiful. "Behold I love the Earth," he says, "which shall be a mansion for the Quendi [elves] and the Atani [men]."[16] Before the awakening of elves and men, the Valar come often to Middle-earth to heal the destruction of Melkor. Aulë comes and in the darkness crafts the dwarves, impatient for children to whom he can teach his crafts. When Ilúvatar asks Aulë why he dares to be so presumptuous as to create a race of beings, the latter answers:

I desired things other than I am, to love and to teach them.
. . . And in my impatience I have fallen into folly. Yet the
making of things is in my heart from my own making by
thee. . . . As a child to his father, I offer thee these things, the
work of the hands which thou hast made.[17]

Here is Tolkien's version of the story of Prometheus, the Greek titan
who created man and stole fire from the gods so that man could enjoy
the arts of civilization. But while Prometheus was punished for his trans-
gression (Zeus had him chained to a rock where an eagle would eat out
his liver daily), Aulë shows humility and is pardoned by Ilúvatar. The
response of Aulë also shows Tolkien exploring the subcreative impulse
of created man: that is, the artist contemplating the origins of art itself.

Prometheus creates man, from a ca. third-century Italian marble relief.

The firstborn

Soon after this comes the appointed hour for the awakening of the
Children of Ilúvatar. First to awake are the elves, who arise on the
shores of a bay in the far east of Middle-earth, where they are greeted
only by starlight and the sound of rushing waters. When they find

their voice they name themselves the Quendi ("those who speak"), but Oromë—who is the first of the Valar to discover them, while out riding his steed Nahar on a hunt—calls them the Eldar ("the people of the stars"). When they first see Oromë many of the Quendi are afraid and flee; Melkor, who had his minions luring and kidnapping elves who strayed into the woods, had sown rumors that a shadow "Rider" was to blame. Melkor had the captive elves brought to Utumno, where, it is believed, they were tortured and corrupted—thus was bred Melkor's slave-race, the orcs. For the sake of all the Quendi, the Valar ride out of the West to war against Melkor. At length they break the walls of Utumno, and Tulkas binds Melkor with the chain Angainor wrought by Aulë—reminiscent of the binding of the Norse wolf Fenrir by the gods of Valhalla with the chain Gleipnir.

After the war, the Valar still fear for the safety of the Quendi, and summon them to Valinor. Most heed the summons, and these are known as the Eldar—the name first given the Quendi by Oromë—or the Calaquendi, "Elves of the Light," while those who feared and stayed behind are the Avari, "the Unwilling." The first of the Eldar to arrive in Valinor are the host of the elf king Ingwë, known as the Vanyar or the Fair Elves, beloved of Manwë and Varda. Next comes the people of Finwë, the Noldor or Deep Elves, beloved of Aulë. Last comes the greatest host, the Teleri, who are led by the brothers Elwë Singolo ("Greymantle") and Olwë. Many of the Teleri are lost on the journey or tarry in the forests or along the seashore, and the Eldar label them—and the Avari, the Unwilling—the Moriquendi, "Elves of the Darkness." Here we see Tolkien after much thought working out the division of the light elves and dark elves he found in his Norse sources (see page 68). Whereas in the Germanic tradition dark elves are often equated with dwarves, Tolkien took another path which, we shall see, brought to the sundering much pathos.

Many of the Teleri linger in the lands west of the Misty Mountains, which come to be called Beleriand. Though Elwë is eager to return to Valinor with his friend Finwë, he happens upon the Maia Melian singing in a glade and falls under her spell. Bound by love of one another, both Melian and Elu Thingol ("King Greymantle") stay in East Beleriand and found the great kingdom of Doriath. His people are known as the Sindar, or Grey Elves. Others of the Teleri linger on the western shores of Beleriand, and learn from Ossë both music and shipbuilding. These elves of the havens become great mariners, and Círdan the Shipwright is their lord. One group of elves beg to remain on the island that Ulmo had used to transport the Vanyar and the Noldor to Aman; this becomes known as Tol Eressëa, "the Lonely Isle."

Fëanor and the Silmarils

The Valar raise a green mound called Túna for the Vanyar and Noldor in Aman, and upon it the elves build the city of Tirion, which has its own white tree named Galathilion. Finwë, king of the Noldor, has three sons: Fingolfin, the strongest and most valiant; Finarfin, the fairest and wisest; and their half-brother Fëanor, who possesses the greatest skills of word and hand. Like the mothers of the Arthurian knights Culhwch and Tristan (whose name means "sadness"), Fëanor's mother dies after giving birth to him. Fëanor grows tall and expert in the crafting of gems, and after long labor in secret he crafts the three jewels known as the Silmarils. Within these crystals he captures the blended light of the Trees of Valinor, and they cannot be destroyed by any power in Arda. But Melkor, who had been recently pardoned by Manwë and freed from his prison, lusts after the Silmarils and seeks to both gain them and turn the Noldor against the Valar. He spreads lies that the Valar want to keep the elves in Valinor so that men can inherit Middle-earth, and also sows discord between Fëanor and his half-brothers. Like the serpent in the Garden of Eden, Melkor tempts Fëanor with promises of power and freedom from the Valar, and tells Fëanor that the Silmarils are not safe from the Valar.

Melkor's lies work. Fëanor forges weapons in secret and in public threatens his brother Fingolfin, resulting in Fëanor's banishment from Tirion. Though the Valar discover that Melkor is behind the strife, and Fëanor realizes that Melkor has betrayed him and desires the Silmarils for himself, the realizations are too late to prevent the Dark Enemy's escape from Aman. Returning to Middle-earth as a cloud, Melkor forms an alliance with the giant spider Ungoliant, and together under a cloak of darkness they make their way to Valinor, destroying the Two Trees. Devouring the blessed light of the trees, Ungoliant is able to escape to Middle-earth with Melkor, untouched by the hunters of Valinor. Manwë summons Fëanor to Valinor, where the Valar ask him to give them the Silmarils, to rekindle the light that has been extinguished. However, with the warnings of Melkor still in his heart, Fëanor refuses. He soon learns that Melkor has gone to his fortress, slain Finwë in his own doorway,

Like Melkor tempting Fëanor, the serpent tempts Eve in Eden, in this ca. 1500 German manuscript engraving.

and stolen the Silmarils. Fëanor, in his grief, curses both Melkor (who he names "Morgoth," the "Black Foe of the World") and the summons of Manwë that had separated him from all he loved. He gathers all of the Noldor and promises them freedom if they will leave Aman with him and pursue Morgoth to Middle-earth. "War shall we have," pledges Fëanor, "and hatred undying." He burns hot in his pursuit of vengeance, like Malory's Sir Gawain, who, when his brothers are killed by Sir Lancelot, brings King Arthur and the knights of the Round Table to France to avenge their death. Neither Fëanor nor Gawain live to see the vengeance fulfilled, and both are the cause of the breaking of fellowship.

The seven sons of Fëanor swear an oath to follow their father in pursuit of the Silmarils, and many more of their kindred are eager to return to Middle-earth—including the fairest woman of all the Noldor, the golden-haired Galadriel, who wished to rule a realm of her own. Even Fingolfin and Finarfin follow their kin reluctantly to the shores of Aman, where Fëanor tries to convince the Teleri to join them, and, failing to do so, seizes their white ships by force, in what comes to be called the Kinslaying. Some ships are wrecked and many elves drown in the storms caused by the tears of the Maia Uinen, a storm as powerful as the one sent by Zeus in *The Odyssey*, which destroys the ships of Odysseus and sends his crew to their deaths. After landing on the shores of Middle-earth, Fëanor burns all of the ships, instead of sending them back across the frigid strait to ferry those Noldor who had to make the journey by land in the North, a long march through killing ice and snow. In medieval Irish mythology, the family of gods known as the Tuatha Dé Danann also sailed from the West to Ireland and burned their ships upon landing.[18]

BEREN AND LÚTHIEN

When the Noldor return to Middle-earth they find that it was no longer a land lit only by ancient stars. For the Valar had, from the last silver flower and golden fruit of the Two Trees, shaped the moon and the sun and set them on their courses by placing them in the care of two Maiar (following Germanic custom, Tolkien makes the moon masculine and the sun feminine).[19] Thingol and Melian had by then founded a mighty kingdom in Beleriand, and the dwarves had awoken and come over the Blue Mountains to Beleriand. Indeed, the dwarves—Khazad in their own tongue, Naugrim ("Stunted People") in Sindarin—had helped Thingol forge weapons and build his underground palace, Menegroth, the Thousand Caves. Melian wove a girdle of protection around her husband's kingdom, called Doriath, so that none could find nor enter it against her will. There was born their only child, Lúthien, fairest of all the Children of Ilúvatar.

After the death of Fëanor, wounded by balrogs at the gates of Angband, Melkor's fortress, his sons and the sons of Fingolfin and Finarfin are for a while reconciled and each seek kingdoms of their own in Middle-earth. Fingolfin and his sons Fingon and Turgon hold Hithlum in the northwest: Fingon's portion is called Dor-lómin, while Turgon rules Nevrast from his halls at Vinyamar by the sea. Later Turgon would build Gondolin in the hidden vale of Tumladen, in memory of Tirion. His friend Finrod Felagund, eldest son of Finarfin, builds the stronghold of Nargothrond with the aid of the dwarves, who also make for him the Nauglamír, the "Necklace of the Dwarves." Finrod's sister Galadriel dwells for a long while with Melian in Doriath, where she falls in love with Celeborn, kinsman of Thingol. The highlands of Dorthonion are held by Angrod and Aegnor, two sons of Finarfin, while the fourth brother Orodreth builds the fortress of Minas Tirith on an island in the river Sirion. In East Beleriand the sons of Fëanor rule: Maedhros and Maglor, Celegorm and Curufin and Caranthir, Amrod and Amras. Lastly, in the southeast lay Ossiriand, home to the Green-elves.

At the first rising of the sun in Middle-earth there also awake the Secondborn, the Atani or Edain, mortal men, far to the east of Beleriand over the Blue Mountains. After long journeying, the people of Balan, later given the name Bëor the Old, come into Beleriand and are discovered by Finrod Felagund, who loves them and teaches them many things. "Westwards our hearts have been turned," explains Bëor to Finrod, "and we believe that there we shall find light."[20] Eventually three kindreds—the "Three Houses of the Elf-friends"—come to Beleriand, and many of the young men of the Edain enter into the service of the lords of the Eldar (and a woman, Haleth, is warrior and chieftain in her own right). But Morgoth spreads lies and deceit among the Edain, causing many men to distrust the Eldar and some to even doubt the existence of Morgoth and the Valar (whom they called gods). A sundering of men occurrs, with some returning east and others departing southward.

The House of Hador Goldenhead is the greatest house of the Edain who stay in the West. From Hador descends Húrin and Túrin Turambar and Eärendil. They faithfully serve King Turgon in the wars against Morgoth, while the House of Bëor serves that of Finrod Felagund. From Bëor comes a great leader of men named Barahir, who is hunted in the wild by Sauron and his orcs until he and all of his companions are slain, save one, his son Beren. In his grief-filled wonderings, Beren comes upon Lúthien singing in the moonlight and is struck dumb in awe. When at last he breaks free from the spell he calls out to her, "Tinúviel!" ("Nightingale"), and when she sees him this daughter of the Eldar and the Maiar falls in love with a mortal man. But her father King Thingol scorns Beren's desire for Lúthien. "Bring me in your hand a Silmaril

from Morgoth's crown," he declares, "and then, if she will, Lúthien may set her hand in yours."[21] The motif of the impossible challenge can be seen in *Culhwch and Olwen*, when Ysbaddaden Chief Giant lays out several seemingly impossible tasks to the hero who asks for his daughter's hand.

"[In 1909] I met the Lúthien Tinúviel of my own 'personal romance' with her long dark hair, fair face and starry eyes, and beautiful voice."[22]

—J. R. R. TOLKIEN DESCRIBING HIS WIFE, EDITH

Whereas Culhwch had the aid of Arthur's knights in accomplishing his tasks, Beren has Finrod Felagund and Lúthien herself. Beren and Finrod are captured by Sauron and thrown into a pit to be devoured by a werewolf. After making a Rapunzel-like escape from Doriath, Lúthien makes her way to Sauron's tower to free Beren with the aid of Huan, a great hound of Valinor. Though Finrod dies in battle with the werewolf, Huan slays the great wolves of Sauron and, after long battle, overwhelms their master. Sauron is forced to yield Beren and the tower to Lúthien, who nurses her lover back to health. After many adventures the lovers come at last to Angband, and Lúthien casts a sleeping spell upon Morgoth and his servants. Beren is then able to pry one Silmaril from the iron crown, but trying for a second rouses Morgoth and his dread guard, the giant wolf Carcharoth. When Beren tries to fend off the wolf with the Silmaril, Carcharoth bites off his hand and consumes the jewel. The Silmaril's fire, however, begins to consume the innards of the beast and it goes on a murderous rampage through Beleriand. Returning to Doriath, Beren and Lúthien stand before Thingol and Beren asks again for Lúthien's hand. "What of your quest?" inquires the king. "Even now a Silmaril is in my hand," says Beren grimly, showing what remains of his right arm.[23] Amazed, Thingol yields to Beren's request.

The hunting of the wolf Carcharoth is taken up by Thingol, Beren, Huan, Mablung Heavyhand, and Beleg Strongbow. When the wolf attacks Thingol, Beren stands between them with his spear, but receives a deadly wound. Huan then tackles Carcharoth and after a great battle, kills him, only to die in turn from the wolf's venom. Mablung cuts the

The giant wolf Carcharoth biting off Beren's hand was likely inspired by the Norse myth of the wolf Fenrir, who bit off the hand of the god Tyr. That scene is shown here in this 1911 illustration by John Bauer from a children's book of Norse mythology, **Our Fathers' Godsaga** *(1887), by Swedish writer Viktor Rydberg.*

Tyr und Fenrir.

Silmaril from the wolf's belly and places it in Beren's hand, and Beren gives it to the king before his spirit leaves his body. Lúthien goes to sing before Mandos himself for the release of her husband from death, and the Valar allows Beren to return to Middle-earth only if Lúthien agrees to give up her birthright and become mortal. So does she choose and she and Beren live out their remaining days together, founding a line of great kings, but ever retreating from the world.

The end of the tale of Beren and Lúthien reads like a gender-reversed version of Orpheus trying to retrieve his wife Eurydice from the Underworld. The tone, however, is unmistakingly Northern. The story was originally outlined in Tolkien's epic poem, *The Lay of Leithian*, which he worked on from 1925–31, but never finished. When Edward Crankshaw, the outside reader for Allen and Unwin, was first presented with *The Lay of Leithian* in 1937, he mistook it for a translation of an authentic Celtic romance (much to Tolkien's amusement).[24] The talking hound Huan has antecedents in both Celtic and Norse myth. The Norse god Tyr lost his hand when it was bitten off by the wolf Fenrir, and many of the deities of Valhalla pleaded tearfully for the release of Balder from Hell.

The Silmarillion then turns to the tale of Túrin Turambar (see discussion of that tale in its expanded version, *The Children of Húrin*, on pages 205–13). After Túrin's death, Morgoth releases Húrin from captivity. Húrin wanders in grief through Beleriand. In the fortress of Nargothrond he slays Mîm the petty-dwarf, who had betrayed his son (banished from the dwarf-cities of the East in ancient days, the petty-dwarves were smaller than their kin and took to lives of stealth), and takes the Nauglamir back to Thingol in Doriath.

Tears and Irony

recurrent image in the Quenta Silmarillion is that of tears, or *Nirnaeth* in Sindarin, which recalls the medieval Welsh word *hiraeth* or "sad longing." Thus for example the Fifth Battle of Middle-earth, the Nirnaeth Arnoediad, "Unnumbered Tears, for no song or tale contain all its grief."[25] This last, desperate attempt by the Eldar to defeat Morgoth was led by Maedhros, son of Fëanor, who had been inspired by the tales of Beren and Lúthien. The forces of Maedhros were joined by those of Fingon and Turgon, as well as by countless men and dwarves. This great host was defeated before the gates of Angband by the fell beasts unleashed by Morgoth and by Easterlings, men who betrayed the sons of Fëanor. And yet strength and loyalty remained in two men, the brothers Huor and Húrin, who stood alone against the enemy so that Turgon could retreat to Gondolin.

Tolkien also employs the Anglo-Saxon device of ironic understatement in *The Silmarillion*, as in the same battle when Fingon faces the Lord of Balrogs: "That was a grim meeting."[26] Grim was the battle, for in it Fingon, High King of the Noldor falls, as does Huor and the dwarf king Azaghâl, and the sons of Fëanor are scattered. Húrin is captured and tortured by Morgoth, but still mocks the Dark Lord and will not betray to him the location of Gondolin. For this Morgoth curses Húrin and all his kin. Then only in the hidden kingdom of Gondolin lay the hope of elves and men.

Thingol summons the dwarves of Nogrod, in the Blue Mountains, into his caves to remake the necklace and set within it the Silmaril. But these dwarves lust after the jewel and murder Thingol while he is alone deep within his caves. Their kin then march to Doriath and kill many of the Sindar, including Mablung. On the way back to Nogrod, these dwarves are ambushed by Beren and his son Dior, who wrest the Nauglamir from the dwaves and bring it to Lúthien in Ossiriand. Dior goes to Doriath to claim the empty throne of his grandfather Thingol. After a time, one evening a messenger delivers a small chest to Dior. Opening it, he discovers the Nauglamir with the Silmaril, which he knows must have been sent to him by his parents Beren and Lúthien just before their deaths. When the sons of Fëanor hear that Dior now possesses the jewel and is rebuilding Doriath, they raise an army and storm the Thousand Caves. Dior slays Celegorm, Carufin, and Caranthir but is himself slain. The Silmaril is entrusted to Dior's daughter Elwing, who escapes the caves and flees to the sea.

the fall of gondolin

Of the great elven kingdoms of Middle-earth, Gondolin alone now stands, and Morgoth turns his hatred there. He captures Turgon's nephew Maeglin, who under threat of torture and promise of lordship, reveals the location of Gondolin. Morgoth sends a great army of balrogs, dragons, and orcs to attack the city. Turgon falls in the great battle, and amid the fire and destruction Tuor, son of Huor, flees with his wife Idril, daughter of Turgon, and their son Eärendil to the mouths of the River Sirion. There, "bright Eärendil" comes of age as ruler of the remnant of Gondolin, and takes as his wife Elwing, daughter of Dior. They have two sons, Elrond and Elros, the Half-elven. Eärendil becomes restless and decides to journey out to sea in search of Aman; while he is gone the sons of Fëanor come to the exiles of Gondolin and demand the Silmaril. They attack his people at the havens and carry off his sons. Elwing, in the likeness of a great white bird, bears the Silmaril away from the battle to Eärendil on his ship. With Elwing at his side, he sails west with the Silmaril on his brow, and at long last lands upon the shores of Aman, the first man to walk in the Blessed Realm. In Geoffrey of Monmouth's *Vita Merlini* (ca. 1150), the Welsh bard Taliesin—whose name means "Shining Brow"—sailed to the Isle of Avalon to petition the fairy-healers to allow him to bring King Arthur back to Britain.

> Eönwë, the herald of Manwë, addressed Eärendil at his landing, Hail Eärendil, of mariners most renowned, the looked for that cometh at unawares, the longed for that cometh beyond hope! Hail Eärendil, bearer of light before the Sun and Moon! Splendour of the Children of the Earth, star in the darkness, jewel in the sunset, radiant in the morning![27]

This is a clear echo of Tolkien's inspiration for the tale of Eärendil, Cynewulf's *Crist* (see page 176):

> Hail Earendel, of angels brightest,
> Over Middle-earth to men sent.

Standing before the Valar in Valinor, Eärendil begs pardon for the actions of the Noldor and seeks pity for elves and men, asking Manwë for help against the growing dark in Middle-earth. Manwë answers his prayers, and sets Eärendil and his ship in the heavens to sail across the sky, with the Silmaril shining on his brow, as the Star of Hope. The ships of the Teleri carry the hosts of the Vanyar and the Noldor of Finarfin to Middle-earth, and this army of the Valar meets that of Morgoth in the War of Wrath. The elves and the Edain defeat the balrogs and orcs of Morgoth, who stays hidden in his fortress but unleashes the first of the winged dragons to appear in Middle-earth. Eärendil and Thorondor, Lord of Eagles, destroy the dragons and the army of the Valar traps Morgoth in his deepest cavern, wresting the two Silmarils from him and throwing him once more in chains.

Eönwë takes possession of the Silmarils and orders the two remaining sons of Fëanor, Maedhros and Maglor, to return to Aman for judgment. But they refuse, and send word demanding that Eönwë give them the Silmarils forged by their father. Eönwë replies that because of their ruthlessness and evil deeds, the brothers have forfeited the ownership of the Silmarils, which instead would be sent into the West. Maedhros and Maglor do not heed this decree either; in disguise, they steal the Silmarils from Eönwë's camp and escape into the wild. The Silmarils, however, do not tolerate being carried by the brothers, and inflict unendurable pain on them. Unable to bear the torment, Maedhros throws himself into a chasm of fire, and likewise Maglor in despair leaps into the sea. Thus do the three Silmarils find their resting places: one in the heavens, one in the fires within the earth, one in the depths of the seas.

Afterward, many of the elves of Beleriand sail into the West to dwell upon the Lonely Isle, but others remain in Middle-earth. Chief among these are Círdan the Shipwright, Celeborn and Galadriel, and the High King of the Noldor, Gil-galad, son of Fingon. Elrond journeys to Lindon in the northwest with the household of Gil-galad, while Elros chooses to stay with the men of the West, and becomes their ruler. Morgoth is cast back into the Timeless Void, and Eärendil is charged to guard the ramparts of the sky against Morgoth's return.

númenor

The fourth section of *The Silmarillion* is called Akallabêth, and concerns mainly the adventures of men in the Second Age. At the end of the First Age, following the second defeat of Morgoth, the Valar summon the Eldar to return to the West.

" *[Those who come] dwelt in the Isle of Eressëa; and there is in that land a haven that is named Avallónë, for it is of all cities the nearest to Valinor, and the tower of Avallónë is the first sight that the mariner beholds when at last he draws nigh to the Undying Lands over the leagues of the Sea.* " [28]

—"Akallabêth," *The Silmarillion*

To reward the valor of the Edain in the wars against Morgoth, the Valar create a new island for them west of Middle-earth, and it is called Andor, "the Land of Gift." Across the Great Sea the Edain sail to Andor, guided by the Star of Eärendil, and on this new land they found the kingdom of Westernesse, Númenórë in the High Eldarin tongue. The Númenóreans (Dúnedain in Sindarin) are tall with bright eyes and given long life, though they are still mortal. They learn many crafts from Eönwë, under the kingship of Elros, the Númenóreans raise a temple to Ilúvatar on their highest mountain, around which eventually are built the tombs of their kings. They also become great mariners, and explore many lands. But they are forbidden by Manwë to sail to Valinor, lest they become enamored with the immortality of the Valar and the Eldar that can never be theirs.

They sail to Middle-earth, where they teach men there how to till the land, grind grain, shape stone and wood, and other hallmarks of civilization (see chart on pages 198–99). But many Númenóreans grow distrustful of the Valar and resent their ban. "Why do the Lords of the West sit there in peace unending," they began asking, "while we must die and go we know not whither, leaving our home and all that we have made?" [29] The messenger of Manwë informs the Númenórean king that even should they sail to Aman they would not gain eternal life, for it was not Ilúvatar's gift to men, and men should not envy the gifts given to others. The king is not satisfied with this answer, and he and others of the royal line become obsessed with extending their lives and cheating death. They spend much time pursing pleasure and revelry, and even preserve their dead through embalming and building lavish houses for them. They also begin establishing fortified harbors in Middle-earth, extracting tribute from those men to whom they had previously been teachers. Only a handful of Númenóreans, called the Faithful, secretly keep their friendship with the Eldar and devotion to the Valar.

Ancient History and *The Silmarillion*

The earliest history of Middle-earth as described in *The Silmarillion* offers striking parallels with biblical history and that of the ancient Mediterranean. It connects to the history of men given in the Appendices of *The Lord of the Rings*, which focuses on the very medieval Third Age.

The Silmarillion	The Bible and Ancient History
Ilúvatar creates the material universe—Eä ("Let it be" in Elvish)—out of the Void.	God creates the heavens and the earth; a dark, formless void until he utters the words "Let there be light." (Genesis 1:1–3)
The Children of Ilúvatar are created, with the deathless Quendi (elves) the first to awake. Unions between the Maiar (lesser spirits) and the elves, and the elves and men, engender heroes and heroines of great renown.	God creates humankind in his image—man (Adam) and woman (Eve)—and the Sons of God take wives from the daughters of Eve, who give birth to the Nephilim, "the heroes that were of old, warriors of renown." (Genesis 1:26, 6:1–4)
When men first come into the world, they fall quickly under the influence of Morgoth, for "they listened to his evil and cunning words."	The first man and the first woman are deceived by the cunning words of the serpent, thought to be Satan. (Genesis 3)
Men in the east dwell in darkness, wandering wild and lawless in unharvested lands, troubled by demons and dragons.	Many of the descendants of Adam wander with their flocks in the east, worshiping dark spirits and encountering giants and beasts. (Numbers 13:32–33)
Civilized men, the Númenóreans, found cities in the east, develop writing, and instruct other men in the sowing of seeds and the grinding of grain.	Civilization arise in the eastern Mediterranean, in Mesopotamia and Egypt, where the first cities are built and writing is invented. (ca. 3500–3000 BC)
The Númenóreans build great stone temples and elaborate tombs for kings like Ar-Pharazôn the Golden.	The Sumerians and the Egyptians build great stone temples and elaborate tombs for kings and gold-clad pharaohs.

The Númenóreans rebel against Ilúvatar, becoming tyrannical, performing atrocities (including human sacrifice) and are destroyed by a great flood.	The peoples east of Eden have tyrannical kings, perform atrocities (especially in Sodom and Gomorrah), and are destroyed by the Great Flood. (Genesis 6–8, 18–19)
Remnant Númenóreans establish the kingdoms of Arnor and Gondor in Middle-earth.	According to legend, refugees from Troy found kingdoms in the West.
Osgiliath and Minas Anor become great cities, full of learning and beautiful buildings.	Athens and Rome become great cities of learning, commerce, and culture.
Osgiliath is replaced by Minas Anor as the capital of the Númenóreans.	Rome replaces Greece as the great power in the Mediterranean.
Gondor establishes relations with some of their less-civilized northern neighbors, e.g., Rohan and Rhovanion.	Rome makes treaties with some of the northern barbarians, e.g., the Franks and the Visigoths.
The line of kings ends in Gondor; Minas Anor is renamed Minas Tirith.	The Roman Empire collapses in the West; the new capital in the East, Byzantium, is renamed Constantinople.
From the Dúnedain rangers of the North comes a leader, Aragorn, who will reestablish the line of kings in Gondor.	From the north come warrior kings (e.g., Theodoric, Clovis, Charlemagne, and Alfred) who establish the medieval kingdoms of the West.

At this time, Sauron emerges from hiding and seeks to become Lord of Middle-earth, building his great Tower of Barad-dûr and forging the One Ring. A lord named Pharazôn seizes the throne of Númenór unlawfully by marrying his cousin Tar-Míriel, the true heir of Elros, and calls himself Ar-Pharazôn the Golden. He amasses a great armada and sails to Middle-earth to challenge Sauron for its lordship. Rather than fighting, Sauron comes and humbles himself before Ar-Pharazôn, pledging to be his vassal. The king takes Sauron as hostage back to Númenór, and there Sauron starts to work his lies. He tells Ar-Pharazôn that there is no Ilúvatar—it is just a lie of the Valar—and that the greatest of all powers was the Dark Lord Melkor. Ar-Pharazôn then begins to worship Melkor, and erects a great temple where Sauron burns the White Tree and performs human sacrifices. One fruit alone from the White Tree is saved by Isildur, son of Elendil of the Faithful.

The corruption of Ar-Pharazôn by Sauron parallels the earlier deceit of Fëanor by Morgoth, and the fate of the Faithful resembles the story of the Israelites fleeing the pharaoh in Exodus.

When Ar-Pharazôn sees death approaching him in his old age, he seeks counsel from Sauron, who convinces him to break the ban and sail west, to demand a share of immortality from the Valar. Amid terrible lightening and storms, Ar-Pharazôn's armada sets sail, and the king himself walks onto the shores of Aman and claims the Blessed Land for his own. At that, the Valar renounce their rule of Arda, while Ilúvatar unleashes his wrath upon the Númenóreans, swallowing up their fleet in a chasm beneath the sea and collapsing the mountains of Aman on top of Ar-Pharazôn and his encampment. The whole island of Andor is sunk beneath a great wave, and the ships of Elendil alone are saved from the destruction of Númenór. Like Noah and his sons, Elendil is carried on the flood for many days before his ships are cast upon the shores of Middle-earth.[30] Sauron's body is destroyed in the catastrophe, but he returns as a dark spirit to Middle-earth and once again takes up his abode in Mordor.

French artist Gustave Doré's Bible illustration from 1866, of Genesis 7:4: "I will cause it to rain upon the earth forty days and forty nights; and every living substance that I have made will I destroy from off the face of the earth." Similarly, the Númenórean kingdom was destroyed in a great flood after they rebelled against Ilúvatar.

The myth of Atlantis can be seen in the fall of Númenór; indeed, this entire part of *The Silmarillion* was called by Tolkien "Akallabêth," "the Downfallen," or "Atalantë" in the Eldarin tongue. So too can be glimpsed parts of the Arthurian myth of Avalon—the paradisiacal island hidden in the mists where King Arthur is taken after his last battle to be healed of his wounds and where he still lives, according to the medieval Britons. The Númenóreans can, on the clearest days, see far to the West the shining Elvish haven of Avallónë on the island of Eressëa. And even after their fall, the Dúnedain survivors in Middle-earth looked often with hope to the West: "Avallónë is vanished from the Earth and the Land of Aman is taken away. . . . Yet once they were, and therefore they still are, in true being and in the whole shape of the world as at first it was devised."[31]

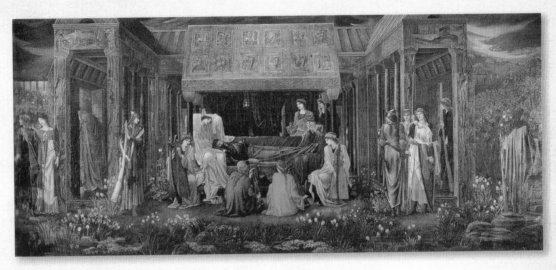

The monumental painting The Last Sleep of Arthur in Avalon *(1881–98),*
by Edward Burne-Jones, now in the Museo de Arte de Ponce, Puerto Rico.

The Rings of Power

In the final section of *The Silmarillion*, Tolkien retells the history of the
Rings of Power, including the events of *The Lord of the Rings*, in the context and style of the greater legendarium. After the defeat of Morgoth,
Sauron makes obeisance to Eönwë, who bids him to go to Manwë for
judgment. Not willing to receive what will likely be harsh sentencing,
Sauron instead hides in Middle-earth until Eönwë departs, and then
appears to the elves in the fair guise of Annatar, the Lord of Gifts. He
teaches the Noldor many things; they become skilled craftsmen, and
create the Rings of Power under his guidance. But Sauron forges the
One Ring in the fires of Mount Doom in order to watch and control the wearers of the other rings. When Sauron puts on the One
Ring, the elves became aware of his intentions and flee with the three
greatest rings—Narya, Nenya, and Vilya—crafted by Celebrimbor, son
of Curufin. While at war with the elves, Sauron gives out the rest of his
rings—seven to the dwarf lords, nine to the kings of men—in order to
bring under his control the rest of the children of Middle-earth.

After the destruction of Númenór, the survivors, members of the
Faithful, make their way to Middle-earth in three ships. Elendil lands on
the western shore, in Lindon, where he is befriended by the High King
Gil-galad; he then establishes the northern realm of Arnor. His sons

Isildur and Anárion land to the south and found the realm of Gondor. In Gondor they build a great city, Osgiliath, the fortresses Minas Anor (later renamed Minas Tirith) and Minas Ithil (later Minas Morgul). They also construct the unbreakable Orthanc tower in the iron fortress of Isengard, and the colossal statues called the Argonath. Isildur plants the White Tree at Minas Ithil, and the seven Seeing Stones (the Palantíri) rescued from Númenór are distributed throughout their lands as a means of communication and defense. Undaunted, Sauron gathers his servants and attacked Minas Ithil, taking the fortress while Isildur escapes to the lands of his father. Elendil and Gil-galad then form the Last Alliance between men and elves and march to meet Sauron at the plain of Dagorlad, northwest of Mordor. Together with the dwarves of Moria they defeat Sauron's army and lay siege to his fortress for seven years. At last Sauron emerges and slays Elendil and Gil-galad in battle, but Isildur cuts the One Ring from his hand and Sauron's spirit flees into shadow to hide for many ages. This is the beginning of the Third Age, the period covered in *The Lord of the Rings*.

Though Elrond and Círdan counsel Isildur to throw the Ring into the fires of Mount Doom and put an end to Sauron's power, Isuldur refuses. "This I will have as a *wergild* for my father's death, and my brother's."[32] The medieval *wergild* was utilized to put an end to constant feuding and to bring social stability; here, however, it leads to the survival of Sauron and the death of Isildur, who is smote by orc arrows in the Great River, where the Ring falls from his finger to the bottom of the river bed. In the remaining brief pages that retell the War of the Ring, there are a few notable variances from *The Lord of the Rings*. Gollum, for example, is not mentioned by name in *The Silmarillion*, and it is said that Frodo *threw* the Ring into Mount Doom. Apart from the members of the White Council, only Frodo and Aragorn are named as heroes of the war. Lastly, Mithrandir (Gandalf) is given most of the credit for the defeat of Sauron and the restoration of Gondor.

THE FIRST WORDS OF THE VALAQUENTA are "In the beginning." These are, of course, also the first words of the Book of Genesis.[33] *The Silmarillion* is not just biblical in its language; genealogical history abounds and nearly all of its major themes are Judeo-Christian. Its earliest parts resemble the creation accounts of ancient peoples including the Hebrews, the Greeks, and the Romans, and the interference of the Valar in the affairs of elves and men will recall for many the writings of Homer and Virgil. Rhona Beare argues that in *The Silmarillion*, Tolkien was trying to subject the wild myths of the Celtic and Germanic North to the clear restraint of the Greco-Roman epic form.[34] The mild climate of England serves then as a middle ground between misty, rainy Ireland and hot, dry Greece, and thus did he want to make his legendarium more "redolent of our 'air.'"[35]

But like *The Hobbit* and *The Lord of the Rings*, *The Silmarillion* derives much of its color and majesty from medieval material. Tolkien told Milton Waldman that he wanted to capture "the fair elusive beauty" of the Celtic, but it also needed to be "high."[36] By "high" I believe that Tolkien meant "of higher purpose," such as that attempted by the writers of medieval hagiography and romance. Like the heraldic banners of the Noldor and the Númenóreans fluttering above the battlefields of Middle-earth, the imagery of *The Silmarillion* brings us back to the Age of Chivalry, when wizards—not to mention kings and priests—could "move Elves and Men and all living things of good will to valiant deeds."[37]

This image from the fifth-century illuminated manuscript of the works of Virgil known as the Vergilius Romanus, *shows a scene from the* Aeneid, *where the Trojan hero Aeneas and Dido, Queen of Carthage, seek refuge from a storm in cave. Some scholars see Greco-Roman mythical epics such as the* Aeneid *and the* Iliad *as structural inspiration for Tolkien in* The Silmarillion.

The Children of Húrin

WHEN IN 1937 J. R. R. TOLKIEN shared the "Quenta Silmarillion" and the poem "The Gest of Beren and Lúthien" with Allen & Unwin, Stanley Unwin respectfully suggested that parts of the material were like jewels that should be mined to produce short adventures. Tolkien had in fact already combined previously separate tales in the "Quenta Silmarillion," and continued to work on these separately for decades. A case in point is *The Children of Húrin*. As discussed in chapter two, Tolkien had become obsessed with the Finnish epic *The Kalevala* during his first years as a student at Oxford (see pages 84–86). He tried his hand at a modern retelling (à la William Morris) of "The Story of Kullervo" from the *Kalevala*, a tale of an orphan and fugitive who unwittingly seduces his own sister, leading to her suicide as well as his own. Garth has suggested that Tolkien's separation from Edith at this time drew him to this dark and strange story.[38] In any case, Tolkien "softened" the story and depicted a more sympathetic Kullervo, but the project was soon abandoned.

Instead of the prose rewrite, Tolkien chose to incorporate elements of the story of Kullervo into an original Middle-earth tale. *The Children of Húrin* began life in the early 1920s as a poem, originally titled "Túrin son of Húrin and Glórund the Dragon." Alliterative and in Old English meter, the poem had reached over two thousand lines before Tolkien abandoned it at the point of the dragon's attack on Nargothrond. A second attempt was even longer and was abandoned at the same point in the narrative. Prose summaries of the adventures were included in the various versions of what would become *The Silmarillion*. After he finished *The Lord of the Rings*, Tolkien spent a great deal of effort composing a detailed narrative of the deeds of Túrin in prose. Christopher Tolkien sewed together a continuous prose narrative from these various threads and published it as *The Children of Húrin* in 2007. It is a dark, complex, and at times thrilling novel, with the mythological sweep of *The Silmarillion* and the depth of character achieved in *The Lord of the Rings*.

húrin

The novel begins with the foundation of the House of Húrin. Húrin's grandfather, Hador Goldenhead, a lord of the Edain loved by the elves, is given lands in Hithlum by the elf-king Fingolfin. Hithlum, translated from Sindarin as "Land of Mists,"[39] also contains the Anglo-Saxon element *hyð*, "landing-place or harbor," and indeed a great firth pierces Hithlum's southwestern border. Hador's son Galdor in turn had two sons, Húrin and Huor. Húrin was short of stature but strong and hardy, while Huor was tall and swift. Húrin married Morwen of the House of Bëor, a stern and proud woman of dark beauty. Morwen bore Húrin a son, Túrin, and a daughter, Urwen, but she was called affectionately Lalaith, "Laughter," by those who knew her. Laughter died early in the House of Húrin. Huor was slain in the Nirnaeth Arnoediad (see page 194), just two months after he wed Rían; Túrin and Morwen were driven out of Hithlum; and Húrin was captured and tortured by Morgoth. For defying the Dark Lord, Húrin was made to watch all of the tragedies that befell his House from a high place on Thangorodrim.

> *"Huor fell pierced with a venomed arrow in the eye, and all the valiant men of Hador were slain about him in a heaps and the Orcs hewed their heads and piled them as a mound of gold in the sunset."* [40]

—Chapter II, "The Battle of Unnumbered Tears," *The Children of Húrin*

This panel of the Bayeux Tapestry depicts the death of King Harold Godwinson at the Battle of Hastings, which was similar to the death scene of Huor in The Children of Húrin. *An arrow pierced the eye of Harold, and his loyal body of huscarls fought around him in a circle until they were all slain.*

Pride and fate are the dominant themes of the novel. Tolkien gives us a glimpse of his theory of fate or doom early on in *The Children of Húrin*. The first extensive dialogue in the book, following a long section of narrative that is very similar to that of *The Silmarillion*, is a conversation between Túrin and his lame mentor Sador, which takes place after the untimely death of Lalaith:

"Was Lalaith indeed like an Elf-child, as my father said? And what did he mean, when he said that she was briefer?"

"Very like," said Sador, "for in their first youth the children of Men and Elves seem close akin. But the children of Men grow more swiftly, and their youth passes soon; such is our fate."

Then Túrin asked him: "What is fate?"

"As to the fate of Men," said Sador, "you must ask those that are wiser. . . . But as all can see, we weary soon and die; and by mischance many meet death even sooner. But the Elves do not weary, and they do not die save by great hurt. . . . "

" . . . I wish, Labadal, that I were one of the Eldar. Then Lalaith might come back, and I should still be here, even if she were long away. . . . "

" . . . They are a fair folk and wonderful, and they have a power over the hearts of Men. And yet I think sometimes that it might have been better if we had never met them, but had walked in lowlier ways. For already they are ancient in knowledge; and they are proud and enduring. In their light we are dimmed, or we burn with too quick a flame, and the weight of our doom lies the heavier on us."[41]

We, the reader, are the young and grieving child with the existential questions; Tolkien is the lame old teacher, with a sense of the great wonders that lie beyond, but never claiming to know all the answers. Tolkien also is like the child who has seen the elves—Sador later calls them the Fair Folk (medieval Welsh *tylwyth teg*)—and longs to be reunited with them, with their undying beauty and ancient wisdom. But the exposure to Faery makes our grief all the greater, for it is our doom to be possessed—enchanted—by a longing that, as C. S. Lewis writes, can never be satisfied in this world.

Pride is the peculiar characteristic of the House of Húrin. Húrin was so proud that he could mock Morgoth to his face, as recounted in *The Silmarillion* (see page 194), and his wife Morwen is called the proudest of all women. Túrin is consumed with pride and personal honor, like the solitary hero of pagan Northern myth. "You think of yourself and your own glory," the elf Gwindor tells him, "but we must think of others beside ourselves, for not all can fight and fall."[42] Pride rules Túrin's heart and causes him often to give ill counsel. Like Odysseus with the Cyclops, he can't stop himself from taunting his enemy, and in the end with the dragon Glaurung (see page 211), this hubris leads to the suicide of Níniel as well as his own. Similar to the Greek concept of hubris is Old English *ofermod*, "overmastering pride," which Tolkien discussed at length in the afterword of his *The Homecoming of Beorhtnoth Beorhthelm's Son* (1953; see page 64). Like Beorhtnoth in *The Battle of Maldon*, Túrin (and his mother and father) are often "too proud, too princely,"[43] leading to bad decisions that place personal honor before family and community. Yet we, the reader, mourn rather than scorn their actions. "Magnificent perhaps, but certainly wrong," as Tolkien writes of Beorhtnoth, ". . . a noble error, or the error of a noble."[44]

Túrin in the Wild

After the imprisonment of Húrin, evil men called Easterlings invade Dor-lómin and threaten Morwen's household. Fearing for the safety of Túrin, she sends him away to seek asylum in Doriath with King Thingol, where the young man is well received in honor of his father. This part of the novel closely follows the plot of *The Odyssey*, in which the household of Odysseus is harassed by the suitors of Penelope in her husband's absence, while her son Telemachus goes to seek aid from his father's friends on the Greek mainland. Like Telemachus, Túrin comes of age in his exile, and indeed becomes a mighty warrior among the Sindar. Armed with sword and dragon-helm, Túrin becomes a renowned march-warden (i.e., guardian of the border), fighting and wandering the wilderness alongside his friend Beleg Strongbow. Beleg's epithet "Strongbow" was borne famously by Richard fitz Gilbert de Clare, 2nd Earl of Pembroke, the Norman baron whose victories in Ireland in 1170 led directly to Henry II's invasion of that island a year later and hence to England's subjugation of the Irish.

Túrin grows in strength and pride but not in wisdom. Saeros, Thingol's haughty counselor, taunts the unkempt Túrin and provokes and attacks him, leading to a humiliating chase and Saeros's accidental death. His name recalls the Anglo-Saxon word *searo*, which can mean skill and cleverness but also cunning and treachery.[45] "His words were cunning," writes Tolkien of Saeros.[46] Saeros calls Túrin "Woodwose," the Middle English name for a wild man of the wood (see page 50). Mablung the Hunter beseeches Túrin to go before King Thingol and trust in his judgment, warning Túrin not to become a "runagate," the Middle English version of "renegade."

Mablung's advice is not heeded, however, for Túrin decides to go into exile rather than ask the pardon of Thingol for a crime he did not commit. Tolkien here explores the life of the outlaw, and, perhaps, postmodern nihilism. Túrin is confronted with the worldview of the criminal when he leaves Doriath and lives in the Wild among the Gaurwaith ("wolf-men"), whose ethos (or lack thereof) is most often expressed by one of their company named Andróg. "Fool!" he yells at Túrin. "You call yourself an outlaw. Outlaws know no law but their needs. Look to your own . . . and leave us to mind ours."[47]

For a while Túrin lives by this code, but Andróg's mistreatment of his old friend Beleg snaps him out of his nihilism:

> "You were cruel . . . without need. Never until now have we tormented a prisoner; but to this Orc-work such a life as we lead has brought us. Lawless all our deeds have been, serving only ourselves, and feeding hate in our hearts."
>
> But Andróg said: "But whom shall we serve, if not ourselves? . . ."
>
> "At least my hands shall not again be raised against Elves or Men," said Túrin. "Angband has servants enough. If others will not take this vow with me, I will walk alone."
>
> Then Beleg opened his eyes and raised his head. "Not alone!"[48]

Beleg and Túrin understand the power of fellowship to blow away the black cloud of nihilism, as did both Tolkien and Lewis (learned in the trenches of the Great War). Túrin joined the outlaws at first simply not to be alone in the wood, but found that it was not enough to just "hang with the crowd." Only true friendship, one of noble purpose, can save a lost soul like Túrin—although in this story, it only saves him for a while.

If the Easterlings and the outlaws represent the darker tendencies in man, then Mîm the petty-dwarf serves the same purpose for his race. His treachery at Amon Rûdh, when he betrays Túrin and Beleg to the orcs, escalates the pathos and tragedy surrounding Túrin, who escapes the orcs only to end up slaying his friend Beleg, albeit unwittingly, with Beleg's black sword, Anglachel. This cursed sword becomes both companion to Túrin and an outward symbol of its new master's character and doom. When he comes into the elven stronghold of Nargothrond, Túrin loses his identity and takes on that of his sword, being called by the elves there Mormegil, the "Black Sword." It is a common trope of chivalric romance to cast the villain as the Black Knight, with armor to match the soul, but it is also used occasionally as a disguise by good knights. Tolkien would have known examples of both through a reading of Malory alone.

Malory may also have provided some inspiration for the madness of both Túrin and his sister Niënor. The madness of Niënor, who runs naked, weeping, through the forest of Brethil, recalls an episode in *Le Morte D'Arthur* when Guinevere chastises Lancelot for his infidelity:

> When [Guenever] heard him so clatter she was nigh wood [i.e., mad] and out of her mind, and for anger and pain wist not what to do. And then she coughed so loud that Sir Launcelot awaked, and he knew her hemming. And then he knew well that he lay not by the queen; and therewith he leapt out of his bed as he had been a wood man, in his shirt, and the queen met him in the floor; and thus she said: False traitor knight that thou art, look thou never abide in my court, and avoid my chamber, and not so hardy, thou false traitor knight that thou art, that ever thou come in my sight. Alas, said Sir Launcelot; and therewith he took such an heartly sorrow at her words that he fell down to the floor in a swoon. And therewithal Queen Guenever departed. And when Sir Launcelot awoke of his swoon, he leapt out at a bay window into a garden, and there with thorns he was all to-scratched in his visage and his body; and so he ran forth he wist not whither, and was wild wood as ever was man; and so he ran two year, and never man might have grace to know him.[49]

Like Lancelot adopting a new name after his experience of being scratched and scarred—*le Chevalier Mal Fet* ("the Ill-Made Knight")—Niënor is given the new name Níniel, "Maid of Tears." Both of these new names serve to hide the true identity of their bearers. Also like Malory's description of Lancelot above, Túrin's recurring madness is described

An illustration of the Black Knight of Arthurian legend by H. J. Ford from
The Book of Romance *(1902), edited by Andrew Lang.*

by Tolkien in alliterative prose: "Then Túrin went as one witless through the wild woods."[50]

The instrument of Túrin's destruction is Glaurung—the Worm of Morgoth—the colossal serpent and father of the race of dragons in Middle-earth. Tolkien, as he demonstrated in *The Hobbit*, was attracted to the tradition of the magic dragon—that is, a terrifying beast who also has the ability to mesmerize its victims through its gaze alone. Glaurung tortures his victim (Túrin) just as the dragon's master Morgoth tortures his victim (Húrin) at the beginning of the novel: by hiding or revealing knowledge of dark deeds, inflicting the poison of despair. Though Túrin can destroy Glaurung through cunning and strength, he cannot, like Sigurd, destroy the curse laid down by Morgoth on Húrin and all his kin. "For see, I am blind!" he tells Mablung after Níniel has thrown herself into the river. "Blind, blind, groping since childhood in a dark mist of Morgoth!"[51] Túrin then takes his own life, by the black sword. "Then they lifted up Túrin," writes Tolkien, "and saw that his sword was broken asunder. So passed all that he possessed."[52]

This dark novel closes not with two suicides, but rather with the sad reunion of Húrin and Morwen at the grave of their son. This scene, which appears in a longer form in *The Silmarillion*, is abbreviated here to provide one brief moment of light and tenderness. Húrin, who had been long imprisoned and separated from Morwen, recognizes his wife and embraces her before she collapses in despair and her last breath is spent.

THERE IS MUCH OF SUBSTANCE in the *The Children of Húrin*, not the least of which are original illustrations by Alan Lee. Tolkien even sneaks an environmental message into the novel. "And we do not teach Men to find them," says Mîm the dwarf of the earth-bread plants (an edible bread-like root), "for Men are greedy and thriftless, and would not spare till all the plants had perished."[53] Given the negative reception and widespread ignoring of *The Silmarillion*, as time goes by it will be interesting to see if readers and critics alike will appreciate the sustained plot and complex characters of this tale plucked from the legendarium. Túrin is unlike any other Tolkien protagonist. He is brave and valorous, but he is also prideful, melancholic, disillusioned, and ultimately a prisoner of a dark fate.

Time and Death in Tolkien's Legendarium

In *The Silmarillion*, Ilúvatar has dictated varying dooms to his children. To the Valar, the Ainur who went to Arda (Earth), immortality was granted as well as to Arda itself. The Quendi (elves) "die not till the world dies, . . . neither does age subdue their strength," "and dying they are gathered to the halls of Mandos in Valinor."[54] But the Atani (men) "die indeed, and leave the world." Yet Ilúvatar "willed that the hearts of Men should seek beyond the world and should find no rest therein."[55] This explains the rebellion of the Númenóreans against the Valar at the beginning of the "Akallabêth:

> Why should we not envy the Valar, or even the least of the Deathless? For
> of us is required a blind trust, and a hope without assurance, knowing not
> what lies before us in a little while. And yet we also love the Earth and would
> not lose it.[56]

Even the Númenóreans, the greatest of men, lack faith. Here Tolkien makes us confront our human obsession with time and mortality, our desire to live forever, and yet be bound to a world that is ever changing. As he describes it in a letter of 1956, it is "the mystery of the Love of the world in the hearts of a race 'doomed' to leave and seemingly lose it."[57] In *Mere Christianity*, C. S. Lewis argues that our constant surprise with the passage of time means that we were not made for this world but rather for a place where time does not exist. In *The Silmarillion*, Tolkien also appears to be suggesting this, though he states that Ilúvatar has not yet revealed the ultimate fate of Men, not even to the Valar. "Many ages of Men unborn may pass ere that purpose is made known; and to you [Men] it will be revealed and not the Valar."[58]

Several characters in *The Lord of the Rings* also seem to be obsessed with time. When Gandalf reports on the return of Sauron to Mordor, Frodo remarks, "I wish it need not have happened in my time." "So do I," replies Gandalf, "and so do all who live to see such times. But that is not for them to decide. All we have to do is to decide what to do with the time that is given us."[59]

Though in part Tolkien is drawing upon both classical and Northern tragic heroes—particularly Beorhtnoth—Túrin is also more like the character of a modern novel or movie. He is, at many points in the story, mad, or as we would say of a contemporary figure, "mentally unstable." There is no eucatastrophe in this book, no "fairy-tale ending," just a spiral of exile, imprisonment, and tragic death. The

Lewis and Tolkien both understood the medieval view of time as linear *devolution*. Like the ancients, medieval man believed in a Golden Age in the past followed by a steady decline, in Christian terms a growing corruption of the world leading to the Apocalypse and the Second Coming. In Middle-earth, men learned from elves "in the days when all the world was wonderful."[60] While Valar dominate the First Age, the greatest elf-lords the Second Age, and an alliance of the races mark the Third Age, the Fourth Age is the time of men and the disappearance of elves, dwarves, and hobbits. Not only do men now struggle to see elves and hobbits, they doubt even the existence of the Valar and Ilúvatar and have all but forgotten myth. This, Tolkien believed (under the influence of his fellow Inkling Owen Barfield), is reflected in the ways in which we have changed language from the literal to the metaphoric. "Man in his beginnings had a vision of the cosmos as a whole, and of himself as a part of it," explains Verlyn Flieger. "We now perceive the cosmos as particularized, fragmented, and wholly separate from ourselves."[61]

One illustration of this point in *The Lord of the Rings* is when Elrond, Celeborn, and Galadriel sit together at night in Eregion during their last journey together to Rivendell:

> If any wanderer had chance to pass, little would he have seen or heard, and it would have seemed to him only that he saw grey figures, carved in stone, memorials of forgotten things now lost in unpeopled lands. For they did not move or speak with mouth, looking from mind to mind; and only their shining eyes stirred and kindled as their thoughts went to and fro.[62]

Modern man is like this wanderer. Of past glories and immortal beauties we see only memorials of forgotten things carved in stone. Most people would not even stop to look let alone engage with the past. And yet we still feel uneasy about the passage of time. This is our doom.

dragon is ultimately slain, but his stain cannot be so easily washed away by either man or elf. One who looks for hope must find it in *The Silmarillion*, where a descendant of Hador named Eärendil helps bring about the defeat of Morgoth and his army of dragons. For Húrin has spent too much time with Morgoth, and Túrin with Glaurung, not to have been tainted by their malice.

Tolkien created a world, and called it Middle-earth. What is Middle-earth? It is more than the Shire; it is more than Doriath. *This* is Middle-earth, it is all around you, whether you live in the English countryside or in a town or country far from the island of Britain. For Middle-earth is, technically, Midgard—the place between Heaven and Hell, where men rule beneath the gods and above the malevolent creatures. It is the world of men, though not exclusively, for, like Sam, we *think* we have seen an elf, we *have* heard stories about dragons and dwarves. We know the world to be numinous, even if we have given scientific names to phenomena once attributed to Fäerie. We know that ancient myths and medieval romances provide us with truths science cannot touch. There are more things in heaven and earth.

Tolkien, like C. S. Lewis, detested "chronological snobbery," the now-common belief that old things are almost always inferior to new, that the present has little to learn from the past. More than once does Tolkien come to the defense of history. "That is a chapter of ancient history which might be good to recall," says Gandalf of the first war against Sauron, "for there was sorrow then too, and gathering dark, but great valour, and great deeds that were not wholly vain."[63] Tolkien was never interested in history as a discipline, as an academic artifact. Historical periods were only interesting to him if they remained alive and relevant. "It is an historical document," he wrote sarcastically of *Beowulf* as seen by modern critics. "Only as such does it interest the superior culture of today."[64]

One fascinating aspect of Tolkien is that, despite his technical/scientific brilliance in philology, he was also an artist. In his short story *Leaf by Niggle* (1945), Tolkien writes a very personal allegory, his own *Portrait of an Artist*, in which the two characters Niggle and Parish are likely the two sides of Tolkien himself. The first, an artist, is a loner, cranky, obsessive, a procrastinator, a perfectionist; the second, a simple English gardener, is married with mundane responsibilities. The story concludes with a reconciliation between these two characters, a reconciliation Tolkien hoped to bring about within his own life.

Reconciling the creative artist, with the demands of publishers and fans, and the teacher/scholar, with *its* demands from colleagues and students, would not have been a simple task. For Tolkien not only created things, but he thought like an artist and he responded the way an artist does to other art, more so than the way a scholar responds when he is merely studying art. Tolkien puts it this way: "[My] typical response upon reading a medieval work was to desire not so much to make a philological or critical study of it as to write a modern work in the same tradition."[65]

We are thankful that he did just that. *The Hobbit*, *The Lord of the Rings*, and indeed most of Tolkien's fiction are modern works in the medieval tradition, books and poems imbued with the peculiar virtues of the heroic verse, chivalric romance, stylized art, and Christian/pagan virtues of northern Europe in the Middle Ages. The modern world had not so much extinguished the medieval as it did create new vehicles—novels, films, the Internet—through which ancient and medieval ideas could be expressed. The enormous popularity of Tolkien's books and Jackson's films would suggest, indeed, that the virtues of Middle-earth are still very much part of our cultural conversation.

appendices

appendix 1

monsters and critics

TOLKIEN ESTABLISHED HIS ACADEMIC reputation and legacy with the article "*Beowulf*: The Monster and the Critics" (see pages 16–18). Monster and critic must have been difficult to separate in the mind of Professor Tolkien following the release of *The Lord of the Rings*. "Some who have read the book, or at any rate have reviewed it," he wrote in the preface to the second edition, "have found it boring, absurd, or contemptible; and I have no cause to complain, since I have similar opinions of their works, or of the kind of writing that they evidently prefer."[1] Or, more poetically, as Tolkien wrote:

> *The Lord of the Rings*
> is one of those things:
> if you like it you do,
> if you don't, then you boo![2]

While Tolkien and his early critics may have been worlds apart in their literary tastes, the ever-expanding readership of *The Hobbit* and *The Lord of the Rings* has caused many critics—including academics—to reexamine the literary merit of Tolkien's fiction. No longer do you find serious writers automatically dismissing the corpus as juvenile and escapist fantasy. Indeed, as the twentieth century came to a close, even onetime skeptics had to ask if there was something to Tolkien being named in so many polls as "The Author of the Century."

Tolkien promised not to allow critical praise to puff him up with vanity like Mr. Toad in *The Wind in the Willows* (though their driving abilities might be comparable)—a work that Tolkien admired. No, Tolkien was a far more practical man than Toadie. He once compared his work to that of Edmund Spenser and Thomas Malory, and Italian Renaissance poet Ludovico Ariosto, simply to get better rooms from the Warden at

Merton College.[3] A man of hobbit-like tastes, Tolkien lived in a modest suburban home long after he had the financial means to do otherwise. Perhaps he remembered Gandalf's warning to Bilbo at the end of *The Hobbit*: "You are a very fine person, Mr. Baggins, . . . but you are only quite a little fellow in a wide world after all!"[4]

The Hobbit and Children's Literature

APART FROM COMMENTS ON his early poetry by his friends in the T.C.B.S. and the Inklings, the first real literary criticism Tolkien received came after the release of *The Hobbit* in 1937. Newspaper and magazine reviews were generally positive, comparing Tolkien's achievement to that of Lewis Carroll and George MacDonald (see, for example, C. S. Lewis's comments on pages 220–23).[5] Anne Carroll Moore, the pioneering children's books librarian at the New York Public Library, placed *The Hobbit*

> in the true tradition of the old sagas. I think it is a mistake to compare *The Hobbit* with *Alice* or with *The Wind in the Willows*. It is unlike either book. It is firmly rooted in *Beowulf* and authentic Saxon lore. . . . There is sound learning behind *The Hobbit*, while a rich vein of humor connects this little being . . . with the strange beings of the ancient world and the world we live in today.[6]

The Hobbit received recognition by winning major children's book awards in both Britain and America, and Tolkien's work soon appeared in syllabi and surveys of important juvenile fiction.[7]

Academic criticism, in contrast, was restrained. Indeed, not much attention was given to *The Hobbit* by academic critics until after the appearance of *The Lord of the Rings*, and almost no discussion of the former could thenceforth be done without reference to the latter. The historian and critic Edmund Fuller, for example, sees *The Hobbit* and *The Lord of the Rings* as a four-part epic, comparable to Wagner's *Ring* cycle, with both *The Hobbit* and *Das Rheingold* acting as the "shorter, relatively childlike wonder tale" introducing a more substantive trilogy.[8] The comparisons continued from Tolkien scholars and English professors on both sides of the Atlantic: Michael N. Stanton believes that *The Hobbit* is marred by "condescension and preciosity" and has one-dimensional characters,

Previous pages:
The road goes on and on . . . a ca. 1900 photochrom of the town of Malvern, in Worcestershire, in the West Midlands, England.

flaws "corrected" in *The Lord of the Rings*.[9] Charles Moseley points out "clumsy and contrived" and clichéd passages early in the book, while admitting that it gets better, as if Tolkien were "learning on the job."[10] Brian Rosebury calls *The Hobbit* "a likeable patchwork of accomplishments, blunders, and tantalizing promises of the Middle-earth to come: flawed by inconsistencies of tone and conception."[11]

Other critics have delved into *The Hobbit*'s hidden treasures. Bonniejean Christensen argues that it is a work that "examines the nature of evil and the limits of man's response to it, a fact often overlooked because the tone of *The Hobbit* identifies it as a fantasy belonging in the nursery."[12] Paul Kocher calls *The Hobbit* "a misunderstood work," full of many effective techniques in storytelling for children (such as sound effects), which also pokes fun at adult conventions.[13] The intrusive narrator, for example, would be taken at face value by children but interpreted as parody by more sophisticated readers. Similarly, Jane Chance proposes that Tolkien's intrusive and patronizing narrator is intended as parody.[14] "*The Hobbit* is seldom far from comedy," concluded Kocher.

Tolkien gives an extensive explanation of his own views on children and children's literature in a letter he wrote to his Aunt Jane Neave (then aged ninety, and demanding more Tom Bombadil) in 1961:

> I am not interested in the "child" as such, modern or otherwise, and certainly have no intention of meeting him/ her halfway, or a quarter of the way . . . [and] I have only once made the mistake of doing it, to my lasting regret . . . in the early part of *The Hobbit*. But I had not then given any serious thought to the matter. . . . Certainly I am 'childish' enough, and that ought to be enough for real children or any one "childish" in the same sort of way, and never mind if the old chap knows a lot of jolly words.[15]

C. S. Lewis as Tolkien Critic

ONE READER WHO CERTAINLY UNDERSTOOD Tolkien's peculiar brand of "childishness" was his friend, colleague, and fellow myth-poet C. S. Lewis. "We feel it to be numinous," says Lewis of myth. "It is as if something of great moment has been communicated to us."[16] This unabashed belief in "the numinous" and "great moment" is precisely what sets Lewis—and Tolkien—apart from most modern literary critics. In *Surprised by Joy* (1955), Lewis writes that it was his Christian friends that he made in Oxford in the 1920s—especially Owen Barfield, Hugo Dyson, and Tolkien—who helped him get over the hurdles necessary to accept first theism and then Christianity. According to Lewis, they also broke down what he called the "chronological snobbery" of his age, "the uncritical acceptance of the intellectual climate common to our own age and the assumption that whatever has gone out of date is on that account discredited."[17] It is this shared belief, even more than their friendship, that makes Lewis an exceptional Tolkien critic.

Tolkien began sharing his writing with Lewis in 1929, starting with the poem that would become "The Lay of Leithian" (see page 193)[18] Lewis's enthusiasm for the poem, as much as his creative and affectionate criticism of certain lines, had a remarkable effect on Tolkien. At last he had found a kindred soul, a lover of Northern myth capable of the kind of verbal sparring that the T.C.B.S. had reveled in. Lewis would describe the benefits of this close friendship in his book *The Four Loves* (1960). According to Humphrey Carpenter, Tolkien was sometimes hurt by Lewis's tougher criticism, especially of the poems in *The Lord of the Rings*.[19] But these criticisms were actually less harsh than Tolkien's own expressions of dislike for *The Screwtape Letters* (1942), which Lewis dedicated to Tolkien, and for the Narnia books.

Lewis nonetheless expressed great admiration for both *The Hobbit* and *The Lord of the Rings*. His reviews of the *The Hobbit* appeared, anonymously, in the *Times Literary Supplement*, on October 2, 1937, and six days later in the *Times* proper. Comparing the work to *Alice's Adventures in Wonderland*, George MacDonald's *Phantastes*, and *The Wind in the Willows*, Lewis remarked on the sense of depth and believability in *The Hobbit*, and Tolkien's "happy fusion of the scholar's with the poet's grasp of mythology." Using the opportunity to both praise Tolkien and take a shot at modern novelists, Lewis concludes, "The Professor . . . has studied trolls and dragons at first hand and describes them with that fidelity which is worth oceans of glib 'originality.'"

Tolkien also shared the complete typescript of *The Lord of the Rings* with Lewis in 1949. In a letter addressed to "My dear Tollers," Lewis wrote:

> I have drained the rich cup and satisfied a long thirst.
> Once it really gets under way the steady upward slope

of grandeur and terror . . . is almost unequalled in the whole range of narrative art known to me. In two virtues I think it excels: sheer sub-creation—Bombadil, Barrow Wights, Elves, Ents—as if from inexhaustible resources, and construction. Also in *gravitas*. . . . I congratulate you. All the long years you have spent on it are justified.[20]

Lewis wrote a review of *The Fellowship of the Ring* for the British literary magazine *Time & Tide* titled "The Gods Return to Earth" (August 14, 1954), followed the next year by a combined review of the second and third volumes titled "The Dethronement of Power" (October 22, 1955). The two reviews have since been republished separately as well as combined. They deserve being quoted from at length. From "The Gods Return to Earth":

This book is like lightning from a clear sky. . . . To say that in it heroic romance, gorgeous, eloquent, and unashamed, has suddenly returned at a period almost pathological in its anti-romanticism, is inadequate. . . . But in the history of Romance itself—a history which stretches back to the *Odyssey* and beyond—it makes not a return but an advance or revolution: the conquest of new territory. . . .

Not content to create his own story, [Tolkien] creates, with an almost insolent prodigality, the whole world in which it is to move, with its own theology, myths, geography, history, palaeography, languages, and order of beings—a world "full of strange creatures beyond count." . . . [H]ere are beauties which pierce like swords or burn like cold iron; here is a book that will break your heart.[21]

From "The Dethronement of Power":

[The War of the Ring] has the very quality of the war my generation knew. It is all here: the endless, unintelligible movement, the sinister quiet . . . , the lively, vivid friendships, the background of something like despair and the merry foreground. . . . The book is too original and too opulent

for any final judgment on a first reading. But we know at
once that it has done things to us. We are not quite the
same men.[22]

In his second review, Lewis focused on three points: moral relativism, war, and the "realism" of myth. One common false criticism
of Tolkien, writes Lewis, comes from mistaking the author's belief in
good and evil for his creating black-and-white characters: Boromir and
Sméagol alone show that the latter is not the case. As for the charge of
escapism, Lewis testifies to Tolkien's grasp of the realities of war (which
both men had seen up close, unlike most of their critics) as well as to
his choice of the fantastic to engage in "serious comment." "The value
of myth," writes Lewis, "is that it takes all the things we know and
restores to them the rich significance which has been hidden by 'the veil
of familiarity.' . . . By dipping them in myth we see them more clearly."
Here we see an echo of Lewis's apologetics as well as Tolkien's essay "On
Fairy-stories."

The first review was excerpted for a blurb that appeared on the
original dust jacket of *The Fellowship of the Rings* along with similar praise
from noted British writer Richard Hughes and Scottish novelist and
poet Naomi Mitchison. Some reviewers reacted—and still react—with
strong criticism to Lewis's description of *The Lord of the Rings*. Tolkien
noted this in a letter to Rayner Unwin, saying that, although the critics'
reviews were better than he feared, they might have been even better

> if we had not . . . got involved at all with the extraordinary
> animosity that C.S.L. seems to excite in certain quarters.
> He warned me long ago that his support might do me as
> much harm as good. I did not take it seriously, though
> in any case I should not have wished other than to be
> associated with him.[23]

Both Tolkien and the critics of "certain quarters" seem to miss the
fact that Lewis's reviews contain some beautiful and powerful language.
Only Lewis and Tolkien, for example, could describe aesthetic heights
as like being pierced by a sword.[24] Lewis's reviews also, and more importantly, contain good insights into how Tolkien wrote and why he made
particular choices of genre, voice, and characterization. Tolkien could

hardly say publicly that his friend's insights were on target; however, we can assume that because Tolkien often shared drafts of his work with Lewis, Tolkien privately recognized the value of Lewis's opinions.

REVIEWS OF THE LORD OF THE RINGS

WHILE C. S. LEWIS admittedly gushed over *The Lord of the Rings*, most early reviews were, to say the least, mixed. In the *Times Literary Supplement* Alfred Duggan, while praising *The Fellowship* as "sound prose and rare imagination," complained about Tolkien's simplistic conception of good and evil and suggested that the novel was a subtle political allegory about the West versus the Communist East.[25] In its review of *The Two Towers*, the same publication hailed it as "a prose epic in praise of courage" and yet lacking in its treatment of women.[26] Writing for the *Nation* in 1956, the American critic Edmund Wilson called the trilogy "juvenile trash," while the British journalist Philip Toynbee celebrated (prematurely) in 1961 that Tolkien's "childish" books "have passed into a merciful oblivion."[27] Robert Flood, a Benedictine priest, even declared *The Fellowship* "pretentious snobbery" and "a fraud."[28] While the academics and other literati were mostly hostile, students on campuses from Britain to America became enamored of Middle-earth in the late 1950s and early '60s. By the time *The Lord of the Rings* appeared in paperback in America in 1965, it had already reached cult status among college students.[29]

By Judith Johnson's count, 340 reviews of *The Hobbit* and *The Lord of the Rings* had appeared by 1964, while the next ten years leading up to Tolkien's death produced nearly 650 critical responses.[30] She refers to this period as "the cult years," when an idealistic and youthful audience worldwide first discovered Tolkien's fiction (many through the Ace paperbacks) and fan clubs and fanzines were founded.

Even fellow-medievalist Norman Cantor, admiring of Tolkien's accomplishment, couldn't help but take a few shots and psychoanalyze his subject:

> Tolkien is a prime example of being what the British
> psychiatrist R. D. Laing called "a successful schizophrenic."
> This is what lies behind *The Lord of the Rings*. It is the most
> astonishing monument to the old historical philology ever
> developed and the most extended and difficult piece of

pseudomedievalism ever imagined. . . . It is genteel Nordic neoracism in the form of neomedievalism.[31]

The poet W. H. Auden, a friend and former student of Tolkien's who called *The Lord of the Rings* "a masterpiece of its genre," gives us some insight into why there are such strong disagreements over the merits of the epic:

> I can only suppose that some people object to Heroic Quests and Imaginary Worlds on principle; such, they feel, cannot be anything but light "escapist" reading. That a man like Mr. Tolkien, the English philologist who teaches at Oxford, should lavish such incredible pains upon a genre which is, for them, trifling by definition, is, therefore, very shocking.[32]

The Silmarillion

The Silmarillion provoked even harsher responses following its publication in 1977. Many reviewers reacted strongly against the biblical style of its prose and the quasi-chivalric tone of its dialogue. "Tolkien pleases not because he is arcane and outlandish but because he is an unadventurous defender of mediocrity," wrote Peter Conrad in the *New Statesman*. "Middle-earth is a suburb; its hobbits are Babbits, homespun, humdrum shopkeepers."[33] Since no hobbits appear in *The Silmarillion*, Conrad's attack reveals resentment left over (maybe even growing) from the still-popular *Lord of the Rings*.

"J. R. R. Tolkien, Author of the Twentieth Century"

Part of the shock and dismay of the critics comes from the enormous popularity of *The Lord of the Rings*. Sales during the first few years of publication were much greater than expected. When in early 1956 Tolkien received his first royalty payment from Allen & Unwin—£3,500—it was considerably more than his annual salary from Oxford. By 1959, the hardback edition had sold 156,000 copies; in the first ten months of the appearance of the paperback edition in America, 250,000 copies were sold.[34] To date, total sales of *The Lord of the Rings* (including sales of both individual and combined volumes) are estimated at over 150 million copies, second only to Charles Dickens's *A Tale of Two Cities*.[35]

Even more shocking to the Tolkien-haters were the results of several polls taken in the UK around the turn of the millennium.[36] First came a joint reader's poll conducted in 1996 by the Waterstone's book chain and the BBC-4 program *Book Choice*. When asked to choose the five greatest books of the twentieth century, more than 5,000 of the 26,000 who responded chose *The Lord of the Rings* (*The Hobbit* came in nineteenth place). A *Daily Telegraph* poll produced the same results, and the paper reported in 1999 that in a MORI (Market & Opinion Research International) poll in the UK, *The Lord of the Rings* had come in second—to the Bible. In 2003, *The Lord of the Rings* won another BBC poll, this time for the best-loved novel from any country or date.

The reaction of the journalists and literary critics to these poll results reached apoplectic heights. Auberon Waugh, editor of the *Literary Review*, suspected that Tolkien's fans had "orchestrated a campaign."[37] Germaine Greer declared that it had been her "nightmare that Tolkien would turn out to be the most influential writer of the twentieth century."[38] "[Why] read ersatz mythology by Tolkien rather than reading Homer?" asked critic A. N. Wilson, while novelist John Bayley described *The Lord of the Rings* as "fantastically badly written."[39] No less than the chief inspector of schools in Britain said that the poll results were proof of low cultural expectations: "If *The Lord of the Rings* is our favourite book, what is it saying about our attitude toward quality in the arts? English teachers ought to be trying to develop discrimination."[40]

Discrimination needs no further development among this group of critics. "Tolkien's critics, not his readers, are out of touch with reality," writes Patrick Curry in response to the outrage. "Never has the intellectual establishment so richly deserved defiance."[41] "The misologists [or 'word-haters,' as Tolkien called them] won, in the academic world;" writes Tom Shippey, "as did the realists, the modernists, the post-modernists, the despisers of fantasy. But they lost outside the academic world."[42]

reappraisal

There are signs, however, that the academic world might be coming around to an appreciation of Tolkien as both writer and thinker. A recent collection of essays by academic philosophers, for example, subjects *The Lord of the Rings* and other Tolkien works to Marxist, Freudian, Existentialist, and other critical lenses.[43] *The Lord of the Rings* "is an ethical

text," declares the University of Virginia's Alison Milbank, "that teaches us to give up dominatory and fixed perceptions in order to receive the world back as gift."[44] Brian Rosebury examines the critical reaction to Tolkien and describes it as more "bemused silence, or tacit dismissiveness" than outright hostility.[45] His own criticism considers Tolkien's fiction within the context of his modernist contemporaries—Kafka, Joyce, Eliot, Faulkner, Rilke—and argues that Tolkien was not so very different than these writers, a "welcome variant" rather than a complete outsider. If a writer is to be "effectively praised," writes Rosebury, "the praise must be justified in terms which bear an intelligible relation to the work of other writers."[46]

the greening of tolkien

ROSEBURY'S NARROW PRESCRIPTION for Tolkien criticism—that he must be compared to other, more acceptable authors—does not represent the great breadth and originality of scholarly approaches to Tolkien that have appeared over the last twenty years. Tolkien has, for example, found his way into "ecocriticism" and "green studies." There is much grist in Tolkien's fiction for this mill. In *The Hobbit*, for example, the mere evocation of nature in song can stir desire in the heart. "Then something Tookish woke up inside him," writes Tolkien of Bilbo, upon hearing the song of the dwarves, "and he wished to go and see the great mountains, and hear the pine-trees and the waterfalls, and explore the caves."[47] "[N]obody cares for the woods as I care for them,"[48] says Treebeard in *The Two Towers* before he marches off to war against the tree-killing Saruman and his orcs.

Patrick Curry has authored the first and most extensive survey of environmental themes in Tolkien's writings.[49] He approaches the material as a "Radical Eclectic," giving a very personal postmodern defense of Tolkien by attacking the titans of modernism: modern science, Marx, Freud, and global capitalism, not to mention the usual literary suspects like Eliot, Ezra Pound, and D. H. Lawrence. But in particular, Curry attempts to depict Tolkien as a conservationist, an ecologically aware author who makes Middle-earth itself a character in his books.

Andrew Light has argued for what he calls "green time" in Tolkien—that is, a geological time scale attuned to the natural world.[50] With Tolkien's emphasis on Bombadil, Fangorn, and the elves, writes Light, "there is a recognizable call here for us to appreciate the longer perspective of other things in the world and to take responsibility for our [human] actions."[51] Yet another school of thought sees Tolkien's environmentalism properly understood as Christian stewardship of living and growing things.[52]

Verlyn Flieger points out, however, that the first real villain met by the hobbits in *The Lord of the Rings* is a tree: Old Man Willow, who was "Huge, hostile, malicious."[53] Departing from the lighthearted tone in which he introduces Willow-man in the early poem "The Adventures of Tom Bombadil" (first published in 1934), Tolkien gives us a description of "the dangerous wilds," a common fear in medieval literature:

> The countless years had filled them . . . with malice. But none were more dangerous than Great Willow: his heart was rotten, but his strength was green. . . . His grey thirsty spirit drew power out of the earth and spread like fine root-threads in the ground, and invisible twig-fingers in the air, till it had under its dominion nearly all the trees of the Forest from the Hedge to the Downs.[54]

Tom Bombadil is needed to protect travelers from the malice of the Old Forest. "Tolkien is not sentimental," writes Fleming Rutledge, referring especially to the eagles. "He never condescends to the animal world . . . for him, as for the psalmists, nature is benign and dangerous in equal parts."[55]

medievalists and medievalism

MANY OF THE MOST PROLIFIC and respected Tolkien critics come from the same academic field as their subject: they are medievalists—literary critics trained in the languages and literature of the European Middle Ages. Of this group, one scholar stands out for his widely recognized accomplishments and for the fact that he is not just a medievalist, but one trained in medieval philology in almost the exact way that Tolkien himself was trained. Tom Shippey's path took him from Birmingham to Oxford and Leeds, with a stop at Cambridge along the way (he was one of C. S. Lewis's last pupils). An Anglo-Saxonist then and now, Shippey nonetheless tried his hand at a piece of Tolkien criticism in 1970, which Tolkien both read and praised. Inspired by Tolkien's supportive comments, Shippey would go on to author dozens of essays and conference papers and two highly influential books: *The Road to Middle-earth* (1992) and *J. R. R. Tolkien: Author of the Century* (2000).

Tom Shippey has his own clear prose style: precise, logically moving the reader along a line of evidence toward proof, or at least substantiated argument. His philological-critical approach to Tolkien can be summed up in one concise sentence from *The Road to Middle-earth*: "Good writing began with right words."[56] After explaining the methodology of the philologist by using examples from the very (medieval) source material used by Tolkien himself, Shippey focuses on the names and words—Earendil, Baggins, hobbit, Frodo, wraith—that launched a thousand stories of Middle-earth.

Very different in tone from his philological exegesis is Shippey's discussion of the broader themes in *The Lord of the Rings*. For instance, he offers a lengthy discussion of the definition of evil in Middle-earth, concluding that Tolkien was caught between two contradictory views of evil: the Boethian, where evil is internal/psychological (and perhaps ultimately nonexistent), and the Manichean, where evil is a real, external, and powerful entity. Shippey argues that Tolkien allowed a tension between these two to exist in *The Lord of the Rings*, a view now challenged by some.[57]

One of Shippey's accomplishments is that he defeats the modernist critics on their own terms. He argues quite convincingly in *Author of the Century* that Tolkien did not simply retreat into the past or into fantasy to escape the modern world, but was himself a modern writer who chose—like Richard Wagner, Aldous Huxley, George Orwell, and others—to address the problems of modernity through the use of the fantastic. "Tolkien was a writer fully in touch with his era," agrees Patchen Mortimer, "and his work reveals modernist attributes—and even ambitions of modernist scope.... His use of fantasy is not escapist, but a strategy for articulating the awful and inexplicable."[58]

Another medievalist with a long and distinguished record of Tolkien criticism is Jane Chance (formerly Nitzsche) of Rice University. In her book *Tolkien's Art* (1979), Chance illustrates the myriad and complex ways in which Tolkien responded to medieval literature—and his theories thereon—through his own fiction. These include a reworking of *Beowulf* in *The Hobbit*, mimesis (parody) of Breton lays and Middle English romance in many of his minor works, and, in *The Lord of the Rings*, an extended exploration of the tension between barbarian valor and Christian charity. On

the last point, Chance argues that Tolkien reconciles these two seemingly conflicting values "through the sacrificial (Christian) act of the free peoples, who heroically battle (in Germanic fashion) Sauron's Lieutenant," while the humble servant Sam aids Frodo in his sacrifice.[59]

One group of Tolkien scholars has provided immense service to students of Middle-earth through the editing of several reference collections and the creation in 2000 of the scholarly journal *Tolkien Studies*, now the most important source for new studies of Tolkien's work. The journal's founding editors are Douglas A. Anderson, Michael D. C. Drout, and Verlyn Flieger. Anderson has given us *The Annotated Hobbit* (2002); Drout has edited an encyclopedia of Tolkien criticism as well as written a detailed study of "*Beowulf*: the Monsters and the Critics;" Flieger has produced a critical edition of *Smith of Wooten Major*; and Flieger and Anderson together have produced a new edition, with commentary, of Tolkien's "On Fairy-stories." These works, together with the guides produced by Wayne G. Hammond and Christina Scull, constitute an indispensable scholarly reference collection covering the entirety of Tolkien's literary output.

Verlyn Flieger has also produced two significant monographs on themes running through the whole of Tolkien's legendarium: *A Question of Time: J. R. R. Tolkien's Road to Faërie* (1997) and *Splintered Light: Logos and Language in Tolkien's World* (2002). In addition to some of the most original and significant criticism of *The Silmarillion*, Flieger also wrote a very interesting essay in which she agrees with Shippey that Tolkien exhibited modernist traits, but goes even further in suggesting that Tolkien also presaged postmodernism. She cites as evidence from *The Lord of the Rings* Tolkien's heavy use of interlace, a medieval literary device but one embraced by many postmodern novelists, and his agility in switching voices from the "high" (the chivalric of Aragorn and Faramir) to the "low" (Sam, the orcs).

As a group, these scholars make little effort in hiding their admiration of Tolkien. Their scholarship has established Tolkien in the center of the emerging academic interest in "medievalism," which has become a subject in its own right. Not all academic medievalists, however, share Tolkien's interpretation of the Middle Ages, and not all are crazy about elevating medievalism to equal footing with medieval studies. The particularly contrarian Norman Cantor reads *The Lord of the Rings* as a counter-romance, focusing on the experiences of Frodo: "not the

Arthurian heroism of golden knights but the wearying, almost endless struggle of the little people against the reality of perpetual war and violence."[60] In addition to Marxist and Freudian interpretations, there have even been efforts to look at Tolkien's fiction in a poststructuralist light.[61]

CHRISTIAN INTERPRETATIONS

MORE PROLIFIC HAS BEEN the school of Christian interpretation of Tolkien's writings. After the success of the first Peter Jackson film, in 2002 the *Chesterton Review* at Seton Hall University dedicated an entire volume to contemporary Christian criticism of Tolkien. Here, editor Stratford Caldecott previews his Tolkien book, *The Power of the Ring* (2005), with an essay focusing on the themes of hope and mercy in Tolkien's writings:

> Frodo is, of course, saved by an apparent accident, for Gollum bites the ring from his finger and falls into the Fire. This is in fact a consequence of Frodo's earlier (and freer) decision to spare Gollum's life. . . . Thus, in the end it is not Frodo who saves Middle-earth at all, nor Gollum. It can only be God himself, working through the love and freedom of his creatures. The scene is a triumph . . . of Mercy.[62]

In his book, Caldecott describes Tolkien's Catholicism as a "hidden presence" within his writings. He finds similarities between Gildor's song to Elbereth in *The Fellowship* ("O Elbereth! . . . The Starlight on the Western seas")[63] and the popular Catholic hymn to the Virgin Mary, *Ave Maris Stella* ("Hail, Queen of Heaven, . . . star of the sea").[64]

Peter Kreeft, a Christian philosopher at Boston College and a popular and prolific apologist, takes Tolkien's worldview as seriously as he does that of Plato. In *The Philosophy of Tolkien* (2005), Kreeft employs an interesting critical strategy: chapters are defined by philosophical categories (metaphysics, cosmology, aesthetics, etc.); subchapters whose headings are philosophical or theological questions (e.g., "Is beauty always good?"); and answers to these questions in the form of quotations from both Tolkien and C. S. Lewis, with commentary. Kreeft is, like the medievalists Tolkien and Lewis, critical of modern progressivism. "We have not progressed in virtue or wisdom," he writes, "only in power and cleverness."[65] In other words, modern man is more Saruman than Gandalf. For Kreeft, *The Lord of the Rings* possesses a different kind of

power: it "heals our culture as well as our souls. It gives us the most rare and precious thing in modern literature: the heroic."[66]

"I shall use the major doctrines of the Christian faith as the template," writes Ralph C. Wood, "for my reading of Tolkien."[67] Wood, professor of theology and literature at Baylor University, believes that *The Lord of the Rings* "discloses—not by overt preachment but by covert suggestion—the principal claims of the Christian faith." He turns to an obscure bit of discarded writing called "The Debate of Finrod and Andreth," published by Christopher Tolkien in *Morgoth's Ring*, which contains a prophecy of Ilúvatar's eventual entry into Middle-earth, and argues that this reveals Tolkien's own thoughts on death and death's defeat.[68] In this work, the mortal woman Andreth instructs the wise elf Finrod that men were "born to life everlasting," and that Melkor has spoiled this by introducing death; and yet, an ancient prophecy among men says that "the One [Eru/Ilúvatar] will himself enter Arda, and heal Men and all the Marring from the beginning to the end."[69] It is hard to argue that here Tolkien did not have the Incarnation of Christ in mind.

Fleming Rutledge, an Episcopal priest, reads what he calls "divine design" in *The Hobbit* and *The Lord of the Rings*. For example, the tripartite division of the Church can be seen in the survivors of Middle-earth battles—be they wizards, hobbits, men, dwarves, or elves—who remain vigilant for the return of evil (the Church Militant); the heroic dead, like Thorin and Théoden and Boromir, in the "halls of waiting" (the Church Expectant); and the future reunion of these two groups as the Second Coming (the Church Triumphant).[70]

Richard Purtill argues that Tolkien made a distinction between primary belief, the category in which Christian scripture would reside for him, and secondary belief, the kind of belief readers give to fiction.[71] C. S. Lewis, as we have seen, placed the Christian story in the second category until Tolkien convinced him that it was a true, or historical, myth. Though perhaps not sharing the same definition of myth, both Lewis and Tolkien, writes Purtill, believed in the "numinous idea." For Tolkien, this was most powerfully expressed in the untold stories, those evoking a lost past, an unrecorded history begging to be discovered.[72] Such longing for vanished lands and cultures, found throughout *The Lord of the Rings* and *The Silmarillion*, is similar to Lewis's concept of joy, realized at an early age with his longing for the vast Northern lands. "Balder the beautiful is dead" (see page 69) worked in Lewis the same magic as did, for Tolkien, the lines "Hail Earendel, brightest of angels, / Over Middle-earth sent to men" (see pages 8 and 59). Hence their friendship first formed while reading Icelandic poetry with the Coal-biters. Like Kreeft, Purtill often turns to the writings of Lewis (especially his literary criticism) to help explain the fiction of Tolkien.

Bradley Birzer, a professor of history at Hillsdale College, sees Tolkien as one of the great Christian humanists of the twentieth century, in the company of such diverse thinkers as Eliot, Lewis, Eric Voegelin, and Russell Kirk.[73] In *J. R. R. Tolkien's Sanctifying Myth* (2002), he argues that Tolkien's goal for his own mythology "was, in short, to revive the northern spirit of courage by infusing it with the Christian doctrine of Grace,"[74] producing what Birzer calls "sanctified myths." This is what Tolkien the scholar observed was happening in the literature of the Middle Ages. "In essence," writes Birzer, "Tolkien's mind remained complexly medieval and oriented toward myth and mystery."[75] As for God, He is there, argues Birzer, as the true "Writer of the Story," "that one ever-present Person who is never absent and never named."[76]

At the risk of oversimplification, the following parallels between Middle-earth and Christianity have been identified by this group of critics:

- God the Father—Ilúvatar
- Christ figures—Gandalf, Frodo, Aragorn (in his second coming)
- Mary, Mother of Christ—Galadriel
- Simon of Cyrene—Sam
- The Cross—the One Ring
- The Via Dolorosa—the journey of Frodo and Sam to Mordor
- The Communion Bread—*lembas*
- Lent—Sam and Frodo's long fast leading to March 25
- The Valley of the Shadow of Death—Mordor, the Grey Havens
- The Assumption—the White Ship
- The Sons of God (angels)—the Valar, the Istari
- Adam—Boromir
- Eve—Galadriel
- Satan/Lucifer—Melkor/Morgoth, Sauron
- Sin—the rings of power
- Abraham—Aulë
- The Israelites—the Eldar, the Númenoreans
- The Prophets—Gandalf, Elrond

I say "parallels" because none of the critics described here argue for exact equation or allegory in the relationship they see between Tolkien's writings and Christian belief. Nor did Tolkien write, as Lewis did in *The Chronicles of Narnia*, with an overt attempt to "reimagine" the Christian story in another world. Obviously, there is some overlapping in these parallels and none of Tolkien's characters is an exact match. But it would be utterly myopic to believe that Holy Scripture and Catholic liturgy did not influence Tolkien's themes, characters, and plots; or that his subcreation was entirely separate from his personal faith. As he wrote in 1953 to Fr. Robert Murray, a family friend who had read galley-proofs of *The Fellowship* and seen an image of the Virgin Mary in the portrayal of Galadriel:

> *The Lord of the Rings* is of course a fundamentally religious and Catholic work; unconsciously at first but consciously in the revision. That is why I have not put in, or have cut out, practically all references to anything like "religion," to cults or practices, in the imaginary world. For the religious element is absorbed into the story and the symbolism.[77]

It was to Mary, Tolkien continued, that he owed his own perception of beauty "both in majesty and simplicity." "Unfortunately," writes Joseph Pearce in the foreword to *J. R. R. Tolkien's Sanctifying Myth*, "those who are blind to theology will continue to be blind to that which is most beautiful in *The Lord of the Rings*."[78]

C. S. Lewis was one of the first to see the beauty in *The Lord of the Rings*, even in its pre-published state and over the objections of some of the other Inklings. One cannot help but think of Morgoth and Sauron when, in *Mere Christianity* (1952), Lewis describes the world as cosmic "civil war, a rebellion" where we all live in "enemy-occupied territory" until the coming of the Messiah, who bears a resemblance to a certain scruffy Ranger from the North. "Christianity is the story of how the rightful king has landed, you might say landed in disguise, and is calling us all to take part in a great campaign of sabotage."[79]

conclusion: tolkien as tolkien critic

OF COURSE, TOLKIEN WOULD HAVE SCOFFED at any suggestion—whether made by Lewis or a modern critic—that Aragorn was Christ.

But then Professor Tolkien does not make it easy for the critic. A private man, he gave few interviews and made known his distrust of literary biographies. More than this, he often purposely confounded attempts to find meaning in his work. "As for any inner meaning or 'message,' it has in the intention of the author none," he wrote in the preface to *The Lord of the Rings*. "It is neither allegorical nor topical. . . . I cordially dislike allegory in all its manifestations." Tolkien much preferred history, he went on to write, whether true or invented: "An author cannot of course remain wholly unaffected by his experience," he admitted, "but the ways in which a story-germ uses the soil of experience are extremely complex."[80]

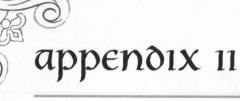

appendix 11

media and middle earth

THE VIVID PROSE OF J. R. R. Tolkien, filled with description of wondrous creatures and dramatic landscapes, begs for illustration and adaptation. Middle-earth has been translated into media ranging from pen-and-ink drawings to HD- and 3D-motion pictures. Tolkien himself began the process with his drawings and sketches dating back to his teenage years, and his readings of his poetry and prose have, since his death, appeared on records and CDs. Doubtful that *The Lord of the Rings* could ever be done successfully on film, Tolkien could hardly have imagined the enormous success, popular and critical, of Peter Jackson's trilogy of films released in 2001–3, followed by the two *Hobbit* films of 2012 and 2013. Now, with a third *Hobbit* film looming on the horizon, it seems that Tolkien's medievalism will continue to attract fresh audiences through new media as well as old.

ILLUSTRATING TOLKIEN

I WILL NOT HERE ATTEMPT a full survey and discussion of the long tradition of Tolkien illustration. Rather, we will look at those illustrators who have been inspired by styles and elements of medieval art and decoration or, in some cases, the "neomedieval" art of the nineteenth century. Like Peter Jackson's films in recent years, some of these artists have produced images of Middle-earth that have become *the* way that many readers visualize Tolkien's characters and landscapes.

TOLKIEN AS ILLUSTRATOR

Ronald Tolkien began drawing and painting from an early age, and in his student days he turned to landscape and later to imaginative drawing (which he called "ishness"). He created original illustrations for *The Hobbit* and *The Lord of the Rings* as well as for *Roverandom* and *The Father Christmas Letters*. Many of Tolkien's paintings, drawings, and designs were published in a series of six calendars from 1973–74 and 1976–79. These were later collected together and published in book form as *Pictures by J. R. R. Tolkien* (London: Allen & Unwin, 1979); two scholarly collections followed, with commentary and criticism, both by Wayne Hammond and Christina Scull.[1]

An amateur artist of limited ability, Tolkien nevertheless was very thoughtful about art and its relation to the fantastic. "In human art Fantasy is a thing best left to words, to true literature," he writes in the essay "On Fairy-stories." "The visible presentation of the fantastic image is technically too easy; the hand tends to outrun the mind, even to overthrow it."[2]

Somewhat surprisingly, Tolkien's style of drawing and painting borrows little from the medieval. His original illustrations for *The Hobbit*, used on the book jacket and as color plates inserted in early hardcover editions, are stylistically reminiscent of nineteenth-century book illustration, show some Art Nouveau influence, and utilize a color palette similar to the paintings of the Scottish symbolist painter John Duncan (1866–1945). Even the heraldic devices he drew for *The Silmarillion* bear almost no resemblance to actual medieval heraldry. However, like medieval tapestries and illuminated manuscripts, Tolkien often employed decorative borders; on *The Hobbit* dust jacket the border is filled with runes, as it is on the title page of *The Lord of the Rings*. Tiles and textiles drawn for *The Silmarillion* show bold symmetrical designs more akin to decoration from the ancient Mediterranean. Tolkien remained modest about his own artistic abilities, but this did not prevent him from being demanding and critical of the work of illustrators brought in by publishers for the many editions and translations of his works. Perhaps his favorite illustrator was Pauline Baynes, recommended to him by C. S. Lewis because of her illustrations for *The Chronicles of Narnia*. Baynes's style is in some ways similar to Tolkien's, and his trust in her work led to several commissions, including illustrations for *Farmer Giles of Ham* and *Smith of Wooten Major*.

The Brothers Hildebrandt and Ted Nasmith

Starting in 1973, Tolkien's publishers began producing illustrated calendars, posters, playing cards, and other Middle-earth memorabilia. Many fantasy artists and book illustrators were commissioned for these works, and now with Tolkien fans able to "publish" their own artwork on the Internet the number of Tolkien illustrators has grown to the hundreds.[3] The first calendar, by Allen & Unwin, featured Tolkien's own illustrations. But in 1975 Ballantine Books commissioned the American artists Greg and Tim Hildebrandt to produce fourteen original paintings for their calendar. The unique style of the Brothers Hildebrandt made the *1976 Tolkien Calendar* the top-selling calendar in the world, and they would follow it with two more highly successful calendars in 1977 and 1978.[4]

Working with acrylic on large sheets of Masonite, the Brothers Hildebrandt were able to produce paintings that combined realism (especially in figure work) with the numinousness of Faërie. Saturated primary colors (especially blues and reds), crisp lines, golden light, and startling whites recall medieval pageantry. Closer examination of clothing, arms, and armor, however, reveals that this is the Technicolor Middle Ages of 1950s films such as MGM's *Knights of the Round Table* (1953) and 20th Century Fox's *Prince Valiant* (1954). The twin brothers' admitted influences include Maxfield Parrish, N. C. Wyeth, Howard Pyle, and Disney.[5] Still, at their best, the Brothers Hildebrandt capture the warmth, humor, and gallantry of *The Hobbit* and *The Lord of the Rings*.

Similar Romantic and cinematic influences can be seen in the work of Canadian artist Ted Nasmith. Beginning in the mid 1980s, Nasmith was given several commissions for Tolkien cover art, Tolkien calendars, and for an illustrated edition of *The Silmarillion* in 1998. He has become a prolific painter of Tolkien-inspired works. Nasmith's landscapes are rich, his architecture detailed, and his scenes vibrant. While his figures are not always consistent in their realism, he is capable of capturing a moment in Tolkien and conveying an "historical" depth in his scenes.

John howe

No artist goes to such lengths to reproduce historical detail as John Howe. Howe, Canadian-born and schooled in France, began contributing to Tolkien calendars in the 1980s and would later get commissions to illustrate the books. Like Ted Nasmith, Howe was inspired by the work of the Brothers Hildebrandt and, in his Tolkien paintings, would carry the degree of realism even further while filling his scenes with great sweeps and swirls of fantasy action. Great battles and confrontations with monsters and the Valar provide the subjects of much of Howe's Tolkien illustration. When not illustrating Tolkien, Howe is often painting medieval cathedrals, fairy tales, and scenes from Arthurian legend.

John Howe describes the relationship between historical objects and his unique approach to illustrating Tolkien:

> When is a sword blade too long or too wide? How is the grip constructed? How do helmets stay on heads? . . . The real answers to these questions are to be found in archaeology, and then getting your hands on it. Of course, you can't (always) pick up museum exhibits . . . but a conscientious reconstruction of an object, one that you can use, abuse and repair, wear and carry around, can be exceedingly instructive. . . . As they no longer exist, nearly all of the items used in living history must be recreated, thus I find enormous satisfaction in making objects. . . . . More importantly, the nature of the materials used will lead the hand and mind to designs inaccessible to a pencil on paper. Our garage and attic are consequently piled high with shields of every period, with lances, spears and bits of armour. . . . Gandalf wears a sword I own.[6]

alan lee

While action scenes and especially battles against the dark denizens of Mordor epitomize the art of John Howe, the British artist Alan Lee is known for his soft, ethereal landscapes and the calm beauty of his watercolor illustrations of Tolkien. Lee was commissioned to do illustrations for the 1991 edition of *The Lord of the Rings*, the sixtieth anniversary edition of *The Hobbit*, and *The Children of Húrin*. His celebrated illustrative career also encompasses original art for editions of *The Mabinogion*, T. H. White's *The Book of Merlyn*, and Rosemary Sutcliff's retellings of *The Iliad* and *The Odyssey*. Alan Lee is a close reader of the texts he illustrates, and like Howe he fills his illustrations with historical detail. Lee is particularly inspired by Celtic and Germanic animal art and interlace. Many motifs from his paintings, as well as his set and costume designs for Peter Jackson's films, come from studying the metalwork and manuscript illumination of early medieval Britain and Ireland.

donato giancola

One of the most recent fantasy illustrators to tackle Tolkien is New Yorker Donato Giancola. His oil paintings in particular reveal a master craftsman at work, exhibiting a realism that rivals that of Renaissance and Baroque painters.[7] His use of shadow and light show the influences of Caravaggio and Vermeer, while the arrangement of figures in his mural scenes is reminiscent of classical relief sculpture. Like Howe and Lee, Giancola is a researcher and seeks a historical feel in his clothing, weapons, and armor. Greek, Roman, medieval, and Renaissance styles are all apparent in his depiction of the men of Gondor, while Éowyn and the Rohirrim are appropriately Anglo-Saxon.

tolkien on the radio

the 1955–56 bbc broadcasts

If Tolkien was critical of the illustrations for his books, he was even more so of radio broadcasts of *The Lord of the Rings* and plans to turn the novel into a motion picture. A condensed version of the epic was broadcast in twelve episodes on BBC Radio in 1955 and 1956.[8] The adaptation was produced by Terence Tiller, close friend of George Orwell and W. H. Auden and one of the leading producers of the Third Programme BBC network. No recording of these live broadcasts survives (it is possible that no recording was ever made), but Tolkien indicated his displeasure with the project in several letters to various people. To a Mrs. Molly Waldron, he wrote, "I think the book quite unsuitable for 'dramatization,' and have not enjoyed the broadcasts . . . the text is (necessarily in the space) reduced to such simple, even simple-minded, terms."[9] In a November 6, 1956, letter to Tiller himself, Tolkien pointedly asked why "this sort of treatment is accorded my book?" He went on, "Here is a book very unsuitable for dramatic or semi-dramatic representation. If that is attempted it needs more space, a lot of space."[10]

the 1981 bbc broadcasts

Tolkien did not live to hear the second BBC radio production of *The Lord of the Rings*, which was broadcast in thirteen episodes on BBC Radio 4 from March 8 to August 30, 1981.[11] It re-aired in 1982 and was released for sale on cassette and (later) CD. The script was an adaptation done by Brian

Sibley and Michael Bakewell. Sibley would also adapt *The Chronicles of Narnia* for radio dramatization and write several works books about Lewis and Tolkien. *The Lord of the Rings* cast featured Ian Holm as Frodo, Michael Hordern as Gandalf, and Robert Stephens as Aragorn—all three, English actors of stage and screen, renowned for Shakespearean roles, and eventually knighted—with narration by Irish actor Gerard Murphy.

animated tolkien

rankin and bass's *the hobbit* (1977) and *the return of the king* (1980)

In 1957 the American science fiction aficionado, writer, and literary agent Forrest J. Ackerman approached Stanley Unwin about purchasing the rights to make an animated film version of *The Lord of the Rings*. Given his criticisms of the BBC attempts to dramatize *The Lord of the Rings*, Tolkien's response is a bit surprising:

> I should welcome the idea of an animated motion picture,
> with all the risk of vulgarization; and that quite apart from
> the glint of money, though on the brink of retirement
> that is not an unpleasant possibility. I think I should find
> vulgarization less painful than the sillification achieved by
> the BBC.[12]

After a visit by Ackerman to Oxford, Professor Tolkien wrote to Christopher that he was impressed by some illustrations shown to him (because they looked more Arthur Rackham than Walt Disney), but that the story line was quite bad. "But it looks as if business might be done. Stanley U[unwin] and I have agreed on our policy: *Art or Cash*."[13] In other words, Tolkien wanted absolute author veto of anything he found objectionable in an adaptation, or else a large sum of money.

But as negotiations with Ackerman continued, Tolkien was shown a revised story line and disliked it intensely. He continued to complain until the deal was off. In 1967, Tolkien finally sold the film rights to both *The Hobbit* and *The Lord of the Rings* to United Artists. Nothing happened for several years until, after Tolkien's death, the rights to *The Hobbit* were licensed to Arthur Rankin and Jules Bass. Best known for their collaboration on American holiday classics like *Rudolph the Red-Nosed Reindeer* (1964), Rankin/Bass Productions turned the animation duties over to the Japanese studio Topcraft. The animating coordinator was Toru Hara, who was inspired by Arthur Rackham's illustrations.[14] Despite a $3 million budget and a distinguished cast that included the voices of Orson Bean (Bilbo), John Huston (Gandalf/Narrator), Richard Boone (Smaug), and Otto Preminger (Elvinking), *The Hobbit* (NBC-TV, 1977) is plagued with two-dimensional animation and silly songs. It is family-friendly fare—*Rudolph and Frosty Visit Middle-earth*—and only the very young will find it tolerable. No attempts were made to make this visit medieval.

Unfortunately, an attempt was made to produce a sequel. *J. R. R. Tolkien's Return of the King—A Tale of Hobbits* was first broadcast on NBC-TV in May 1980. Other distinguished actors joined their voices to those of Bean and Huston, including Theodore Bikel (Aragorn), William Conrad (Denethor), and Roddy McDowall (Sam). Screenwriter Romeo Muller does a decent job in figuring out ways to condense all of *The Lord of the Rings* into a ninety-seven-minute television production. And while the song "Frodo of the Nine Fingers and the Ring of Doom," has a resonance with the book, neither the music nor the animation will impress adult viewers.

Ralph Bakshi's *The Lord of the Rings* (1978)

Acclaimed animator Ralph Bakshi sought for years to acquire the rights to *The Lord of the Rings* in order to produce a grown-up animated version. Ultimately, with the backing of producer Saul Zaentz, who had provided financial backing for Bakshi's X-rated *Fritz the Cat* (1972), Bakshi got the rights to create three (later reduced to two) animated films. The first was released in November of 1978 with the title *The Lord of the Rings*. Its cast featured the voices of British actors John Hurt (Aragorn) and Anthony Daniels (Legolas), who had starred the previous year as C-3PO in *Star Wars*. Noted fantasy writer Peter Beagle helped Chris Conkling with the script. Bakshi used the technique of rotoscoping in order to bring a painterly realism to his animation, "like Rembrandt in motion."[15] Shooting at the fifteenth-century Belmonte Castle in Cuenca, on the La Mancha plains of Spain, is perhaps the only thing medieval about the enterprise, and it certainly lacked Cervantes' ability to parody romance. Some of the battle scenes borrow footage from

Sergei Eisenstein's classic medieval epic, *Alexander Nevsky* (1938).[16] But in
the end (though the film itself has no real conclusion), the first film was
a commercial and critical flop, and a second was never produced. One
of the only significant outcomes of the project is that the film inspired
a teenage boy in New Zealand named Peter Jackson to, in the famous
words of St. Augustine, *tolle lege* (Latin), "pick up and read" the book.

Peter Jackson's Trilogy

The filmmaking techniques of the 1950s and '60s did not impress
Tolkien, nor did the desire of the Beatles to make a *Lord of the Rings* film
(with John as Gollum, of course). For any dramatic adaptation of fantasy
to be successful, Tolkien said, disbelief would not have to be suspended
but "hanged, drawn, and quartered."[17]

Because Tolkien sold the film and licensing rights to *The Hobbit* and
The Lord of the Rings to United Artists in 1967, after his death the Tolkien
Estate had no legal rights to money or artistic decisions in future
film adaptations. Rather, these were and are in the hands of Tolkien
Enterprises, a company owned by the American film and music mogul
Saul Zaentz. Zaentz had backed the film adaptation of *One Flew Over the
Cuckoo's Nest* (1975) and the aforementioned Ralph Bakshi 1978 animated
film. Most recently, Zaentz coproduced the stage musical *The Lord of
the Rings*, which premiered in Toronto in 2006 and experienced a short
run in London's West End (see pages 265–66). In the 1980s, Zaentz was
interested in filmmaker John Boorman (*Excalibur*) doing a Tolkien film,
but Boorman became frustrated with attempts to condense the epic
into one film.

Enter New Zealand filmmaker Peter Jackson. Known for his
low-budget horror comedies (*Bad Taste, Meet the Feebles*) and the Oscar-
nominated *Heavenly Creatures* (1994), Jackson had been a Tolkien fan
for years but only turned to serious contemplation of doing a Tolkien
film in 1995 as a vehicle for his collaborators, the special-effects effects
studio Weta Workshop in New Zealand, run by Richard Taylor and
Tania Rodger. Jackson and his partner Fran Walsh approached Zaentz
with the idea of filming two live-action *Lord of the Rings* films in New
Zealand. Zaentz agreed to option the film rights to Jackson if he could
find a studio to finance his films. Miramax was the first to show interest,
but producers Harvey and Bob Weinstein would only agree to finance
one film, and so allowed Jackson to look for another studio (asking for

reimbursement and 5 percent of the gross in return). New Line Cinema, under the advice of CEO Bob Shaye, shocked the world by agreeing to finance Jackson's project to the tune of $270 million, but only if *three* films were shot simultaneously.

screenplay

Peter Jackson and Fran Walsh produced a ninety-page treatment of *The Lord of the Rings* and shared that, in 1997, with New Zealand playwright Philippa Boyens, who would join them to form the writers' trio responsible for the screenplay for the three films. In interviews, Jackson and Boyens consistently speak with deference to and respect for "Professor Tolkien." Jackson and the actors were frequently seen on set pouring over copies of the novel, which Orlando Bloom (Legolas) refers to in an interview on the DVD as "the Bible." "As filmmakers, as writers, we had no interest whatsoever in putting our junk, our baggage into these movies," explains Jackson. "We just thought that we should take what Tolkien cared about clearly and put them into the film. This should ultimately be Tolkien's film, it shouldn't be ours."[18] It is hard to imagine a Hollywood writer or *auteur* director making such a statement.

That does not mean that changes, deletions, and additions were not made. Old Man Willow, Tom Bombadil, and the Barrow-wights are gone (or at least not mentioned in the films), and the character of Arwen was greatly expanded. The Scouring of the Shire was another casualty of the script-writing process. While these choices have upset Tolkien purists, what is often overlooked is the original writing done for the film, including new dialogue that is not only consistent with Tolkien's writing but which occasionally evokes the medieval and romantic spirit of the book.

concept art and design

One of the aspects of Tolkien's writing that most appealed to Jackson was the believability of his sub-created world. It *feels* like history, says Jackson, like Tolkien really did discover some lost medieval manuscript. Thus the verisimilitude of Middle-earth dictated to a great extent Jackson's choice of conceptual artists as well as his direction to the legion of set, prop, and costume designers who worked on the three films. The Tolkien illustrations of Alan Lee and John Howe were most influential to the writing team as they worked on the script, and thus

Jackson worked hard to bring both artists to New Zealand as conceptual artists working primarily with Weta. Sets, costumes, weapons, creatures, and just about every physical part of the films can be traced to drawings by Lee and Howe, who produced new work for the film that was still very much under the influence of Roman, Celtic, Germanic, and high medieval motifs and styles. Lee and Howe speak of giving "a sense of art history" and "layers of civilization" in their depiction of Gondor, for example, while Hobbiton was made to look like a thatched-roof, homely Midlands hamlet from pre-industrial times. "It's almost as if you are digging things up out of the ground," states Howe, "rather than creating them."[19]

Richard Taylor, who supervises Weta Workshop, shares this passion for "historical" detail in his work. Etchings in swords and armor, tapestries hanging on the walls, motifs on belts and boots, and many other things that are barely noticeable in the film: all had to carry this since of believability. For the plate armor in the films (worn primarily by the Urûk-hai and the men of Gondor), Weta hired professional armorsmiths and built a forge in the studio so that each plate of each suit was made using medieval techniques of heating, cooling in water, and hammering. Taylor's designers carried all of this off so well that they would attract the attention of the producers of *The Chronicles of Narnia* films, and thus history seemed to be repeating itself when production design inspired by the words of Tolkien was influencing the production design of movies inspired by the words of C. S. Lewis!

casting

With rumors flying around the Internet as soon as it became known that Jackson was tackling *The Lord of the Rings*, casting for the films was crucial. While Jackson naturally wanted to employ Australian and Kiwi actors—e.g., Australians Cate Blanchett (Galadriel), Hugo Weaving (Elrond), David Wenham (Faramir), and Miranda Otto (Éowyn), Kiwis Karl Urban (Éomer) and Craig Parker (Haldir)—he also wanted English actors in key roles so as to be true to Tolkien's Shire. Sean Connery, Peter O'Toole, and Anthony Hopkins—not English but Scottish, Irish, and Welsh, respectively—were all reportedly offered the role of Gandalf but turned it down. Whether any of this is true or not, the eventual casting of Englishman Sir Ian McKellen was near perfect. While less of a "box office" name, McKellen had an impeccable resume of stage and

screen success. He studied the novel carefully and often, and threw himself completely into the role of Gandalf, even mimicking Tolkien himself in the performance. (McKellen studied English literature at St. Catharine's College, Cambridge, in the late 1950s, where he attended lectures by C. S. Lewis.) McKellen also lends an undeniable gravitas to the whole project, but especially to the first film, for which he received a Lead Actor Oscar nomination. The eventual additions of Sir Ian Holm (Bilbo), Sir Christopher Lee (Saruman), John Rhys-Davies (Gimli), Bernard Hill (Théoden), and John Noble (Denethor) gave the films a solid foundation of seasoned thespians.

Riskier was the casting of the four younger hobbits. Diminutive and relatively unknown northern Britons Billy Boyd (Pippin) and Dominic Monaghan (Merry) certainly looked the part, as did the youngest member of the fellowship, Elijah Wood (Frodo). But casting a recognizable American actor in arguably the lead role was a risk as big as Wood's piercing blue eyes. The role of Samwise Gamgee went ultimately to another American actor, Sean Astin, who, like Wood, was recognizable from childhood roles. Astin, "Hollywood" born and bred (he is the son of actors John Astin and Patty Duke), is telling in his admission of ignorance upon being offered the role of Sam:

> I pulled into the Barnes and Noble parking lot, jumped out of the car, and practically sprinted to the front counter. Then I made a fool out of myself.
>
> "Excuse me, do you have anything by Tolkien? . . . It's J. R. Tolkien . . . or J. R. R. . . . something like that?"
>
> . . . How, I wondered, did I get to this point? Here I was, twenty-eight years old, with a degree in history and literature from a major institution of higher learning [UCLA]. I had graduated with honors, for Pete's sake. I considered myself a pretty well-read person. So how did I miss this *thing*? This movement in publishing? This cultural phenomenon? . . . and all I could do was scratch my head and wonder, *What else am I missing?*[20]

These films would also require true action stars, but again Jackson avoided big names. Orlando Bloom (Legolas) was plucked straight out of a London drama school, while Sean Bean (Boromir) was a respected actor best known for his lead role in the British television series *Sharpe*. The crucial role of Strider/Aragorn was originally given to the British actor Stuart Townsend, but it was felt he was too young for the part. Already well into the shooting of the first film, the role was recast and went to Danish-American actor/artist/musician Viggo Mortensen. Coincidentally, as noted in chapter four, Vigo was originally one of the names of the hobbits in an early draft of *The Lord of the Rings*.[21] The relatively unknown Mortensen also immersed himself in the role, carrying his prop sword with him everywhere and sleeping in the stable with his stunt horse. Soft-spoken but with command presence, he brings a tenderness to Aragorn, a bit of Rivendell to smooth the rough edges of the Ranger. Mortensen also does a good job throughout the trilogy of betraying the uncertainty within Aragorn. His face clearly shows "Did I make the right decision?"

The final piece of the puzzle was "casting" Gollum. Jackson's intent was to use the sketches of Lee and Howe along with sculpted models to create a CGI (computer-generated image) for all three films. "Gollum is one of the most iconic and loved folklore characters of the twentieth century," admitted Richard Taylor. "To be tasked with the job of designing the definitive, quintessential fantasy characters from our literary past was tough."[22] The studio, however, had other ideas. "He's a CG character who has to deliver a dramatic performance," stated the New Line executives. "Weta is going to do shots for this film, but they're not going to do Gollum."[23] While the designers eventually convinced New Line, Jackson viewed an audition tape for Gollum's voice done by British character actor Andy Serkis and decided that he wanted a live actor in the Gollum scenes. Serkis was hired and placed in a motion-capture suit, so that his acting—his physical movement—was digitized to create a hybrid human-digital character.[24] His very physical, expressive performance brought the technically impressive animation to life. Rather than a machine replacing a human, Serkis became the human replacement for the machine, a thing of which Tolkien would likely have approved.

the fellowship of the ring

How does one begin an epic? Unlike Homer, who opened *The Iliad* melodramatically with the line "Sing, oh Muse, the rage of Achilles," Tolkien began *The Lord of the Rings* quietly, with an essay about hobbits

followed by the description of a hobbit birthday party. Jackson debated over the beginning of his epic trilogy. Should he begin as Tolkien had, in Hobbiton, or was it necessary to provide a backstory for the film viewers? The studio demanded a prologue, and so Jackson edited together a narration (by Cate Blanchett's Galadriel) voiced over an intense battle sequence depicting the defeat of Sauron by the armies of Gil-galad and Elendil. *The Fellowship of the Ring*, premiering in London on December 10, 2001, begins in blackness, with the line, "The world is changed; I feel it in the water, I smell it in the air." The history of the Ring is told by Galadriel, ending with Bilbo's taking of the ring from Gollum's pool. "For the time will soon come," says Galadriel, "when hobbits will shape the fortunes of all."[25]

History, epic battle, treachery, and prophecy give way to the humble surroundings of Bag End, as the next scene begins as Tolkien did with "Concerning Hobbits," here the first chapter of Bilbo's book. Hobbiton is vividly constructed (or planted, in the case of much of the grass and shrubbery) by the production team according to the drawings of Alan Lee. Amid the lush greens and ale and pipe-weed cheerfulness of the Shire, Jackson introduces most of the prominent players of *Fellowship*: Bilbo, Frodo, Gandalf, Sam, Merry, and Pippin. Gandalf's appearance at Bilbo's party provides the viewer with scale (he squeezes into Bilbo's "hobbit hole") and offers Bilbo and Frodo information about the Ring. Compressing the time period of the book, Jackson has Frodo's escape from the Shire following hard on the heels of Bilbo's own disappearance.

Even more compression occurs in the following scenes, as Frodo, Sam, Merry, and Pippin escape the Black Riders and venture beyond the borders of the Shire. The complete omission from the film of their adventures before Bree—with Old Man Willow, the Barrow-wights, and especially Tom Bombadil—proved the most controversial of Jackson's choices. Many of Tolkien's readers are fans of Bombadil (as, it seems, was Tolkien himself) and were looking forward to his appearance in the film, but Jackson and his writing partners felt strongly that these episodes were not directly related to the Ring and therefore would not advance the drama of the storyline.[26] For pacing, therefore, Jackson chose to omit them and instead to intercut Gandalf's encounters with Saruman with the journey of the hobbits and Strider to Rivendell, an elegantly filmed version of Alan Lee's Celtic/Art Nouveau architectural designs for "the last Homely House in the West" (more city than house in the film).

The omission of Tom Bombadil from Peter Jackson's films is probably the most obvious and commented upon change from the novel. But many readers also point to the important character of Glorfindel, an elf-lord from Rivendell who plays a crucial role in *The Fellowship* (book). Here it is more a case of compression than omission. Though Glorfindel does not appear in the film, Arwen (Liv Tyler) is given some of his part in the story and the role of Haldir is elevated, with actor Craig Parker made-up to resemble Tolkien's description of Glorfindel:

> Glorfindel was tall and straight; his hair was of shining gold,
> his face fair and young and fearless and full of joy; his eyes
> were bright and keen, and his voice like music; on his brow
> sat wisdom, and in his hand was strength.[27]

Another controversy was the enlargement of the role of Arwen, who appears first in the "Flight to the Ford" scene, replacing Glorfindel. Arwen takes Frodo on her own horse, protects him from the ringwraiths, and prays for his healing, asking that the grace bestowed upon her flow to him. Tolkien fans feared rumors circulating before the film's release that Arwen would be transformed into a Xena-type warrior princess, who seem almost obligatory now in Hollywood action films. Jackson felt that he needed to both reduce the number of characters and increase the role of Aragorn's love-interest, and thus Arwen was used throughout the trilogy to explain Aragorn's motivation. The writers felt justified in this change because much of the love story derived from Tolkien's own material as found in *The Lord of the Rings*'s appendices; they were also able to make connections between Arwen's romance with Aragorn and that of Lúthien and Beren. After training Tyler in sword fighting in preparation for her to appear in a battle scene in film two, Jackson thought better of this change to Arwen. As Tyler herself explains, "You don't have to put a sword in [Arwen's] hand to make her strong."[28]

Alison Milbank points out how effectively Jackson "fetishizes" the Ring in the first film, especially in the Council of Elrond scene, when it remains glowingly in the center of the frame while the actors fade to soft-focus in the background.[29] In Bag End, at the beginning of the film, Jackson emphasized how unusually heavy the Ring was and gave it a voice; in the snowy path toward Caradhras, when Boromir picks up the Ring, an extra large prop is used for a close-up to emphasize the increasing power it has over him.

Boromir is the first to express the dual theme of despair and hope, prominent in the novel. He tells Aragorn that Galadriel spoke to his mind: "'Even now there is hope left,'" she said, "but I can't see it. It is long since there has been hope among my people."[30] Jackson then establishes the first sign of true friendship—or even kinship—between the two men of Gondor, as Boromir (in the extended edition) describes the White Tower of Gondor to Aragorn and promises to take him back to the city. Mortensen's face reveals Aragorn almost allowing himself to believe that this could happen.

GREATLY CONTRASTING ARE THE SET DESIGNS for Moria and Lothlorien, the crowning architectural achievements respectively of dwarves and elves in Middle-earth. Moria is all solid stone, angular, dark, and cold, while Lothlorien is curvilinear, organic, soft, and light. Whereas the dwarf-tongue sounds harsh to human ears, the speech of the elves—mostly Sindarin in the films—sounds soft and melodic. Blanchett, Mortensen, and Tyler each tackled Sindarin, with a speech coach, with varying degrees of success. Mortensen, Tyler, and Boyd also provide vocals for songs.

The final scenes in *The Fellowship of the Ring* film, "The Departure of Boromir" and "The Road Goes Ever On," vary in significant ways from the books. Partly this is due to the screenwriters' reorganization, as, for example, Boromir's death and the capture of Merry and Pippin, from the second book, are included in the first film. This makes great sense from a dramatic standpoint, for it wraps up Boromir's storyline and does so in a moving death scene, highlighted by some of the best original dialogue from the screenplay. Tolkien's description of Boromir's death, as we saw earlier, is sparse and heroic, with clear references to *The Song of Roland*. Jackson films the sequence close to Tolkien's description, but the extended dialogue (with a nod to Walt Whitman) deepens both Boromir's tragedy and Aragorn's promise to take his place as defender of Gondor:

BOROMIR, *leaning against a tree with three arrows in him.* Forgive me, I did not see. I failed you all.

ARAGORN, *at his side.* No, Boromir. You fought bravely. You have kept your honor.

BOROMIR Leave it. *He stays Aragorn's hand as he grasps the arrow in Boromir's chest.* It is over. The world of men will fall, and all will come to darkness, and my city to ruin.

ARAGORN I do not know what strength is in my blood, but I swear to you, I will not let the White City fall, nor our people fail.

BOROMIR Our people. *Aragorn nods.* Our people! *Boromir reaches for his sword and Aragorn places it in his hand.* I would have followed you my brother, my captain, my king. *Boromir dies.*

ARAGORN, *signing an elvish blessing.* Be at peace, son of Gondor. *He kisses Boromir's brow, then stands as Legolas and Gimli look on.* They will look to his coming from the White Tower, but he will not return. *He cries.*[31]

Just as Aragorn asserts his loyalty to Gondor in this scene (symbolized by strapping on Boromir's Gondorian vambraces, or forearm armor), Sam displays his loyalty to Frodo in the next by walking steadfastly into the lake (and nearly drowning!) in pursuit of his friend. "I made a promise, Mr. Frodo, a *promise*," states Sam (Sean Astin). "'Don't you leave him, Samwise Gamgee.' And I don't mean to. I don't mean to."[32] Tolkien's scene, however, is more humorous than heroic, with Frodo chiding Sam ("Don't pinch, lad!") as he pulls him from the water.

The Two Towers

The second film in the trilogy, *The Two Towers*, premiered in New York on December 5, 2002. It opens with a somber tone. We see Gandalf's fall in Moria, the capture of Merry and Pippin, and Frodo and Sam wondering lost in Emyn Muil. There they encounter Gollum, and we begin to see his sad story. There is a very poignant moment when the starving Gollum tells Frodo that he knows what suffering under the power of the Ring is like, that "once it gets hold of you, it never lets you go."[33] As the camera pulls back we see Frodo, Sam, and Gollum—arranged dramatically in a triangle—each struggling privately with their own doubts and fears. In the Dead Marshes, Gollum saves Frodo's life by pulling him out of the water and away from grasping specters in mail, cinematic phantoms from the Middle Ages as epitomized in Laȝamon's *Brut* (see page 71):

> *Hu liged I þan stræme stelene fisces*
> *mid sweorde bi-georede; heore sund is awemmed,*
> *heore scalen wleoted swulc gold-faye sceldes,*
> *þer fleoted heore spiten swulc hit spæren weoren.*

> "How steel fishes lie in the stream,
> girt with sword; their swimming is spoiled,
> their scales float like gold-bright shields,
> their fins drift there as if it were spears." [34]

This departure from the novel was perhaps intended to make apparent to the viewer the growing link between Frodo and Gollum. In *The Two Towers*, Andy Serkis plays Gollum as a wild addict, and his frantic performance inspired screenwriter Fran Walsh to write a more expansive and complex part for Gollum. A two-camera technique is used at one point to depict a schizoid conversation between the remaining goodness (Sméagol) and the lost addict (Gollum) within the wretched creature. This scene resonated with a lot of filmgoers and critics. It represents perhaps the height of cinematic fantasy achievement, building from a medieval base and adding twentieth-century writing (from both Tolkien and the screenwriters), contemporary method acting by a fine actor, ultra-realistic CGI, and a talented director who knows how and when to present the package to the viewer.

Much of film two deals with the domestic and foreign affairs of the vassal state of Rohan. While Tolkien completely separated the Frodo/Sam/Gollum section from that dealing with Rohan and Fangorn, Jackson had to intercut the action throughout, which is actually closer to the medieval romance technique of intricate "interlacing" used in the Arthurian Vulgate cycle (and which Tolkien himself employs, for example, in *The Silmarillion*). The set design for Meduseld, the palace of the king of Rohan, goes beyond the description provided by Tolkien in the published version of the epic. The Saxon/Norse animal-style interlace, seen in the exterior carvings, actually illustrates what Tolkien describes in an early draft of *The Lord of the Rings*:

> Before Théoden's hall there was a portico, with pillars made
> of mighty trees hewn in the upland forests and carved with
> interlacing figures gilded and painted. The doors also were
> of wood, carven in the likeness of many beasts and birds and
> jeweled eyes and golden claws.[35]

Composer Howard Shore's musical theme for Rohan, played every time the scene shifts back to Meduseld, employs the unique Norwegian fiddle, a folk instrument, to enhance the feeling of "Northernness."

Jackson found it very difficult to include all of the material from Tolkien's *The Two Towers* in his second film, even in the extended edition. Because of this and because of time-sequence purposes he moved, for example, the Shelob scenes to the third film. Still, he found room for some original scenes and dialogue, even if much of it appeared only on the extended edition DVD. One of these scenes is "The Funeral of Théodred," which features Éowyn (Miranda Otto) singing an elegy in Old English as her cousin is laid to rest in a burial mound. Afterward Théoden (Bernhard Hill), king of Rohan, laments the passing of his son and heir:

> THÉODEN Alas that these evil days should be mine!
> The young perish, and the old linger. That I should live
> to see the last days of my House.
> GANDALF Théodred's death was not of your making.
> THÉODEN No parent should have to bury their child.
> *He breaks down weeping.*
> GANDALF He was strong in life. His spirit will find its
> way to the halls of your fathers.[36]

Not only is this original scene a very poignant and human moment, but it serves as a needed counterbalance to the battle scenes that dominate the second half of the film. Just like Faramir's musing over the dead Haradrim boy-soldier—he wonders what the boy is named, where he is from, and if he was truly evil or just a victim of circumstance—it shows Jackson—like Homer in *The Iliad*—steering clear of the pure glorification of war by asking, in its midst, the tough questions about its necessity and its casualties.

One of the most egregious departures of script from book in this second film is the depiction of Faramir (David Wenham). In *The Two*

Towers (the book), when Faramir meets Frodo he is not tempted by the Ring, and makes a strong declaration against ever wanting to possess it (see page 151).

Peter Jackson moves this speech (in shortened form) to the extended edition of the third film, but in the second film Faramir is not only tempted by the Ring, he captures Frodo and Sam (and the ambushed Gollum), allows his men to treat them roughly, and ultimately drags them unwillingly back to Osgiliath in a desperate attempt to please his father. Peter Kreeft sees this as a gratuitous change "from heroic, honorable medieval knight to suspicious, uncertain fool."[37] "We see neither the true heroic faith in Faramir," agrees David Rozema, "nor the tragedy in Boromir's lack of the same."[38] While this criticism may be a bit too strong, it is puzzling that Faramir should undergo such a shift; his close relationship with Mithrandir (Gandalf) is completely ignored in the film, and many Tolkien fans were disappointed not to see the humble scholar-knight portrayed on screen. Was this done intentionally so as not to deflect our affections from Aragorn, Gandalf's other pupil? Screenwriter Philippa Boyens explains that to stick to the book here would have diminished the power of the Ring, while Wenham believes that the change gives Faramir on-camera emotional growth.[39]

The centerpiece of the film is the Battle of Helm's Deep, with parallel conflicts at Isengard and Osgiliath. With Helm's Deep we see Jackson both continuing cinematic convention and displaying technological invention. Saruman sends his Uruk-hai troops off to war in a scene whose aesthetics are reminiscent of Leni Riefenstahl's Nazi propaganda films. Christopher Lee makes the most of his vocal gifts and Brad Dourif (Wormtongue), a single tear trickling down his cheek, represents the awe and terror of the spectator. Helm's Deep's night battle in the mud and rubble recalls scenes in many films about twentieth-century warfare. The second film's visual and emotional climax—Gandalf suddenly appearing on the hill astride a rearing white horse leading the cavalry of Rohan—is an obvious nod to Hollywood westerns. The Weta team employed a new artificial intelligence software program called Massive to build a realistic-looking army of fifty thousand orcs, with each digital warrior moving independently and reacting to virtual sights and sounds. Jackson confessed that the 1964 film *Zulu* provided the pattern for his Battle of Helm's Deep, with its slow buildup and "all hell's broke loose" depiction of one hundred British soldiers desperately defending their fort against four thousand Zulus warriors.

As much as the second film is about war, it is also about hope. Early in the film the exiled Éomer (Karl Urban) tells Aragorn, "Look for your friends, but do not trust to hope. It is forsaken in these lands."[40] But Aragorn is the carrier of hope in the film. Bound together by love, Aragorn and Arwen express their shared allegiance to hope at nearly the same time in the film, though they are separated geographically. Elrond (Hugo Weaving), trying to convince his daughter to leave Rivendell for the Undying Lands, asks her, "Why do you linger here when there is no hope?" "There is still hope," she asserts,[41] though Aragorn left her with little at their last parting. For his part, Aragorn awaits seemingly certain death on the walls of Helm's Deep, yet he has promised Gandalf that the defenses will hold. A frightened boy (Haleth son of Hamma, from Old English hæleð, "hero") arming for his first battle expresses his desperation to Aragorn: "They say that it is hopeless." Aragorn, after testing the boy's sword, looks him in the eyes and replies, "There is always hope."[42]

Aragorn's courage and leadership are needed at Helm's Deep because the king's are failing. Théoden teeters on the brink of inaction and despair as he sees his men slaughtered by Saruman's vicious, soulless, creatures. "So much death," he laments. "What can men do against such reckless hate?" "Ride out with me," urges Aragorn. "Ride out and meet them!" "For death and glory?" asks a smiling king. "For Rohan, for your people," answers Aragorn.[43] As Strider he must take orders from the king of Rohan, but as the heir of Gondor he is Théoden's lord, and it is here, near the end of film two, that Aragorn assumes the mantle of statesmanship as promised to Boromir at the end of film one.

The choice of hope over despair, hinted at in the final dialogue between Frodo and Sam in film one, is made explicit by Sam in his speech at the end of film two:

> SAM It's like in the great stories, Mr. Frodo, the ones
> that really mattered. . . . Folk in those stories had lots of
> chances of turning back, only they didn't. They kept goin',
> 'cause they were holdin' on to something.
> FRODO What are we holding on to, Sam?
> SAM That there's some good in this world, Mr. Frodo, and
> it's worth fightin' for![44]

Sam's assertion (a line invented by scriptwriter Philippa Boyens), made here in the face of Frodo's growing despair in war-torn Osgiliath, that there *is* good in the world, seems to convince Frodo. Gollum, looking on, is not convinced, for he is so far under the power of the Ring that he cannot hope for goodness within himself or in other people. Frodo has apparently betrayed him, and the film ends with Gollum convincing Sméagol to lead the hobbits to certain death in Shelob's lair.

The Return of the King

The dark tone of film two, arguably reflecting Tolkien's own pessimism, carries over to the opening of film three. Jackson made a bold choice to begin the last part of his trilogy with a flashback sequence showing the transformation of Sméagol into Gollum. A sunny fishing expedition on Sméagol's birthday quickly gives way to a violent portrayal of addiction: Sméagol strangles his friend Déagol, accompanied by a throbbing and screeching soundtrack, and seizes the Ring. The Ring then seizes him, and film three continues the schizophrenic dialogues between good Sméagol and evil Gollum. Jackson exaggerates the rift between Gollum and Sam to the point of Gollum convincing Frodo that it is Sam who wants the Ring for himself. As many critics have pointed out, this is a major change to the story in book three, and though it seems a natural development in the film's plot, Frodo's eventual dismissal of Sam does not quite resonate with the relationship as developed in the books.

Film three also develops the close relationship between Aragorn and Éowyn, with the latter and her uncle expecting a formal bond to occur. But the viewer is taken back to Rivendell and reminded of Arwen, who glimpses a future with Aragorn and a son of *their* union. That future is all but gone, her father tells her, though nothing is certain. "Some things are certain," she responds, asserting her belief in the hope that comes from loving. While her love is symbolized by the Evenstar jewel she gave to Aragorn, which he wears on a chain around his neck, her hope is manifest in the reforging of the Shards of Narsil into the newly christened sword Andúril, and the delivering of Andúril to Aragorn by Elrond. "I give hope to men,"[45] declares Elrond as he gives the sword to Aragorn. Jackson invents this sequence so that Aragorn's assumption of the sword of kingship can come at a climactic moment in the trilogy, though in the film he seems ultimately convinced to do so in order to save a dying Arwen.

In Minas Tirith it is the tree of kings that is dying, the White Tree, which represents the hope of the people of Gondor, who guard it still out of a faint hope, Gandalf tells Pippin, that it will flower when a king returns to Gondor. But the city is now in the hands of a steward, Denethor (John Noble), who tries to unravel Gandalf's plans for Aragorn and the defense of the city. "Authority has not been given you to deny the return of the king!"[46] shouts Gandalf, confirming Denethor's suspicions. As the shadow of Mordor looms over Gondor, Pippin asks Gandalf if he believes whether there is any hope for the Frodo and Sam and their quest. "There was never much hope," responds Gandalf, his mind clouded by pipe smoke, "only a fool's hope."[47] Even Gandalf the White and the prophetic Elrond cannot see, with certainty, the outcome of the events about to unfold.

But Denethor, who has been using the Seeing Stone, thinks he can. His grieving for the dead Boromir makes him inactive, or else drives him to bad decisions, such as sending his surviving son, Faramir, to retake Osgiliath. The near-fatal wounding of Faramir sends Denethor over the edge into utter despair and, eventually, suicide.

The sets and miniatures of Minas Tirith and Minas Morgul (based on the drawings of Alan Lee and John Howe) are some of the greatest achievements of the production team working on this film. For Minas Tirith and Osgiliath, the designs seem inspired by Byzantine and Romanesque architecture, with solid walls and columns, brick domes, and rounded arches.[48] Minas Tirith was, according to the set designers, a combination of Mont Saint-Michel and medieval Sienna, complete with craft guilds emblems above the shops, while the throne room was based on Charlemagne's chapel at Aix-la-Chapelle (present-day Aachen, Germany). The sound and light effects for Minas Morgul stand out in particular, heightening the tension as Frodo attempts to smuggle the Ring into Mordor while a frightened Pippin watches from afar on the *palantír* he took from Gandalf. Pippin begins to redeem himself (for disobeying Gandalf with the seeing stone) by offering his service (homage and fealty) to Denethor and by climbing a perilous height to light the tower beacon. Though orcs now descend on Gondor, hope also spreads as breathtaking aerial shots show us beacon fires erupting on snow-covered mountaintops high above the clouds. Some archaeologists

believe that the hill forts of Iron Age Britain may have communicated with each other through similar signal fires.[49]

"The men have found their captain," Éowyn tells Aragorn as the Rohirrim answer Gondor's call for help. "You have given us hope."[50] Merry in turn offers his service to Théoden, but later both he and Éowyn are told they cannot take part in the coming battle. To make matters worse for the White Lady of Rohan, Aragorn suddenly decides to leave camp and spurns the love offered by Éowyn. "It is but a shadow and a thought that you love," he tells her. "I cannot give you what you seek."[51] As Aragorn (accompanied by Legolas and Gimli) leave for the Dimholt, Théoden bestows his authority on the saddened Éowyn as he leaves for his doom, and urges her not to despair.

Théoden has encountered despair but conquered it. Denethor, who has also lost a son, has succumbed to it, as he sends Faramir off on a suicide mission to retake Osgiliath. When a grievously wounded Faramir returns to the citadel, Denethor chooses death for himself and his son and orders the Gondorian soldiers to flee for their lives. "Gondor is lost," he declares. "There is no hope for men."[52] But as he says this he is walking past the White Tree, where we glimpse a single white flower blossoming. There *is* still hope, for we the viewers have seen it in the strength of Gandalf, the bravery of Pippin, the loyalty of Sam and Merry, and the perseverance of Frodo and Aragorn.

But there is also the betrayal of Sméagol/Gollum, which becomes clear to Frodo only after he has been lured, alone, into Shelob's cave. Even an apparition of Galadriel and the Light of Eärendil are not enough to save Frodo from Shelob's stinger. Nor is the staff of the White Wizard enough to defeat the Witch-king of Angmar, who suddenly appears on a fell beast and (in the extended edition) breaks Gandalf's staff along with Pippin's courage. However, once again the viewer is saved from despair by the editing of the film. Sam arrives, bearing the Light and Sting, to save Frodo from Shelob, while horns announce the arrival of the Rohirrim just in time to save a falling Minas Tirith. As in classic Western films (and the end of film two), the cavalry saves the day— here, the largest cavalry charge ever assembled for film, involving over 250 real horses and riders enhanced by CG to a total of six thousand.[53] Éowyn urges Merry to stay brave as Théoden delivers the war cry: "Ride now! Ride for ruin, and the world's ending!"[54] While it is not quite Ragnarok—the world-ending battle of Norse myth—the look of terror on the orcs' faces does give the audience some feel for the awesome might of a heavily armed cavalry assault in the Middle Ages.

The first heavy-armored cavalry in ancient warfare was war elephants, and Sauron sends his giant oliphaunts into the fray at this time to meet the force from Rohan. As the Nazgûl and oliphaunts sweep down on the Rohirrim and a giant troll beats on the door of the citadel, Gandalf delivers a speech to Pippin about death. White shores, a far green country, and a swift sunrise—lines taken from Frodo's vision in the house of Bombadil, repeated at the Grey Havens—encourage us, as it does Pippin: "That doesn't sound so bad?" "No, it doesn't,"[55] responds a smiling Gandalf, who knows something of the afterlife. But though Théoden has been felled by the Nazgûl, we are not ready to embrace death yet. Éowyn intercedes to save her uncle, and Aragorn appears with the Black Fleet and the army of the dead (a slightly different scene than the actual book, where the dead were not in the ship at Pelennor, only Aragorn's allies). An unusual return for the king of Gondor, but a return nonetheless.

"You fool," sneers the Witch-king as he grabs Éowyn by the throat, "no man can kill me." Indeed. But what about a hobbit and a woman? Merry stabs him in the leg, while Éowyn removes her helmet and, with the words "I am no man,"[56] runs him through with her sword. A faint echo here, perhaps, of Odysseus in the cave of Polyphemus—"My name is Nobody," says the hero, leaving the Cyclops to shout, "Nobody is hurting me!" when Odysseus drives the stake into his eye. This thrilling movie moment is soon followed by another: a spectacular effects shot of Legolas, with elvish super agility, climbing a charging oliphaunt from tail to tusk and bringing it down with his bow. The graceful turn by Orlando Bloom is here reminiscent of Errol Flynn in *The Adventures of Robin Hood* (1938) and Mark Hamill in *The Empire Strikes Back* (1980), and Jackson and his production team have given us a similarly iconic moment for the twenty-first century.

Though the battle is won, it is a costly victory. "My body is broken," Théoden tells his niece. "I go to my fathers, in whose mighty company I shall not now feel shamed."[57] Éowyn too has received a grievous wound; her recovery, along with that of Merry and Faramir, was chronicled in great detail by Tolkien in "The Houses of Healing" episode of book three. Jackson, however, chooses to condense or discard much of this part of the book. Aragorn's "healing hand," which harkens back to the sacral power of ancient Germanic kings, is not explained here; the romance of Éowyn and Faramir is shown through montage (accompanied by a Liv Tyler song); and the formal assumption of Aragorn's kingship—replete with ceremonies of vassalage and heraldic devices in the book—is ignored. Fans of the book will miss Prince Imrahil, Ghân-buri-Ghân and the Wild Men, the Dúnedain, and the sons of Elrond, whose assistance with the victory at Pelennor is sacrificed in the name of simplification.

The rest of the film is concerned with Frodo's growing "addiction" to the Ring, and to Aragorn showing himself to Sauron as the returned King of Gondor. Gandalf worries that Frodo, in Mordor, is past hope—though we have just witnessed Sam's rescue of the Ring and the Ring-bearer—while Aragorn reassures him that hope remains. The Gondorian king *is* the hope, along with the rest of Frodo's friends, who ride off to face an overwhelmingly superior enemy force on its own territory, solely as a distraction. Frodo needs this, and he needs Sam, who in the end must carry Frodo and the Ring himself up the slopes of Mount Doom. "Come on, Mr. Frodo. I can't carry it for you, but I can carry you!"[58] This is a powerfully acted moment for Astin, who convincingly embodies Sam's undaunted optimism, his determination, and above all his loyalty.

Aragorn has also grown more determined, for it is he who assures a grieving Gandalf before the Black Gates that Frodo is not dead, despite the *mithril* shirt displayed by the taunting Mouth of Sauron. Jackson abandoned the idea of having Aragorn engage in single combat with Annatar—that is, Sauron in the fair guise with which he fooled the elves (see page 201)—and instead made the climactic moment a speech given by Aragorn to his terrified troops (portrayed by real soldiers from the New Zealand army):

> Sons of Gondor, of Rohan, my brothers, I see in your eyes the same fear that would take the heart of me. A day may come when the courage of men fails, when we forsake our friends and break all bonds of fellowship. But it is not this day. An hour of wolves and shattered shields, when the Age of Men comes crashing down. But it is not this day! This day we fight! By all that you hold dear, on this good earth, I bid you stand, Men of the West![59]

Compare this speech—with its echoes of Winston Churchill and *Henry V*'s St Crispin Day speech—to these words (see page 68) from the Old Norse *Poetic Edda*:

> Hard is it in the world,
> great whoredom,
> an axe age, a sword age,
> shields will be cloven,
> a wind age, a wolf age,
> ere the world sinks.[60]

The ascent of Frodo and Sam up Mount Doom is a masterpiece of cinematography, aided by the location of the shoot on a real volcano. Jackson's interpretation of the events at the Crack of Doom varies again from the book. Instead of Gollum falling accidentally into the fire, in the film Frodo struggles with him to regain the Ring, and both fall over the cliff (Frodo grabs onto the edge but Gollum falls into the fire). Frodo then becomes a more active player in the destruction of the Ring (Jackson carefully avoids making it appear that Frodo pushes Gollum), and it gives Sam another opportunity to save his friend by pulling him up to safety. Stranded on a rocky outcrop surrounded by rushing lava, Frodo and Sam await "the end of all things" by recalling images from the Shire, a device employed by the writers to remind viewers why these Halflings left at the beginning of film one: to preserve their good green earth from the shadow of evil.

The most common criticism of the third film concerns the multiple endings employed by Jackson. Like the deceptive cadences at the end of a Beethoven symphony, these multiple "goodbyes" and fade-outs annoyed many reviewers. But how does one say goodbye to Middle-earth, to a world which many people gave many years of their lives to create on screen? Having long ago decided to discard "The Scouring of the Shire," Jackson still had to film the reunion of the Fellowship, the coronation of Aragorn (and reunion with Arwen), the return home of the hobbits, and the departure of Frodo and the elves from the Grey Havens. This last scene elicited strong emotions from Astin, Boyd, and Monaghan, whose tears viewers could well believe. When Sam, returning to the Shire, utters the last words of the film (and book)— "Well, I'm back"—viewers who themselves had invested more than

three years in anticipation of the films (and then of their extended DVD versions) are both happy and sad to leave the high adventure to return to the comfort of their own shires and hobbit-holes.

Box Office and Reviews

Peter Jackson's trilogy has, to date, earned more than $1 billion in US box office receipts, while millions more continue to come in from the VHS, DVD, and Blu-Ray versions (cinematic and extended) and rentals. It is in the top ten film franchises in terms of both US and worldwide gross receipts. As one Dutch study has shown, many viewers responded that watching the films was nothing less than a spiritual experience.[61] Harder to discern are the trends in the reviews of the movie critics, given their widely divergent readership and the fact that they are reviewing three different films. Like the critics of the reader's polls, they are also often reacting to the whole Tolkien phenomenon—books, Internet chatter, fans showing up to viewings in costume—and seldom are neutral on Tolkien at the outset. Furthermore, Jackson in particular had to face the challenge of producing a serious filmic adaptation after decades of film studios producing bad sword-and-sorcery movies, many of which were viewed by these same critics.

Overall, however, Jackson's movies earned a good deal of critical praise.[62] Roger Ebert (*Chicago Sun Times*) wrote that *The Fellowship of the Ring* is "an awesome production" that transcends its genre, but ultimately it is not "a true visualization of Tolkien's Middle-earth."[63] *Rolling Stone*'s Peter Travers praises the acting of McKellen, Mortensen, and Bean as well as Jackson's ability to root *The Fellowship* in emotion,[64] while Stephanie Zacharek of Salon.com believes that "Jackson captures the spirit and flavor of Tolkien's storytelling."[65] The technological achievement of Jackson and Weta received nearly universal praise, especially with the appearance of Gollum in *The Two Towers*. Ebert calls *Towers* "one of the most spectacular swashbucklers ever made" with "scenes of breath-taking beauty."[66] Philip French (the *Observer*) sees the influence of the Pre-Raphaelites and Art Nouveau children's book illustrations in the design and photography of *Towers*, while the "New Zealand settings have a rugged, primeval grandeur."[67] While many now consider *Towers* the best movie of the trilogy, Ebert gives that title to *The Return of the King*, calling it "a work of bold ambition" despite lacking "truthful emotion thought-fully paid for."[68] J. Hoberman (*Village Voice*) sees "stray shards of character psychology" in Gollum, Denethor, and Éowyn, but warns us about this "exhausting and riveting . . . technological marvel." "Look, don't listen," writes Hoberman, for "Aragorn's Agincourt speech is not exactly Shakespeare."[69] No, but it is, as we have seen, the Old Norse *Poetic Edda*.

awards

While the first two films earned many technical awards, Peter Jackson and the actors were given little recognition by the Hollywood mainstream. Ian McKellen, for example, was the only actor even nominated for an Academy Award (for *Fellowship*). These were truly ensemble films, and so there was little discussion over the lack of Oscar nominations for the actors. Most surprising, perhaps, was the failure to recognize Sean Astin with a Best Supporting Actor nomination for *Return of the King*. Jackson and his crew, however, would finally get their due with the 2004 Academy Awards. *Return of the King* was nominated in eleven categories and swept them all, including Oscars for Best Director and Best Picture. It also won five BAFTAs, Director's Guild of America and Director's Guild of Great Britain Awards (for Jackson), four Golden Globes, two Grammys, a Screen Actor's Guild Award for Best Cast in a Motion Picture, and dozens of others. In 2007, the American Film Institute ranked *The Fellowship of the Ring* as number fifty in its list of Top 100 films, and nearly every viewer's poll lists the films even higher.[70]

the hobbit films

No sooner had the glitter settled from Oscar Night than did Peter Jackson and the cast get questions regarding a "prequel"—would *The Hobbit* be coming soon to a New Zealand shire? While all parties seemed willing, several legal battles stood in the way. The first was between Saul Zaentz and New Line Cinema, the former asking in 2004 for royalties from the three films. Peter Jackson followed suit in 2005, claiming that he did not receive all of the profits due to him from New Line.[71] In December 2007 a settlement was reached and New Line announced that it would finance, together with MGM (which had purchased United Artists), two hobbit films with Jackson as executive producer.[72]

Additional legal action was taken by Tolkien's heirs, who also were claiming that they did not receive adequate compensation for material used in the Jackson films. A suit was filed in February 2008 by the Trustees of the J. R. R. Tolkien Estate and HarperCollins Publishers

Ltd. (coplaintiffs) against New Line, now a division of Warner Bros. A settlement was reached in September 2009, with an undisclosed amount of the proceeds going to the Tolkien Trust to further its charitable objectives. Commenting on the settlement, Christopher Tolkien said: "The Trustees regret that legal action was necessary but are glad that this dispute has been settled on satisfactory terms that will allow the Tolkien Trust properly to pursue its charitable objectives. The Trustees acknowledge that New Line may now proceed with its proposed films of *The Hobbit*."[73]

After the Jackson/New Line feud was resolved, it was announced that the two new films, *The Hobbit* and a sequel to *The Hobbit*, would be shot in 3-D simultaneously in New Zealand. New Line would distribute in North America and MGM internationally. It was also announced that Jackson would not direct the films, but rather serve as coexecutive producer along with Fran Walsh. Guillermo Del Toro was then hired in 2008 to direct and cowrite the films. Best known for *Pan's Labyrinth* and the *Hell Boy* films, Del Toro described the assignment as "an absolute dream come true." "I'm eager to explore themes that lend themselves easily to metaphor," he said in an interview. "The fantastic is the only tool we have nowadays to explain spirituality to a generation that refuses to believe in dogma or religion. Superhero movies create a kind of mythology. Creature movies, horror movies, create at least a belief in something beyond."[74]

The script was written by a team consisting of Del Toro, Jackson, Walsh, and Philippa Boyens. Preproduction work, including costume and creature designs, was completed by Weta and preliminary discussions were held with some of the principle actors, including Ian McKellen and Andy Serkis. But the financial troubles and pending sale of MGM in 2010 delayed casting and production of the films, leading Del Toro to walk away from the project at the end of May. Jackson agreed to serve once again as director, and the casting of the major roles was completed in early 2011. Martin Freeman (*Hitchhiker's Guide to the Galaxy*) was chosen to play Bilbo and Richard Armitage (*Robin Hood*) was tapped as Thorin Oakenshield, while McKellen, Serkis, Christopher Lee, Ian Holm, Cate Blanchett, and Hugo Weaving agreed to reprise their roles from *The Lord of the Rings*, as did Elijah Wood (although Frodo did not appear in *The Hobbit* book). Some surprising cast additions were Sylvester McCoy as Radagast the Brown, Barry Humphries as the Great Goblin, and for the second film, Evangeline Lilly as a Mirkwood elf named Tauriel (not in any Tolkien book). Even more surprising was Jackson's announcement, just months before the first film's release, that there would now be *three Hobbit* films.

The Hobbit: An Unexpected Journey appeared on screens around the world on December 14, 2012. While it had a strong opening weekend and has grossed nearly $1 billion worldwide, both fans and critics have been less impressed than they were with *The Lord of the Rings* trilogy. Slow pacing and Jackson's choice to film at forty-eight frames per second were the most common complaints. "The movie looks so hyper-real," writes *Rolling Stone*'s Peter Travers, "that you see everything that's fake about it, from painted sets to prosthetic noses."[75] While dwarf silliness and Radagast's eccentricities also proved distracting to some, the film's major departure from Tolkien was in depicting a warrior Bilbo who takes on wargs and giant orcs with his newfound sword. Freeman is otherwise convincing as a fussy Bilbo, and once again Serkis's Gollum nearly steals the show. Seeing Wood, McKellen, and Blanchett again felt like returning home, and the mere glimpse of Smaug's nostril at the end of the film gives one hope that some of the old magic will cloak the sequels.

stage productions

"DRAMA IS NATURALLY HOSTILE TO FANTASY," wrote Tolkien. "Fantastic forms are not to be counterfeited. Men dressed up as talking animals may achieve buffoonery or mimicry, but they do not achieve Fantasy."[76] Such a challenge has perhaps scared off serious attempts to bring *The Lord of the Rings* to the stage (not to mention the licensing fees). Children's theater, therefore, may seem a more natural fit, more capable of achieving fantasy for at least the very young. British playwright Glyn Robbins adapted *The Hobbit* for the stage, and Roy Marsden's productions of the adaptation have toured Britain since 1999. Reviewers, mostly mildly appreciative, have commented on its Gothic stage designs and Pre-Raphaelite costuming.

Much more ambitious is *The Lord of the Rings*, a musical produced by Kevin Wallace and Saul Zaentz, directed by Matthew Warchus, with book and lyrics by Warchus and Shaun McKenna and music by A. R. Rahman, Värttinä, and Christopher Nightingale. After a successful trial run of more than six months in Toronto, the musical came to the

Theatre Royal, Drury Lane, in June 2007 (when I caught a performance) and ran for 492 performances until it closed in July 2008. At £12 million it was one of the most expensive musicals ever produced in London's West End. The star of the London production was Laura Michelle Kelly (Galadriel), fresh from originating the title role in the London production of *Mary Poppins*. Her singing is the highlight of an otherwise forgettable collection of songs.

In the tradition of *The Lion King* and other West End/Broadway musical spectacles, *The Lord of the Rings* attempted to wow audiences with its large and elaborate sets and special effects. Hobbits frolicked in the aisles just before the curtain rose on Bilbo's party, orcs with crutches for arms snuck up on spectators in the balcony, and the balrog jumped out at the audience with an adrenaline rush of smoke and confetti. It is now well known that Tolkien loved trees, and this was taken to heart by the set and costume designers. Almost every set looked organic, with twirling vines and twisting trees spilling out all over the theater. Costuming for the warriors—especially Strider, Boromir, and Gimli—incorporated several historical pieces from the arms and armor of the Middle Ages. In my opinion, the condensation and conflation of the novel produced a confusing mess and the acting was of the quality of the typical "sword-and-sorcery" movie; it never reached the power or intimacy of the Peter Jackson films. There was talk of a world tour in 2011, but a more serious rewrite would seem warranted. If mimicry and buffoonery on stage can ever be a good thing, it is achieved by Canadian actor/playwright Charles Ross. Ross debuted his one-man version of Jackson's *Lord of the Rings* films at the Edinburgh Fringe Festival in 2009, after working on it for nearly five years and trying to secure the rights. Condensing eleven hours and twenty-three minutes into a sixty-five-minute performance results not only in a manic whirl-wind but also a loving tribute to Tolkien and the films. Ross plays all the major roles and many of the minor ones—from orcs to Gandalf's moth to the bucket that falls down the well in Moria! He also sings the soundtrack—or hums it as the case may be—while acting out battle scenes and all the now-iconic moments from Peter Jackson's trilogy. There are lots of funny moments, but a warning: you will be lost if you have not seen the films (sorry, the books won't help much with the visual gags). This is not medieval but medievalism at several removes. And it is hilarious.

musical inspiration

FROM THE CREATION OF ARDA to the adventures of the hobbits, music and songs are clearly an integral part of Tolkien's sub-creation. "I have little musical knowledge," admitted Tolkien in a 1964 letter. "Music gives me great pleasure and sometimes inspiration."[77] In his own house he enjoyed the piano-playing of his wife and daughter, and he was a regular concertgoer in Oxford. He knew little about opera, though he attended a performance of part of Wagner's *Der Ring des Nibelungen* at Covent Garden with C. S. Lewis in the 1930s. (Tolkien and Wagner were both reworking many of the same themes from the ca. 1200 *Nibelungenlied*, though there are important differences in their respective interpretations.[78]) He preferred old popular ballads to the American-inspired pop and rock music of his later years, his secretary claiming that he loathed the Beatles and John Lennon in particular.[79]

Tolkien did not live to hear most of the music that his books inspired, but there is one notable exception. Oxford graduate Donald Swann composed a song-cycle titled *The Road Goes Ever On* by composing music to the lyrics in Tolkien's works, and played it privately to Tolkien during a visit to Oxford in 1965. The professor enjoyed the songs and suggested to Swann a Gregorian-type chant for the lament "Namárië." Swann included his edit and performed the songs, with accompanying baritone William Elvin, at Ronald and Edith's Golden Anniversary celebration at Merton College in 1966. According to musician Simon Machin, "Swann viewed Tolkien's work not as escapist fantasy, but as a paradigm of human life with its sense of destiny and purpose."[80]

Many musical genres are represented by the dozens of original songs inspired by Tolkien that have appeared since the late 1960s. Robert Plant and Jimmy Page of Led Zeppelin, for example, were both fans of *The Lord of the Rings*, and in their early years they wrote Tolkien-themed songs.[81] Tracks like "Ramble On" (from *Led Zeppelin II*) and "The Battle of Evermore" (on *Led Zeppelin IV*) feature lyrics about Mordor, Gollum, and ringwraiths. Marc Bolan, a regular at London's Middle Earth club, formed the glam-rock band T. Rex with a drummer named Steve Peregrin Took. Rick Wakeman, keyboardist for the rock group Yes, wrote several synth-rock pieces inspired by Tolkien in the 1990s. Synth, New Age, and contemporary Celtic music are filled with albums and songs bearing Middle-earth names.

More than a few classical composers have also produced Tolkien-inspired works. Dutch composer Johan de Meij, English composers Carey Blyton and Stephen Oliver, and the Tolkien Ensemble from Denmark are some of the more notable examples. However, Canadian Howard Shore's compositions for Peter Jackson's three films stand alone as the most ambitious and celebrated of all. Shore combined folk instruments, choirs, well-known Irish singer Enya, little known Icelandic vocalist Emiliana Torrini, and Scottish rock diva Annie Lennox with classical orchestration to produce a powerful aural accompaniment to Jackson's images. His Academy Award—winning scores are regularly performed now by orchestras, and Shore has most recently written *The Lord of the Rings Symphony: Six Movements for Orchestra & Chorus.*

TOLKIEN HAD ONCE IMAGINED that he would lay the foundations of a new mythology for England, and from his stories other writers and artists would add their own interpretations and grow the mythology the way countless Greek and Roman writers and artists built upon the stories of Homer and Hesiod. Not only did this come true in the art and cinema discussed here, but also, as evident in the next appendix, in myriad ways of which even Professor Tolkien could not have dreamed.

appendix III

tolkieniana

J. R. R. TOLKIEN was many things: an orphan, a soldier, a father, a devout Catholic, an academician, a medievalist, an artist, a best-selling novelist. But he has also become a phenomenon; or rather it is the countless ripples spread from the splash of his Middle-earth writings in the pool of modern literature that can be described as such. This ripple-effect continues with the boost given by Peter Jackson's films, so much so that the worldwide viewer reaction to the third installment, *The Return of the King*, was the subject of a social science research project whose questionnaire yielded a dataset of nearly 25,000 valid responses![1] "Tolkieniana"—as clumsy as that term is—perhaps best describes the effects that Tolkien had and continues to have on politics, popular culture, and new media. Each of these waves carries a little bit of the medieval into our world in some very unexpected ways.

"frodo Lives!": tolkien and hippie culture

MUSIC WAS JUST ONE PART of the "cult of Tolkien," which began to spread rapidly (especially in America) in the late 1960s. Biographer Humphrey Carpenter attributes much of this to the success of the affordable paperback editions of Tolkien's books on American college campuses, first with the release of a "pirated" Ace edition of *The Lord of the Rings* in 1965 and then with the authorized Ballantine editions of *The Hobbit* and *The Lord of the Rings* which followed later that year.[2] Tolkien's assiduously answering of fan mail from America led to the formation of the "Tolkien Society of America," and soon fan clubs popped up on both coasts along with buttons reading "Frodo Lives" and "Gandalf for President."

Closer to home, Tolkien witnessed a corresponding rise in British sales and the formation of a Tolkien Society in London. London in the

1960s was home to the Middle Earth club, a Covent Garden venue where David Bowie and the Doors (among others) played; and Gandalf's Garden, a magazine, shop, and commune originally based in Chelsea whose objective was "to bring beautiful people together."[3] The "flower children" were drawn to Tom Bombadil and the tree-herding ents, and so a romanticized environmentalism became linked with Tolkien wherever his books were read. In 1972, David McTaggart, one of the founders of Greenpeace, wrote about how reading *The Lord of the Rings* inspired his own eco-politics.

That is not to say that Tolkien would have joined Greenpeace or attended fantasy conventions. "Many young Americans are involved in the stories in a way that I am not," he told one reporter."[4] "Being a cult idol in one's own lifetime I am afraid is not at all pleasant." Tolkien was, for the most part, annoyed by his cult-status, rejected the hippies, and blamed both on American cultural soil.[5] His irritability on the subject went beyond irrational prejudices and donnish crankiness, for overenthusiastic fans were constantly showing up at his door asking for autographs and calling him on the phone in the middle of the night. Rather than enjoying the life of a celebrity in his retirement, he became increasingly private. He had no wish to serve as guru to the groovy.

fantasy before and after tolkien

HE DID, HOWEVER, POLITELY RECEIVE VISITS from a handful of academics and journalists. He also, with the help of Allen & Unwin, continued to answer letters from his fans. In the 1960s and '70s a generation of young people who had grown up reading his books became artists and writers themselves, and the fantasy publishing industry exploded with titles inspired by and in imitation of *The Lord of the Rings*. Tolkien did not inherit a market-defined genre with readers already accustomed to buying fantasy fiction. Rather, he took the essentially Victorian genres of children's stories and adult heroic romance and combined them into something utterly new for *The Hobbit*, developing this further still in *The Lord of the Rings*.

We have already discussed the influence of Andrew Lang's fairy books and George MacDonald's *Princess* books on the young Tolkien. He was also a fan of Lewis Carroll, especially his lesser-known poetry like *Sylvie and Bruno* (1889), and Kenneth Grahame's *The Wind in the Willows* (1908). He records in his diary for April 1910 his reaction at seeing a performance of J. M. Barrie's *Peter Pan*: "Indescribable but I shall never forget it as long as I live."[6] As Garth points out, Barrie's famous play was "aimed squarely at an orphan's heart," and may have been an inspiration for Tolkien's love poem "You and Me / and the Cottage of Lost Play" (1915).[7] As for more adult fare, William Morris, as we have seen, was a particular favorite, and he enjoyed Rudyard Kipling and Arthur Conan Doyle. For adventure he seems to have preferred H. Rider Haggard's novels, especially *King Solomon's Mines* (1885) and *She* (1887), about a mysterious African queen who rules the lost city of Kôr. The latter provided the image of the ancient ruined city for Tolkien's sonnet "Kôr: In a City Lost and Dead" and his painting *Tanaqui*, both from 1915, and Haggard's word "Kôr" even appears in the Quenya lexicon.[8]

As is evident from this brief list,[9] there is not much commonality between these works, and thus no simple genre formula for Tolkien to follow. And yet his own books have provided just this: a "fantasy template" for writers and game designers to follow as they will, to pick and choose words, settings, creatures, and characters. Simply listing such fantasy writers would run to several pages, but the more prominent authors who have admitted to being influenced by Tolkien in one way or another include Michael Moorcock, Ursula K. Le Guin, David Eddings, Stephen R. Donaldson, Terry Brooks, Terry Pratchett, Guy Gavriel Kay, Philip Pullman, and J. K. Rowling (see below). Of these authors, Brooks is perhaps the most imitative, in his *The Sword of Shannara* series (1977–present), while others, like Donaldson and Pullman, have attempted to distance themselves from their literary parent (or grandparent, in some cases). "I do not think that any modern writer of epic fantasy has managed to escape the mark of Tolkien," comments Tom Shippey, "no matter how hard many of them have tried."[10] Most are like the critics in Tolkien's *Beowulf* essay, dismantling the tower and building other structures with its parts, never reaching the heights—nor sharing the purpose—of the master architect.

harry potter and middle-earth

In her creation of the Harry Potter series (1997–2007), British author J. K. Rowling drew inspiration from a wide variety of literary sources, including medieval Arthurian legend, T. H. White, C. S. Lewis, and of course J. R. R. Tolkien. The house-elf named Kreacher bears many similarities to Gollum, including his appearance and his tendency to lie. Boromir calls Sauron, the Dark Lord, "h[e] that we do not name," while the Voldemort, the Dark Lord in Harry Potter, is often called "He-Who-Must-Not-Be-Named." The Horcruxes are like the One Ring in that they capture the malevolent spirit of their creator and, in the case of the locket Horcrux, exploit the weaknesses of the wearer—Harry, Hermione, and especially Ron—to the point of breaking up the fellowship. Dumbledore and Harry are a parallel of Gandalf and Frodo. Dumbledore, like Gandalf, experiences a death and resurrection (of sorts), while the hobbit Frodo, like the child Harry, is the only one who can complete the task of destroying the enemy.

gaming and the merchandising of middle-earth

So WIDE, VARIED, AND PROLONGED have been the responses to Tolkien's fiction that "Tolkieniana" can legitimately be placed under the lens of cultural studies. Brian Rosebury has done this for his discussion of Tolkien-related games and merchandise, coming up with three categories of interpretation: relabeling, assimilation and imitation, and adaptation.[11] In simple terms, this distinguishes between products that have little to do with Tolkien's books (or Jackson's films) other than the name and image on the package or screen; those products that imitate (to varying degrees) Tolkien's writing or characters; and serious attempts to adapt Tolkien's stories to other media, especially film. The first of these we can ignore, and the third has already been examined in Appendix II. It is the large middle group that bears discussion, especially regarding products that are close imitations of the medieval dimensions of Middle-earth.

As noted earlier, Tolkien's impact on the publishing industry has been enormous and perhaps taken too much for granted. In the contemporary fantasy genre, which he virtually created (though not intentionally), one can easily find many imitative novelists in many different countries. But in America in particular, the enormous growth of science fiction and fantasy has led directly to two other cultural phenomena: fantasy role-playing games and reenactment. Of all the role-playing games that have emerged since the 1970s, *Dungeons and Dragons*, cocreated by E. Gary Gygax and Dave Arneson, is both the most influential and the most infamous. Gygax was not just an enthusiastic Tolkien reader; he acted much like Tolkien and Lewis as a "sub-creator."[12] The *D&D* world is a backdrop, with simple rules and equipment, upon which creative individuals (especially the "Dungeon Masters" who build and referee individual games) can create complex scenarios filled with characters and creatures of ancient myth and medieval history. *D&D* books like *Monster Manual* and *Deities and Demigods* demonstrate a wide, if not deep, reading of ancient and medieval texts. The game is, of course, almost purely imitative, so much so that Gygax's original use of "hobbits" had to be removed from the game for legal reasons and replaced by "halflings."

D&D's encouragement of players to see things from the perspective of their characters has led to dangerous identity-confusion among some adolescent players, though this is rare. More frequent is the lampooning of those who play or have played *D&D*. Also, as Rosebury points out, many critics' dismissed Tolkien's books by association with *D&D*, even though Tolkien died before Gygax produced his game; *had* Tolkien lived to see costumed *D&D* players he would likely have dismissed them himself as typically American and part of his "deplorable cultus." Likewise, Tolkien probably would have been shocked to see the growth of the SCA (Society for Creative Anachronism), with its role-playing expanded to include staged combats; hobbyist medieval "reenactors" in many countries; and the more commercial "Renaissance faires" that have popped up all over the United States.[13] A serious academic and a soldier who saw death up close, Tolkien was no escapist in party dress. If many of his readers, in more peaceful times and circumstances, choose to adopt Middle-earth names and costumes, one can hardly blame Tolkien. And, in any case, is the "smart and cynical" stance adopted by wannabe novelists and critics who imbibe the modernist canon really any different?

Imaginative role-playing games have given way in recent years to computer action games, whose realistic graphics are testimony to the talents of engineers and programmers. The images of Middle-earth characters and landscapes are often directly taken from Tolkien illustrators and now the Jackson films. But though these games test the hand-eye coordination and memories of players, they do not engage their imaginations the same way that the far simpler role-playing games do.[14] While occasionally such games can explore characters and scenarios only hinted at in Tolkien's books (the way imitative novels and fan films do), often they do not logically follow Tolkien's narrative and are interchangeable with other computer action and video games.[15] Nevertheless, many computer programmers—and hackers—are Tolkien fans and have, since the 1960s, taken elements of Middle-earth into the cyber-realm, from peripherals that understand Elvish to the "Great Worm" (an extremely destructive 1988 computer virus) to hacker slang like "the Elder Days" (i.e., before the Internet).[16]

tolkien on the internet

Internet searches for "Tolkien," "Middle-earth," and "*The Lord of the Rings*" will conjure up thousands of web sites created by fans of the books, or devoted to the Jackson films, as well as those trying to sell you computer games and Middle-earth merchandise. Companies that create museum replica arms and armor have devoted many resources to creating swords, axes, and helmets inspired by the Jackson films. Like the gaming and fantasy conventions that preceded it (e.g., "Dragon*Con," held annually in Atlanta since 1987), the Web provides an important link between Tolkien fans, a way for them to communicate and share Tolkien trivia, Tolkien-inspired art and fiction, and news about upcoming films and computer games. With the advent of video-sharing sites like YouTube, the Web also serves as a "virtual cinema" for amateur filmmakers producing their own low-budget odes to Middle-earth.

While it is easy to snicker at the "geek factor" in these Tolkien web sites, and difficult to wade through the truly silly or overtly commercial, one should not underestimate the educative dimension of the Internet. Readers new to Tolkien's books now have the ability to see pictures from their homes, anywhere in the world, of Tolkien's Oxford, to read the very medieval texts (in the original languages and in translation) that inspired Tolkien, to view the work of Tolkien illustrators, and to see behind-the-scenes video clips of the special-effects techniques employed by Peter Jackson and Weta. Students and scholars can access important critical essays and monographs online through search engines (a phrase Tolkien would likely have thought menacing). The exclusivity of British public schools and Oxbridge is breaking down in the democratic Web, and there are countless realms to explore through the history, archaeology, and literature collections online. We are living in an age of information abundance, but more than ever it requires the language and critical reading skills that were at the heart of the medieval university—nowhere more institutionalized than at Oxford—to sort through all of this material to find the authentic, the historical, and the truly creative.

ᴄhe pasᴄ anᴅ fuᴄuʀe

IN 2003, THE YEAR THAT THE FILM *The Return of the King* first appeared in theaters, the world learned that hobbits indeed lived "down under"—in Indonesia, about 95,000 to 17,000 years ago.[17] On the island of Flores, archaeologists identified the bones of diminutive hominids with oversized feet and small brains, seemingly six skeletons of the Ebu Gogo—small, hairy cave-dwellers of Indonesian myth. Some scientists have interpreted the remains as those of a different species from ours, the now extinct *Homo floresiensis*, but could not resist calling the first female find "the Hobbit." Standing upright just over three feet tall, *Homo floresiensis* may have used tools and hunted, but in turn *they* may have been hunted by giant storks and Komodo dragons. While the parent of Hobbit may have been a much taller *Homo erectus*, during hundreds of thousands of years of isolation on the island of Flores the *Homo floresiensis* dwindled in size. Hobbits "seldom now reach three feet," wrote Tolkien, "but they have dwindled, they say, and in ancient days they were taller."[18]

Middle-earth too has dwindled in size, or at least the Shire that Tolkien knew and loved as a boy. Sarehole Mill is now run as a museum by the Birmingham City Council, but it is surrounded by indistinct suburban homes and shops. The Tolkien Society and other groups are campaigning for a Tolkien park to be created in Sarehole. Adjacent to the Mill, the park would include a Tolkien center. While this might become a nice pilgrimage destination for Tolkien fans, it is unlikely to coax any remaining hobbits out of their hiding places.

In a 1966 interview given to the BBC, Tolkien admitted that "Hobbits are just rustic English people, small in size because it reflects (in general) the small reach of their imagination—not the small reach of their courage or latent power."[19] Because he considered himself a hobbit "in all but size,"[20] Tolkien partly indicts himself here. He seldom traveled far from Oxford, nor did he care much for the culture and politics of the wider world. And yet he traveled far in his mind and showed great courage in war. He is both Samwise ("Half-wise") and one of the Wise (Gandalf, Elrond). In his fiction he gives us a world of hierarchies

and a warrior aristocracy, and yet he himself was a poor orphan, a slight commoner with common tastes (in food, house, etc.) who made a great impact in the wider world.

THE ONE RING WAS DESTROYED at the end of the Third Age of Middle-earth. And yet, an inscribed gold ring discovered in the Roman town of Silchester (Calleva Atrebatum) in 1785 may have inspired Tolkien, according to a Ring-themed exhibition created in conjunction with the Tolkien Society, which opened in April 2013 at the Vyne mansion in nearby Basingstoke.[21] The Latin inscription on the large ring (approximately one inch in diameter and weighing almost one-half ounce) bears a portrait of Venus crowned, and reads: "Senicianus live well in God."

The archaeologist Sir Mortimer Wheeler believed that the ring was tied to a lead curse-tablet found at a Romano-Celtic temple at Lydney Park, built ca. AD 364 on an Iron Age promontory fort in Gloucestershire. The fort, known locally as Dwarf's Hill, is on a hill riddled with tunnels, mines, and crumbling ruins left by the Romans, which were rumored by villagers to be inhabited by dwarves, goblins, and little people—perhaps an inspiration for Hobbiton?[22] The Latin inscription on the tablet is a curse issued by one Silvianus, apparently the ring's previous owner: "Among those who bear the name of Senicianus to none grant health until he bring the ring to the temple of Nodens." Wheeler, who excavated at the Lydney site, called on Tolkien's expertise in 1929 to explain the name of the otherwise obscure god Nodens. Tolkien wrote a brief etymological note for Wheeler's excavation report in which he linked Nodens with the Irish god Nuadu Airgetlám and the Welsh hero Nudd Law Eraint (both epithets mean "Silverhand").[23]

This convoluted theory is worthy of its own chapter in *The Silmarillion*. Dwarves and hobbits, a mysterious gold ring stolen from its original owner who calls on an ancient native god to cast a curse on the one who stole it, the cursed thief struck down and the ring lost for centuries amid the ruins of a once mighty Roman town. Such a tale would surely have captured the imagination of Professor Tolkien. The problem is, Tolkien may never have even seen the ring. It can, however, stand as a symbol for the whole Tolkien phenomenon. For the ring is a mysterious object wrapped in layers of ancient history, bearing strange and divine words telling a partial story, a story now spread to millions of readers (through the Internet), and being used to raise funds. Tolkien himself has become mythologized, commoditized, and repackaged for a new age raised on high-speed and high-def images. But whether the words are inscribed in gold or on parchment or assembled from pixels, they must be assembled to tell a good story.

appendix iv

the moral virtues of middle earth

> *"There is indeed no better medium for moral teaching than the good fairy-story, by which I mean a real deep-rooted tale, told as a tale, and not a thinly disguised moral allegory."*[1]

—Tolkien, "Sir Gawain and the Green Knight"

While many have pointed out the lack of religion in *The Lord of the Rings*, few would doubt that there is a strong and clear ethics system in the novel. When Tolkien described it as a very Catholic novel, this may be in part what he had in mind. Aristotle's "virtue ethics," adapted by Church Fathers like Ambrose and Thomas Aquinas to produce the four cardinal virtues—prudence, justice, temperance, and fortitude— would have been part of the young Ronald Tolkien's catechism. These virtues may be associated with one or more characters in his Middle-earth writings. The contrasting values of the Northern world, a barbarian ethos criticized by Aristotle and other classical writers, are equally important in Tolkien's mythopoeia. Lastly, a partial synthesis of these two traditions was brought about in the chivalry of the High Middle Ages, most evident in the heavily French-influenced Arthurian romances with which Tolkien had a love-hate relationship.

We can, therefore, propose a tentative list of Tolkien characters whose actions and/or character exhibit specific moral virtues. This is what follows, with the classical and medieval terms given where appropriate:

BILBO: hospitality, mercy (L *clementia*), cleverness. Bilbo also possesses courage, but it is situational. Giant spiders and dragons bring it out of him, but not battles.

GANDALF: intelligence, knowledge (L *scientia*), wisdom (Gk *sophia*), boldness (Gk *thumos*), clarity.

FRODO: compassion, responsibility to the community, self-sacrifice.

SAM: bravery (Gk *tharsos*), loyalty, service, wonder (OE *wundor*, "marvel, miracle"). Sam sees Frodo as his "other self," Aristotle's description of true friendship.

LEGOLAS AND GIMLI, MERRY AND PIPPIN: love of a friend (Gk *philia*).

BOROMIR: military prowess, protecting the weak (OFr *noblesse oblige*), patriotism.

FARAMIR: brotherly love, duty to family and country, the scholarly pursuit of truth. Faramir has the makings of a philosopher-king, but the humility to settle for service to the true king of Gondor.

ÉOWYN: fearlessness, filial love. Éowyn, like Boromir, is a fiercely proud person, displaying her boldness in the face of enemies but also letting it blind her to other concerns. She is keenly aware of societal injustices, and effectively argues for equal opportunity for women and hobbits (i.e., commoners).

ARAGORN: love, courtesy, humility, practical wisdom (Gk *phronesis*, L *prudentia*), generosity (OFr *largesse*). Aragorn also represents the "magnificence" of kingship, a synthesis of many virtues in the one virtuous ruler.

Tom Bombadil is described as "Master" by Goldberry, yet he does not possess or have power over anything in his forest. This enigmatic passage in *The Fellowship* may indicate that Tom has mastery over himself—his inner regime—a control over his passions and the ability to resist temptations such as the One Ring. Is Tom indeed the "great souled-man" (*megalopsuchos*) of Aristotle, an honor the latter bestows on Socrates in the *Posterior Analytics*?

Many dwarves as well as men like Bard and Aragorn possess purely Germanic virtues. Tolkien describes them often as "grim-faced," while similar adjectives are discussed in his *The Homecoming of Beorhtnoth Beorhthelm's Son* (1953) with its inclusion of the Anglo-Saxon aphorism from *The Battle of Maldon* (tenth century):

> *Hige sceal þe heardra, heorte þe cenre,*
> *mod sceal þe mare þe ure maegen lytlað.*

> Will shall be the sterner, heart the bolder,
> spirit the greater as our strength lessens.[2]

One of the greatest virtues for Tolkien is hope, as we have discussed. Hobbits possess a natural cheerfulness that makes them a good vehicle for carrying hope. "While there's life there's hope!" exclaims Bilbo when the dwarves believe that they are trapped under the mountain.[3] In *The Lord of the Rings*, both hobbits and men struggle against despair to maintain hope.

Appearance versus reality is a common motif in *The Lord of the Rings*. Tolkien makes much of the Strider/Aragorn paradox in *Fellowship*, going so far as to reword the "all that glitters is not gold" parable. Similarly, Sam is, despite his harsh words and humble background, a poet and a "gentle *homme*." "Sam was gentler than his words," Tolkien writes succinctly[4]; here we can glimpse the thematic thread running throughout the work: what makes a gentle-man? The hobbits are constantly misjudged in *The Lord of the Rings*. When Denethor meets Pippin and sees his sword he says "once again it is shown that looks may belie the man—or the Halfling."[5] Pippin a bit later warns one of the boys of Gondor who was threatening him: "when you are older, you will learn that folk are not always what they seem."[6] Finally, Aragorn delivers this same message to all of those gathered at his coronation by choosing Frodo to carry his crown and by bowing before Frodo and Sam and placing them on his own throne.

Many critics have compared Sam's relationship with Frodo to that of a batman or military servant to an officer in the English army of Tolkien's day. I believe that it goes beyond this, however, and resembles the devotion of the saints to Christ, especially "at the end of all things," during the eruption of Orodruin:

> "Master!" cried Sam, and fell upon his knees. In all that ruin of the world for the moment he felt only joy, great joy....
> "Your poor hand!" he said. "And I have nothing to bind it with, or comfort it. I would have spared [Gollum] a whole hand of mine rather . . . "[7]

Through his particular journey, Sam develops the habits of thought and action that make one, according to Aristotle, virtuous. On Mount Doom, he matches Frodo's agape for the Shire with his own selfless love, for his master.

A Tolkien Timeline

Jan. 3, 1892   John Ronald Reuel Tolkien is born in Bloemfontein.

1895   Mabel Tolkien returns to England with her sons Ronald and Hilary.

1896   Arthur Tolkien dies in South Africa.

1900   Ronald Tolkien is admitted to King Edward's School and moves with his mother and brother to Birmingham.

1904   Mabel Tolkien dies at the age of thirty-four.

1908   Ronald Tolkien meets Edith Bratt.

1911   Ronald begins his first term at Exeter College, Oxford.

1914   Ronald and Edith are formally betrothed. The Great War begins.

1915   Ronald is awarded First Class Honours in English. He is commissioned in the Lancashire Fusiliers.

1916   Ronald and Edith are married. Ronald leaves for France and sees action in the Battle of the Somme.

1917   While in the hospital in England recovering from trench fever, Ronald begins writing tales that will become *The Silmarillion*. His eldest son, John, is born.

1918   The end of the Great War. Ronald moves to Oxford and joins the staff of the *Oxford English Dictionary*.

1920   Ronald is appointed Reader in English Language at Leeds University. His second son, Michael, is born.

1924   Ronald is appointed Professor of English Language at Leeds. A third son, Christopher, is born.

1925   Ronald is appointed Rawlinson and Bosworth Professor of Anglo-Saxon at Oxford. His edition of *Sir Gawain and the Green Knight*, with notes by E. V. Gordon, is published.

1926   J. R. R. Tolkien meets C. S. Lewis at an English faculty meeting at Oxford.

1929   Daughter Priscilla is born.

1937   *The Hobbit* is published by Allen & Unwin.

1939   Tolkien delivers his lecture "On Fairy-stories" at St. Andrews University. Charles Williams moves to Oxford and joins the Inklings.

1945	Tolkien is elected Merton Professor of English Language and Literature at Oxford. The death of Charles Williams.
1949	Tolkien finishes writing *The Lord of the Rings*, publishes *Farmer Giles of Ham*.
1954	Publication of *The Fellowship of the Ring* and *The Two Towers*.
1955	Publication of *The Return of the King*.
1959	Tolkien retires from his professorship.
1962	Publication of *The Adventures of Tom Bombadil*.
1963	The death of C. S. Lewis.
1964	Publication of *Tree and Leaf*.
1967	Publication of *Smith of Wootton Major*.
1968	Ronald and Edith move to the town of Poole.
1971	Edith Tolkien dies at the age of eighty-two.
1972	Ronald returns to Oxford. He is awarded by Queen Elizabeth the C.B.E. (Commander of the British Empire) and Oxford bestows an honorary Doctorate of Letters upon him.
Sept. 2, 1973	J. R. R. Tolkien dies in a nursing home in Bournemouth.
1976	Publication of *The Father Christmas Letters*.
1977	Publication of *The Silmarillion* (edited by Christopher Tolkien). An animated version of *The Hobbit* appears on television.
1978	Ralph Bakshi's animated *Lord of the Rings* appears in theaters.
1980	Bass and Rankin's animated *The Return of the King* appears on American television. Publication of *Unfinished Tales*.
1983–96	Publication of *The History of Middle-earth*, twelve volumes (edited by Christopher Tolkien).
2001–3	Peter Jackson's *The Lord of the Rings* trilogy appears in theaters.
2006–7	The musical *The Lord of the Rings* premieres in Toronto, then moves to London's West End. Publication of *The Children of Húrin* (edited by Christopher Tolkien).
2009	Publication of *The Legend of Sigurd and Gudrún* (edited by Christopher Tolkien).
2012–14	Peter Jackson's *The Hobbit* trilogy appears in theaters.

NOTES

EPIGRAPH AND PREFACE:

1. J. R. R. Tolkien, *The Silmarillion*, 2nd edition, edited by Christopher Tolkien (Boston: Houghton Mifflin, 2001), 38. All subsequent references are to this edition unless otherwise stated.

2. *The Lord of the Rings: The Fellowship of the Ring* (New Line Cinema, 2001), screenplay by Fran Walsh, Philippa Boyens, and Peter Jackson; novel by J. R. R. Tolkien.

3. Humphrey Carpenter and Christopher Tolkien (eds), *The Letters of J. R. R. Tolkien* (Boston: Houghton Mifflin, 2000), 64; hereafter *Letters*.

4. Tolkien, describing the Welsh language, in "English and Welsh," in *The Monsters and the Critics and Other Essays*, ed. by Christopher Tolkien (London: HarperCollins, 1997), 162–97.

5. *J. R. R. Tolkien: A Biography* (Boston: Houghton Mifflin, 1977; 2000); hereafter *Biography*.

6. In *J. R. R. Tolkien: Author of the Century* (Boston: Houghton Mifflin, 2001) but even more so in *The Road to Middle Earth* (Boston: Houghton Mifflin, 2003); hereafter *Author* and *Road*.

7. This list includes Daniel Grotta, *J. R. R. Tolkien: Architect of Middle Earth* (Philadelphia: Running Press, 1992); Joseph Pearce, *Tolkien: Man and Myth* (San Francisco: Ignatius Press, 1998); and Michael White, *Tolkien: A Biography* (New York: New American Library, 2003). To be fair, these authors did not have the access to the Tolkien family and private papers that Carpenter and Garth enjoyed.

8. Popular audience periodicals such as *Amon Hen* and *Mythlore* are now joined by hundreds of Tolkien websites (enthusiasm—if not original criticism—guaranteed), and 2004 witnessed the launch of a peer-reviewed academic journal, aptly named *Tolkien Studies* (West Virginia University Press).

9. See, for example, Jim Smith and J. Clive Matthews, *The Lord of the Rings: The Films, the Books, the Radio Series* (London: Virgin Books, 2004); Kristin Thompson, *The Frodo Franchise: The Lord of the Rings and Modern Hollywood* (Berkeley: University of California Press, 2007); and *The Rough Guide to* The Lord of the Rings (London: Penguin, 2003).

10. "*Beowulf*: The Monsters and the Critics," *Proceedings of the British Academy*, vol. 22 (1936): 245–95.

CHAPTER 1: LEARNING HIS CRAFT

1. *Letters*, p. 56.

2. See *Letters*, pp. 37, 410: "[*Tolkien*] is not Jewish in origin, though I should consider it an honour if it were."

3. *Letters*, p. 54.

4. John and Priscilla Tolkien, *The Tolkien Family Album* (London: HarperCollins, 1992), 21. *Wench* is a Middle English word for young girl or prostitute, perhaps related to Old English *wancol*, "unstable, vacillating." Tolkien worked on the W words for the *Oxford English Dictionary*.

5. 1965 interview with Denys Gueroult, BBC Sound Archives, quoted in John Garth, *Tolkien and the Great War* (Boston: Houghton Mifflin, 2003), 12.

6. *Letters*, 390; Angela Gardner (ed) and Jef Murray (illustrator), *Black & White Ogre Country: The Lost Tales of Hilary Tolkien* (Moreton-in-Marsh, UK: ADC Publications, 2009).

7. Biography, 33.

8. J. R. R. Tolkien, *The Lord of the Rings Fiftieth Anniversary Deluxe Edition*. London: HarperCollins, 2004), 987; hereafter *LOTR*.

9. Garth, *Tolkien and the Great War*, 6.

10. *Letters*, p. 52.

11. *J. R. R. Tolkien, Life and Legend: An Exhibition to Commemorate the Centenary of the Birth of J. R. R. Tolkien (1892–1973)* (Oxford: Bodleian Library, 1992), 25.

12. *Road*, 245–47.

13. *Letters*, pp. 277–83.

14. *Biography*, 78.

15. See *Chronology*, 78ff.

16. Quoted by Humphrey Carpenter in *Biography*, 97.

17. *Letters*, p. 303.

18. Ibid., p. 78.

19. *LOTR*, 225.

20. *Biography*, 81.

21. See Mark T. Hooker, "Frodo's Batman," *Tolkien Studies*, Vol. 1 (2004): 125–136.

22. John Garth, *Tolkien and the Great War: The Threshold of Middle-earth* (Boston: Houghton Mifflin, 2003).

23. Ibid., 38, 218.

24. Ibid., 214ff.

25. *Chronology*, 104.

26. *Biography*, 110.

27. *Letters*, pp. 55–6.

28. For examples of Tolkien's work on the *OED* and related discussion, see Peter Gilliver, Jeremy Marshall, and Edmund Weiner, *The Ring of Words: Tolkien and the Oxford English Dictionary* (Oxford: Oxford Univ. Press, 2006).

29. Wayne G. Hammond, *J. R. R. Tolkien: A Descriptive Bibliography* (Kent: St. Paul's Bibliographies, 1993). Lee and Solopova (2005, 6) estimate the total number of "notes, published lectures, articles and various forewords to academic publications, plus his scholarly 'books,' they number around thirty (and that is stretching the point)."

30. Michael D. C. Drout, "J. R. R. Tolkien's Medieval Scholarship and its Significance." *Tolkien Studies*, Vol. 4 (2007), 113–76.

31. Published first as a separate book (London: Humphrey Millford, 1937), the essay has since appeared in *Proceedings of the British Academy*, Vol. 22 (1937), 245–95; *The Monsters and the Critics and Other Essays* (New York: HarperCollins, 1983), 5–48; and Seamus Heaney (trans), *Beowulf: A Verse Translation* (New York: W.W. Norton, 2002), 103–30. The lecture materials from which the essay was derived have been published as Michael D. C. Drout (ed), *Beowulf and the Critics* (Tempe, AZ: Arizona Center for Medieval and Renaissance Studies, 2002).

32. Tolkien, "*Beowulf*: The Monsters and the Critics," in Heaney (trans), *Beowulf*, 105.

33. Ibid.: "The lovers of poetry can safely study the art [of *Beowulf*], but the seekers after history must beware lest the glamour of Poesis overcome them."

34. Ibid., 107ff, quoting R. W. Chambers and W. P. Ker.

35. Ibid., 112–14.

36. Ibid., 115.

37. Ibid., 117, quoting Ker.

38. Ibid., 119.

39. Ibid., 112.

40. J. R. R. Tolkien, "On Fairy-stories," in *Essays Presented to Charles Williams* (Oxford: Oxford University Press, 1947); *Tree and Leaf* (London: Allen & Unwin, 1964; Boston: Houghton Mifflin, 1965). Quotations here are from J. R. R. Tolkien, *The Tolkien Reader* (New York: Ballantine, 1966), hereafter, "On Fairy-stories," *Tolkien Reader*.

41. See Verlyn Flieger and Douglas A. Anderson (eds), *Tolkien On Fairy-stories: Expanded Edition, with Commentary and Notes* (London: HarperCollins, 2008).

42. "On Fairy-stories," *Tolkien Reader*.

43. Tolkien does not give a full history of fairies in the essay. However, C. S. Lewis, in the chapter "The *longaevi*" in his *The Discarded Image*, goes into more detail about their origins and shows that Milton alone gives us three different versions of fairies.

44. "On Fairy-stories," *Tolkien Reader*, 38–9.

45. Ibid., 67.

46. Ibid., 69.

47. Ibid., 72.

48. Ibid., 75.

49. "On Fairy-stories," *Tolkien Reader*, 77.

50. Ibid., 79ff.

51. Joseph Pearce, "Foreword" in Bradley J. Birzer, *J. R. R. Tolkien's Sanctifying Myth: Understanding Middle-earth* (Wilmington, DE: ISI Books, 2002), x. See also ibid., 26.

52. Walter Hooper (ed), *The Letters of C. S. Lewis to Arthur Greeves* (New York: Collier Books, 1986), 427.

53. "On Fairy-stories," *Tolkien Reader*, 85–6.

54. Ibid., 86. Tolkien here uses "Joy" in the same way C. S. Lewis does in *Surprised by Joy*, a book which owes its existence in part to an argument between Tolkien and Lewis on the nature of myth (to which Tolkien refers in both "On Fairy-stories" and his poem "Mythopoeia").

55. Ibid., 87–90.

56. *Biography*, 195.

57. Flieger and Anderson (eds), *Tolkien On Fairy-stories*, 9–10.

58. See *Reader's Guide*, 688.

59. *Biography*, 112.

60. Ibid., 118–19.

61. A good collection of anecdotes from Tolkien's students and colleagues can be found in Birzer, *J. R. R. Tolkien's Sanctifying Myth*, 3–6.

62. Unfinished poem from MS (Estate of J. R. R. Tolkien), quoted in Carpenter, *The Inklings*, 176 (author's translation).

63. C. S. Lewis, *All My Road Before Me: The Diary of C. S. Lewis 1922–1927* (Boston: Mariner Books, 1992), 392–3.

64. See *Reader's Guide*, s.v. societies and clubs.

65. *Letters*, p. 36.

66. John Wain, *Sprightly Running: Part of an Autobiography* (New York: St. Martin's, 1962), 181.

67. Walter Hooper (ed), *The Collected Letters of C. S. Lewis*, Vol. II (San Francisco: HarperCollins, 2004), p. 16.

68. See Diana Pavlac Glyer, *The Company They Keep: C. S. Lewis and J. R. R. Tolkien as Writers in Community* (Kent, OH: Kent State University Press, 2007).

69. *Letters*, p. 388.

70. For membership, see *Reader's Guide*, s.v. Inklings.

71. Review of *The Inklings* by Humphrey Carpenter: "Oxford's Magic Circle," *Books and Bookmen* 24, no. 4 (Jan. 1979), 10.

72. Colin Duriez, *J. R. R. Tolkien and C. S. Lewis: The Story of Their Friendship* (Stroud, UK: Sutton, 2005; originally HiddenSpring, Mahwah, NJ 2003), viii.

73. Scott Calhoun, "C. S. Lewis and J. R. R. Tolkien: Friends and Mutual Mentors," in *An Examined Life: C. S. Lewis, Life, Works, and Legacy*, Vol. 1, edited by Bruce L. Edwards (Westport, CT: Praeger, 2007), 263.

74. *Letters*, pp. 29, 89.

75. Calhoun, 265.

76. Duriez, *Tolkien and Lewis*, viii.

77. Richard Sturch, "Common Themes Among Inklings." In Brian Horne (ed), *Charles Williams: A Celebration* (Leominster, UK: Gracewing, 1995), 154.

78. On the influence of Owen Barfield's *Poetic Diction* on Tolkien, see Verlyn Flieger, *Splintered Light: Logos and Language in Tolkien's World*, 2nd edition (Kent, OH: Kent State University Press, 2002).

79. See *Reader's Guide*, s.v. fandom.

80. Writing to his successor at Oxford, Norman Davis (quoted in *Biography*, 233.)

81. *Biography*, 237.

82. Published (with alterations) in Christopher Tolkien (ed), *The Monsters and the Critics and Other Essays* (London: George Allen & Unwin, 1983), 224–40.

83. Shippey, *Road*, 338.

84. *Letters*, p. 341 (written to his daughter four days after Lewis's death).

85. *Biography*, 287–8.

86. Preface to the second edition of *LOTR*, xxiii–xxiv.

87. In Henry Resnik, "An Interview with Tolkien," *Niekas* 18 (1967), 37–43 (38). See Fimi, Dimitra. *Tolkien, Race and Cultural History: From Fairies to Hobbits* (New York: Palgrave Macmillan, 2009), 7.

88. Garth (21) quoting from the Stapledon Society minutes, Dec. 1 and Nov. 7, 1913.

89. *Letters*, p. 246.

90. See "The Great War," 7–15 of this book; and "Magic and Machines," 79.

91. *LOTR*, 357.

92. Ibid., 48.

93. Ibid., 815.

chapter 2: tolkien's middle ages

1. A spirited defense of Tolkien source criticism has just been made by the authors of the essays in Jason Fisher (ed), *Tolkien and the Study of His Sources: Critical Essays* (Jefferson, NC: McFarland, 2011).
2. Shippey, *Author*, xxvii.
3. Somewhat, it must be admitted, to the chagrin of Tolkien (see *Reader's Guide*, 969–70), who claimed to be "growing" stories out of "the leaf-mould of the mind" (i.e. things seen or read but long since descended into the depths of his mind).
4. The distinction may even be a false one: see Birzer, *Sanctifying Myth*, 25.
5. Jane Chance Nitzsche, *Tolkien's Art* (London: Macmillan, 1979), ch. 4. Tolkien's *The Lay of Aotrou and Itroun*, for example, is modeled upon the medieval Breton lay.
6. *Letters*, p. 239.
7. The Book of Job has also been claimed, and Tolkien appears to have made comments on the other translators' work to the general editor, Fr. Anthony Jones. See *Letters*, p. 378.
8. *Letters*, p. 281.
9. Ibid., p. 376.
10. Carpenter, *Biography*, 41–44.
11. Richard L. Purtill, *J. R. R. Tolkien: Myth, Morality, and Religion* (San Francisco: Harper & Rowe, 1984), 88ff.
12. In *Letters*, pp. 177–78, he says that "Orc" was derived from the Old English *orc*, which meant "demon." Tolkien words and concepts often blended influences; it is also possible that the Roman deity influenced the Germanic word.
13. Ibid., p. 172.
14. Ibid., p. 176.
15. Ibid., p. 107.
16. Ibid., p. 89.
17. Ibid., p. 157.
18. The term "barbarian" was first used by the ancient Greeks to describe anyone who did not speak Greek (and were thus usually considered inferior). For the Romans it came to be used especially of Celts, Germans, and other cultures occupying lands beyond the northern and western frontiers of the empire.
19. See Walter Goffart, *Barbarians and Romans, A.D., 418–584: Techniques of Accommodations* (Princeton, NJ: Princeton Univ. Press, 1987); and Thomas S. Burns, *Barbarians Within the Gates of Rome* (Bloomington, IN: Indiana Univ. Press, 1994).
20. Tolkien's lack of clarity on the subject of orcs and goblins is apparent in Wayne G. Hammond and Christina Scull, *The Lord of the Rings: A Reader's Companion* (Boston: Houghton Mifflin, 2005), 165.
21. *Reader's Guide*, 466–7; Shippey, *Road*, 14ff.
22. See Sandra Ballif Straubhaar, "Myth, Late Roman History, and Multiculturalism in Tolkien's Middle-earth," in Jane Chance (ed), *Tolkien and the Invention of Myth: A Reader* (University Press of Kentucky, 2004), 101–18.
23. The historiography of "the Fall of Rome" is long and complex, beginning with Edward Gibbons' *The Decline and Fall of the Western Roman Empire* (1776–88). Many new studies appeared in and around the anniversary year 2010: see Chris Wickham, *Framing*

the Early Middle Ages: Europe and the Mediterranean, 400–800 (Oxford: Oxford Univ. Press, 2005); Bryan Ward-Perkins, *The Fall of Rome and the End of Civilization* (Oxford: Oxford Univ. Press, 2006); Peter Heather, *The Fall of the Roman Empire: A New History of Rome and the Barbarians* (Oxford: Oxford Univ. Press, 2007); Guy Halsall, *Barbarian Migrations and the Roman West 376–568* (Cambridge: Cambridge Univ. Press, 2007); Edward James, *Europe's Barbarians AD 200–600* (London: Longman, 2009); and Adrian Goldsworthy, *How Rome Fell: The Death of a Superpower* (New Haven: Yale Univ. Press, 2010).

24. For the Greek and Roman sources on the Celts, see H. D. Rankin, *Celts and the Classical World* (London: Croom Helm, 1987); and John Koch (ed), *The Celtic Heroic Age* (Celtic Studies Publications, 1995). A good archaeological overview is Barry Cunliffe, *The Ancient Celts* (Oxford: Oxford Univ. Press, 1997). For the recent scholarly debate on the terms "Celts," see Simon James, *The Atlantic Celts* (London: British Museum Press, 1999); John Collis, *The Celts: Origins, Myths and Inventions* (Stroud: Tempus, 2003); and Christopher A. Snyder, "Celts," in Snyder (ed), *The Early Peoples*, I: 126–7.

25. Most recently genetic studies and other biological methods have been employed to determine, for example, the origins and extent of "Celtic" and "Germanic" populations in medieval (and modern) Europe, but there is no agreed upon methodology and the results have often been contradictory.

26. For analysis of these events, see N. J. Higham, *Rome, Britain, and the Anglo-Saxons* (London: Routledge, 1992); K.R. Dark, *Civitas to Kingdom: British Political Continuity 300–800* (Leicester: Leicester Univ. Press, 1993); Michael Jones, *The End of Roman Britain* (Ithaca, NY: Cornell Univ. Press, 1996); and Christopher A. Snyder, *An Age of Tyrants: Britain and the Britons, AD 400–600* (University Park, PA: Penn State Univ. Press, 1998).

27. "Britons" is the term Caesar uses to describe the natives of Britain, and it continues in use well into the Middle Ages to refer to the Welsh and other Brittonic speakers (as opposed to those speaking Anglo-Saxon or Old English). See Christopher A. Snyder, *The Britons* (Oxford: Blackwell, 2003).

28. Gildas, *On the Ruin of Britain*, 20.1 and 24.3–4 (trans. Michael Winterbottom).

29. See *Angles and Britons: O'Donnell Lectures* (Cardiff: Univ. of Wales Press, 1963), pp. 1–41.

30. Peter Gilliver, Jeremy Marshall, and Edmund Weiner, *The Ring of Words: Tolkien and the Oxford English Dictionary* (Oxford: Oxford Univ. Press, 2006), 98–99. *Carrek* is the root word of The Carracks, a group of rocky islands off Cornwall.

31. A hill or mountain may euphemistically be called a cairn, hence The Carracks (Cornwall), Carreg Cennnen (Carmarthenshire), and Carrock Fell (Cumberland). See J. R. R. Tolkien, *The Annotated Hobbit*, rev. and expanded ed., annotated by Douglas A. Anderson (Boston: Houghton Mifflin, 2002), 164, and John Rateliff, *The History of the Hobbit, Part One: Mr. Baggins* (Boston: Houghton Mifflin, 2007), 261ff.

32. *Letters*, p. 26.

33. Ibid., p. 144. In another letter (p. 227) to Allen & Unwin in October of 1955, Tolkien says that he wishes to connect "'Celticness' . . . as a linguistic pattern" to *The Return of the King*.

34. E.g. Prince Imrahil and Gimli in *The Return of the King* (*LOTR*, 872 and 874).

35. On Tolkien's use of Welsh language and literature, see Carl Phelpstead, *Tolkien and Wales: Language, Literature and Identity* (Cardiff: University of Wales Press, 2011).

36. *Biography*, 168.

37. Dimitra Fimi, "Tolkien's '"Celtic" type of legends': Merging Traditions," *Tolkien Studies* 4 (2007), 51–71.

38. Christina Scull and Wayne G. Hammond, *The J. R. R. Tolkien Companion and Guide*, vol. 1 (New York: Houghton Mifflin, 2006), 56.

39. J. R. R. Tolkien, "English and Welsh," in *The Monsters and the Critics and Other Essays*, ed. by Christopher Tolkien (London: HarperCollins, 1997), 162–97.

40. *Letters*, pp. 175–6.

41. Ibid., pp. 134, 219, 289, and 385.

42. Edmund Wainwright, *Tolkien's Mythology for England: A Middle-Earth Companion* (Hockwold cum Wilton, UK: Anglo-Saxon Books, 2004), 21.

43. Ibid., 87. Tolkien claimed OE *pûcel* referred to a devil or minor spirit.

44. *The Book of Lost Tales Part Two*, 290. See Marie Barnfield, "More Celtic Influences: Númenor and the Second Age," *Mallorn* 29 (Aug. 1992), 6–13; and Tom Shippey, "Tolkien and Iceland: The Philology of Envy," Symposium at the Árni Magnússon Institute of Icelandic Studies, Reykjavík, Iceland (Sept. 13–14, 2002) http://www2.hi.is/Apps/WebObjects/HI.woa/wa/dp?detail=1004508&name=nordals_en_greinar_og_erindi

45. *Letters*, pp. 55–56. Beginning only after 597 AD, the formal conversion of the Anglo-Saxons to Christianity was hardly the earliest among the barbarians. Missionaries were active among the Goths in the late fourth century, St. Patrick had converted a large number of Irish well before 500, and the Frankish king Clovis converted to Catholicism in 496.

46. Ibid., p. 144.

47. Ibid., p. 108.

48. The story appears in the *Anglo-Saxon Chronicle* under the year 449. On the beginnings of Anglo-Saxon England, see Stephen Bassett (ed), *The Origins of the Anglo-Saxon Kingdoms* (Leicester: Leicester Univ. Press, 1989); Barbara Yorke, *Kings and Kingdoms of Early Anglo-Saxon England* (London: Routledge, 1990); John Hines (ed), *The Anglo-Saxons from the Migration Period to the Eighth Century* (Woodbridge: Boydell, 1997); and John Blair, *The Church in Anglo-Saxon Society* (Oxford: Oxford Univ. Press, 2005).

49. See Shippey, *Road*, 102. OE *mearc* means "boundary," which would also be appropriate for a hobbit who founded the border of the Shire.

50. See R. L. S. Bruce-Mitford, *The Sutton Hoo Ship Burial*, 3 vols. (London: British Museum Press, 1975–83); and Martin Carver, *Sutton Hoo: A Seventh-Century Princely Burial Ground and its Context* (London: British Museum Press, 2005).

51. Hall, John Lesslie, trans. *Beowulf: An Anglo-Saxon Poem* (Boston: D.C. Heath & Co., 1892). http://www.gutenberg.org/files/16328/16328-h/16328-h.htm

52. Alfred's first biography was written by the Welsh cleric Asser in 893. The best modern study of Alfred is Richard Abels, *Alfred the Great: War, Kingship and Culture in Anglo-Saxon England* (London: Longman, 1998).

53. *Letters*, p. 108.

54. See John Tinkler, "Old English in Rohan," in Neil D. Isaacs and Rose A. Zimbardo (eds), *Tolkien and the Critics* (University of Notre Dame Press, 1968), 164–69.

55. Wainwright, *Tolkien's Mythology*, 98.

56. See Daniel Donoghue, *Old English Literature: A Short Introduction* (Oxford: Blackwell, 2004); and Peter Goodrich, "Literature," in Snyder (ed), *The Early Peoples*, II: 365–6.

57. Translation by author.

58. *LOTR*, 284. See Shippey, *Road*, 33.

59. Translation by author.

60. *LOTR*, p. 508.

61. Translation by author.

62. *LOTR*, 474, 485.

63. See Anderson, *Annotated Hobbit*, 125.

64. See Andy Orchard, *A Critical Companion to Beowulf* (Woodbridge, UK: D.S. Brewer, 2005); and Patrick W. Conner, "*Beowulf*," in *Early Peoples*, I: 69–71.

65. See *Reader's Guide*, 91.

66. Translation by author.

67. *LOTR*, 177. See *Reader's Companion*, 24–26.

68. For *Homecoming* and Tolkien's *Maldon* criticism, see now Tolkien, *The Tolkien Reader* (New York: Ballantine, 1966), 1–27.

69. See Steve Morillo (ed), *The Battle of Hastings, Sources and Interpretations* (Woodbridge: Boydell and Brewer, 1996).

70. See Gwyn Jones, *A History of the Vikings* (Oxford: Oxford Univ. Press, 1968); Jesse Byock, *Viking Age Iceland* (New York: Penguin, 2001); and Benjamin Hudson, *Viking Pirates and Christian Princes* (Oxford: Oxford Univ. Press, 2005).

71. *Letters*, p. 281.

72. See Rory McTurk, *A Companion to Old Norse-Icelandic Literature and Culture* (Oxford: Blackwell, 2005).

73. *Letters*, p. 119.

74. *LOTR*, 838.

75. Translated by Benjamin Thorpe (1866), http://www.northvegr.org/secondary%20 sources/eddic%20poetry/the%20voluspa/v002.html

76. See Shippey, "Light-elves, Dark-elves, and Others: Tolkien's Elvish Problem," *Tolkien Studies*, vol. 1 (2004), 1–15.

77. Shippey, *Road*, 246.

78. *Letters*, pp. 150, 385. Tolkien translates the Old English word *earendel* as "'ray of light,' applied sometimes to the morning-star." See also Shippey, *Road*, 246ff.

79. *Biography*, 30.

80. Ruth S. Noel, *The Mythology of Middle-earth* (Boston: Houghton Mifflin, 1978), 87–88.

81. C. S. Lewis, *Surprised by Joy* (New York: Harcourt, 1955).

82. C. S. Lewis, "The Dethronement of Power," in Neil D. Isaacs and Rose A. Zimbardo (eds), *Tolkien and the Critics* (University of Notre Dame Press, 1968), 15.

83. Shippey, *Road to Middle-earth*, 39–41.

84. Translation by author.

85. See Shippey, *Road*, 348–9.

86. Lewis wrote the intro to G. L. Brook's translation, a lengthy essay on Laȝamon and a smaller version that appears in *The Discarded Image*, and, according to Walter Hooper (pers. com.), was planning his own edition of the *Brut* the year he died.

87. *Letters*, p. 317.

88. The translation is included in Christopher Tolkien (ed), *Sir Gawain and the Green Knight, Pearl and Sir Orfeo* (London: Allen & Unwin, 1975; New York: Ballantine, 1980). The radio adaptation was done by Kevin Crossley-Holland.

89. J. R. R. Tolkien and E. V. Gordon (eds), *Sir Gawain and the Green Knight*, 2nd ed, edited by Norman Davis (Oxford: Oxford University Press, 1967).

90. Later edited by Christopher Tolkien and published in *The Monsters and the Critics and Other Essays* (London: Allen & Unwin, 1983).

91. *LOTR*, 888.

92. Tolkien and Gordon (eds), *Sir Gawain*, p. 20.

93. Tolkien (trans), *Sir Gawain*, p. 51.

94. For these and other comparisons, see Michael D. C. Drout (ed), *J. R. R. Tolkien Encyclopedia: Scholarship and Critical Assessment* (New York: Routledge, 2007), pp. 615–17.

95. *Letters*, p. 39.

96. *Biography*, 36, 42.

97. Ibid., 218.

98. Fimi, *Tolkien, Race and Cultural History*, 38.

99. Alfred W. Pollard, ed., *The Works of Geoffrey Chaucer* (London: Macmillan, 1899), 166. http://books.google.com/books?id=g09BnIGEkN0C&dq=%22with+hir+joly+compa ignye%22+bath&source=gbs_navlinks_s

100. Tolkien's comments are taken from a 1951 letter to Milton Waldman (*Letters*, p. 144 and a draft of "On Fairy-stories" (Tolkien Papers, Bodleian Library, Oxford). See *Reader's Guide*, 56. Compare this to the attitude of his close friend G. B. Smith, who preferred the native Celtic Arthurian tales to the French versions: see Garth, 32.

101. See Christopher A. Snyder, *The World of King Arthur* (New York: Thames and Hudson, 2000); and Snyder, "Arthurian Origins," in Norris J. Lacy (ed), *A History of Arthurian Scholarship* (Cambridge: D. S. Brewer, 2006), 1–18. Also, there has been much debate among historians about the accuracy and usefulness of these dates: see Snyder, "Arthurian Origins," passim.

102. Shippey, *Road*, 160

103. See Richard Barber, *The Holy Grail: Imagination and Belief* (Cambridge, MA: Harvard Univ. Press, 2005).

104. *Morgoth's Ring* (i.e. Volume 10 of *The History of Middle-earth*), 365–6.

105. See, for example, Wainwright, *Tolkien's Mythology*, 20 and 28–9.

106. J. R. R. Tolkien, *The Hobbit: or, There and Back Again* (Boston: Houghton Mifflin, 1997), 263. All *Hobbit* citations in this chapter are to this edition unless otherwise stated.

107. *Letters*, p. 182. As far as I know, this is Tolkien's only reference to Merlin and Gandalf together.

108. The story became part of *Akallabêth* in *The Silmarillion*. See the comments of Christopher Tolkien in *The Lost Road and Other Writings*, vol. 5, p. 260; and Doughan, "An Ethnically Cleansed Faery?"

109. Parzifal is the German version of Parsifal/Perceval. The Knight of the Swan first appears in *chansons de geste* related to Godfrey of Bouillon, hero of the First Crusade.

110. See *Reader's Companion*, 16.

111. *LOTR*, 362.

112. *The Book of Lost Tales*, Part Two, 170. See Garth, *Tolkien and the Great War*, 220–21.

113. Garth, *Tolkien and the Great War*, 221.

114. *Letters*, p. 64.

115. *The Book of Lost Tales*, Part Two, 159–60.

116. *LOTR*, 473.

117. For a survey of historical Arthur theories, see Snyder, "Arthurian Origins."

118. See Shippey, *Road*, 38.

119. See ibid., *Road*, 160ff.

120. See Shippey, *Author*, 105; and Richard C. West, "The Interlace Structure of *The Lord of the Rings*, in Jared Lobdell (ed), *A Tolkien Compass* (La Sall, IL: Open Court, 1975), 77–94.

121. In 1934 the Winchester Malory, a manuscript that differs organizationally from the book as published by Caxton, was discovered and subsequently edited by Eugène Vinaver. C. S. Lewis reviewed Vinaver's edition of Malory for the *Times Literary Supplement* in June 1947 and, since he already owned a copy, sold the review copy to Tolkien. *Le Morte d'Arthur* was one of the subjects discussed by Lewis and Tolkien in their last meeting, three months before Lewis's death. See *Chronology*, 316, 607.

122. Noel, *The Mythology of Middle-earth*, 164–5.

123. His T.C.B.S. friend G. B. Smith had composed a long Arthurian poem entitled "Glastonbury" in 1915.

124. Unpublished, Tolkien Papers, Bodleian Library, Oxford.

125. Quoted in *Biography*, 171.

126. *Letters*, p. 349.

127. See ibid., p. 377.

128. Ralph C. Wood, *The Gospel According to Tolkien* (Louisville, KY: Westminster John Knox Press, 2003), 6.

129. See *Reader's Guide*, s.v. "Reading." The last three authors in this list are more properly termed writers of juvenile fiction, but their literary creations have taken on something like fairy tale status.

130. See Anne C. Petty, "Identifying England's Lönnrot," *Tolkien Studies* 1, no. 1 (2004), 69–84.

131. *Letters*, p. 176 and 214.

132. John Ruskin, *Modern Painters*, vol. 1 (1873).

133. John Ruskin, *Lectures on Architecture and Painting* (1854).

134. See Jessica Yates, "William Morris's Influence on J. R. R. Tolkien," in Sarah Wells (ed), *The Ring Goes Ever On*, 204–19. Yates points out that Tolkien's favored illustrator, Pauline Baynes, was of the Arts and Crafts tradition of Morris and Burne-Jones.

135. Simon Machin, "Brothers in Arms," *Oxford Today* 20, no. 1 (Michaelmas 2007) http://www.oxfordtoday.ox.ac.uk/2007-08/v20n1/08.shtml; Garth, 14.

136. See Jan Marsh, *The Pre-Raphaelites*, 150. Morris returned to Iceland in 1873.

137. Marjorie Burns, *Perilous Realms: Celtic and Norse in Tolkien's Middle-earth* (Toronto: Univ. of Toronto Press, 2005), 75ff; *Reader's Guide*, 603.

138. *Chronology*, 36, 383.

139. *Letters*, p. 417.

140. Jane Farrington, *The Pre-Raphaelites at Birmingham Museum and Art Gallery* (Birmingham: BM&AG, 2003), 62.

141. *Reader's Guide*, 816.

142. Ibid., 604.
143. See Yates, "William Morris's Influence," 209.
144. See *Biography*, 30.
145. Salomon Reinach in *Reader's Guide*, 456.
146. Fimi (*Tolkien, Race and Cultural History*, 34) argues that Tolkien's opinions on fairies evolved over time.
147. See *Reader's Guide*, 685, and Shippey, *Road to Middle-earth*, 51–54.
148. For similarities and differences, see Colin Manlove, "How Much Does Tolkien Owe to the Work of George MacDonald?" in Sarah Wells (ed), *The Ring Goes Ever On: Proceedings of the Tolkien 2005 Conference*, vol. 2 (Coventry, UK: The Tolkien Society, 2008), 109–16.
149. See Gisela Kreglinger's article on MacDonald in Drout, *J. R. R. Tolkien Encyclopedia*, 399–400.
150. See *Reader's Guide*, 567ff. Tolkien would later be critical of this aspect of his early writing, and does not adopt the tone in the *Lord of the Rings*.
151. See, for example, *Letters*, p. 185
152. "On Fairy-stories," *Tolkien Reader*, 28.
153. Shippey, *Road*, 70.
154. Talk given at Church House, Westminster on Sept. 16, 1977. See *Reader's Guide*, 655.

Chapter 3: "There and Back Again"

1. See *Biography*, 180–1.
2. The chronology is somewhat unclear: see J. R. R. Tolkien, *The Annotated Hobbit*, rev. and expanded ed., annotated by Douglas A. Anderson (Boston: Houghton Mifflin, 2002), 5–12; *Reader's Guide*, 385–93; and John Rateliff, *The History of the Hobbit, Part One: Mr. Baggins; Part Two: Return to Bag-end* (Boston: Houghton Mifflin, 2007).
3. Carpenter, *Biography*, 175. See also Tolkien's 1955 letter to W. H. Auden, *Letters*, p. 215.
4. *Letters*, p. 215.
5. See Rateliff, 47.
6. See Shippey, *Road*, 66.
7. For these and other possibilities, see Hammond and Scull, *Reader's Companion*, 1–8. The English folk sprite known as Puck may ultimately derive from Welsh fairies called *pwca*.
8. *Annotated Hobbit*, 9. The word appears in volume II.
9. Shippey, *Road*, 67–68; Drout, *Rings, Swords, and Monsters*, lecture four.
10. See *Annotated Hobbit*, 35. In *LOTR* we meet Tooks named Isumbras, Peregrin, and Mirabella. Baggins, like most hobbit surnames, is English slang.
11. Christopher Tolkien *The History of Middle-earth: The Return of the Shadow*, vol 6. (New York: Houghton Mifflin, 1988), 7.
12. *Letters*, p. 176.
13. *LOTR*, Appendix F, 1137.
14. *Letters*, p. 236.
15. *LOTR*, 2.
16. *Letters*, p. 274.
17. See *Reader's Companion*, 375–77.

18. For the case of Valacar of Gondor and Vidumavi of Rhovanion, see Straubhaar, "Myth, Late Roman History, and Multiculturalism."

19. Translated by Henry Adams Bellows (1936), http://www.sacred-texts.com/neu/poe/poe03.htm.

20. See *Annotated Hobbit*, 98.

21. See ibid. 7–8; Rateliff, *The History*, Part 1, 48ff.

22. The likeliest candidate is *Der Berggeist* (ca. 1925) by the German artist Josef Madlenner. See *Annotated Hobbit*, 37–8.

23. Drout, "Rings, Swords, and Monsters," lecture four.

24. *The Hobbit*, 34.

25. The classifications "trooping fairies" and "solitary fairies" are employed by the poet W. B. Yeats (in 1888) and the folklorist K. M. Briggs.

26. *The Hobbit*, 48.

27. See *Annotated Hobbit*, 94–5.

28. *The Hobbit*, 50.

29. *Letters*, pp. 31–32.

30. Ibid., pp. 391–93. Anderson (*Annotated Hobbit*, 102) points out that nearly all of the mountains in Tolkien's own drawings resemble Alpine peaks.

31. Shippey, *Road*, 70.

32. *Letters*, pp. 318, 449.

33. Ibid., p. 31.

34. The Narnian giants live in "Ettinsmoor," while Tolkien's live in "the Ettenmoors or troll-fells" (*Fellowship*, 200).

35. See *Annotated Hobbit*, 106–9.

36. *The Hobbit*, 67.

37. *Annotated Hobbit*, 120.

38. *Letters*, p. 32.

39. See *Annotated Hobbit*, 120ff.

40. *The Hobbit*, 67.

41. *LOTR*, 48. Gandalf suspects that the ring exerted an "unwholesome power" over Bilbo from the very beginning.

42. See Eric Katz, "The Rings of Tolkien and Plato: Lessons in Power, Choice, and Morality," in Gregory Bassham and Eric Bronson (eds), The Lord of the Rings *and Philosophy* (Chicago: Open Court, 2003), 5–20; and discussion in ch. 5 below.

43. *The Hobbit*, 80.

44. C. S. Lewis, "The Necessity of Chivalry," in Walter Hooper (ed), *C. S. Lewis: Present Concerns* (London: Harcourt, 1986), 13–16.

45. See *Annotated Hobbit*, 146–7.

46. *The Hobbit*, 95.

47. *Annotated Hobbit*, 156–7.

48. See Gilliver, Marshall, and Weiner, *The Ring of Words*, 98–99; *Annotated Hobbit*, 164; and Rateliff, *The History*, Part 1, 261ff.

49. See Rateliff, *The History*, 228ff, 253ff.

50. *Annotated Hobbit*, 164–5.

51. Shippey, *The Road to Middle-earth*, 80.

52. *The Hobbit*, 114–5.

53. Ibid., 126.

54. *Annotated Hobbit*, 183.

55. *The Hobbit*, 126.

56. *Annotated Hobbit*, 199. Rateliff (402) also suggests Marie de France's "Guigemar" and "Pwyll, Prince of Dyfed," from the *Mabonogi*, as possible medieval influences.

57. *The Hobbit*, 137.

58. The meaning of *attercop* is discussed at length by Lizzie Wright, the wife of Tolkien's undergraduate mentor Joe Wright, who had Ronald over for her "huge Yorkshire teas" on Sunday afternoons. See E. M. Wright, *Rustic Speech and Folk-Lore* (1913), quoted and discussed in John S. Ryan, *The Shaping of Middle-earth's Maker: Influences on the Life and Literature of J. R. R. Tolkien* (Highland, MI: American Tolkien Society, 1992), 35–7.

59. *The Hobbit*, 151

60. Ibid., 160, 173.

61. Richard Hayman, "Green Men and the Way of All Flesh," *British Archaeology* 100 (May/June 2008): http://www.britarch.ac.uk/ba/ba100/feat5.shtml (accessed May 22, 2011).

62. *The Hobbit*, 177.

63. C. S. Lewis, *The Chronicles of Narnia 5: Voyage of the Dawn Treader* (New York: HarperCollins, 1994), 450.

64. *The Hobbit*, 226.

65. Rateliff, *The History*, Part 1, 453–4. Like the communes (towns) of medieval Italy, Esgaroth seems to have maintained its independence from the feudal lordship of Dale.

66. The dragon in the earliest fragment of *The Hobbit* appears as Pryftan. See Rateliff, *The History*, Part 1, 3ff.

67. *Biography*, 30.

68. *The Hobbit*, 193.

69. Ibid., 194.

70. *Letters*, p. 31.

71. Shippey, *Road*, 82. See also Tolkien's letter to Naomi Mitchison, December 18, 1949.

72. See *Annotated Hobbit*, 309.

73. *The Hobbit*, 258–9.

74. Brian Rosebury (*Tolkien: A Cultural Phenomenon*, 113) points out that this is a reference (perhaps accidental) to the "good thief" who asks Jesus' forgiveness at the Crucifixion (Luke 23).

75. See Aeon J. Skoble, "Virtue and Vice in *The Lord of the Rings*," in Gregory Bassham and Eric Bronson (eds), The Lord of the Rings *and Philosophy* (Chicago: Open Court, 2003), 110–19.

76. *Letters*, p. 310.

77. Quoted by Philip Norman in "The Prevalence of Hobbits," *New York Times Magazine* (January 15, 1967), 100.

78. Anonymous review of *The Hobbit* (Oct. 2, 1937), 714. See *Annotated Hobbit*, 362.

79. Jane Chance Nitzsche, *Tolkien's Art: 'A Mythology for England'* (London: Macmillan, 1979), 31ff.

80. Tolkien in Norman, "The Prevalence," 100.

chapter 4: tales of the third age

1. *Letters*, p. 23.

2. Ibid., p. 24. See also *Reader's Companion*, xviii.

3. Birzer, *Sanctifying Myth*, 27.

4. *LOTR*, 988.

5. See George Sayer, "Recollections of J. R. R. Tolkien," in Joseph Pearce (ed), *Tolkien: A Celebration* (London: HarperCollins, 1999), 8.

6. *Reader's Companion*, xxxii–xxxiii.

7. *LOTR*, 1. In a 1955 letter to his publisher (*Letters*, p. 230) Tolkien states that the Shire is "more or less a Warwickshire village of about the period of the Diamond Jubilee [i.e. 1897]."

8. See Thomas Shippey, "Thegns," in Christopher A. Snyder (ed.), *The Early Peoples of Britain and Ireland: An Encyclopedia*, vol. II (Oxford: Greenwood, 2007), 495–6.

9. On Middle-earth, see Chapter One. While many of these place names have Old English roots, several have Celtic (specifically British) origins—e.g. Bree, Chetwood, and Crickhollow—which Shippey suggests that Tolkien employed in order to show that the hobbits, like the English, had "invaded" territory occupied by an older people. See Shippey, *Road*, 114; and *Reader's Companion*, 16.

10. See note 8.

11. John and Priscilla Tolkien, *The Tolkien Family Album*, 22. Garth (*Tolkien and the Great War*, 206) points out that the army surgeon at the Birmingham University Hospital, where Tolkien invalided in 1914, was Major Leonard Gamgee, a relative of the inventor.

12. *Letters*, pp. 244–5.

13. Ibid., p. 28.

14. *LOTR*, 45.

15. Ibid., 53.

16. Ibid., 48.

17. Ibid., 53.

18. Ibid., 50.

19. *Reader's Companion*, xx.

20. No. 14 in the *Dyrham Proverbs*: see Shippey, *Road*, 137.

21. *LOTR*, 64.

22. As opposed to the attitude of his father, Hamfast "Gaffer" Gamgee. OE *hāmfæst* means "stay at home," while a "gaffer" is English slang for a rustic old man: see *Reader's Companion*, 55.

23. *LOTR*, 119.

24. Ibid., 123. Cf. Goldeboru in the Middle English romance *Havelok the Dane* (thirteenth century).

25. *Letters*, p. 26; Shippey, *Road*, 107.

26. See *Reader's Companion*, 128.

27. *Letters*, p. 272.

28. See Shippey, *Author*, 63; and *Reader's Companion*, 116, 122, 779.

29. See Blackham, *Tolkien's Oxford*, 103–11.

30. *LOTR*, 137

31. *Reader's Companion*, 147–8.

32. *LOTR*, 149.

33. Ibid., 171.

34. *LOTR*, 170.

35. *Reader's Companion*, 261.

36. *LOTR*, 994.

37. Literal translation, http://en.wikipedia.org/wiki/Erlkonig and other online sources.

38. See John and Priscilla Tolkien, *The Tolkien Family Album*, 31; and *Reader's Companion*, 203, 266–7.

39. *LOTR*, 243.

40. Ibid., 261.

41. Patrick Ford (trans), *Culhwch and Olwen*, 148.

42. *LOTR*, 257.

43. Ibid., 259.

44. Ibid., 24.

45. Ibid., 472.

46. Ibid., 433.

47. Ibid., 83.

48. Ibid., 661.

49. See Shippey, *Road*, 119.

50. *LOTR*, 270.

51. Ibid., 329.

52. Shippey, *Author*, 85–6.

53. *LOTR*, 354, 357.

54. Ibid., 366.

55. Later, in *The Two Towers*, Galadriel even sends word to Gimli speaking like a courtly lover: "To Gimli son of Glóin, . . . give his Lady's greeting. Lockbearer, wherever thou goest my thought goes with thee." (*LOTR*, 503).

56. For Celeborn and Galadriel as gift-givers, see Alison Milbank, "'My Precious': Tolkien's Fetishized Ring," in Gregory Bassham and Eric Bronson (eds), The Lord of the Rings *and Philosophy* (Chicago: Open Court, 2003), 40. For the Marian interpretation of Galadriel, see discussion on page 233.

57. *LOTR*, 392.

58. So it has been traditionally thought; recent studies say it more likely was erected on a pedestal beside the harbor. See "Colossus of Rhodes" in Brian Fagan (ed), *The Seventy Great Mysteries of the Ancient World* (London: Thames and Hudson, 2001).

59. *LOTR*, 406.

60. *Reader's Companion*, xxxii–xxxiii.

61. *Letters*, pp. 170–1.

62. *LOTR*, 413–4.

63. Trans. by Charles Scott Moncrief, 1919. *Olifant* is the name of Roland's horn.

64. *LOTR*, 430.

65. *Letters*, pp. 382–3.

66. See Snyder, *The Britons*, 153ff. The poem "Armes Prydein Vawr" calls these Bretons "warriors on war-horses."

67. Shippey (*Road*, 123) points out that many Rohan names come specifically from the Mercian dialect.
68. *LOTR*, 522–23.
69. Among the subjects they discuss are myths, political isolationism, just war, and moral relativism, all themes discussed in this book.
70. *Enta* and *eoten* are forms of the same word, which is variously translated giant, ogre, and troll.
71. *LOTR*, 463. Treebeard says (486) that trolls were made by the enemy as a mockery of ents.
72. Hammond and Scull (*Reader's Companion*, 392) compare Gandalf's combat with the balrog with that between Beowulf and Grendel's mother.
73. *Letters*, pp. 201–2.
74. *LOTR*, 135.
75. Ibid., 676.
76. *Letters*, p. 243. The letter, never published, was written in reply to a January 22, 1956, *New York Times* review by W. H. Auden.
77. *LOTR*, 530.
78. Ibid., 579–80.
79. Anonymous review of *LOTR* in the *Times Literary Supplement*, August 27, 1954, p. 541.
80. Scott A. Davison, "Tolkien and the Nature of Evil," in Gregory Bassham and Eric Bronson (eds), The Lord of the Rings *and Philosophy* (Chicago: Open Court, 2003), 99–109.
81. For the scholarly debate on this issue, see Shippey, *Road to Middle Earth*, 140–46; Rose Zimbardo, "Moral Vision in *The Lord of the Rings*," in *Understanding* The Lord of the Rings: The Best of Tolkien Criticism, Rose A. Zimbardo and Neil D. Isaacs (eds) (Boston: Houghton Mifflin, 2004), 73; John Wm. Houghton and Neal K. Keesee, "Tolkien, King Alfred, and Boethius: Platonist Views of Evil in *The Lord of the Rings*," *Tolkien Studies* 2 (2005): 131–59.
82. Kreeft, *Philosophy of Tolkien*, 176.
83. *LOTR*, 243.
84. *Letters*, p. 243.
85. "Foreword" in Bradley J. Birzer, *J. R. R. Tolkien's Sanctifying Myth: Understanding Middle-earth* (Wilmington, DE: ISI Books, 2002), xii.
86. Augustine puts forward his theory particularly in *Confessions* and *On the Free Choice of the Will*. See also Davison, "Tolkien and the Nature of Evil," 102–3.
87. Exemplified by Henri IV in France and, some would say, by Elizabeth I in England. The French *politiques* would influence Cardinal Richelieu in the seventeenth century as he developed the similar philosophy of *raison d'état*.
88. *LOTR*, 581.
89. Ibid., 581.
90. Lewis utilizes such contrasts on occasion in both *Narnia* and the Space Trilogy. In *Out of the Silent Planet*, the scientist Weston is similar to the Tolkien villain Saruman.
91. *LOTR*, 59.
92. Ibid., 615.
93. Ibid., 627–28.
94. Ibid., 623.
95. Ibid., 664.

96. Ibid., 665. See also Beregond's description of Faramir: *LOTR*, 766.

97. *LOTR*, 671.

98. Ibid., 681.

99. Ibid., 672.

100. *LOTR*, 702.

101. Forman, Harry Buxton, ed. *The Works of Percy Bysshe Shelley in Verse and Prose.* (London: Reeves and Turner, 1880).

102. *LOTR*, 723.

103. See Arwen van Zanten, "Going Berserk: in Old Norse, Old Irish and Anglo-Saxon Literature," *Amsterdamer Beiträge zur älteren Germanistik*, 63, no. 1 (August 2007), 43–64.

104. *LOTR*, 730–31.

105. Ibid., 753, 771.

106. Ibid., 756.

107. The letter is preserved in the *Libri Feudorum* as well as Gratian's *Decretum*. Trans. here by Kenneth Pennington: http://faculty.cua.edu/pennington/Feudal%20 OathBrundage.htm.

108. *LOTR*, 777.

109. See further Shippey, *Author*, 98–9; and Sarah Beach, "Specific Derivation," *Mythlore* 12, no. 4 (Summer 1986): 16.

110. *LOTR*, 779.

111. Ibid., 784–5.

112. *LOTR*, 809.

113. Versions of the story appear in Jean Froissart, *Chronicles* (ca. 1370) and John Barbour, *The Brus* (1375). It was embellished later by Sir Walter Scott and others.

114. *LOTR*, 812.

115. Miryam, Librán-Moreno, "Parallel Lives: The Sons of Denethor and the Sons of Telamon," *Tolkien Studies* 2 (2005): 15–52.

116. Judy Ann Ford, "The White City: *The Lord of the Rings* as an Early Medieval Myth of the Restoration of the Roman Empire," *Tolkien Studies* 2 (2005): 53–73.

117. *LOTR*, 824.

118. Ibid., 818, 819, 824.

119. *Letters*, no. 183.

120. *LOTR*, 758.

121. Ibid., 836.

122. Ibid., 976.

123. Ibid., 841.

124. Ibid., 842.

125. Ibid., 849.

126. Ibid., 844.

127. Ibid., 847.

128. For the medieval antecedent, see discussion in Chapter Two, page 81.

129. *LOTR*, 865.

130. Ibid., 866.

131. See *Reader's Companion*, 564–71.

132. See John. Pryor and Elizabeth M. Jeffreys, *The Age of the* ΔΡΟΜΩΝ: *The Byzantine Navy ca. 500–1204* (Leiden, Netherlands: Brill, 2006).

133. *LOTR*, 867.

134. Ibid., 960.

135. *Letters*, p. 323.

136. *LOTR*, 870.

137. Peter Kreeft, *The Philosophy of Tolkien* (San Francisco: Ignatius Press, 2005), 44.

138. *The Hobbit*, 45.

139. David Rozema observes that Frodo's "charity has a salutary effect upon the other kinds of loving relationships in the story," especially upon Sam. See Rozema, "*The Lord of the Rings*: Tolkien, Jackson, and 'The Core of the Original,'" *Christian Scholar's Review*, 443.

140. *LOTR*, 55.

141. *The Hobbit*, 256.

142. Hammond and Scull (*Reader's Companion*, 603–4) believe that Frodo's responding to Sam's song was inspired by the story of the imprisoned King Richard the Lionheart and his loyal minstrel Blondel.

143. *LOTR*, 911–12.

144. See Derek S. Brewer, "*The Lord of the Rings* as Romance," in Mary Salu and Robert T. Farrell (eds), *J. R. R. Tolkien, Scholar and Storyteller: Essays in Memoriam* (Ithaca, NY: Cornell Univ. Press, 1979), 249–64.

145. *LOTR*, 937–8.

146. *LOTR*, 945.

147. See discussion in Chapter One, page 20.

148. *The Hobbit*, 101.

149. *LOTR*, 954.

150. Ibid., 999.

151. Ibid., 996.

152. Ibid., 56.

153. J. R. R. Tolkien, "Fate and Free Will," edited by Carl F. Hostetter, *Tolkien Studies* 6 (2009): 183–88.

154. In a letter to *Beyond Bree* (June 1991), 10. Quoted in *Reader's Companion*, 200.

155. Kreeft, *Philosophy of Tolkien*, 167.

156. Norman F. Cantor, *Inventing the Middle Ages* (New York: William Morrow, 1991), 231–2.

157. Ibid. Cantor calls Tolkien "an archaeologist of medieval society."

158. I use here C. S. Lewis's four categories, based on the Greek and Latin terms for love (there are, in fact, many more). Lewis includes patriotism under the category *storge* (Affection). See also pp. 166–67.

159. *The Lord of the Rings: The Two Towers* (New Line Cinema, 2002), screenplay by Fran Walsh, Philippa Boyens, Stephen Sinclair, and Peter Jackson; novel by J. R. R. Tolkien.

160. *Letters*, p. 179.

161. *LOTR*, 1019.

162. María José Álvarez-Faedo, "Arthurian Reminiscences in Tolkien's Trilogy: *The Lord of the Rings*," in María José Álvarez-Faedo (ed), *Avalon Revisited: Reworkings of the Arthurian Myth* (Bern: Peter Lang, 2007), 185–210.

163. *LOTR*, 309–10.

164. Patchen Mortimer, "Tolkien and Modernism," *Tolkien Studies* 2 (2005), 126.

165. *LOTR*, 1030.

166. Lewis, *Abolition of Man*; idem, *A Grief Observed*.

chapter 5: the song of ilúvatar

1. Carpenter, *Biography*, 72.

2. Quoted in Garth, 45.

3. Carpenter, *Biography*, 83.

4. See *Reader's Guide*, 901ff.

5. Rhona Beare, "A Mythology for England," in Allan Turner (ed), *The Silmarillion—Thirty Years One* (Walking Tree Publishers, 2007), 1–31. Beare corresponded with Prof. Tolkien and wrote some of the first published criticism of *The Silmarillion*.

6. J. R. R. Tolkien, *The Silmarillion*, 2nd edition, edited by Christopher Tolkien (Boston: Houghton Mifflin, 2001), 15. All subsequent references are to this edition unless otherwise stated.

7. Eru first shows the Ainur an unfolding vision of what Arda will become, i.e., a globe. Tolkien does not explain until much later in *The Silmarillion* that Arda is "rounded" after the wars with Melkor.

8. *The Silmarillion*, 18.

9. Ibid., 29.

10. In *The Mabinogi and Other Medieval Welsh Tales*, trans. and ed. by Patrick K. Ford (Berkeley: Univ. of California Press, 1977), 135.

11. *The Silmarillion*, 30.

12. See Flieger, *Splintered Light*, 57ff.

13. Trans. Albert S. Cook, Yale Studies in English (http://www.gutenberg.org/catalog/world/readfile?fk_files=1500641&pageno=1).

14. Trans. Susan Oldrieve (http://homepages.bw.edu/~uncover/oldrievegenesisb.htm).

15. Arda is the Little Kingdom presumably because Eru's throne is in the Big Kingdom.

16. *The Silmarillion*, 41.

17. Ibid., 43.

18. See Beare, "A Mythology for England," 3–4.

19. Ibid., 28–9; Beare points to the twelfth-century English alliterative romance, *The Wars of Alexander*, as a possible source for Tolkien's myth of the origins of the Sun and Moon.

20. *The Silmarillion*, 141.

21. Ibid., 167.

22. *Letters*, p 417.

23. Ibid., 184.

24. *Letters*, pp. 25–26.

25. *The Simarillion*, 192.

26. Ibid., 193.

27. Ibid., 248–9.

28. Ibid., 260.

29. Ibid., 264.

30. Tolkien (*Letters*, 156) calls Elendil "a Noachian figure." Beare ("A Mythology for England," 19) also points out the similarities between Elendil and Aeneas.

31. *The Silmarillion*, 281.

32. Ibid., 295.

33. See Michaël Devaux, "The Origins of the *Ainulindalë*: The Present State of Research," in Allan Turner (ed.), The Silmarillion—*Thirty Years On* (Zollikofen, Switzerland: Walking Tree Publishers, 2007), 81–110.

34. See Beare, "A Mythology for England," esp. 29.

35. Tolkien, *Letters*, p. 144.

36. Ibid.

37. *The Silmarillion*, 299.

38. Garth, *Tolkien and the Great War*, 26.

39. See *The Silmarillion*, Appendix s.v. *hîth.* "Hith" and *hyð* are homophonic (pronounced the same way).

40. J. R. R. Tolkien (edited by Christopher Tolkien), *The Children of Húrin* (Boston: Houghton Mifflin, 2007), 59. Hereafter *Children*.

41. *Children*, 42–44.

42. *Children*, 162.

43. J. R. R. Tolkien, *The Homecoming of Beorhtnoth*, in Tolkien, *The Tolkien Reader* (New York: Ballantine Books, 1966), 16.

44. Ibid., 24–25.

45. In a similar way did *searo/searu* inspire Saruman, "cunning man."

46. *Children*, 82.

47. Ibid., 104.

48. Ibid., 114.

49. Malory, *Le Morte d'arthur* (Ware, Hertfordshire: Wordsworth, 1996), book 11, chapter 8.

50. *Children*, 253.

51. Ibid., 255.

52. Ibid., 257.

53. Ibid., 134.

54. *The Silmarillion*, 41–2.

55. Ibid., 41

56. Ibid., 265.

57. *Letters*, p. 246.

58. *The Silmarillion*, 265

59. *LOTR*, 51.

60. *The Hobbit*, 194.

61. Flieger, *Splintered Light*, 39.

62. *LOTR*, 985

63. *LOTR*, 52.

64. "*Beowulf*: The Monsters and the Critics," in Seamus Heaney (trans), *Beowulf: A Verse Translation*, 104.

65. Quoted in Cantor, *Inventing the Middle Ages*, 227.

appendix 1: monsters and critics

1. J. R. R. Tolkien, *The Lord of the Rings* (Boston: Houghton Mifflin, 2004), xxiii.
2. Carpenter, *Biography*, 226.
3. See *Letters*, pp. 181–2.
4. *The Hobbit*, 272.
5. Anderson (*The Annotated Hobbit*, 18–9) records thirty reviews of the first British edition and another twenty of the first American edition.
6. *Horn Book* (March–April 1938), quoted in *The Annotated Hobbit*, 21.
7. See *Reader's Guide*, 398–401.
8. Edmund Fuller, "The Lord of the Hobbits: J. R. R. Tolkien," in Isaacs and Zimbardo (eds.), *Tolkien and the Critics*, 18.
9. Michael N. Stanton, *Hobbits, Elves, and Wizards: Exploring the Wonders of the Worlds of J. R. R. Tolkien's* The Lord of the Rings (New York: Palgrave Macmillan, 2001), 7–8.
10. Charles Moseley, *J. R. R. Tolkien* (Plymouth: Northcote House, 1997), 44, 48.
11. Brian Rosebury, *Tolkien: A Cultural Phenomenon* (London: Palgrave Macmillan, 2003), 114.
12. Bonniejean Christensen, "Gollum's Character Transformation in *The Hobbit*," in Lobdell (ed.), *A Tolkien Compass*, 9–10.
13. Paul Kocher, *Master of Middle-earth: The Achievement of J. R. R. Tolkien* (London: Pimlico, 2002), 19ff.
14. Jane Chance Nitzsche, *Tolkien's Art* (London: Macmillan, 1980), ch. 2.
15. *Letters*, pp. 309–11.
16. C. S. Lewis, *An Experiment in Criticism* (Cambridge: Cambridge Univ. Press, 1961), 44. See also Purtill, *J. R. R. Tolkien: Myth, Morality, and Religion*, 9, 26.
17. Lewis, *Surprised by Joy*, 206–7.
18. See Carpenter, *The Inklings*, 29–32.
19. *Biography*, 226.
20. The letter is included in full in *Biography*, 230–231.
21. Lewis, "The Gods Return to Earth," reprinted in the *Chesterton Review* 28, nos. 1 & 2 (2002), 73–77.
22. Lewis, "The Dethronement of Power," in Rose A. Zaimbardo and Neil D. Isaacs, *Understanding* The Lord of the Rings: *The Best of Tolkien Criticism* (Boston: Houghton Mifflin, 2004), 11–15.
23. *Letters*, p. 184.
24. Compare to Tolkien's phrase "their joy was like swords" (*LOTR*, 954).
25. "Heroic Endeavor," *Times Literary Supplement* (Aug. 27, 1954), 541.
26. "The Epic of Westernesse," ibid. (Dec. 17, 1954), 817.
27. Edmund Wilson, "Oo, Those Awful Orcs!" *Nation* 182, no. 15 (April 14, 1956); Philip Toynbee, "Dissension Among the Judges," *Observer* (Aug. 6, 1961).
28. Robert H. Flood, C.S.B., "Hobbit Hoax? The Fellowship of the Ring," *Books on Trial* (Feb. 1955), quoted in Birzer, 14.
29. See Birzer, 13–17.
30. Judith A. Johnson, *Six Decades of Tolkien Criticism* (London: Greenwood, 1986), 50.
31. Norman F. Cantor, *Inventing the Middle Ages* (New York: William Morrow, 1991), 226. There are factual mistakes in Cantor's biographical discussion of Tolkien and Lewis.

32. Review of *The Return of the King* in the *New York Times* (Jan. 22, 1956).

33. Peter Conrad, "The Babbit," *New Statesman* (Sept. 23, 1977), 408–9, quoted in Birzer, 21.

34. Birzer, 15.

35. *The Hobbit* is third at over 100 million copies, while not far behind is C. S. Lewis's *The Lion, the Witch and the Wardrobe* at 85 million copies.

36. See Pearce, *Tolkien: Man and Myth*; Shippey, *Author*, xx–xxi; and *Reader's Guide*, 551.

37. See Pearce, *Tolkien: Man and Myth*, 3.

38. Interviewed in *W: The Waterstone's Magazine* (Winter/Spring 1997).

39. Both comments are in A. N. Wilson, "Tolkien was not a writer," *Daily Telegraph*, Nov. 24, 2001.

40. *Reader's Guide*, 551.

41. Patrick Curry, "Why Tolkien is for the real grown-ups," *New Statesman* 126, no. 4319 (Jan. 31, 1997), 47.

42. Shippey, *J. R. R. Tolkien: Author of the Century*, xvii. Unfortunately, such misinformed criticism continues in journalistic circles: see, for example, Adam Gopnik, "The Dragon's Egg: High Fantasy for Young Adults," *New Yorker* Dec. 5, 2011 (http://www.newyorker.com/arts/critics/atlarge/2011/12/05/111205crat_atlarge_gopnik?currentPage=all).

43. Gregory Bassham and Eric Bronson (eds.), The Lord of the Rings *and Philosophy* (Chicago: Open Court, 2003).

44. Milbank, "'My Precious,'" in Bassham and Bronson, 44.

45. Brian Rosebury, *Tolkien: A Cultural Phenomenon* (London: Palgrave Macmillan, 2003), 3.

46. Rosebury, *Tolkien*, 5.

47. *The Hobbit*, 45.

48. *LOTR*, 472.

49. Patrick Curry, *Defending Middle-Earth* (London: HarperCollins, 1997).

50. Andrew Light, "Tolkien's Green Time: Environmental Themes in *The Lord of the Rings*," in Bassham and Bronson, 150–63.

51. Light, "Tolkien's Green Time," 162–63.

52. See Matthew Dickerson and Jonathan Evans, *Ents, Elves, and Eriador: The Environmental Vision of J. R. R. Tolkien* (Lexington: University of Kentucky Press, 2006).

53. Verlyn Flieger, "Taking the Part of Trees: Eco-Conflict in Middle-earth," in Clark and Timmons (eds.), *J. R. R. Tolkien and His Literary Resonances*, 148.

54. *LOTR*, 130.

55. Fleming Rutledge, *The Battle for Middle-earth: Tolkien's Divine Design in* The Lord of the Rings (Grand Rapids, MI: Eerdman's, 2004), 29.

56. Shippey, *Road*, 57.

57. See John Wm. Houghton and Neal K. Keesee, "Tolkien, King Alfred, and Boethius: Platonist Views of Evil in *The Lord of the Rings*," *Tolkien Studies* 2 (2005): 131–59; and pp. 146–47.

58. Patchen Mortimer, "Tolkien and Modernism," *Tolkien Studies* 2 (2005): 113, 121.

59. Nitzsche, *Tolkien's Art*, 6.

60. Cantor, *Inventing the Middle Ages*, 229.

61. See, for example, Robert Giddings (ed.), *J. R. R. Tolkien: This Far Land* (1990).

62. Stratford Caldecott, "The Horn of Hope," *Chesterton Review* 28, nos. 1 and 2 (Feb/May 2002), 37.

63. *LOTR*, 79.

64. Stratford Caldecott, *The Power of the Ring: The Spiritual Vision Behind* The Lord of the Rings (New York: Crossroad, 2005), 54–5.

65. Kreeft, *Philosophy of Tolkien*, 180.

66. Ibid., 16.

67. Wood, *The Gospel According to Tolkien*, 9.

68. Ibid., ch. 5.

69. *Morgoths's Ring* (i.e. Volume 10 of *The History of Middle-earth*), 321.

70. Fleming, *The Battle*, 42.

71. Richard L. Purtill, *J. R. R. Tolkien: Myth, Morality, and Religion* (San Francisco: Harper & Rowe, 1984), 3.

72. Ibid., 10.

73. Birzer, *J. R. R. Tolkien's Sanctifying Myth: Understanding Middle-earth* (Wilmington, DE: ISI Books, 2002).

74. Ibid., xxv.

75. Ibid., 23.

76. Quoting Tolkien from *Letters*, 145, 253.

77. *Letters*, p. 172.

78. Pearce, "Foreword," in Birzer, *J. R. R. Tolkien's Sanctifying Myth*, xiii.

79. C. S. Lewis, *The Complete C. S. Lewis Signature Classics* (New York: HarperCollins, 2007), 46.

80. Preface to the second edition of *LOTR*, xxiii–xxiv.

appendix II: media and middle-earth

1. Wayne G. Hammond and Christina Scull, *J. R. R. Tolkien: Artist and Illustrator* (Boston: Houghton Mifflin, 2000); id., The Art of The Hobbit by J. R. R. Tolkien (London: HarperCollins, 2011).

2. Tolkien, "On Fairy-stories," 70.

3. The website Tolkien Gateway (http://tolkiengateway.net/wiki/Portal:Images) has samples from over 160 different artists.

4. An entertaining account of the Brothers Hildebrandt's method of painting is provided by Greg Hildebrandt Jr.: *Greg and Tim Hildebrandt: The Tolkien Years*, exp ed (New York: Watson-Guptill, 2002).

5. Hildebrandt, *The Tolkien Years*, 6.

6. John Howe, "Getting it Right" (http://www.john-howe.com/medieval/), excerpted from *Myth & Magic: The Art of John Howe* (New York: HarperCollins, 2001).

7. See Donato Giancola, *Middle-earth: Visions of a Modern Myth* (Nevada City, CA: Underwood Books, 2010).

8. For discussion see Jim Smith and J. Clive Matthews, *The Lord of the Rings: The Films, the Books, the Radio Series* (London: Virgin Books, 2004), 15–16.

9. *Letters*, pp. 228, 229, 254.

10. A 1966 BBC Radio treatment of *The Hobbit* seems to have been more faithful to Tolkien's book. In 1954 the BBC Third Programme broadcast dramatic readings of Tolkien's translations of *Sir Gawain and the Green Knight* and *The Homecoming of Beorhtnoth*.

11. See Smith and Matthews, *The Films*, 71–88.
12. *Letters*, p. 257 (to Rayner Unwin).
13. Ibid., p. 261.
14. Smith and Matthews, *The Films*, 19.
15. See Smith and Matthews, *The Films*, 54.
16. *The Rough Guide to* The Lord of the Rings (London: Penguin, 2003), 116.
17. Tolkien, "On Fairy-stories," 71.
18. *The Fellowship of the Ring*, Extended DVD Edition, Appendices, Part One.
19. Ibid.
20. Sean Astin (with Joe Layden), *There and Back Again: An Actor's Tale* (New York: St Martin's, 2005), pp. 84–5.
21. *Reader's Companion*, p. xx.
22. Quoted in Joe Fordham, "Middle-earth Strikes Back," *Cinefex* 92 (Jan. 2003), 74.
23. *Two Towers*, Extended Edition DVD, Appendices, Part Three.
24. Roto-animation was also used, and Elijah Wood's eyes and Peter Jackson's feet were given to Gollum.
25. *The Lord of the Rings: The Fellowship of the Ring* (New Line Cinema, 2001), screenplay by Fran Walsh, Philippa Boyens, and Peter Jackson; novel by J. R. R. Tolkien.
26. Surprisingly, Tolkien may have agreed with Jackson: "Tom Bombadil is not an important person—to the narrative" (*Letters*, p. 178).
27. Tolkien, *LOTR*, 226–7.
28. *Two Towers*, Appendices, Disc Three.
29. Alison Milbank, "'My Precious': Tolkien's Fetishized Ring," in Gregory Bassham and Eric Bronson (eds), The Lord of the Rings *and Philosophy* (Chicago: Open Court, 2003), 33.
30. *Fellowship* (New Line, 2001).
31. Ibid.
32. Ibid.
33. *Two Towers* (New Line, 2002).
34. Layamon, *Brut*, ll. 21323–30, trans. by C. S. Lewis in his essay "The Genesis of a Medieval Book," in C. S. Lewis, *Studies in Medieval and Renaissance Literature* (Cambridge: Cambridge Univ. Press, 1998), 33.
35. Quoted in *Reader's Companion*, 400.
36. *Two Towers* (New Line, 2002).
37. Peter Kreeft, *The Philosophy of Tolkien* (San Francisco: Ignatius Press, 2005), 168.
38. See Rozema, "*The Lord of the Rings*: Tolkien, Jackson, and 'The Core of the Original,'" *Christian Scholar's Review*, 437.
39. *Two Towers*, Appendices, Disc Three.
40. *Two Towers* (New Line, 2002).
41. Ibid.
42. Ibid.
43. Ibid.
44. Ibid.
45. *The Lord of the Rings: The Return of the King* (New Line Cinema, 2003), screenplay by Fran Walsh, Philippa Boyens, and Peter Jackson; novel by J. R. R. Tolkien.
46. Ibid.

47. Ibid.

48. The architectural details of the Minas Tirith set bear a striking resemblance to the city architecture in the background of John Maler Collier's painting, *Lady Godiva* (1898). The historical Lady Godiva was an Anglo-Saxon noblewoman, the wife of Earl Leofric of Mercia, who died in 1067.

49. Successfully proven in a recent experiment in North Wales: see http://www.bbc.co.uk/news/uk-wales-north-east-wales-11832323 (accessed May 5, 2011).

50. *Return of the King* (New Line, 2003).

51. Ibid.

52. Ibid.

53. *Return of the King* (Extended Edition DVD), Appendices.

54. *Return of the King* (New Line, 2003).

55. Ibid.

56. Ibid.

57. Ibid.

58. Ibid.

59. Ibid.

60. Translated by Benjamin Thorpe, (1866), http://www.northvegr.org/secondary%20sources/eddic%20poetry/the%20voluspa/v002.html.

61. See Jeroen de Kloet and Giselinde Kuipers, "Spirituality and ·Fan Culture around the *Lord of the Rings* Film Trilogy," *Fabula* 48 (2007), 1–20. This article uses the dataset from a University of Wales, Aberystwyth global survey on viewer response to Jackson's *The Return of the King* as well as interviews with a segment of the Dutch respondents.

62. It is perhaps too early to assess the scholarship on Jackson's films. For a sampling, however, see Janet Brennan Croft (ed), *Tolkien on Film: Essays on Peter Jackson's "The Lord of the Rings"* (Altadena, CA: The Mythopoeic Press, 2004); Thomas Honegger (ed), *Translating Tolkien: Text and Film*. Zurich: Walking Tree Publishers, 2004); Christopher Garbowski, *Spiritual Values in Peter Jackson's Lord of the Rings* (Lublin, Poland: Marie Curie-Skłodowska University Press, 2005); Lynnette R. Porter, *Unsung Heroes of* The Lord of the Rings: *From the Page to the Screen* (Westport, CT: Praeger, 2005); and Ernest Mathijs and Murray Pomerance (eds), *From Hobbits to Hollywood: Essays on Peter Jackson's* Lord of the Rings (Amsterdam and New York: Rodopi, 2006).

63. *Chicago Sun Times*, Dec. 19, 2001.

64. *Rolling Stone*, Dec. 19, 2001.

65. Salon.com, Dec. 18, 2001; http://www.salon.com/2001/12/18/lord_of_the_rings.

66. *Chicago Sun Times*, Dec. 18, 2002.

67. *Observer*, Dec. 15, 2002.

68. *Chicago Sun Times*, Dec. 17, 2003.

69. *Village Voice*, Dec. 16, 2003.

70. http://www.afi.com/100years/movies10.aspx

71. "The Lawsuit of the Rings," *New York Times*, June 27, 2005; see http://www.nytimes.com/2005/06/27/business/media/27movie.html?pagewanted=all

72. For a timeline of these suits and settlements, see Mike Ryan, "TIMELINE: The Hobbit's Troubled 75-year Journey from Page to Screen," *Movieline*, March 23, 2011 (http://

movieline.com/2011/03/23/timeline-the-hobbits-troubled-75-year-journey-from-page-to-screen/).

73. *Reuters*, Sept. 8, 2009 (http://www.reuters.com/article/pressRelease/idUS180663+08-Sep-2009+PRN20090908). This settlement did not prevent the Tolkien Estate and publisher HarperCollins from suing Zaentz and Warner Bros. over licensing slot machines and online games, resulting in counter-suits from the two defendants: see *The Hollywood Reporter*, March 13, 2013 (http://www.hollywoodreporter.com/thr-esq/warner-bros-claims-tolkien-estate-428390). The case is unresolved as of this writing.

74. "*Hellboy II* director del Toro takes his demons seriously," July 2008 interview by Anthony Breznican in *USA Today* (http://www.usatoday.com/life/movies/news/2008-07-07-del-toro-hellboy_N.htm) .

75. *Rolling Stone*, Dec. 13, 2012.

76. Tolkien, "On Fairy-stories," 70–71.

77. *Letters*, p. 350.

78. See Shippey, *Road*, 343–4; and Jamie McGregor, "Two Rings to Rule Them All: A Comparative Study of Tolkien and Wagner," *Mythlore* 29, nos. 3/4 (Spring/Summer 2011).

79. See *Reader's Guide*, 617.

80. Simon Machin, "Brothers in Arms," *Oxford Today* 20, no. 1 (Michaelmas 2007); see https://www.oxfordtoday.ox.ac.uk/page.aspx?pid=1099.

81. Errigo, *Rough Guide*, 286–7.

appendix iii: tolkieniana

1. See Martin Barker and Ernest Mathijs (eds), *Watching* The Lord of the Rings (New York: Peter Lang, 2008).

2. *Biography*, 258ff.

3. Ibid., 261; Errigo, *Rough Guide*, 276.

4. *Biography*, 262.

5. *Letters*, p. 412; Birzer, 16–17.

6. *Chronology*, 19.

7. Garth, *Tolkien and the Great War*, 72-73.

8. Ibid., 79–80.

9. For more titles see *Reader's Guide*, 814–7.

10. Shippey, *Author*, 326.

11. Rosebury, *Tolkien: A Cultural Phenomenon*, ch. 6.

12. Before *D&D*, Gygax developed war games based on historically accurate miniatures, like the medieval-themed *Chainmail* (1971).

13. Most participants now prefer the term "living history," and many of them are serious about their research and construction of arms and costumes.

14. Some role-playing games have been adapted for computer and Internet play, allowing for more complex scoring and play between individuals geographically separated.

15. Rosebury, *Tolkien: A Cultural Phenomenon*, 194–5.

16. Errigo, *Rough Guide*, 281–3.

17. See http://ngm.nationalgeographic.com/features/world/asia/georgia/flores-hominids-text; and http://www.livescience.com/history/091109-human-origins-family-tree.html. For the work on *Homo floresiensis* by the Smithsonian's Matt Tocheri and others, see http://humanorigins.si.edu/research/hop-team/matt-tocheri.

18. *LOTR*, 2.

19. Quoted in *Reader's Companion*, 27.

20. *Letters*, p. 288: "I am in fact a *Hobbit* (in all but size). I like gardens, trees, and unmechanized farmlands; I smoke a pipe, and like good plain food."

21. See the *Guardian*, April 1, 2013 (http://www.guardian.co.uk/books/2013/apr/02/hobbit-tolkien-ring-exhibition).

22. See http://www.bbc.co.uk/gloucestershire/films/tolkien.shtml.

23. J. R. R. Tolkien, "The Name Nodens," Appendix I in R. E. M. Wheeler and T. V. Wheeler, *Report on the Excavation of the Prehistoric, Roman, and Post-Roman Site in Lydney Park, Gloucestershire* (London: Society of Antiquaries, 1932), 132–37.

appendix iv: the moral virtues of middle earth

1. J. R. R. Tolkien, "Sir Gawain and the Green Knight," in *The Monsters and the Critics*, ed. by Christopher Tolkien, 73.

2. In Tolkien, *The Tolkien Reader*, 5.

3. *The Hobbit*, 210.

4. Ibid., 617.

5. Ibid., 756.

6. Ibid., 769.

7. Ibid., 947.

BIBLIOGRAPHY AND TOLKIEN RESOURCES

ABBREVIATIONS

Annotated Hobbit	Tolkien, J. R. R. *The Annotated Hobbit*. Rev. and expanded ed. Annotated by Douglas A. Anderson. Boston: Houghton Mifflin, 2002.
Biography	Carpenter, Humphrey. *J. R. R. Tolkien: A Biography*. Boston: Houghton Mifflin, 2000.
Chronology	Hammond, Wayne G. and Christina Scull. *The J. R. R. Tolkien Companion and Guide: Chronology*. Boston: Houghton Mifflin, 2006.
Encyclopedia	Drout, Michael D. C. (ed.). *J. R. R. Tolkien Encyclopedia: Scholarship and Critical Assessment*. New York: Routledge, 2007.
Gr	Greek
Ir	Irish
L	Latin
Letters	Carpenter, Humphrey and Christopher Tolkien (eds.). *The Letters of J. R. R. Tolkien*. Boston: Houghton Mifflin, 2000.
Life and Legend	*J. R. R. Tolkien, Life and Legend: An Exhibition to Commemorate the Centenary of the Birth of J. R. R. Tolkien (1892–1973)*. Oxford: Bodleian Library, 1992.
LOTR	Tolkien, J. R. R. *The Lord of the Rings Fiftieth Anniversary Deluxe Edition*. London: Harper Collins, 2004.
OE	Old English
OFr	Old French
ON	Old Norse
Q	Quenya
Reader's Companion	Hammond, Wayne G. and Christina Scull. *The Lord of the Rings: A Reader's Companion*. Boston: Houghton Mifflin, 2005.
Reader's Guide	Hammond, Wayne G. and Christina Scull. *The J. R. R. Tolkien Companion and Guide: Reader's Guide*. Boston: Houghton Mifflin, 2006.
S	Sindarin
W	Welsh

BIBLIOGRAPHIES, GUIDES, AND REFERENCE WORKS

Blackwelder, Richard E. *A Tolkien Thesaurus*. New York: Garland, 1990.

Day, David. *Guide to Tolkien's World: A Bestiary*. London: Bounty Books, 1979.

Drout, Michael D. C. "J. R. R. Tolkien's Medieval Scholarship and its Significance."*Tolkien Studies* 4, 2007, Appendices.

Drout, Michael D.C. (ed.). *J. R. R. Tolkien Encyclopedia: Scholarship and Critical Assessment*. New York: Routledge, 2007.

Drout, Michael D. C., Hilary Wynne, and Melissa Higgins. "Scholarly Studies of J. R. R. Tolkien and His Works (in English): 1984–2000." *Envoi* 9, no. 2, Fall 2000, 135–67.

Duriez, Colin. *Tolkien and* The Lord of the Rings. *A Guide to Middle-earth*. Stroud, UK: Sutton, 2004.

The Encyclopedia of Arda: An Interactive Guide to the Works of J. R. R. Tolkien. CD- ROM. (http://www.axiomtoolworks.com/encarda.htm)

Hammond, Wayne G. (with Douglas Anderson). *J. R. R. Tolkien: A Descriptive Bibliography*. Winchester: St. Paul's Bibliographies, 1993.

Hammond, Wayne G. and Christina Scull. *The J. R. R. Tolkien Companion and Guide*. 2 vols. Boston: Houghton Mifflin, 2006.

Jönsson, Åke. *A Tolkien Bibliography 1911–1980: Writings by and about J. R. R. Tolkien*. 1984, rev. ed., 1986.

Middle English Dictionary. University of Michigan, 2001. (http://quod.lib.umich.edu/m/med/)

Noel, Ruth S. *The Languages of Tolkien's Middle-earth*. Boston: Houghton Mifflin, 1980.

Onions, C. T. *The Oxford Dictionary of English Etymology*. Oxford: Clarendon Press, 1966.

Sibley, Brian. Illustrated by John Howe. *West of the Mountains, East of the Sea: The Map of Tolkien's Beleriand*. London: HarperCollins, 2010.

Simpson, Jacqueline and Steve Roud. *Oxford Dictionary of English Folklore*. Oxford: Oxford Univ. Press, 2003.

Snyder, Christopher A. (ed.). *The Early Peoples of Britain and Ireland: An Encyclopedia*. 2 vols. Oxford: Greenwood International, 2008.

Tolkien Gateway. (http://www.tolkiengateway.net/wiki/Main_Page)

THE WRITINGS OF J. R. R. TOLKIEN

The Tolkien Manuscripts, which include extensive notes for and drafts of both his academic and popular publications, are held in the Modern Papers collection of the Department of Western Manuscripts at the Bodleian Library, Oxford. Not all are accessible to the public. Manuscripts and drafts of *The Hobbit*, *The Lord of the Rings*, *Farmer Giles of Ham*, and *Mr. Bliss* (including original Tolkien drawings and paintings) were bequeathed by the author in 1957 to Marquette University in Milwaukee, Wisconsin. The Marquette collection was developed by Richard E. Blackwelder (see http://www.marquette.edu/library/collections/archives/Mss/JRRT/mss-blackwelder.html). Another significant body of Tolkien papers can be found at the Marion E. Wade Center at Wheaton College in Wheaton, Illinois (see http://www.wheaton.edu/wadecenter). For a detailed discussion of these and smaller collections, see Wayne G. Hammond, "Special Collections in the Service of Tolkien Studies," in Wayne G. Hammond and Christina Scull (eds.), The Lord of the Rings *1954–2004: Scholarship in Honor of Richard E. Blackwelder* (Milwaukee, WI: Marquette Univ. Press, 2006), 331–40. For a complete bibliography of Tolkien's scholarship, see Michael D. C. Drout, "J. R. R. Tolkien's Medieval Scholarship and Its Significance." *Tolkien Studies* 4 (2007), Appendices.

Carpenter, Humphrey with Christopher Tolkien (eds.). *The Letters of J. R. R. Tolkien.* Boston: Houghton Mifflin, 2000.

Sisam, Kenneth (ed.). *Fourteenth-Century Verse and Prose.* With *A Middle English Vocabulary* by J. R. R. Tolkien. Oxford: Clarendon Press, 1922.

Tolkien, Baillie (ed.). *J. R. R. Tolkien: Letters from Father Christmas.* Boston: Houghton Mifflin, 1999.

Tolkien, Christopher (ed.). *The Monsters and the Critics and Other Essays.* London: Allen & Unwin, 1983.

Tolkien, J. R. R. "*Ancrene Wisse* and *Hali Meiðhad*." *Essays and Studies,* vol. 14, 1929, 104–26.

———. "*Beowulf*: The Monsters and the Critics." *Proceedings of the British Academy,* vol. 22, 1937, 245–95.

———. *The Hobbit: or There and Back Again.* London: Allen & Unwin, 1937.

———. "Prefatory Remarks" to J. R. Clark Hall (rev. by C. L. Wren), *Beowulf and the Finnesburg Fragment.* London: Allen & Unwin, 1940, pp. ix–xliii.

———. "Leaf by Niggle." *Dublin Review,* January 1945, 46–61.

———. "On Fairy Stories." *Essays Presented to Charles Williams.* London: Oxford Univ. Press, 1947, pp. 38–89.

———. *Farmer Giles of Ham.* London: Allen & Unwin, 1949.

———. "The Homecoming of Beorhtnoth Beorhthelm's Son." *Essays and Studies,* N.S. vol. 6, 1953, 1–18.

———. *The Fellowship of the Ring.* London: Allen & Unwin, 1954.

———. *The Two Towers.* London: Allen & Unwin, 1954.

———. *The Return of the King.* London: Allen & Unwin, 1955.

———. *The Adventures of Tom Bombadil and Other Verses from the Red Book.* London: Allen & Unwin, 1962.

———. "English and Welsh." In *Angles and Britons: O'Donnell Lectures.* Cardiff: Univ. of Wales Press, 1963, pp. 1–41.

———. *Tree and Leaf.* London: Allen & Unwin, 1964; Boston: Houghton Mifflin, 1965.

———. *A Tolkien Reader.* New York: Ballantine, 1966.

———. *Smith of Wootton Major.* London: Allen & Unwin, 1967.

———. *The Road Goes Ever On: A Song Cycle* (with music by Donald Swann). London: Allen & Unwin, 1968.

——— (trans. and intro., ed. by Christopher Tolkien). "*Sir Gawain and the Green Knight,*" "*Pearl,*" and "*Sir Orfeo.*" London: Allen & Unwin, 1975.

———. *The Father Christmas Letters.* London: Allen & Unwin; Boston: Houghton Mifflin, 1976.

——— (ed. by Christopher Tolkien). *The Silmarillion.* London: Allen & Unwin; Boston: Houghton Mifflin, 1977; 2nd edition, 1999.

——— (ed. with intro., commentary, index, and maps by Christopher Tolkien). *Unfinished Tales of Númenor and Middle-earth.* London: Allen & Unwin, 1980; Boston: Houghton Mifflin, 1990.

———. (illustrated by Pauline Baynes). *Poems and Stories.* London: Allen & Unwin, 1980.

———— (ed. by Joan Turville-Petre). *The Old English Exodus*. New York: The Clarendon Press; London: Oxford University Press, 1981.

————. *Mr. Bliss*. London: Allen & Unwin, 1982; Boston: Houghton Mifflin, 1983.

———— (ed. by Alan Bliss). *Finn and Hengest: The Fragment and the Episode*. New York: Houghton Mifflin, 1983.

———— (ed. by Christopher Tolkien). *The History of Middle-Earth*. 12 vols. London: Allen & Unwin; Boston, Houghton Mifflin, 1983–96. The individual volumes are titled as follows:
1 *The Book of Lost Tales, Part One* (1983).
2 *The Book of Lost Tales, Part Two* (1984).
3 *The Lays of Beleriand* (1985).
4 *The Shaping of Middle-Earth: The Quenta, the Ambarkanta and the Annals* (1986).
5 *The Lost Road and Other Writings: Language and Legend before the Lord of the Rings* (1987).
6 *The Return of the Shadow: The History of the Lord of the Rings, Part One* (1988).
7 *The Treason if Isengard: The History of the Lord of the Rings, Part Two* (1989).
8 *The War of the Ring: The History of the Lord of the Rings, Part Three* (1990).
9 *Sauron Defeated: The End of the Third Age (The History of the Lord of the Rings, Part Four)* (1991).
10 *Morgoth's Ring: The Later Silmarillion, Part One, The Legends of Aman* (1993).
11 *The War of the Jewels: The Later Silmarillion, Part Two, The Legends of Beleriand* (1994).
12 *The Peoples of Middle-Earth* (1996).

———— (ed. by Michael D. C. Drout). *Beowulf and the Critics*. Tempe, AZ: Arizona Center for Medieval and Renaissance Studies, 2002.

————. *The Lord of the Rings Fiftieth Anniversary Deluxe Edition*. London: HarperCollins, 2004.

———— (ed. by Christopher Tolkien). *The Children of Húrin*. Boston: Houghton Mifflin, 2007.

————. *Tales from the Perilous Realm*. Illustrated by Alan Lee. Boston: Houghton Mifflin, 2008.

———— (ed. by Christopher Tolkien). *The Legend of Sigurd and Gudrún*. London: HarperCollins, 2009.

———— (ed. by Carl F. Hostetter). "Fate and Free Will." *Tolkien Studies* 6, 2009, 183–88.

Tolkien, J. R. R. and E. V. Gordon (eds.). *Sir Gawain and the Green Knight*. Oxford: Clarendon Press, 1925.

Tolkien, J. R. R., E. V. Gordon, et al. *Songs for the Philologists*. Private Printing: Dept. of English, University College, London, 1936.

FILMOGRAPHY AND DISCOGRAPHY

For an exhaustive and detailed discography, see *The Tolkien Music List* (http://www.tolkien-music.com/).

Arkenstone, David. *Music Inspired by Middle-Earth*. Neo Pacifica, 2001.

Bakshi, Ralph (dir.). *The Lord of the Rings*. Animated. Fantasy Films/Saul Zaentz, 1978.

Bass, Jules and Arthur Rankin, Jr. (dir.). *The Hobbit*. Made for TV, animated. Rankin/Bass Productions, 1977.

————. *The Return of the King*. Animated. Rankin/Bass Productions, 1979.

Beyond the Movie: The Lord of the Rings: Fellowship of the Ring (National Geographic, 2002).

Beyond the Movie: The Lord of the Rings: Return of the King (National Geographic, 2003). http://www.snagfilms.com/films/title/beyond_the_movie_lord_of_the_rings_return_of_the_king/

De Menj, Johan (composer). *Symphony Nr. 1:* The Lord of the Rings. Performed by the Koninklijke Militaire Kapel (Netherlands), Pierre Kuijpers, conductor. The Hague: Ottavo, 1988.

Enya. "Lothlórien." *Shepherd Moons.* Reprise Records, 1991.

Everstar. *Enchanted Journey: Music Inspired by the Lord of the Rings.* Sequoia Records, 2003.

Glass Hammer. *Journey of the Dunadan.* 2003.

———. *The Middle Earth Album.* 2001.

Hargrove, Gene. *The Music of Middle-earth.* 2 vols. http://www.oldforestsounds.com/

Hewitt, Harry. "A Tolkien Tapestry" (solo work for piano). 1958.

The Hollywood Studio Orchestra and Singers. *The Lord of the Rings: The Return of the King.* Laser Light Digital, 2004.

Hruby, Jan and Kukulin. *Silmarillion.* Orchard, 2004.

The Hunt for Gollum (online fan film). 2009. http://www.thehuntforgollum.com/

Jackson, Peter (dir.). *The Lord of the Rings: The Fellowship of the Ring.* New Line Cinema, 2001.

———. *The Lord of the Rings: The Two Towers.* New Line Cinema, 2002.

———. *The Lord of the Rings: The Return of the King.* New Line Cinema, 2003.

Kilgarriff, Michael. *BBC Radio Presents: The Hobbit.* New York: Bantam Audio, 1988.

Lewis, Bob. *The Hobbit: A Dramatization of J. R. R. Tolkien's Classic.* St. Paul, MN: HighBridge Co., 2001.

Monsters of Middle-earth. The History Channel (first aired October 5, 2009).

Mostly Autumn. *Music Inspired by the Lord of the Rings.* Classic Rock Legends, 2002.

Reiff, Caspar and Peter Hall (composers). *A Night at Rivendell with the Tolkien Ensemble.* Classico, 2000.

Roseman, Leonard (composer). *J. R. R. Tolkien's Lord of the Rings: Original Soundtrack Recording.* Berkeley: Fantasy Records, 2001.

Shore, Howard (composer). *The Lord of the Rings: The Fellowship of the Ring (Soundtrack).* Warner Bros., 2001.

———. *The Lord of the Rings: The Two Towers (Soundtrack).* Warner Bros., 2002.

———. *The Lord of the Rings: The Return of the King (Soundtrack).* Warner Bros., 2003.

———. *The Lord of the Rings: The Fellowship of the Ring (The Complete Recordings).* Warner Bros., 2005.

———. *The Lord of the Rings: The Two Towers (The Complete Recordings).* Warner Bros., 2006.

———. *The Lord of the Rings: The Return of the King (The Complete Recordings).* Warner Bros., 2007.

Sibley, Brian, et al. *BBC Radio Presents: The Lord of the Rings.* North Kingstown, RI: BBC Audiobooks America, 2002.

The Tolkien Ensemble. *24 Songs from the Lord of the Rings.* Classico, 2001.

The Tolkien Ensemble and Christopher Lee. *Lord of the Rings: At Dawn in Rivendell.* Decca U.S., 2003.

Tolkien, J. R. R. *J. R. R. Tolkien Reads and Sings from His* Lord of the Rings. New York: Caedmon, 1975.

———. *The J. R. R. Tolkien Soundtrack.* New York: Caedmon Records, 1977.

———. *The Fellowship of the Ring: A Dramatization.* New York: Random House, 1981.

———. *The Hobbit: A Dramatization.* New York: BBC Worldwide, 1988.

————. *Of the Darkening of Valinor and Of the Flight of the Noldor from* The Silmarillion. Read by Christopher Tolkien, 1978.

————. *The Silmarillion.* Read by Martin Shaw, 1998.

————. *The Silmarillion: Of Beren and Lúthien.* Read by Christopher Tolkien, 1977.

Tolkien, J. R. R. and Christopher (narrators). *The J. R. R. Tolkien Audio Collection* (Abridged). Caedmon, 2001.

Wakeman, Rick. *Songs of Middle Earth: Inspired by The Lord of the Rings.* BMG, 2002. Consists of songs previously released (differently titled) on *Heritage Suite* (1993) and *The Seven Wonders of the World* (1995).

ORGANIZATIONS, PODCASTS, AND WEB SITES

ADC Promotions (Tolkien books and Tolkien inspired art): http://www.adcbooks.co.uk/

Arthedain (the Tolkien Society of Norway): http://www.arthedain.org/english.html

The Bird and the Baby: http://www.tc.umn.edu/~d-lena/BirdnBab.html

Brothers Hildebrandt (Tolkien illustrators): http://www.brothershildebrandt.com/

C. S. Lewis and the Inklings: http://personal.bgsu.edu/~edwards/lewis.html

The Council of Elrond: www.councilofelrond.com

The Elvish Linguistic Society: http://www.eldalamberon.com

The Encyclopedia of Arda: A Reference Guide to the Works of J. R. R. Tolkien: http://www.glyphweb.com/arda/

The Forodrim (the Stockholm Tolkien Society): http://www.forodrim.org/

The Frodo Franchise (Tolkien blog): http://www.kristinthompson.net/blog/

The Gathering of the Fellowship (Tolkien fan community): http://gatheringofthefellowship.org/

Donato Giancola (Tolkien illustrator): http://www.donatoart.com/

The Grey Havens: Songs and Tales: http://tolkien.cro.net/talesong.html

The Hobbit Blog (Peter Jackson's official blog for the *Hobbit* films): http://www.thehobbitblog.com/

The Hobbit Movie (unofficial site): http://the-hobbit-movie.com/

John Howe (Tolkien illustrator): http://www.john-howe.com/

J. R. R. Tolkien: A Collection (rare editions and collectables): http://www.themoment.co.uk/tolkien/

J. R. R. Tolkien: An Imaginative Life (Gnostic Society lecture series by Lance Owens): http://gnosis.org/wgs/Tolkien.html

The Lord of the Rings (official site of the musical): http://www.lotr.com/home/

The Lord of the Rings Fanatics Network: http://www.lordotrings.com/

The Lord of the Rings.Net (official movie site): http://www.lordoftherings.net/

The Lord of the Rings Soundtrack: http://www.lordoftherings-soundtrack.com/

The Lord of the Rings Radio Network (podcasts): https://itunes.apple.com/us/podcast/lord-rings-radio-network-return/id74843234

The Mathom House (collectibles): http://www.the-mathom-house.com/

Middle-earth Enterprises (licensing): http://www.middleearth.com/

The Music of The Lord of the Rings: see: http://en.wikipedia.org/wiki/Music_of_The_Lord_of_
the_Rings_film_series#External_links

The Mythopoeic Society: http://www.mythsoc.org/

Ted Naismith (Tolkien illustrator): http://www.tednasmith.com/

Northeast Tolkien Society (formerly *Heren Istarion*): http://herenistarionnets.blogspot.com/

TheOneRing.net: www.theonering.net

Ring Lord (fan site): http://ring-lord.tripod.com/

Sacnoth's Scriptorium (website of Tolkien scholar John D. Rateliff):
http://www.sacnothscriptorium.com/

Secrets of the Lord of the Rings (podcast lectures by Fr. Roderick Vonhogen):
https://itunes.apple.com/us/podcast/sqpn-secrets-of-middle-earth/id252800456

Shiro no Norite (Japanese Tolkien Society): http://smialjapan.exblog.jp/

Teaching Tolkien (maintained by Prof James McNelis): http://teachingtolkien.org/

The Tolkien Archives (sponsored by the *New York Times*):
http://www.nytimes.com/specials/advertising/movies/tolkien/index.html

Tolkien at Oxford (iTunesU podcast):
https://itunes.apple.com/us/itunes-u/tolkien-at-oxford/id381700970

Tolkien, C. S. Lewis and the British Literary Tradition (iTunesU podcast No. 11):
https://itunes.apple.com/us/itunes-u/c.s.-lewis/id391568426/

Tolkien Gateway (encyclopedia): http://www.tolkiengateway.net/wiki/Main_Page

Tolkien Genootschap Unquendor (site of the Dutch Tolkien Society): http://www.unquendor.nl/

The Tolkien Library (Tolkien book collecting site): http://www.tolkienlibrary.com/

The Tolkien Music List: http://www.tolkien-music.com

The Tolkien Professor (podcast lectures by Dr. Corey Olsen of Washington College, MD):
http://www.tolkienprofessor.com/

The Tolkien Sarcasm Page: http://flyingmoose.org/tolksarc/tolksarc.htm

The Tolkien Shop (books and collectables): http://www.tolkienshop.com/

The Tolkien Society: www.tolkiensociety.org

Tolkien Society on Twitter: http://twitter.com/TolkienSociety

The Tolkien Wiki Community: http://www.thetolkienwiki.org/wiki.cgi?FrontPage

Tolkien.co.uk (the HarperCollins site): http://www.tolkien.co.uk/

Tolkien's Oxford: http://users.ox.ac.uk/~tolksoc/TolkiensOxford/

PERIODICALS

Amon Hen: The Bulletin of the Tolkien Society (London) (published bimonthly):
http://www.tolkiensociety.org/ts_info/amonhen.html

Arda (the journal of the Swedish Tolkien Society, published annually, Stockholm: Forodrim,
1981–)

Beyond Bree (newsletter of the Tolkien Special Interest Group of American Mensa, published
monthly, Sherman Oaks, CA, 1981–): http://www.cep.unt.edu/bree.html

In Fellowship (journal published by the Gathering of the Fellowship Community, 2005–)

The Journal of Inkling Studies: http://www.inklings-studies.com/index.html (2011–)

Mallorn: The Journal of the Tolkien Society (London) (published bi-annually, 1971–): http://www.tolkiensociety.org/ts_info/mallorn.html

Minas Tirith Evening-Star (published quarterly by the American Tolkien Society, 1967–): http://www.americantolkiensociety.org/MTES.htm

MythCon Proceedings (Los Angeles: Mythopoeic Society, 1970–72)

The Mythic Circle (a literary magazine published annually by the Mythopoeic Society)

Mythlore (published quarterly by the Mythopoeic Society, 1969–)

Mythprint (the monthly bulletin of the Mythopoeic Society)

The New Tolkien Newsletter (Bath: Widcombe Press, 1980–82)

Orcrist: The Bulletin of the University of Wisconsin Tolkien Society (published irregularly 1967–)

Parma Eldalamberon: The book of Elven-tongues (the journal of the Elvish Linguistic Fellowship, published by the Mythopoeic Society, 1971–)

Parma Nölé (journal of the Northeast Tolkien Society)

Silver Leaves: http://www.whitetreefund.org/silver_leaves.html

The Tolkien Journal (published by the Tolkien Society of America, 1965–72)

Tolkien Studies (published annually by West Virginia University Press, 2004–): http://www.wvupress.com/journals/details.php?id=3

Vinyar Tengwar (the journal of the Elvish Linguistics Fellowship): http://www.elvish.org/

Other periodicals, like the *Chesterton Review*, the *Saint Austin Review*, *Seven: An Anglo-Saxon Literary Review*, and *Inklings: Jahrbuch für Literatur und Asthetik*, frequently include articles and special issues devoted to Tolkien.

INTERVIEWS WITH J. R. R. TOLKIEN AND THE TOLKIEN FAMILY

Resnik, Henry. "An Interview with Tolkien." *Niekas* 18, 1967, 37–43.

CHAPTER SOURCES

The best general biography of J. R. R. Tolkien is Humphrey Carpenter, *J. R. R. Tolkien: A Biography* (Boston: Houghton Mifflin, 1977; 2000). For a more detailed, "intellectual biography," nothing can compete with Tom Shippey, *The Road to Middle Earth* (Boston: Houghton Mifflin, 2003). Both works are essential. The following are some good general and accessible works covering both Tolkien's writings and Tolkien phenomena:

Carter, Lin. *Tolkien: A Look Behind the Lord of the Rings*. New York: Ballantine Books, 1969.

The Rough Guide to The Lord of the Rings. London: Penguin, 2003.

CHAPTER 1: LEARNING HIS CRAFT

Anderson, Douglas A. (ed.). *Tales Before Tolkien: The Roots of Modern Fantasy.* New York: Ballantine Books, 2005.

Blackham, Robert S. *Tolkien's Oxford.* Stroud, UK: The History Press, 2010.

Calhoun, Scott. "C. S. Lewis and J. R. R. Tolkien: Friends and Mutual Mentors," 249–74 in *An Examined Life: C.S. Lewis, Life, Works, and Legacy*, vol. 1. Edited by Bruce L. Edwards. Westport, CT: Praeger, 2007.

Cantor, Norman F. *Inventing the Middle Ages.* New York: William Morrow & Co, 1991.

Carpenter, Humphrey. *J. R. R. Tolkien: A Biography.* Boston: Houghton Mifflin, 1977; 2000.

————. *The Inklings.* London: Allen & Unwin, 1978.

Carpenter, Humphrey and Christopher Tolkien (eds.). *The Letters of J. R. R. Tolkien.* Boston: Houghton Mifflin, 2000.

Chance, Jane (ed.). *Tolkien the Medievalist.* New York: Routledge, 2003.

Collier, Ian, Richard Crawshaw and Andrew Butler (eds.). *Tolkien Society Guide to Oxford.* Tolkien Society, 2005.

Drout, Michael D. C. "J. R. R. Tolkien's Medieval Scholarship and its Significance." *Tolkien Studies* 4, 2007, 113–176.

Drout, Michael D. C. (ed.). *Beowulf and the Critics*, by J. R. R. Tolkien. Tempe, AZ: Arizona Center for Medieval and Renaissance Studies, 2002.

Duriez, Colin. *J. R. R. Tolkien and C. S. Lewis: the Story of a Friendship.* Stroud, UK: Sutton, 2005.

Evans. G. R. *The University of Oxford: A New History.* London: I. B. Tauris, 2010.

Flieger, Verlyn and Douglas A. Anderson (eds.). *Tolkien On Fairy-stories: Expanded Edition, with Commentary and Notes.* London: HarperCollins, 2008.

Gardner, Angela and Neil Holford. *Wheelbarrows at Dawn: The Memories of Hilary Tolkien.* Moreton-in-Marsh, UK: ADC Publications, 2010.

Gardner, Angela (ed.) and Jef Murray (illustrator). *Black & White Ogre Country: The Lost Tales of Hilary Tolkien.* Moreton-in-Marsh, UK: ADC Publications, 2009.

Garth, John. *Tolkien and the Great War: The Threshold of Middle-earth.* Boston: Houghton Mifflin, 2003.

Gilliver, Peter. "At the Wordface: J. R. R. Tolkien's Work on the Oxford English Dictionary." In Patricia Reynolds and Glen GoodKnight (eds.), *Proceedings of the J. R. R. Tolkien Centenary Conference 1992.* Milton Keynes: Tolkien Society, 1996, 173–86.

Gilliver, Peter, Jeremy Marshall, and Edmund Weiner. *The Ring of Words: Tolkien and the Oxford English Dictionary.* Oxford: Oxford Univ. Press, 2006.

Glyer, Diana Pavlac. *The Company They Keep: C. S. Lewis and J. R. R. Tolkien as Writers in Community.* Kent, Ohio: Kent State University Press, 2007.

Grotta, Daniel. *J. R. R. Tolkien: Architect of Middle Earth.* Philadelphia: Running Press, 1992.

Hooker, Mark T. "Frodo's Batman." *Tolkien Studies* 1, 2004, 125–136.

Hooper, Walter. *C. S. Lewis: The Companion and Guide.* London: HarperCollins, 2005.

Mitchell, Bruce. "J. R. R. Tolkien and Old English Studies: An Appreciation." In Patricia Reynolds and Glen GoodKnight (eds.), *Proceedings of the J. R. R. Tolkien Centenary Conference 1992.* Milton Keynes: Tolkien Society, 1996, 206–12.

Poe, Harry Lee. Photos by James Ray Veneman. *The Inklings of Oxford*. Grand Rapids, MI: Zondervan, 2009.

Pollard, Alfred W. (ed.), *The Works of Geoffrey Chaucer*.London: Macmillan, 1899, 166.

Ryan, John S. *The Shaping of Middle-earth's Maker: Influences on the Life and Literature of J. R. R. Tolkien*. Highland, MI: American Tolkien Society, 1992.

Shippey, Tom. *J. R. R. Tolkien: Author of the Century*. Boston: Houghton Mifflin, 2001.

Sturch, Richard. "Common Themes Among Inklings." In Brian Horne (ed.), *Charles Williams: A Celebration*. Leominster, UK: Gracewing, 1995, 153–75.

Tolkien, John and Priscilla Tolkien. *The Tolkien Family Album*. London: HarperCollins, 1992.

Tolley, Clive. "Tolkien's 'Essay on Man': A Look at *Mythopoeia*." *The Chesterton Review* 28, nos. 1 & 2 (Feb. & May 2002): 79–96.

White, Michael. *Tolkien: A Biography*. New York: New American Library, 2003.

Wood, Steve. "Tolkien and the O.E.D." *Amon Hen* 28, August 1977.

CHAPTER 2: TOLKIEN'S MIDDLE AGES

Barber, Richard. *The Holy Grail: Imagination and Belief*. Cambridge, MA: Harvard Univ. Press, 2005.

Burns, Marjorie. *Perilous Realms: Celtic and Norse in Tolkien's Middle-earth*. Toronto: Univ. of Toronto Press, 2005.

Campbell, James (ed.). *The Anglo-Saxons*. Ithaca, NY: Cornell University Press, 1982.

Cunliffe, Barry. *The Ancient Celts*. Oxford: Oxford University Press, 1997.

Doughan, David. "An Ethnically Cleansed Faery? Tolkien and the Matter of Britain." *Mallorn* 32, September 1995.

Drout, Michael D. C. (ed.). *J. R. R. Tolkien: Beowulf and the Critics*. Medieval & Renaissance Texts & Studies, vol. 248. Tempe, AZ: Arizona Center for Medieval and Renaissance Studies, 2002.

Fimi, Dimitra. "'Mad' Elves and 'Elusive Beauty': Some Celtic Strands of Tolkien's Mythology." *Folklore* 117, August 2006, 156–70.

———. "Tolkien's '"Celtic" type of legends': Merging Traditions." *Tolkien Studies* 4, 2007, 51–71.

———. "Material Culture and Materiality in Middle-earth: Tolkien and Archaeology." Pp. 339–43 in Sarah Wells (ed.), *The Ring Goes Ever On: Proceedings of the Tolkien 2005 Conference*, vol. 2. Coventry: The Tolkien Society, 2008.

———. *Tolkien, Race and Cultural History: From Fairies to Hobbits*. New York: Palgrave Macmillan, 2009.

Flieger, Verlyn. "J. R. R. Tolkien and the Matter of Britain." *Mythlore* 23, no. 1, whole no. 87, Summer/Fall 2000.

Heaney, Seamus (trans.). *Beowulf: A Verse Translation*. New York: W. W. Norton, 2002.

James, Simon. *The World of the Celts*. New York: Thames and Hudson, 1993.

Leahy, Kevin and Roger Bland. *The Staffordshire Hoard*. London: British Museum Press, 2009.

Lee, Stuart and Elizabeth Solopova. *The Keys of Middle-earth: Discovering Medieval Literature through the Fiction of J. R. R. Tolkien*. New York: Palgrave Macmillan, 2005.

Malory, Sir Thomas. *Le Morte d'Arthur*. New York: The Modern Library, 1999.

Manlove, Colin. "How Much Does Tolkien Owe to the Work of George MacDonald?" Pp. 109–16 in Sarah Wells (ed.), *The Ring Goes Ever On: Proceedings of the Tolkien 2005 Conference*, vol. 2. Coventry: The Tolkien Society, 2008.

Marsh, Jan. *The Pre-Raphaelites: Their Lives in Letters and Diaries*. London: Collins and Brown, 1996.

Noel, Ruth S. *The Mythology of Middle-earth*. Boston: Houghton Mifflin, 1978.

Rankin, H. D. *Celts and the Classical World*. London: Croom Helm, 1987.

Scull, Christina. "The Influences of Archaeology and History on Tolkien's World." In K. J. Battarbee (ed.), *Scholarship and Fantasy: Proceedings of the Tolkien Phenomenon, May 1992, Turku, Finland*. Turku, Finland: University of Turku, 1993, 33–51.

Shippey, Tom. "Tolkien and Iceland: The Philology of Envy," Symposium at the Árni Magnússon Institute of Icelandic Studies, Reykjavík, Iceland (Sept. 13–14, 2002).

Snyder, Christopher A. *An Age of Tyrants: Britain and the Britons, AD 400–600*. University Park, PA: Penn State University Press, 1998.

———. *The World of King Arthur*. New York: Thames and Hudson, 2000.

———. *The Britons*. Peoples of Europe Series. Oxford: Blackwell, 2003.

The Staffordshire Hoard: http://staffordshirehoard.org.uk/

Straubhaar, Sandra Ballif. "Myth, Late Roman History, and Multiculturalism in Tolkien's Middle-earth." In Jane Chance (ed.), *Tolkien and the Invention of Myth: A Reader*. University Press of Kentucky, 2004, 101–18.

Tinkler, John. "Old English in Rohan." In Neil D. Isaacs and Rose A. Zimbardo (eds.), *Tolkien and the Critics*. University of Notre Dame Press, 1968, 164–69.

Vinaver, Eugène (ed.). *Malory: Works*. 2nd ed. New York: Oxford University Press, 1978.

Wainwright, Edmund. *Tolkien's Mythology for England: A Middle-Earth Companion*. Hockwold-cum-Wilton, Norfolk: Anglo-Saxon Books, 2004.

Wilson, David M. (ed.). *The Northern World: The History and Heritage of Northern Europe, AD 400–1100*. New York: Harry N. Abrams, 1980.

Yates, Jessica. "William Morris's Influence on J. R. R. Tolkien." In Sarah Wells (ed.), *The Ring Goes Ever On: Proceedings of the Tolkien 2005 Conference*, vol. 2. Coventry: The Tolkien Society, 2008, 204–19.

CHAPTER 3: "THERE AND BACK AGAIN"

Abels, Richard. "Franks Casket." In Christopher A. Snyder (ed.), *The Early Peoples of Britain and Ireland: An Encyclopedia*. Oxford: Greenwood International, 2008, vol. I, 236–37.

Bibire, Paul. "By Stock or By Stone: Recurrent Imagery and Narrative Pattern in *The Hobbit*." In K. J. Battarbee (ed.), *Scholarship and Fantasy: Proceedings of the Tolkien Phenomenon, May 1992, Turku, Finland*. Turku: Univ. of Turku, 1993, 203–15.

Cofield, David. "Changes in Hobbits: Textual Differences in Editions of *The Hobbit*." *Beyond Bree*, April 1986.

Green, William. *The Hobbit: A Journey into Maturity*. New York: Twayne, 1994.

O'Brien, Donald. "On the Origin of the Name 'Hobbit.'" *Mythlore* 16, no. 2, whole no. 60, Winter 1989.

Rateliff, John. *The History of the Hobbit, Part One: Mr. Baggins; Part Two: Return to Bag-end*. Boston: Houghton Mifflin, 2007.

Scull, Christina. "*The Hobbit* Considered in Relation to Children's Literature Contemporary with Its Writing and Publication." *Mythlore* 14, no. 2, Winter 1987.

Tolkien, J. R. R. *The Hobbit: or, There and Back Again*. Boston: Houghton Mifflin, 1997.

———. *The Annotated Hobbit*. Rev. and expanded ed. Annotated by Douglas A. Anderson. Boston: Houghton Mifflin, 2002.

CHAPTER 4: TALES OF THE THIRD AGE

Álvarez-Faedo, María José. "Arthurian Reminiscences in Tolkien's Trilogy: *The Lord of the Rings*." Pp.185–210 in María José Álvarez-Faedo (ed.), *Avalon Revisited: Reworkings of the Arthurian Myth*. Bern: Peter Lang, 2007.

Bassham, Gregory and Eric Bronson (eds.). The Lord of the Rings *and Philosophy*. Chicago and LaSalle, IL: Open Court, 2003.

Chance, Jane. *The Lord of the Rings: The Mythology of Power*. New York: Twayne, 1992.

Ford, Judy Ann. "The White City: *The Lord of the Rings* as an Early Medieval Myth of the Restoration of the Roman Empire." *Tolkien Studies* 2, 2005, 53–73.

Hammond, Wayne G. and Christina Scull. *The Lord of the Rings: A Reader's Companion*. Boston: Houghton Mifflin, 2005.

Librán-Moreno, Miryam. "Parallel Lives: The Sons of Denethor and the Sons of Telamon." *Tolkien Studies* 2, 2005, 15–52.

Scull, Christina. "A Preliminary Study of Variations in Editions of *The Lord of the Rings*." *Beyond Bree*, April and August 1985.

Stanton, Michael N. *Hobbits, Elves, and Wizards: Exploring the Wonders and Worlds of J. R. R. Tolkien's* The Lord of the Rings. New York: Macmillan Palgrave, 2001.

West, Richard C. "The Interlace Structure of *The Lord of the Rings*." Pp. 77–94 in Jared Lobdell (ed.), *A Tolkien Compass*. Chicago and LaSalle, IL: Open Court, 1975.

CHAPTER 5: THE SONG OF ILÚVATAR

Flieger, Verlyn. *Interrupted Music: The Making Of Tolkien's Mythology*. Kent, OH: Kent State University Press, 2005.

Flieger, Verlyn and Carl F. Hostetter (eds.). *Tolkien's "Legendarium": Essays on the History of Middle-earth*. Westport, CT: Greenwood, 2000.

Helms, Randel. *Tolkien and the Silmarils*. Boston: Houghton Mifflin, 1981.

Jensen, Keith W. "Dissonance in the Divine Theme: The Issue of Free Will in Tolkien's *Silmarillion*." In Bradford Lee Eden (ed.), *Middle-earth Minstrel: Essays on Music in Tolkien*. Jefferson, ND: McFarland, 2010, 102-13.

Kilby, Clyde. *Tolkien and* The Silmarillion. Berkhamsted: Lion Publishing, 1977.

Lewis, Alex and Elizabeth Currie. *The Epic Realm of Tolkien: Part One—Beren and Lúthien*. Moreton-in-Marsh: ADC Publications, 2009.

Noad, Charles E. "On the Construction of *The Silmarillion*." In Verlyn Flieger and Carl F. Hostetter (eds.), *Tolkien's "Legendarium": Essays on the History of Middle-earth.* Westport, CT: Greenwood, 2000, 31–68.

The Silmarillion by J. R. R. Tolkien: A Brief Account of the Book and Its Making. Boston: Houghton Mifflin, 1977.

Tolkien, J. R. R. (ed. by Christopher Tolkien). *The Silmarillion,* 2nd edition. Boston: Houghton Mifflin, 1999.

Turner, Allan (ed.). *The Silmarillion: Thirty Years On.* Zollikofen, Switzerland: Walking Tree Publishers, 2007.

APPENDIX 1: MONSTERS AND CRITICS

Arthur, Sarah. *Walking with Frodo: A Devotional Journey through* The Lord of the Rings. Wheaton, IL: Tyndale House Publisher, 2003.

Birzer, Bradley J. *J. R. R. Tolkien's Sanctifying Myth: Understanding Middle-earth.* Wilmington, DE: ISI Books, 2002.

Bramlett, Perry C. *I Am in Fact a Hobbit: An Introduction to the Life and Work of J. R. R. Tolkien.* Macon, GA: Mercer University Press, 2003.

Caldecott, Stratford. "The Horns of Hope: J. R. R. Tolkien and the Heroism of Hobbits." *The Chesterton Review* 28, nos. 1 and 2, 2002.

———. *The Power of the Ring: The Spiritual Vision Behind the Lord of the Rings.* New York: Crossroad, 2005.

Cantor, Norman F. *Inventing the Middle Ages.* New York: William Morrow, 1991.

Chance, Jane (ed.). *Tolkien and the Invention of Myth: A Reader.* University Press of Kentucky, 2004.

Chance, Jane and David D. Day. "Medievalism in Tolkien: Two Decades of Criticism in Review." *Studies in Medievalism* 3,1991, 375–87.

Chance, Jane and Alfred Siewers (eds.). *Tolkien's Modern Middle Ages.* New York: Palgrave Macmillan, 2005.

Clark, George and Daniel Patrick Timmons (eds.). *J. R. R. Tolkien and His Literary Resonances: Views of Middle-earth.* Westport, CT: Greenwood, 2000.

Colebatch, Hans. *Return of the Heroes: The Lord of the Rings, Star Wars, and Contemporary Culture.* Perth: Australian Institute for Public Policy, 1990.

Curry, Patrick. *Defending Middle-Earth.* London: HarperCollins, 1997.

———. "Tolkien and His Critics: A Critique." In Thomas Honeggar, *Root and Branch: Approaches Towards Understanding Tolkien* (Zurich: Walking Tree, 1999), 81–148.

Dickerson, Matthew and Jonathan Evans. *Ents, Elves, and Eriador: The Environmental Vision of J. R. R. Tolkien.* Lexington: University of Kentucky Press, 2006.

Drout, Michael D. C. *Rings, Swords, and Monsters: Exploring Fantasy Literature.* The Modern Scholar; Recorded Books, 2006.

Drout, Michael D. C. and Hilary Wynne. "Tom Shippey's *J. R. R. Tolkien: Author of the Century* and a Look Back at Tolkien Criticism Since 1982." *Envoi* 9, no. 2, Fall 2000, 101–34.

Flieger, Verlyn. *Splintered Light: Logos and Language in Tolkien's World.* Grand Rapids, MI: Eerdman's, 1983.

———. *A Question of Time: J. R. R. Tolkien's Road to Faërie.* Kent, OH: Kent State University Press, 1997.

———. "A Postmodern Medievalist?" In Jane Chance and Alfred Siewers (eds.), *Tolkien's Modern Middle Ages*. New York: Palgrave Macmillan, 2005, 17–28.

Giddings, Robert (ed.). *J. R. R. Tolkien: This Far Land*. London: Vision Press, 1983.

Hammond, Wayne. "The Critical Response to Tolkien's Fiction." In Patricia Reynolds and Glen GoodKnight (eds.), *Proceedings of the J. R. R. Tolkien Centenary Conference 1992*. Milton Keynes: Tolkien Society, 1996, 226–32.

Hammond, Wayne G. and Christina Scull (eds.). The Lord of the Rings *1954–2004: Scholarship in Honor of Richard E. Blackwelder*. Milwaukee, WI: Marquette Univ. Press, 2006.

Helms, Randel. *Tolkien's World*. Boston: Houghton Mifflin, 1974.

Honegger, Thomas (ed.). *Reconsidering Tolkien*. Zurich: Walking Tree Publishers, 2005.

Houghton, John Wm. and Neal K. Keesee. "Tolkien, King Alfred, and Boethius: Platonist Views of Evil in *The Lord Of The Rings*." *Tolkien Studies* 2, 2005, 131–159.

Isaacs, Neil D. and Rose A. Zimbardo (eds.). *Tolkien and the Critics: Essays on J. R. R. Tolkien's* The Lord of the Rings. South Bend, IN: Univ. of Notre Dame Press, 1968.

Johnson, Judith A. *J. R. R. Tolkien: Six Decades of Criticism*. London: Greenwood Press, 1986.

Kocher, Paul. *Master of Middle-Earth: The Achievement of J. R. R. Tolkien*. London: Pimlico, 2002.

Kreeft, Peter. *The Philosophy of Tolkien: The Worldview Behind the Lord of the Rings*. San Francisco: Ignatius Press, 2005.

Lewis, C.S. Review of *The Fellowship of the Ring* by J. R. R. Tolkien. *Time and Tide*, Aug. 1954, 1082.

Lobdell, Jared (ed.). *A Tolkien Compass*. Chicago and La Salle, IL: Open Court, 2003.

Milbank, Alison. *Chesterton and Tolkien as Theologians: The Fantasy of the Real*. London and New York: T&T Clark, 2009.

Mortimer, Patchen. "Tolkien and Modernism." *Tolkien Studies* 2, 2005, 113–129.

Moseley, Charles. *J. R. R. Tolkien*. Writers and Their Work Series. Plymouth, UK: Northcote, 1997.

Nitzsche, Jane Chance. *Tolkien's Art: "A Mythology for England."* London: Macmillan, 1979.

Pearce, Joseph. *Tolkien: Man and Myth, A Literary Life.* San Francisco: Ignatius Press, 1998.

Podles, Mary. "Tolkien and the New Art: Visual Sources for *The Lord of the Rings*. *Touchstone*, Jan/Feb 2002. http://touchstonemag.com/archives/article.php?id=15-01-041-f

Purtill, Richard L. *J. R. R. Tolkien: Myth, Morality, and Religion*. San Francisco: Harper & Rowe, 1984.

Reynolds, Patricia and Glen GoodKnight (eds.). *Proceedings of the J. R. R. Tolkien Centenary Conference 1992*. Milton Keynes: Tolkien Society, 1996.

Rosebury, Brian. *Tolkien: A Critical Assessment*. London: Macmillan, 1992.

Rutledge, Fleming. *The Battle for Middle-earth: Tolkien's Divine Design in* The Lord of the Rings. Cambridge: Eerdmans, 2004.

Salu, Mary and Robert T. Farrell (eds.). *J. R. R. Tolkien, Scholar and Storyteller: Essays in Memoriam.* Ithaca, NY: Cornell Univ. Press, 1979.

Shippey, Tom. *The Road to Middle Earth*. Boston: Houghton Mifflin, 2003.

Wells, Sarah (ed.). *The Ring Goes Ever On: Proceedings of the Tolkien 2005 Conference*. 2 vols. Coventry: The Tolkien Society, 2008.

West, John G., Jr. (ed.). *Celebrating Middle-earth: The Lord of the Rings as a Defense of Western Civilization*. Inkling Books, 2002.

West, Richard C. *Tolkien Criticism: An Annotated Checklist*. 1970; rev. ed. 1981.

———. "A Tolkien Checklist: Selected Criticism 1981–2004." *MFS: Modern Fiction Studies* 50, no. 4, Winter 2004, 1015–28.

Williams, Donald T. *Mere Humanity: G. K. Chesterton, C. S. Lewis, and J. R. R. Tolkien on the Human Condition.* Nashville: B and H Publishing, 2006.

Wood, Ralph C. *The Gospel According to Tolkien: Visions of the Kingdom in Middle-earth.* Louisville: Westminster John Knox Press, 2004.

Zimbardo, Rose A. and Neil D. Isaacs (eds.). *Understanding* The Lord of the Rings: *The Best of Tolkien Criticism.* Boston: Houghton Mifflin, 2004.

APPENDIX II: MEDIA AND MIDDLE-EARTH

Adams, Doug. *The Annotated Scores of* The Lord of the Rings *Films.* 2007. http://www.musicoflotr.com/

———. *The Music of* The Lord of the Rings *Films: A Comprehensive Account of Howard Shore's Scores.* Carpentier/Alfred Music Publishing, 2010.

Astin, Sean (with Joe Layden). *There and Back Again: An Actor's Tale.* New York: St. Martin's Griffin, 2004.

Braun, J. W. *The Lord of the Films: The Unofficial Guide to Tolkien's Middle-earth on the Big Screen.* Toronto: ECW Press, 2009.

Catalogue of an Exhibit of the Manuscripts of J. R. R. Tolkien. Milwaukee, WI: The Marquette Univ. Dept. of Special Collections and Univ. Archives, 1983.

Croft, Janet Brennan (ed.). *Tolkien on Film: Essays on Peter Jackson's* The Lord of the Rings. Altadena, CA: Mythopoeic Press, 2004.

Drawings by J. R. R. Tolkien: Catalog of an Exhibition of Drawings by J. R. R. Tolkien at the Ashmolean Museum, Oxford. Introduction by Baillie Tolkien. Oxford: The Ashmolean Museum; London: National Book League, 1976.

Entertainment Weekly *Special Collector's Issue:* The Lord of the Rings *Ultimate Viewer's Guide,* May 2004.

Fisher, Jude. The Lord of the Rings *Complete Visual Companion.* Boston: Houghton Mifflin, 2004.

Garbowski, Christopher. *Spiritual Values in Peter Jackson's* Lord of the Rings. Lublin: Marie Curie-Skłodowska University Press, 2005.

Giancola, Donato. *Middle-earth: Visions of a Modern Myth.* Nevada City, CA: Underwood Books, 2010.

Hammond, Wayne G. and Christina Scull. *J. R. R. Tolkien: Artist and Illustrator.* Boston: Houghton Mifflin, 2000.

Hildebrandt, Gregory, Jr. *Greg and Tim Hildebrandt: The Tolkien Years.* Expanded Edition. New York: Watson-Guptill Publications, 2002.

Honegger, Thomas (ed.). *Translating Tolkien: Text and Film.* Zollikofen, Switzerland: Walking Tree Publishers, 2004.

The Invented Worlds of J. R. R. Tolkien: Drawings and Original Manuscripts from the Marquette University Collection. Milwuakee, WI: Marquette University, 2004.

J. R. R. Tolkien: The Hobbit *Drawings, Watercolors, and Manuscripts, June 11–September 30, 1987.* Milwaukee, WI: Marquette University, 1987.

J. R. R. Tolkien, Life and Legend: An Exhibition to Commemorate the Centenary of the Birth of J. R. R. Tolkien (1892–1973). Oxford: Bodleian Library, 1992.

Lacôn, Ruth. *The Art of Ruth Lacôn: Illustrations inspired by the works of J. R. R. Tolkien.* Moreton-in-Marsh, UK: ADC Publications, 2006.

Lee, Alan. *The Lord of the Rings Sketchbook*. Boston: Houghton Mifflin, 2005.

The Lord of the Rings: *Trilogy Photo Guide*. London: HarperCollins, 2004.

Machin, Simon. "Brothers in Arms." *Oxford Today* 20, no. 1, Michaelmas 2007. https://www.oxfordtoday.ox.ac.uk/page.aspx?pid=1099.

Margolis, Harriet, et al. (eds.). *Studying the Event Film:* The Lord of the Rings. Manchester, UK: Manchester University Press, 2009.

Mathijs, Ernest and Murray Pomerance (eds.). *From Hobbits to Hollywood: Essays on Peter Jackson's* Lord of the Rings. Amsterdam and New York: Rodopi, 2006.

Myth and Magic: The Art of John Howe. Foreword by Peter Jackson. New York: Barnes and Noble, 2006.

Naismith, Ted. "Similar but Not Similar: Appropriate Anachronism in My Paintings of Middle-earth." In Jane Chance and Alfred Siewers (eds.), *Tolkien's Modern Middle Ages*. New York: Palgrave Macmillan, 2005, 189–204.

Porter, Lynnette R. *Unsung Heroes of* The Lord of the Rings: *From the Page to the Screen*. Westport, CT: Praeger, 2005.

Pryor, Ian. *Peter Jackson: From Prince of Splatter to Lord of the Rings*. New York: St. Martin's Press, 2004.

Rateliff, John D. Review of Peter Jackson, *The Lord of the Rings* (2000–2002). In seven parts: http://www.wizards.com/dnd/article.asp?x=dnd/dx20020111x

Rosebury, Brian. *Tolkien: A Cultural Phenomenon*. London: Palgrave Macmillan, 2003.

Russell, Gary. *The Art of the Lord of the Rings*. Boston: Houghton Mifflin, 2004.

Sibley, Brian. The Lord of the Rings *Official Movie Guide*. London: HarperCollins, 2001.

———. *Peter Jackson: A Film-Maker's Journey*. London: Harcourt, 2006.

Sibley, Brian, et al. *BBC Radio Presents: The Lord of the Rings*. North Kingstown, RI: BBC Audiobooks America, 2002

Shippey, Tom. "Another Road to Middle-earth: Jackson's Movie Trilogy." In Rose A. Zimbardo and Neil D. Isaacs (eds.), *Understanding* The Lord of the Rings: *The Best of Tolkien Criticism*. Boston: Houghton Mifflin, 2003, 233–54.

Smith, Jim and J. Clive Matthews. The Lord of the Rings: *The Films, the Books, the Radio Series*. London: Virgin Books, 2004.

Thompson, Kristin. *The Frodo Franchise: The Lord of the Rings and Modern Hollywood*. Berkeley: University of California Press, 2007.

Tolkien, J. R. R. (foreword and notes by Christopher Tolkien. *Pictures by J. R. R. Tolkien*. London: Allen & Unwin, 1979; London: HarperCollins; Boston: Houghton Mifflin, 1991.

APPENDIX III: TOLKIENIANA

Barker, Martin and Ernest Mathijs (eds.). *Watching* The Lord of the Rings. New York: Peter Lang, 2008.

Bates, Brian. *The Real Middle-Earth: Magic and Mystery in the Dark Ages*. London: Pan Books, 2002.

Beahm, George. *The Essential J. R. R. Tolkien Sourcebook: A Fan's Guide to Middle-earth and Beyond*. Franklin Lakes, NJ: New Page, 2004.

Desanto, Tom, et al. *Ringers: Lord of the Fans*. Feature-length documentary, 2005.

Lloyd, D. R. *The Sillymarillion: An unauthorized parody of J. R. R. Tolkien's* The Silmarillion. Cold Spring Press, 2004.

Mathijs, Ernest (ed.). The Lord of the Rings: *Popular Culture in Global Context*. London: Wallflower Press, 2006.

Rosebury, Brian. *Tolkien: A Cultural Phenomenon*. Basingstoke: Palgrave Macmillan, 2003.

Shippey, Tom. *The Oxford Book of Fantasy Stories*. Oxford: Oxford University Press, 1994.

APPENDIX IV: THE MORAL VIRTUES OF MIDDLE EARTH

Tolkien, J. R. R. *The Hobbit: or, There and Back Again*. Boston: Houghton Mifflin, 1997.

————. "Sir Gawain and the Green Knight," in *The Monsters and the Critics and Other Essays*, ed. by Christopher Tolkien. Boston: Houghton Mifflin, 1983.

————. *A Tolkien Reader*. New York: Ballantine, 1966.

CONTACT INFORMATION

HarperCollins (UK)
http://www.tolkien.co.uk/Pages/Home.aspx
Tel: +44 (0)2 087-417-070
E-mail: enquiries@harpercollins.co.uk
HarperCollins Publishers (US)
10 East 53rd Street
New York, NY 10022
Tel: (212) 207-7000

Houghton Mifflin
http://www.houghtonmifflinbooks.com/
222 Berkeley Street
Boston, MA 02116
Tel: (617) 351-5000

The J. R. R. Tolkien Estate
http://www.tolkienestate.com/home/

The J. R. R. Tolkien Trust
c/o Manches LLP
9400 Garsington Road Oxford Business Park
Cowley, Oxford
Oxfordshire OX4 2DQ
Tel: +44 (0)1-865-722-106
Fax: +44 (0)1-865-201-012

index

A

Ackerman, Forrest J., 130, 241
Adam and Eve, 182
Adrian I, Pope, 55
Ainur, 179, 181, 212
Aislabie, Michael, 98
Alfred the Great, 55, 64
Allen & Unwin, 96, 124, 125, 193, 203. *See also* Rayner Unwin, Stanley Unwin
Anderson, Douglas, 108, 230
Anglo-Saxons
    Beowulf and, 61–64
    fortifications of, 144–45
    heritage, 71
    history and language of, 51–65
    mead halls, 111
    Normans and, 64
    poetry, 182
    rabbits and hobbits and, 98
    riddles of, 108, 116
    runes of, 105
    study of, 44, 45
    Tolkien and, 42
    understatement of, 194
Antiquity, 39–40, 138
Aquinas, Thomas, 169, 278
Aragorn
    Arwen and, 80, 101
    as Arthurian, 165
    as Christ figure, 233, 234
    as ideal monarch, 162, 162
    coronation of, 170
    Éowyn and, 142
    healing hands of, 81, 162
    in *The Lord of the Rings*, 132, 136, 137, 139, 140–43, 158, 162, 163, 170
    inspirations for, 55, 80
    King Arthur and, 77
    Lancelot and, 80
    Mouth of Sauron and, 73
    qualities of, 74, 77
    Old English poetry and, 59
    on women, 158
    sword of, 77
    throne of, 50
Architecture. *See specific groups; specific places*
Aristophanes, 5
Aristotle, 119, 278, 280, 281
Ar-Pharazôn, 199–200
Arwen, 72, 80, 101, 134
Asimov, Isaac, 83
Auden, W. H., 24, 69, 225, 240

Aurelianus, Ambrosius, 45
Aurvandil, 68

B

Baggins, Bilbo. *See* Bilbo
Baggins, Frodo. *See* Frodo
Bakshi, Ralph, 242–43
Balrog, 137, 181
Bard, 118
Barfield, Owen, 27, 31, 221
Barnsley, T. K. "Tea-cake," 4–5
Barrovian Society. *See* T.C.B.S.
Barrowclough, Sidney, 4
Barrow-downs, 130–31
Bass, Jules, 241–42
Battle of Hastings, 39, 64, 65
Beare, Rhona, 178, 203
Bede, Venerable, 53, 57, 126
Beorn, 110–11
Beowulf
    history of, 52, 57
    parallels to, 118, 140
    Tolkien and, 16–18, 24, 25, 61–64, 81, 89
Beren, 50, 184, 191–93, 194
Bible, 40, 105, 198–200
Bilbo
    adventures in *The Hobbit*, 105–7, 110–13, 116, 118
    character development, 120
    history of character, 98–99
    naming of, 97
    reaction to dwarves, 102–3
    returning, 120
    "Riddles in the Dark" and, 108–9
Birmingham, 2–3, 4, 5, 34, 127, 275
Birzer, Bradley, 124, 233
Blackwood, Algernon, 107
Bliss, Alan "A. J.", 24, 72
Bloemfontein, 2
Boethius, 55
Book of Kells, 112
Book of Lost Tales, The, 14–15, 51, 86, 177
Bombadil, Tom, 129, 132
Boromir
    characteristics of, 151–52
    death of, 63, 139–40, 156, 160
    doubt of, 164
    in *The Lord of the Rings*, 134, 166
    One Ring and, 146
Bratt, Edith, 5. *See also* Tolkien, Edith; Tolkien, J. R. R
Bree, 132–33
Brideshead Revisited (Waugh), 6
Brighton, 4

PICTURE CREDITS